DOING EDUCATIONAL RESEARCH

Sara Miller McCune founded SAGE Publishing in 1965 to support the dissemination of usable knowledge and educate a global community. SAGE publishes more than 1000 journals and over 800 new books each year, spanning a wide range of subject areas. Our growing selection of library products includes archives, data, case studies and video. SAGE remains majority owned by our founder and after her lifetime will become owned by a charitable trust that secures the company's continued independence.

Los Angeles | London | New Delhi | Singapore | Washington DC | Melbourne

DOING EDUCATIONAL RESEARCH

OVERCOMING CHALLENGES IN PRACTICE

EDITED BY **MARIT HONERØD HOVEID** ■ **LUCIAN CIOLAN** ■
ANGELIKA PASEKA ■ **SOFIA MARQUES DA SILVA**

EERA
EUROPEAN EDUCATIONAL
RESEARCH ASSOCIATION

SAGE

Los Angeles | London | New Delhi
Singapore | Washington DC | Melbourne

Los Angeles | London | New Delhi
Singapore | Washington DC | Melbourne

SAGE Publications Ltd
1 Oliver's Yard
55 City Road
London EC1Y 1SP

SAGE Publications Inc.
2455 Teller Road
Thousand Oaks, California 91320

SAGE Publications India Pvt Ltd
B 1/I 1 Mohan Cooperative Industrial Area
Mathura Road
New Delhi 110 044

SAGE Publications Asia-Pacific Pte Ltd
3 Church Street
#10-04 Samsung Hub
Singapore 049483

Editor: James Clark
Assistant editor: Diana Alves
Production editor: Katherine Haw
Copyeditor: Gemma Marren
Proofreader: David Hemsley
Indexer: Silvia Benvenuto
Marketing manager: Lorna Patkai
Cover design: Naomi Robinson
Typeset by: C&M Digitals (P) Ltd, Chennai, India
Printed in the UK

Library of Congress Control Number: 2018966738

British Library Cataloguing in Publication data

A catalogue record for this book is available from the British Library

ISBN 978-1-5264-3553-8
ISBN 978-1-5264-3554-5 (pbk)

CONTENTS

ABOUT THE EDITORS

Marit Honerød Hoveid is Professor of Pedagogy at the Department of Education and Lifelong Learning at the Norwegian University of Science and Technology (NTNU). Her first degree (Cand.Polit) in Social Pedagogy is from the University of Oslo in 1989, and her PhD is from NTNU in 2009. She has worked in teacher education for over 16 years but is now working with a disciplinary approach to pedagogy/education at NTNU. Her research is centred around foundational questions related to education, teaching and learning, and to methodology of research. Hoveid has a longstanding relationship with the European Educational Research Association (EERA), her term as secretary general ended in 2016. She is now a senior fellow of the Emerging Researchers group.

Lucian Ciolan, PhD is Professor of Educational Research and Policy at the University of Bucharest, Faculty of Psychology and Educational Sciences, where he is also serving as dean. His main academic fields of interest include (but are not limited to): influencing decision-making through public/educational policy, cognitive neurosciences applied in behavioural change, learning research and teacher education. Starting in 2014, Lucian became a member of the EERA council, representing Romania and now he is president of ARCE – the Romanian Educational Research Association. Alongside his academic activity, Lucian was extensively involved in consultancy and capacity building programmes in Europe and beyond, mainly focused on public policy and educational reforms. In this capacity, he is a member of a professional network of trainers and consultants on policy change called International Centre for Policy Advocacy.

Angelika Paseka is Professor for Educational Science with a bias on school education and professionalism at the University of Hamburg, Germany. She holds a doctorate in Sociology and has a post-doctoral lecture qualification (Habilitation) in Educational Science. She has been working in teacher education since 1992 at several institutions in Austria (College of Teacher Education/Vienna, University of Vienna and Linz) before changing to the University of Hamburg in 2010. Her current research interests focus on teacher professionalism, uncertainty and family–school partnership and she is an expert in qualitative methods in educational research. She was a council member of the Austrian Society for Research and Development in Education for eight years and in this time represented Austria in the EERA council. She is co-founder and co-editor of the *Zeitschrift für Bildungsforschung* as well as author and co-author of several publications.

Sofia Marques da Silva is Assistant Professor of the Faculty of Psychology and Educational Sciences, University of Porto, Portugal, in the field of Research Methodologies and Sociology of Education and is a member the Educational Research and Intervention Centre. She holds a PhD in Educational Sciences since 2008 and has been doing research in the field of inclusion, diversity and youth and is published at both national and international level. She is coordinator of the national project GROW:UP – Grow Up in Border Regions in Portugal: young people, educational pathways and agendas (FEDER/FCT). She is editor-in-chief of the journal *Ethnography & Education*. She is convenor of EERA and represents of the Portuguese Society of Education Sciences, representing it in the EERA council. She is deputy coordinator of the initiative Portugal INCoDe.2030, coordinating activities on digital inclusion and gender gap in digital technologies.

ABOUT THE CONTRIBUTORS

Liselott Aarsand is Professor at the Department of Education and Lifelong Learning, Norwegian University of Science and Technology, Trondheim, Norway. Her research takes a discourse analytical perspective and comprises ethnographic works and qualitative interviews with a particular interest in adult learning, subjectification, and social norms and order in everyday practices.

Pål Aarsand is Professor at the Department of Education and Lifelong Learning, Norwegian University of Science and Technology, Trondheim, Norway. His research interest concerns children's digital media practices and phenomena such as gaming, identity work and literacy. He is also interested in methodological and ethical dilemmas in research with children.

Herbert Altrichter is Professor of Education and Educational Psychology, Director of the Linz School of Education, Department of Educational Research, Johannes Kepler University, Austria. His research interests include educational governance studies (school development and system reform), evaluation, teacher education and qualitative research methodology.

Sonja Bauer-Hofmann is a member of the NOESIS evaluation project and doctoral researcher at the University of Vienna, Department of Education, with a thematic focus on the history of comprehensive schooling, theories of schooling, international comparative research and educational policy-making.

Antje Brock is a research assistant at the Freie Universität Berlin, Department of the scientific advisor of the UNESCO Global Action Programme on Education for Sustainable Development in Germany. Her main research focus is monitoring of education for sustainable development as well as questions of justice and social inequality.

Perry den Brok is Professor and Chair of the Education and Learning Sciences group at Wageningen University and Research, and Chair of the 4TU Centre for Engineering Education, an innovation centre for the four universities of technology in the Netherlands.

Javier Díez-Palomar is Associate Professor for Didactics of Mathematics at the University of Barcelona, Faculty of Education, Spain. He is the Spanish representative in the Commission Internationale pour l'Ètude et l'Armélioration de l'Enseignement des Mathématiques (CIEAEM). His expertise focuses on successful pathways in teaching and learning in mathematics education.

Karin Doolan is Associate Professor at the University of Zadar's Department of Sociology, Croatia. Her research has engaged with a Bourdieusian lens to explore how social class and gender intersect in shaping young people's educational experiences. More recently she has examined how social class differences are reinforced by natural disasters such as floods.

Nadine Etzkorn holds a Master in educational science. She works at the Institut Futur at the Freie Universität Berlin to monitor the national implementation of the Global Action Programme on Education for Sustainable Development and to develop recommendations on scaling-up ESD in the German education system.

Maria P. Figueiredo is Associate Professor of Educational Sciences at the School of Education of the Polytechnic of Viseu, and Researcher at the CI&DEI/IPV, Portugal. She is Secretary General of the European Educational Research Association. Main research interests are focused on improving quality in childhood services and teacher education.

Miriam Galvin is Senior Research Fellow at the Academic Unit of Neurology, Biomedical Sciences Institute, Trinity College Dublin and Atlantic Fellow for Equity in Brain Health, at the Global Brain Health Institute, University of California San Francisco and Trinity College Dublin. Her research interests include research methodology, philosophy of social sciences, health services research, psychosocial studies and discourse.

Rocío García-Carrión is Ramon y Cajal Fellow in Educational Psychology, focused on the study of dialogic learning environments for academic and social success, University of Lleida, Faculty of Education, Spain. She has been Marie Curie Fellow at Cambridge University where she transferred this knowledge to several schools in the UK.

Corinna Geppert is a member of the NOESIS evaluation project at the University of Vienna, Department of Education and post-doctoral researcher with a thematic focus on educational transitions and trajectories, equality of opportunity, international comparative research and educational policy-making.

Nelson Gonçalves is Lecturer of Animation at the School of Education of the Polytechnic of Viseu, and freelancer 3D Artist. His work on architecture visualisation and digital heritage is deeply connected to his commitment to Free Culture.

Aitor Gómez González is Associate Professor for Research Methods and specifically methodologies oriented towards social transformation and social impact, at the University Rovira i Virgili, Faculty of Education, Spain. His expertise is based on innovative methodologies to overcome social inequalities in learning communities.

Gábor Halász is Doctor of the Hungarian Academy of Sciences. He is Professor of Education at the Faculty of Education and Psychology of the University Eötvös Loránd in Budapest where he is leading a Centre for Higher Educational and Innovation Research and the Doctoral School in Educational Sciences.

Romiță Iucu is Professor of Educational Sciences at the Faculty of Psychology and Educational Sciences, University of Bucharest, with main research interests in teacher education, higher education policy and institutional management in the higher education area.

Tamara Katschnig is deputy project leader of the NOESIS evaluation project at the University of Vienna, Department of Education, and Professor for Research in Further and Continuing Education at the University College of Teacher Education Vienna/ Krems (KPH).

Michaela Kilian is a member of the NOESIS evaluation project and doctoral researcher at the University of Vienna, Department of Education, with a thematic focus on the research of transitions in education, class climate and longitudinal research, as well as a teacher at a new middle school.

Mariella Knapp is a member of the NOESIS evaluation project and doctoral researcher at the University of Vienna, Department of Education, with a thematic focus on the research of school leadership, regional school development and educational trajectories of students.

Sabine Krause is Professor for Education Science with a focus on general education and epistemic cultures at University of Innsbruck, Faculty of Education Science, Austria. Research interests also include culture in education and cultures of remembrance.

Gertraud Kremsner is PostDoc and Senior Lecturer with a research focus on inclusive research (with persons with learning difficulties) as well as Dis/Ability Studies at the University of Vienna, Centre for Teacher Education, Austria.

Sarah Désirée Lange, PhD, is Academic Counsellor at the Chair for Primary School Education and Didactics at the Faculty of Education at the University of Wuerzburg, Germany. Her research interests include multi-lingualism, migration and digitalisation in primary schools, teaching quality and teacher professionalisation and international and comparative research.

Linda Liebenberg, PhD, is a researcher focused on youth with complex needs. Her work explores the promotion of positive youth development and mental health as well as how best to conduct research with children and their communities, including the use of participatory image-based methods.

Christoph Maeder is Professor of Sociology of Education and a member of the Children – Childhood – Schooling research centre at the University of Teacher Education Zürich, Switzerland. He is interested in the everyday life inside 'people processing organisations', the sociology of knowledge and ethnographic research methods.

Tim Mainhard is Associate Professor at the Department of Education at Utrecht University. His research focuses on social dynamics in educational settings and their impact on student and teacher outcomes. He teaches in the Utrecht Graduate School for Teaching.

Gerry McNamara is Professor of Educational Evaluation at the School of Policy and Practice, DCU Institute of Education and Co-Director of the Centre for Evaluation, Quality and Inspect. His research interests include educational evaluation including programme evaluation, inspection and self-evaluation in schools, leadership and school governance.

Anca Nedelcu is Professor at the Faculty of Psychology and Educational Sciences, University of Bucharest, with main research interests in pedagogy of diversity, comparative education, educational management and reflective practice in education.

Joe O'Hara, PhD, is Professor of Education, Director, EQI – Centre for Evaluation, Quality and Inspection, School of Policy and Practice, Dublin City University Institute of Education, DCU St Patrick's Campus, Dublin. He is President of the European Educational Research Association. His research interests include school evaluation and inspection, teacher education and culturally responsive evaluation and assessment.

Michelle Proyer is Assistant Professor in the area of Inclusive Education at the Centre for Teacher Education, University of Vienna. Her research interest focuses on the intersection of disability and culture in Austria.

Anja Sieber Egger is Social Anthropologist and Co-Director of the Children – Childhood – Schooling research centre at the University of Teacher Education Zürich, Switzerland. She explores the everyday culture in school including processes of difference and recognition.

Mandy Singer-Brodowski did her PhD project at the Leuphana University of Lüneburg. She now works at the Institut Futur at the Freie Universität Berlin, monitoring the Global Action Programme on Education for Sustainable Development. Her main research interests are ESD, transformative science and transformative learning.

Cătălina Ulrich-Hygum is Professor of Sociology of Education at the Faculty of Psychology and Educational Sciences, University of Bucharest, with main research interests in sociology of childhood, policy and programme evaluation.

Gisela Unterweger is European Ethnologist and Co-Director of the Children – Childhood – Schooling research centre at the University of Teacher Education Zürich, Switzerland. She has a strong research interest in the anthropology of childhood. She explores and investigates through ethnographic research the cultural dimensions of schooling.

Tanja Werkl is project coordinator of the NOESIS evaluation project and doctoral researcher at the University of Vienna, Department of Education, with a thematic focus on higher education and scientific management, project management and externally funded research.

Theo Wubbels is Emeritus Professor at the Department of Education at Utrecht University. He participates in several national committees on (teacher) education and quality assurance. Theo was President of the European Educational Research Association (EERA) until September 2018.

Raphael Zahnd is Professor in the area of Inclusive Education at the School of Education, University of Applied Sciences and Arts Northwestern Switzerland. His research interests focus on inclusive education, processes of social inclusion/exclusion and disability discourse.

ABOUT EERA

EERA – EUROPEAN EDUCATIONAL RESEARCH ASSOCIATION: RESEARCH FOR THE BENEFIT OF EDUCATION AND SOCIETY

EERA, the European Educational Research Association, is an association of European educational research associations. It was established to further high quality educational research for the benefit of education and society. EERA argues that high quality research not only acknowledges its own context but also recognises wider, transnational contexts with their social, cultural and political similarities and differences. Founded in 1994, EERA has grown into a network of over 40 educational research associations in more than 35 European countries. While many of EERA's member associations have long histories, some are still young associations and the dynamic interaction between the members creates a unique and vibrant scholarly community. EERA continues to support the establishment of educational research associations in European countries without such organisations and welcomes applicants. While primarily focused on the development of European educational research, EERA promotes collaboration and ties with other associations inside and outside of Europe. The association's activities, such as the annual European Conference on Educational Research (ECER), seasonal schools for emerging and experienced researchers, academic writing workshops and publishing, build on, and promote, free and open dialogue and critical discussion and take a comprehensive and interdisciplinary approach to theory, methods and research ethics.

EERA is a democratic organisation run by the Council, consisting of representatives of EERA member associations who meet twice a year. Council members also contribute to standing working groups in between Council meetings and take an active role in promoting the Association in their own local contexts. EERA also has an executive committee which meets four times per year. EERA networks, which number 33 in 2019, are scholarly communities committed the development of areas of educational research at a European level. They play a vital role in the life of the Association and are central to the organisation and running of the annual ECER.

The most important event on the EERA calendar is the European Conference on Educational Research (ECER). Welcoming between 2500–3000 participants from about 70 countries per year, ECERs are a cooperative venture between EERA, a hosting university and a national research association who all contribute to the academic and administrative success of the event. The annual ECER is always preceded by the Emerging Researchers Conference (ERC) offering special activities for early career researchers. This focus on researchers in their early careers is a central part of EERA's mission, which seeks to support this community through a range of activities including season schools, bursaries, etc.

The annual seasonal schools for emerging and experienced researchers throughout Europe are important elements of EERA mission, too. Among the most important of these is the annual EERA Summer School, which in recent years has been hosted in Czechia, Austria, the UK, Norway and Sweden. In addition, a handful of EERA networks organise smaller season schools in areas such as Histories of Education, Mathematics Education and Curriculum Studies.

EERA also takes great pride in the EERJ – the *European Educational Research Journal*, an online peer-reviewed journal with a unique focus on Europeanisation of education and educational research. Published since 2003, it welcomes papers presented in ECERs but is also open for all submissions from within and outside EERA. In addition, some EERA networks have developed cooperative relationships with subject specific journals that encourage conference participants to submit their work for publication.

While these activities are all directed towards individual researchers, EERA is also active in organising support for educational research as collective endeavour. EERA continues to cooperate with European networks such as ISE (Initiative of Science in Europe) and EASSH (European Alliance for Social Sciences and Humanities) in order to raise awareness about the importance of research in the Social Sciences and Humanities and to raise their profile within EC funding mechanisms.

PART I

GETTING READY FOR THE UNEXPECTED

AN INTRODUCTION TO CHALLENGES IN EDUCATIONAL RESEARCH

Sofia Marques da Silva and Lucian Ciolan

'First and foremost: have fun!'

'So watch out for methodological watchdogs!' (Pierre Bourdieu in Wacquant, 1989: 54)

Vividly lived experiences and decisions taken while doing research persist largely unexplored and unaccounted. Research trajectories are not linear and are shaped by a wide scope of influences, judgements, issues of credibility, competing interests or of limits in addressing specific education questions. Decisions we make when conducting research are rarely divorced from concerns related to the social implications of our research. New developments related to the politics of financing research, to higher education institutions competing globally, to the use of new technologies to generate data, to the inclusion of participants in the research design, or to education taking place in a diversity of new contexts are introducing new questions that need to be addressed. This book has the overarching aim to provide a collection of chapters that may work as a guide to better understand and reflect on our decisions and to become more focused on identifying and dealing with different types of challenges.

WHAT IS THIS BOOK ABOUT?

The focus of this book is on discussing challenges selected by contributors, which have emerged within a research project. This book provides the reader with different types of compromises and negotiations that researchers make either to maintain high quality standards or to design research that makes sense to their contexts and participants.

This book brings together a group of researchers from the field of education to share their views and generate knowledge about challenges while enrolled in a research project. We asked for their narratives and accounts on their processes of transformation while doing research. The aim was to have a collection of contributions focused on different challenges, using a diversity of methodologies and, thus, accounting for research activity within a diversity of designs in educational research. Alongside this, a dual aim was to have a diversity of countries represented and to illustrate the value of contributions of researchers from different nationalities, generations, schools of thought and research cultures. This edited book is designed around cases, each one providing a detailed discussion focused on research challenges and the scenarios in which they are disclosed. It is aimed to assist particularly PhD students and emerging researchers, and is directed to those who need to find answers and elucidations to assist their on-going or starting research project.

WHAT IS THE FOCUS? CHALLENGES AND CASES

What qualifies as a challenge? Doing educational research is about constructing pathways and possibilities for human understanding, making sense of educational and social phenomena, interactions, policies and practices. Today, researchers are being challenged by new and multi-sited contexts and phenomena, collective definitions of agendas, dealing with the multi-modal nature of the information that affects education practices, policies and discourses. Research conditions, organisations and cultures have also increasingly changed over the past decades. Research may have become a standardised application of techniques and instrumental solutions, through an increased pressure on delivering outcomes that have a market value; or it may have become a more transparent and negotiated process, involving research participants working collaboratively, against dominant forms of thinking. These are two very different frames of reference for educational research.

We understand that methodological challenges are also theoretical challenges: these might be the challenge of engaging participants; of negotiation and dealing with different powers – institutional, contextual, political; of maintaining a methodological critical perspective; of understanding our own agency; of developing equitable partnerships; of doing educational research in familiar contexts and the difficulty in creating the necessary analytical strangeness (Silva, 2011). Challenges might be at an epistemological level and demand epistemic disruptions (Meneses, 2008; Santos, 2008) or may be everyday life decisions aimed at sustaining participants' commitment during the process, evoking researchers' feelings of vulnerability (Dickson-Swift et al., 2007). Doing research involves experimenting in awkward situations and often finding ourselves in uncomfortable places, making controversial decisions, often challenging methodological prescriptions (Bourdieu and Wacquant, 1992). Either way, while undertaking an enquiry, researchers are always embarking on both an arduous and gratifying endeavour.

We consider of equal importance the capacity of the researcher to understand the challenges of the research process as they occur in practice and the capacity to make decisions to overcome these challenges. Researchers need to be reflective practitioners themselves and have the capacity not just to carefully design and conduct the process to obtain valid and reliable data and results to advance knowledge and/or improve policy and practice. They also need the capacity to be reflexive in relation to their own process of research, in order to understand what they have done as well as imagine and predict challenges they may encounter, what decisions they make and what can be learnt for their own future projects or for other researchers facing similar challenges.

This is not a common methods book. Other excellent publications already cover different methods and methodologies, from classic approaches to the most up to date research designs and innovative techniques for collecting and analysing data. In the past decade we have seen a proliferation of books and handbooks on methods with an increasing interest from different generations of researchers. This book is not dedicated to methods and respective techniques nor is it about decisions at every step of a research process. Other books dedicated to methods already cover topics on how to design and conduct a research project in education.

WHY IS THIS BOOK UNIQUE?

This book focuses on a European dimension of doing educational research. This is understood not as a celebratory, Europeanised or exclusionary perspective, as problematised by Philippou (2005), but as a global and 'joint project that envisages democracy, pluralism and an intercultural approach to diversity' (Enache, 2011: 110). In this introduction the editors would like to allude to the fact that this is an international collection of contributions, with a diversity of cultural, linguistic styles and institutional backgrounds. A question raised in a publication accounting for a roundtable during the ECER 2014 anniversary celebrations in Porto, is very much adequate to this book: 'Who is given voice within this forum?' As explained in the publication, 'This question is specific for the EERA and ECER, and is maybe a question we need as a constant reminder of the multiple landscapes of nationalities and languages we operate in' (Hoveid, 2015: 23). This plurality of belongings is at the centre of the attempt to create understandings and agreements on interpretations (Gadamer, 1989), and it reminds us of, and keeps us awake to, the power relations within the dialogic process of reaching a common meaning through an hermeneutic understanding (Habermas, 1984, 1988).

The book draws on a diversity of researchers' experiences while developing their research within specific projects and it represents the opportunity to demonstrate how a networked collaboration may be cultivated across diversity. The European dimension has been a central discussion for a long time within EERA, fostering vivid discussions and controversies about the meaning underlying this idea, which is influencing research policies and communities at European level (Moos and Wubbels, 2014). This book is a contribution to develop a bit further what might be included and framed by this dimension, of an inherently blurred, yet distinctive, but never complete, nature. By doing this we are not seeking isolation, by just including research projects uniquely developed on European soil, but we are making space for educational researchers across Europe. This is also our tribute to EERA history and a contribution to the construction of a European educational research space (Keiner and Hofbauer, 2014; Lawn et al., 2003; Sirota et al., 2002). The European dimension will hopefully be seen both in this and other publications from EERA and in the organisation itself frequently inviting 'researchers to share the journey undertaken so far and through this become engaged in the future development of the association' (Hoveid, Keiner and Figueiredo, 2014: 401).

EERA has been fostering high-quality education since its foundation in 1994 (Madalińska-Michalak, 2018); and in 2014, when celebrating its twentieth anniversary, the opportunity to debate it again arose in the light of that year's conference theme: *Past, Present and Future* (Hoveid Keiner and Figueiredo, 2014). Aligned with this structural and intergenerational effort, EERA is increasingly enhancing emerging researchers' participation, trying to address their needs, providing open spaces and opportunities to raise questions related to education and to discuss critical points such as those concerning research quality and processes. In fact, the quality of research was the specific theme of the ECER in 2007 in Ghent. In that year, Jenny Ozga in her keynote discussed what she called 'the "moral panic" around the quality of research in education' (Ozga, 2008: 261). This book continues from this statement and aims to discuss and develop collaborative understandings of social life and experiences within educational research.

This book is distinctive. The purpose of this book is to illuminate different ecologies of engagement within the research process, by accounting, interpreting and framing specific challenges. Each contributor delved into selected challenges that are contextualised into specific social, educational, political and historical contexts, but that may provide us with reflections beyond the immediate context and expand the reflection to global narratives and understandings about educational development and educational research in the global framework of research agendas.

HOW DID WE GET HERE? IMAGINING A BOOK

The European Educational Research Association has been encouraging editorial projects in order to give a clear and strong voice to the current status and prospects of educational research in Europe. In 2016, EERA was invited by SAGE to develop a proposal for a book aiming to promote researchers outside of the Anglo-American context, some regular attendants at ECER.

The origins of this book are also sustained in the relationship that the editors have through participation in the EERA council, as executive members, representatives of national associations or through involvement in EERA network activities. The EERA council empowered the four editors, more than three years ago, to develop a proposal and address the call from the publisher.

Our aim was to have a contribution grounded in educational research in Europe and sustained in lived experience and research activities taking place in a diversity of contexts and types of projects. This ethnomethodologically grounded approach led us to privilege practical reasonings and implicit knowledge, meaning that we were looking for processes of interpretation through which actors, in this case researchers, give meaning to challenges in the course of action and made their options accountable and justifiable (Boltanski and Chiapello, 1999). This is one of the strengths of the book and would influence our standpoint.

We started by asking the following questions: what would be a good methods book for PhD students? What would be a relevant, interesting and helpful tool for those enrolled in different stages of a PhD/post-graduate process? The challenge of the editorial team was, from the very beginning, to come up with an innovative idea, which would also fit the requests of the potentially interested target groups. There were two sources of inspiration for that: our own experience as researchers, academics teaching educational research, (meta)analysing the existing knowledge base; and an exploratory research involving Master students, PhD students and emerging researchers. In the next section we will explain the different steps we took.

STEP 1: AN EXPLORATORY RESEARCH

We started by developing an exploratory research with the purpose of understanding what could be missing in other methods books. In the summer of 2016 we involved 94 students from approximately 20 different countries, not only European, enrolled in different stages of their research and with different experience. Of these, 56 were PhD students involved in the EERA Summer School[1] at Johannes Kepler University Linz; 14 were PhD students from the Doctoral Programme in Sciences of Education of the University of Porto; and 24 were Master students of Education and Management from Johannes Kepler University Linz. We developed a small questionnaire (N = 80) and focus group discussions (two groups with 14 students[2]) aiming to discuss three questions:

1   What type of resources/tools/help do you search for/use when it comes to decide which methodology/methods/design you will use in your research?
2   Which are the most significant difficulties you face/faced when making decisions on methodology/methods/design for your research?
3   What, in your opinion, would make an excellent textbook on methodology/methods?

SETTING THE TONE: 'WE HIDE WHAT WE KNOW'

Results of this limited study were already a relevant indication on how to proceed. Students considered that techniques and methods used in educational research were, in general, already well documented. Additionally, they highlighted the fact that procedures and how methodological decisions were taken were not so well explained. They were eager for something that would explore the know-how of research, through real experiences and narratives. As it was voiced, they were seeking a 'textbook that wouldn't separate everything, but that would guide you through the process'.

We understand that a good textbook gives information about difficulties, and how to deal with the unexpected. A student participating in a focus group discussion (FDG) asks the question: 'What to do when you have your script well done and then an unexpected topic, outside the script, comes up'. Necessarily, challenges bring additional tensions and complexity to the research process and this is often less discussed and sometimes silenced. Therefore, a new book would be relevant if it could be a place to ignite a collective discussion: 'Something that at some point is not an individual discussion, but a collective discussion. Something that would connect people to discuss a case' (FGD).

THE NEED FOR AN INTERCULTURAL APPROACH

One of the most vigorous statements made by students during our small enquiry on what would be a good research methods book was the need to have an intercultural approach and awareness about our own cultural positioning while making decisions and constructing scientific arguments. Educational research, like every research project, is never neutral, as a participant of our exploratory study considers: 'there is a bias in the methodological approaches' and 'behind those options we have worldviews, and we usually are not aware of that' (FGD student). Accounting how we, as researchers, engage with a conversation and explore a form of interpretation may constitute an ethical effort to make visible how those that own a stronger voice try to dominate the real world through their rationale in the communicative interaction (Fonseca, 1992). It is developed through a dialogic understanding of a diversity of intersubjective encounters.

The exploratory research with emerging researchers provided us with key findings to set fundamental and structural options that guided our work, framing the scope of the book, its structure and tone. It is, therefore, a book organised around cases and focused on specific challenges and strategies to solve them. With students' perspectives focusing on the idea of challenges within projects and processes, diversity and interculturality of standpoints, methods and decisions, we approached the EERA thematic networks,[3] through a call for proposals.

STEP 2: A NETWORKED REALITY

EERA has 33 networks organised under different topics in educational research. They are diverse in their organisation, members' composition, schools of thought and participants' countries. The call addressing networks was designed to encourage the submission of proposals that were focused on challenges emerging from a research project. Over two years we got involved with contributors, working closely with them on the proposals, we organised workshops and meetings during ECER 2017 and ECER 2018 to further discuss the cases and put them into a wider perspective.

This is a book with meta-reflections on researchers' intellectual trajectories and their situated positions (Haraway, 1988; Harding, 2003; Silva and Parker Webster, 2018). It deals with the options researchers have, and the choices they make, and how these influence the research journey and, above all, the knowledge that is produced: 'positionality and knowledge production are linked, such that knowledge is positioned and situated and therefore context specific, limited, and partial, but not completely relativist' (Silva and Parker Webster, 2018: 504–505). This book provides guidance and critical reflection on practical challenges and accounts for researchers' commitments and limits while doing research. But it goes further, as it highlights a broader challenge of interrogating traditional approaches, models and assumptions regarding inquiry.

THE FINAL OUTCOME

All the chapters of this book contribute to the perspective of research for interpretation and understanding, achieving a balance between the need for a socially responsible research approach and the current instrumentalisation and over-standardisation, dominated by principles of efficiency, performance and impact. As editors, we consider a composite perspective to be more in line with the pedagogical tradition of Europe, centred primarily on the essential role of education, on wellbeing, freedom and diversity of societies and individuals.

All chapters of this book have the same structure. Each one includes an introductory clarification of the chapter, followed by a more developed presentation of the project. The next section looks in depth at the challenges that are addressed in the chapter, and these will vary in number. Each contribution then discusses and reflects on the chosen challenges and clarifies strategies for responses and further discussions. Before the concluding remarks, each chapter provides the reader with a checklist for guidance. After the conclusion, additional readings that authors consider relevant to further explore similar challenges are given.

The different contributions have been organised into different parts. Part I, Getting Ready for the Unexpected, is intended to work as a reminder that in a research venture there is a lot that can't be prefigured. Dealing with sensitive issues, research fatigue or participants' refusal, unexpected findings, over-researched contexts, surprising theoretical solutions or conceptual dilemmas, among others, may cause difficulties for researchers, in general, but also among those undertaking postgraduate and doctoral research. Educational research is a non-linear process, with different levels of unpredictability. However, researchers may anticipate a diversity of challenges such as those presented, described and discussed in the following parts.

Part II, Negotiating Research Contexts and Demands from the Field, has chapters discussing challenges that emerge from the negotiation and power relations across different cultural structures. As a researcher one may be confronted with the negotiation of meanings, resulting from a multi-sited experience of following and mapping networks in unfamiliar contexts. In other cases, we may need to deal with tensions and demands resulting from over familiarity with educational settings and actors or with sensitive issues related to negotiating representation of experiences and voicing those we study.

Part III, Exploring Other Paths for Interpretation, signposts challenges coming from the complex process of interpretation in research. Challenges may be found in the process of selecting the right model for doing literature reviews to theorise complexity; in the implications that sampling and related findings may have in the interpretation; in the process of constructing new narratives for illuminating and understanding less heard voices, by engaging participants in the research process; in the existence of multi-layered, integrated analysis, resulting from collaborative, and sometimes conflicting, analytical work towards a knowledge-building community.

Part IV, Building a Common Ground for Understanding, has a collection of contributions that outline challenges that appear in international collaboration and cross-national research endeavours. Chapters included in this part dwell on different conceptual and theoretical positionalities posed when establishing a common arena for collaboration and for incorporating international and global dimensions. Issues explored relate to mediating, reconciling multiple visions or dealing with theoretical gaps while interpreting multidimensional and complex phenomena or creating end products. The contributions open space to discuss the appropriated competences that in those settings a researcher needs to develop either related to the construction of instruments, dissemination or to establish ethical guidelines.

Part V, Bridging Research and Policy, puts forward contributions for a discussion of challenges emerging from different layers of expectations, demands and pressures, allowing us to further reflect on how educational researchers are engaging in policy-relevant research. Research for generating change has a particularly important role in education. Not only the levels of data and translation of findings will meet different expectations regarding the research, but also the meaning-making and accountability may intensify already existing tensions, in particular when responding to the demands of applied research, or to academic goals. Making sense and translating complex processes and results is a challenge, especially when different actors are involved and evidence-based knowledge to inform policies and influence decisions needs to be communicated.

The last part VI, Getting Ready for an Open Future, includes a short chapter by the editors intended to close the book, but also points forward in relation to educational research.

The series of 'exercises' involved in the making of this book has in itself been a process of generating new knowledge: about emerging researchers engaged in EERA activities and about new research trends, pressures and politics of research and educational research drivers. The book represents a collective reflection similar to a community of practice, understanding community as a 'resource and a repository of meaning' (Cohen, 1985: 45). It has given us as editors the opportunity to relate to researchers' praxis, which will hopefully enable readers to make reinterpretations of their own research endeavours. As editors we also integrated our individual perspectives, ontological and epistemological standpoints, contexts, backgrounds and cultural diversity into an integrated narrative. Our aim is that the different narratives may resonate with the reader and be part of an ongoing conversation. It is hoped that this book will make a contribution to research communities in education and that we all may learn from differing experiences and contexts. As editors we hope you will enjoy this book and we hope it will help you navigate some of the challenges you are confronted with in your own project(s). At least knowing that the phenomena you are struggling with is also common to other projects, is sometimes a consolation. Happy reading!

NOTES

1   Since 2011 EERA has, together with different higher education institutions, and regional/national research associations, promoted a summer school for emerging researchers in education, mainly focused on providing methodological support to participants and has created a platform for exchange, debate and advice for their projects. For more details see https://eera-ecer.de/season-schools/eera-summer-school-2019/ (accessed 20 January 2019).

2   We would like to acknowledge the persons and organisations that, besides EERA, facilitated the development of this exploratory research: the Director of the Doctoral Programme in Education Research, from the Faculty of Psychology and Education Sciences of the University of Porto, Professor Isabel Menezes and all doctoral students that in 2016 participated in the focus group discussions; Professor Herbert Altrichter from the Johannes Kepler University Linz and Master students of Education and Management; all students participating in EERA Summer School that took place in 2016 at Johannes Kepler University Linz.

3   EERA is organised in 33 thematic networks and one emerging researchers' group. See https://eera-ecer.de/networks/ (accessed 20 January 2019).

REFERENCES

Boltanski, L. and Chiapello, È. (1999) *Le Nouvel Esprit du Capitalism*. Paris: PUF.

Bourdieu, P. and Wacquant, L. (1992) *Invitation to Reflexive Sociology*. Chicago: University of Chicago Press.

Cohen, A. P. (1985) *The Symbolic Construction of Community*. London and New York. Tavistock Publications.

Dickson-Swift, V., James, E.L., Kippen, S. and Liamputtong, P. (2007) 'Doing sensitive research: what challenges do qualitative researchers face?', *Qualitative Research*, 7(3): 327–353. DOI: 10.1177/1468794107078515.

Enache, R. (2011) 'Possible orientations of the European dimension in Romanian educational policy', *Policy Futures in Education*, 9(1): 109–113.

Fonseca, I. (1992) *Deixis, Tempo e Narração*. Porto: Fundação Engenheiro António de Almeida.

Gadamer, H.-G. (1989) *Truth and Method*. London: Sheed & Ward.

Habermas, J. (1984) *Sociologie & Théorie du Langage*. Paris: Armand Colin.

Habermas, J. (1988) *On the Logic of the Social Sciences*. Cambridge: Polity Press.

Haraway, D. (1988) 'Situated knowledge: the science question in feminism as a site of discourse on the privilege of partial perspective', *Feminist Studies*, 14(3): 575–599.

Harding, S. (2003) *The Feminist Standpoint Theory Reader: Intellectual and Political Controversies*. London: Routledge.

Hoveid, M. H. (2015) 'Past, present and future of the European Educational Research Association (EERA) and European Conference on Educational Research: Roundtable with former EERA presidents and secretary generals about the significance of the EERA and its future', *European Educational Research Journal*, 14(1): 23–25. DOI: 10.1177/1474904114565527.

Hoveid, M. H., Keiner, E. and Figueiredo, M. P. (2014) 'The European Educational Research Association: people, practices and policy over the last 20 years', *European Educational Research Journal*, 13(4): 399–403.

Keiner, E. and Hofbauer, S. (2014) 'EERA and its European Conferences on Educational Research: a patchwork of research on European educational research', *European Educational Research Journal*, 13(4): 504–518.

Lawn, M., Agalianos, A., Brinet, O. and McGaw, B. (2003) 'Is there an emerging education research space?', *European Educational Research Journal*, 2(1): 180–188.

Madalińska-Michalak, J. (2018) 'Fostering quality education research: the role of the European Educational Research Association as a scientific association', *European Educational Research Journal*. DOI: 10.1177/1474904118797735.

Meneses, M. P. (2008) 'Epistemologias do Sul', *Revista Crítica de Ciências Sociais*, 80: 5–10.

Moos, L. and Wubbels, T. (2014) 'EERA: a participant or an agent in European research policy? A governance perspective', *European Educational Research Journal*, 13(4): 451–463.

Ozga, J. (2008) 'Knowledge: research steering and research quality', *European Educational Research Journal*, 7(3): 261–272.

Philippou, S. (2005) 'The problem of the European dimension in education: a principled reconstruction of the Greek Cypriot curriculum', *European Educational Research Journal*, 4(4): 343–367.

Santos, B. S. (2008) 'A Filosofia à venda, a douta ignorância e a aposta de pascal', *Revista Crítica de Ciencias Sociais*, 80: 11–43.

Silva, S. M. (2011) 'Getting closer to the stranger? Methodological and conceptual challenges in educational contexts', in T. Werler (ed.), *Heterogeneity: General Didactics Meets the Stranger*. Munster: Maxmann. pp. 55–64.

Silva, S. and Parker Webster, J. (2018) 'Positionality and standpoint', in D. Beach, C. Bragley and S. Marques da Silva (eds), *The Wiley Handbook of Ethnography of Education*. Medford, MA: Wiley Blackwell. pp. 501–512.

Sirota, R., Zay, D., Lawn, M. and Keiner, E. (2002) 'European Networking in Education. Report on Roundtable 2, held at ECER 2001, Lille, 7 September 2001', *European Educational Research Journal*, 1(3): 566–592.

Wacquant, L. T. D. (1989) 'Towards a reflexive sociology: a workshop with Pierre Bourdieu', *Sociological Theory*, 7(1): 26–63.

1

DOING EDUCATIONAL RESEARCH

Marit Honerød Hoveid and Angelika Paseka

Educational research goes far beyond technical and methodological skills and this book aims to address the *process* of doing educational research, meaning what happens in *practice*. The objective throughout the chapters of this book is to analyse challenges that educational researchers encounter and have to overcome in a very diverse typology of research projects, and to demonstrate that there are lessons to be learned for other researchers in these analyses. In this first chapter, two of the editors of the book discuss some of these challenges in relation to each other and discuss some of the broad, overarching themes of the book.

1.1 INTRODUCTION

This book speaks from three perspectives within the broad field of educational research: the first is the perspective of the *researcher* with a special focus on an emerging researcher in the process of conducting a research project. In doing educational research, one comes up against a variety of challenges: some are more common while others are specific to the given project and context. The second perspective is related to how one delimits *educational* research. It is necessary to define what is meant by education and educational research – not an easy task given the broadness and transformations continuously happening within this field. Finally, the third is the perspective of *international* research. Whereas national particularities and territorialism in doing research have made it possible for local traditions to evolve, through the influence of globalisation in research and the launch of large projects by global players, such as the EU and OECD, new topics have emerged. With this development new demands and challenges concerning research in general, and more specifically in terms of theoretical, methodological and ethical questions in educational research, arise.

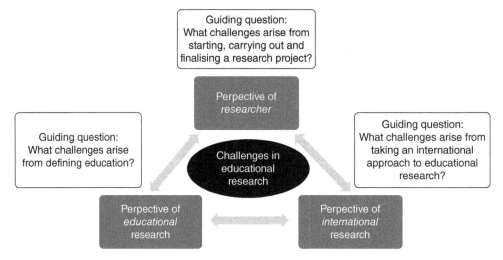

Figure 1.1   Three perspectives on challenges in doing educational research

1.2 THREE PERSPECTIVES ON CHALLENGES IN EDUCATIONAL RESEARCH

Let us address these three perspectives in more detail. Looking at the *first* perspective – from the researcher's point of view, especially the *emerging researcher*, it is sometimes rather confusing and difficult to grasp what one has become engaged in and it takes time to get to grips with the complexities of doing educational research. You must allow yourself the time, and have the patience, to let the field open itself to you. However, if one accepts uncertainty in the course of doing research, we think a future filled with many exciting and challenging moments is guaranteed.

We acknowledge that doing educational research is challenging. This is also one of the reasons why this book has materialised. In the introduction, we addressed the process that led to this book being written. A research process is full of uncertainties in all the stages of the project. The belief that there exists just one solution for a research challenge is an illusion, the reality is quite the opposite, many different ways of how to proceed and to find solutions exist. Therefore, we wanted to write a methods book that avoided simply discussing the *dos* and *don'ts* of conducting educational research, as found in manuals and procedural guidelines for researchers. There is an abundance of these books, some directed especially at the field of educational research (Conrad and Serlin, 2016; Creswell, 2015), others more directed at various ways of carrying out qualitative and quantitative research (Flick, 2014; Silverman, 2017).[1]

In order to get a better insight into the actual process of research we asked for the experiences of researchers on how they handled challenges that occurred in a project they had done. By addressing research projects and the processes entailed in doing research, we asked researchers to do a meta-analysis of one of their own research projects and use it as a case study. We asked them to reflect on how they handled the untidiness of doing research and the uncertainties in the different phases of a research project in the field of education and consequently how they found solutions to the challenges they encountered.

In relation to the *second* perspective, how one delimits what is meant by *educational research*, we argue that this will have an impact on the research conducted. It is not an easy task to do this and looking at other methods books, which address education as a research field, we saw that there are various difficulties involved in how one delimits the field. A common approach is that doing educational research is not addressed specifically; it is instead subsumed under ways of doing social science research in general. What we found was that some of the volumes relevant for educational research describe generic research methods, which might be useful in other research fields as well (e.g. Arthur et al. 2012; Cohen, Manion and Morrison, 2018). Believing that the field is important and will have an impact on the research, it became pertinent for us to try to delimit what we mean by educational research. What characterises educational research as a field is (1) the fact that it does not belong to one disciplinary field, rather you may find entries into educational research through most disciplinary fields of academia thus making it a multi-faceted and multi-disciplinary field of research. It is also a field, which has (2) a strong practical component, meaning that education refers to something one does – it is a practical activity, taking place in and out of the designated institution called school.[2] This activity is commonly referred to as teaching and learning on its most fundamental level and will involve organisational and political activities on more superior levels. All these levels of practice can be studied through educational research. This practical component influences the research in terms of asking for research that aims to improve or make changes to education. Finally, and connected to this last aspect, (3) education always has a normative component which emphasises norms and values that should be taken into account in educational processes. In the continental European tradition this has been addressed through *bildung* theories. However, educational research requires an analytical distance when one assesses what happens in teaching and learning or in implementing education programmes and policies. How normative aspects of education plays with and into educational research is sometimes difficult to discern.

By bringing these three characteristics together, some transformations of topics can be traced if we take a short glimpse at the history of educational research. At an early *first stage*, what can be traced is considerations and philosophical reflections around education that had a strong normative bias. This accounted primarily for the relationships that educators are involved in. Mostly it dealt with the direct relation between teacher and student, and with what teachers needed to instil in students for them to become 'valuable' citizens and good humans. Examples of these approaches are Jean Jacques Rousseau's considerations about the education of Emile (France), Johann Friedrich Herbart's lectures about pedagogical tact (Germany) and from the twentieth century considerations related to the reform of pedagogy, which analyses different ways of encouraging children to learn, like Maria Montessori (Italy) or Rudolf Steiner (Germany). In these approaches the child was at the centre of the pedagogies and educational programmes. This normative underpinning of pedagogical processes was in line with the meaning of 'pedagogy', deriving from the Greek words *país* (boy, child) and *ágō* (leading) with the meaning: leading a child. If this first phase had a more pedagogical approach to education and also was to some degree gradually influenced by developmental psychology, the next stage was the era of educational sociology.

In a next *second stage*, one can see that the view on education was broadened, by introducing the organisation, in most cases schools, in which the personal relationship between teachers and students is embedded. A well-known example is Michael Rutter's (Rutter et al., 1982) study of secondary schools, *Fifteen Thousand Hours* (United Kingdom). By focusing on the structures inherent in the organisation he and his team found out that schools make a difference and that this has an influence on the children and the teaching and learning processes. This is also somewhat in line with the Swedish study, 'Why are schools different?' by Gerhard Arfwedson (1984), discussing questions of culture and organisation in light of the concept school codes (Sweden/Scandinavia). Paul Willis's (1978) critical study *Learning to Labour* (United Kingdom) analyses the dialectic of control within the school setting. The teachers and the students and especially those boys who form a counter-culture to the formal culture of the school know how to cope, to resist as well as to push the limits of rules and norms within their power (see also Giddens, 1984/2009).

Inspired by Willis's study, Werner Helsper (Germany) started, in the 1980s, to analyse school cultures as symbolic orders of single schools: how they shape the learning atmosphere, the ways of instruction, the practices of interacting, giving recognition and care or not, the rules and regulations and how they are negotiated in schools – having in mind that Germany has a highly segregated school system (with academic versus general secondary schools), which are situated in different areas (rural versus urban). Several research teams have in accordance with this addressed how different schools' cultures depend on the school type and the students' social background, and how the *habitus* of students are shaped by this (e.g. Helsper, 2008).[3]

At this second stage of educational research, schools and their local contexts were researched by carrying out case studies often using different qualitative methods for data collection and analyses. Schools were mostly seen as part of a national educational system and their function in society was critically assessed. Over the last decades this has changed dramatically. Instead of focusing on schools, school systems have become a primary focus of educational research. We identify this as a *third stage* of educational research. In this transition of focus, the outcome of education and the idea of using education as a vehicle for economic growth have been increasingly emphasised. A combination of economic reasoning, statistics and psychometrics has begun to dominate as educational research.

The efficiency of school systems is underlined, and the idea seems to be that measurements through testing of students' learning results can predict better efficiency of the system (Hoveid and Hoveid, 2018). Powered by the idea of international competition, economic reasoning and the neo-liberal ideas related to the outcome of education, high stakes testing like PISA or TIMSS has developed on a global scale and these tests have started to dominate educational research (Rizvi, 2009). However, such testing and rankings produce ordinal positions and a hierarchical relationship between the countries involved. At the same time, they flatten differences within one country and reduce complexity. The embeddedness of the grammar of marketisation and market governance into research has created a blind spot (Robertson, 2018).[4] For higher education such an economic objective was installed with the Bologna Declaration from 1999, emphasising the importance of student mobility and employability for an overall development in Europe. The declaration was followed up by the *qualification framework* aiming to align higher education in Europe and beyond.

In summing up this short and very condensed historical overview, what becomes evident is that different purposes and research orientations dominate different periods within the field of educational research. One conclusion we draw is that topics as well as research methods have changed more profoundly within the last decades. The emphasis on doing quantitative and empirical research is probably the most prevalent in relation to earlier research within the educational field. Consequently, and with a critical stance towards educational research, we have to admit that a generic or uniform understanding of what educational research is or might be does not exist, although we realise that some macro-trends can be identified. What we contend is that educational research addresses the field of education in a multi-faceted way, and it is this complexity that characterises educational research and what makes it different from many other fields of research.

Let us now return to Figure 1.1, mentioned above, and highlight educational research from the *third* perspective – internationalisation of research, where some specific challenges arise. This volume covers *international research* from three dimensions: (1) the authors are international, meaning: coming from (predominantly) different European countries; (2) research projects are (partly) carried out by international teams; and (3) the international interrelatedness is explicitly described in the context of globalisation and put into a critical research discourse. A point of departure for this methods book on educational research is the multi-national and multi-lingual context of European researchers, not speaking English as their first language. Having a background in one national system of education, researchers in international research are frequently faced with challenging demands related to cultural sensitivity, different research traditions as well as different ethical considerations pertaining to different cultural contexts, if not before, then as soon as they want to publish their research in the *lingua franca* of research – English. We think there is something to be learned about doing research in general from this situation within educational research, namely that one should not take things for granted and generally become more sensitive towards ways in which research, and especially research findings, can appropriate the understanding and interpretation of phenomena within the field. Operating as researchers in what we could name a multi-cultural context and sensitivity towards the other (student, teacher, parent, etc.) and that which is studied, often overlooked if one operates within a single or hegemonic paradigm. This is not to say that if you are a researcher who has the traits of a non-fluent (*broken* in colloquial terms) English writer, you are necessarily aware of all the difficulties involved in translating and interpreting from one context to another. Being open to and acknowledging that you do not hold the key to a right interpretation, a correct or true way of doing educational research is also connected with the scientific foundations of your research (*wissenschaftsphilosophie*), and what kind of beliefs you yourself hold about the relations of an empirical and/or (social) constructed reality.

In this volume an opportunity has been given in terms of providing a voice to European educational research contexts that are not so visible and which are easily neglected or marginalised for different reasons, language being one of them. We strongly believe that mapping out as much as possible of the educational research terrain in Europe is a valuable undertaking and that this will bring strength to the field. Educational research is a field under pressure, if we look to the way educational research is (not) prioritised by, for instance, supra-national research funding agencies, such as the EU and OECD. Research funding agencies seem to think that large quantitative research projects are more important than genuine pedagogical questions. We claim that genuine pedagogical questions have become a blind spot on the international research agenda. Although education is highly prioritised as a practice and as a field of political governance, it is primarily seen as a field of dissemination and thus for some reason less attention is given to the need for a broad range of educational research.[5]

In the next three sections, we will address challenges in educational research using the frame we have drawn above by referring to three different perspectives on challenges in doing educational research: the researcher (emerging), the field (educational research) and the context (national/international). We will try to address these perspectives in terms of the challenges discussed in this volume. This is not intended as a comprehensive undertaking in terms of listing and categorising what the different chapters address. It is a rather loose and more interpretive linking of some of the themes that run across the chapters of the book, while also trying to clarify certain aspects of undertaking educational research.

1.3 CHALLENGES FOR EMERGING RESEARCHERS

To address the magnitude of challenges encountered in doing educational research a much bigger volume than this book would be needed, and even then, we would not be able to cover everything. The difficulties and challenges that postgraduates (Master, PhDs and post-docs) face as emerging researchers in their own research projects do not seem to focus on knowledge about methods, epistemological considerations or knowing about the stages they must go through in order to conduct their research. Through a small survey made by the editors of this book we gained feedback on what students wanted to learn and know more about. As we have explained earlier (see Introduction) the idea for the foci of this book derived from some of the wishes these students formulated. They articulated a want for a methods book that gives them concrete examples, explanations and practices, encouraging them to find solutions for concrete problems.

Making this kind of methods book on educational research required that researchers were willing to share some of their own queries and challenges, in short that they were willing to open up to the untidiness of what it means to do research. When the findings and sometimes conclusions are on the table, the process leading up to the final stages of a research project is often forgotten. We asked researchers who responded to the call to write a chapter in this book to reflect back on the research process of a project they were engaged in and to highlight some of the challenges they encountered and what choices they had to make. This kind of reflexivity, looking back on what was done, describing and assessing the given actions, is not a common activity for researchers.[6] Furthermore, they were also asked to present their descriptions of challenges and solutions in a way that could be made accessible and provide possible insight for emerging researchers. Such insights into research processes are quite unique. There are aspects and variations of doing educational research, which are not covered in this approach. Below we have tried to address some of the common and important aspects of this reflexive approach to doing educational research.

1.3.1 CARRYING OUT A RESEARCH PROJECT

At the outset of a new project, the tasks sometimes seem overwhelming, whether this is an individual PhD study or a large-scale international research project. Starting, carrying out and finalising a study are stages or rather periods in a process, each of them with their own specificities. In light of this, what the researchers in Chapter 4 describe is perhaps very important to remember: allow for *time* to pass. This might sound strange, why is it important to let time pass? It means that you must allow for processes to evolve, and this takes time. Why, you might ask. Well, for the simple reason, that if you allow time to pass, something which looked difficult at first glance might have solved itself after some time – that happens sometimes. What seemed very strange and unfamiliar the first time it came up in your analyses, for example, might after some time have become the main point you are making. And if you are working with people, as one often does in fieldwork or in research groups, this often means there are different worldviews and opinions, and your research might challenge some beliefs in the field or among the researchers involved. This is what the researchers of Chapter 4 experienced, when they entered the field. Then it is important to have time to get used to and to acknowledge what these differences are, and to decide how they are best solved. You might have to negotiate and adapt the roles of the researchers when you are in close collaboration with a research field, especially if there are strong normative perspectives in the field.

Therefore, before you enter a field, do a deep screening of the context you are going to study, which is good advice from the authors of Chapter 12. It might, in the longer perspective of your project, spare you some challenges you did not need, because you were prepared and anticipated what would come. However, avoiding differences or challenges is not necessarily the point, but being prepared for what they might be and how they are going to intervene with the project is important, not least in terms of how it might influence what kind of data you will be able to gather and what restrictions these differences might put on your analyses and discussions. Remember, as the authors of Chapter 11 claim: 'Research is not a neutral activity' (p. 243).

1.3.2 HOW TIME INTERVENES

Time is an essential factor in research, in so many ways. Who has not, at the start of their PhD, thought they had all the time in the world, three or maybe four years ahead, and then gradually realised that there is not enough time for all there is to do? Most of the projects that are used as cases in this book argue in some form or other about the need to be systematic, thorough, transparent. Research requires that throughout the different phases of the research process you will have to substantiate all the choices and decisions you make, and, of course, all the claims you put forward in the name of research. There are some fairly strict rules on what is seen as good conduct in research. For instance, for the sake of transparency you make visible how you generated and validated results by sharing them with scientific communities of practice, but also ensure that all the authors you cite are authors whose work you have read and know. This can sometimes make research a tedious and slow business, it takes time, and this is something everyone with research experience will tell you. This requires a methodical attitude, something that might throw many researchers off, but it is a necessary part of good conduct in doing educational research. Having said this, also remember, as the authors of Chapter 7 underline, the need to have fun while you do research. Through being prepared for what you might expect, such as the time-consuming aspects of 'preparing your data and figuring out what model is best suited to answer your research question' (p. 150), you can become more relaxed about the workload of the project. A research process seldom follows a straight line, a lot of unexpected things will happen. Remember, sometimes it is the accidents, the unexpected, that create the basis of new knowledge.

1.3.3 WHAT KIND OF RESEARCHER ARE YOU? ABOUT COLLABORATION INHERENT TO RESEARCH

The author of Chapter 5 uses two different metaphors for doing literature reviews, 'net fishing' and 'whale hunting', which are just as descriptive of the whole process of doing research: 'While fishermen who do "net fishing" throw their net and filter the sea with it, whale hunters direct their boats to places where the chance of encountering these big animals is greater, they wait for them to appear and then they concentrate their efforts on catching them', Halász writes (p. 93). In front of, as well as during, a research project it might be worthwhile pondering what kind of 'fisher(wo)man' you are. In times of mixed methods, it might be that you do a little bit of both. Another possible scenario is that you start out doing 'net fishing' and later, when you know more about what you are looking for, become a 'whale hunter'. If nothing else this is a reminder of the dynamics and different roles in the different stages of doing educational research.

The classical image of an academic researcher is the one situated in his ivory tower, all by himself (and yes, this stereotype is predominantly a man). In educational research you will address a field, both in and out of school. This usually involves people participating and being addressed, who are within a context: a practice, an institution, a nation. This often-underestimated part of a research undertaking, the fact that in most cases your (educational) research deals with humans, is frequently overlooked. From humans the unexpected can be expected, they are unpredictable, as Hanna Arendt reminds us (1989). Working with people also raises ethical obligations, which one takes on as a researcher and it underscores that if your research involves close collaboration with children, students, teachers, parents and so forth, and you are dependent on them to get data for your research project, then how you conduct yourself in the field will have what we could call a 'backwash effect'. The authors of Chapter 6 discuss a project working with storytelling, and they emphasise the importance of providing a safe space for participants to tell their stories: 'To [e]nable safe spaces for storytellers, listeners and the developers of the research process: feeling safe, acknowledged and understood is crucial for enabling the sharing of stories as this can be intimate process' (p. 127). So, the backwash effect you might experience, if you are not able to provide this kind of space, is that your research participants will hold back and refrain from telling you their stories.

Another collaborative aspect of doing research is addressed by the authors of Chapter 8, pertaining to the actual doing of the research – how to analyse data: 'By assuming the role of a co-participating researcher in data sessions, [the researcher] is expected to carefully, empathically and critically listen, observe and be engaged in a dialogue aimed at supporting other people's research by introducing various skills and multiple perspectives to the process' (p. 172). This important collaborative aspect of doing research, that research is something you do together with others, is paramount. Although other chapters in this book do not address the collaborative aspects of their research projects, this seems to be an underlying way of working within most of the projects.

In the various stages of doing educational research we have above highlighted what we find are the most important aspects, running through the whole research process from the beginning until you finish: time, yourself as a researcher and relations between yourself, other researchers and the research participants. There are of course a lot of technicalities and tools you must learn in order to do your research, and these are more easily learned – we think. The real challenges are encountered in the way time and people play a part in what you are doing in educational research. How to handle this is not so easily learned, you must experience it, and through your experiences you will hopefully and gradually acquire the knowledge needed to handle the dynamic and unpredictable aspects of social interaction in research settings.

1.4 THE CHALLENGES OF A MULTI-FACETED RESEARCH FIELD

Trying to delimit what educational research is in generic terms is difficult, as we have already stated. It is a multi-faceted research field. There are many challenges inherent to doing research within education, and some aspects stand out more. In this part we address three different aspects or challenges that are recurring. The first is related to the variety of disciplinary methodological approaches. The second is related to the difficulties of making comparisons across cultural and scientific contexts, something that threatens to make educational research insignificant. And a third aspect highlights the interface between educational research and implementation, the policy–practice interface.

1.4.1 DIFFERENT DISCIPLINARY APPROACHES AND METHODS IN EDUCATIONAL RESEARCH

To systematise research procedures, different categories are used concerning design, methods for data collection or data analyses, partly going along the quantitative and qualitative paradigms. Some commonly applied designs in research are cross-sectional studies, longitudinal studies, studies with an experimental design and case studies. In this volume we have focused on challenges deriving from working with longitudinal data (Chapter 10); a combination of longitudinal study and case studies (Chapter 13); mixed methods research design (quasi-experimental and action research) (Chapter 12); several case studies carried out in different institutions: kindergarten (Chapter 4), schools and community (Chapter 11) and university (Chapter 3); and research with a control-group design (Chapter 9).

Concerning data acquisition, the authors worked out challenges using questionnaires (Chapters 3, 7, 9, 10, 11), tests (Chapter 9), standardised scales (Chapter 12), interviews (Chapters 3 and 11) and observations (Chapter 4), but also existing documents were collected (Chapters 5 and 14). Concerning data analysis, the researchers used statistical procedures in combination with questionnaires and tests, and a variety of qualitative methods in combination with observation, interviews and the analysis of videotapes and photographs.

However, there are some chapters that cannot be systematised in a more traditional manner since they use alternative methods and ways of getting accesses in research. In Chapter 6 a participatory approach is carried out analysing not only the data that were produced but also the way these data were produced. In Chapter 3 researchers work with interviews and photos produced by the interviewees to get a deeper understanding of the social background of students and in Chapter 2 the authors discuss the challenges of entering the fluid research field of an online community.

This volume shows the large diversity and polymorphic nature of disciplinary approaches (pedagogy, sociology, psychology, history and so on) and methods used in educational research and makes evident that existing systematisations are exceeded in many projects. By presenting such a diversity we hope to overcome the existing dichotomy between qualitative and quantitative methods and instead look at challenges that arise from using various approaches and their commonalities.

1.4.2 NON-COMPATIBILITY AND COMPARABILITY – A CHALLENGE?

Researchers must be sensitive about the connections between languages, expressions, methods and their strengths and weaknesses. What is compatible and what is not? In Chapter 13 the authors describe how they adapted methods to motivate teachers, students, headteachers and parents to take part and to get data with which they were able to answer the research questions. These different data had to be triangulated. This raised the question of compatibility. The same happened in an EU project in which 14 higher education institutions were involved. In Chapter 10 the authors describe how they tried to find a consensus concerning key concepts, instruments for data acquisition as well as data analysis. A similar challenge arose for the authors of Chapter 11 when they carried out an international research project, having in mind not only different nations but also the local needs of vulnerable groups and communities. The question of compatibility also arises in Chapter 4 when research results were presented: how does one present research findings if the researcher thinks that they might offend those who opened up their kindergarten classes for observations? In this way the ethos of the researchers was challenged. At the end of the project referred to in Chapter 4, a change in perspective took place and the results were presented with another focus, which was part of the research project, but not a central interest of the researchers. Another kind of compatibility emerges when the research field does not exist physically. The authors of Chapter 2 describe how they had to find new methods to grasp and identify a fluid community. In considering a non-material object of research, common methods did not work, and so traditional methods had to be adapted and alternative methods invented. At the same time the authors had to keep in mind existing theoretical categories for the analysis. More practical challenges occur at the interface between the context of research and the reality of politics.

1.4.3 THE INTERFACE BETWEEN EDUCATIONAL RESEARCH AND POLICY

A major theme running through many of the projects highlighted in this book has to do with translation – between people, systems and languages. This translation challenge produces the question: what might reality or – even more provocatively – 'truth' be? In Chapter 13 the authors carried out a research project about experiences with a new type of school in Austria. At the end the results had to be presented: to the government, the stakeholders and participants in schools and the scientific community. Each of these groups had different expectations: related to the format of the presented results, the language used as well as the content. So, the authors had to think about different formats in their presentation of the research. For instance, they had to adapt the language and specialist terms as well as the focus of their presentation: more general with a focus on ideas for political decisions and a change for the better, more specific and concrete with a focus on usefulness for handling the situation in school, or more elaborated with a focus on scientific demands, transparency and theoretical embeddedness. A similar situation had to be mastered in Chapter 4 when access to a research field was threatened because the expectations of the participants in the field were not met. The research participants wanted confirmation of their work whereas the researchers were interested in questioning practice. Chapter 13 describes the effects of different methods of analysing quantitative data. Depending on the method, the results differ and lead to different consequences for the practitioners in the field. In each of the chapters we become aware as readers that the complexity of reality can hardly be mapped in its totality, quite the opposite, by choosing one focus and pushing others into the background, different 'realities' seem to occur. So, the researchers – and we with them – experience that site-dependency and choice of perspective are a fundamental challenge in carrying out research.

Chapter 14 addresses a large-scale research project at the education research–policy interface. The authors point to a number of challenges they come up against, one being the challenge of tensions between complexity and simplicity, which in this case was connected to the design of the project as indicator-based monitoring. They regard this as a generic type of tension in this kind of research, and in their case, it had to do with a tension ranging from the establishing of the research design to the point of science communication. For instance: '[T]he comprehensiveness of the monitoring project meant that the results needed to be condensed to a level that could be handled, reproduced and communicated. The database was characterised by a high complexity, e.g. given the five educational areas it encompassed and the federal structure of the educational system in Germany. The quantity and highly diverse set of documents had to be tackled at the level of document selection and acquisition as well as at the level of analysis', the authors write (p. 300).

Research communication and popularised accounts of research findings is a field of its own. Several of the projects in this book address the challenges entailed in communicating research findings in one form or another. One could of course also turn this around and ask if politicians and others, the media in particular, should have a responsibility for not turning questions concerning education into simplistic or means–ends accounts. Education, as we have now said several times, is a complex field, with complex challenges related to time, place and people, which means there are no simple solutions. As the authors of Chapter 15 write, what might happen is that 'the use of certain indicators might run the risk that value is placed only on what can be measured, thereby losing sight of what counts in the end in education' (p. 301).

1.5 CHALLENGES IN DOING EDUCATIONAL RESEARCH IN AN INTERNATIONAL CONTEXT

We asked earlier: which challenges arise from taking an international approach to educational research? The usual trajectory of an emerging researcher is first to do research within a national context, where one knows the education system, the language and generally what professionals mean when they speak about education.

Some may not venture beyond this. Doing educational research in an international context usually involves a larger team, in collaboration with one or more teams. This immediately calls for a common language, common conceptualisations, understanding of differences and agreements about research procedures, methods and so forth. One of the things one detects early in these processes is that concepts and words have different meanings and needs to be addressed specifically. Also, research traditions within the different education systems across Europe are quite diverse, both in terms of how research is conducted, what kind of research is valued and what status educational research holds. There is obviously a tension in this, especially since some of the European (and American) traditions of doing research seem to be defined as more democratic, open and rigorous. This raises questions as to whether general scientific standards can be found and, furthermore, as to what good educational research is.

A way of answering this is to say that the hierarchies among research institutions/ universities based on various indicators and the impact of academics' scientific publishing (h-index) is an indicator of high-quality research. But, when we know that many of the highest-ranking universities and research journals are situated within the English-speaking world, then perhaps the indicators used to make these evaluations are skewed in favour of English-speaking researchers. Speaking from a small language community like Romania, Croatia or Norway, the idea that competition in the academic world happens on equal terms is misleading.

In educational research there are many challenges on many levels that become even more accentuated in an international research project. For instance, there are some institutions within academia that have long traditions of doing educational research, and others where doing research is new. In Norway, the tradition of doing research within teacher education for instance, which is now situated for the most part in universities, is still underdeveloped, simply because doing research has not been an essential part of the academic activity in these institutions, their primary objective was educating teachers. Today this is on the agenda in Norway and across Europe, and the objective is to develop better research qualifications of academics and students within these institutions. Our point here is merely that research qualifications and ways of doing educational research are unequally distributed, between nations, but also between institutions within nations. Deciding what high-quality research is, in other words, is difficult – using one golden standard is not the solution, we claim.

1.5.1 THE EUROPEAN CONTEXT – NOT ONE UNITARY EDUCATION SYSTEM

One of the effects of the European idea was the Bologna Process, which attempted to unify the different European education systems. Such alignments can be observed at the universities where the Bachelor, Master and PhD (3+2+3) programmes/ degrees replaced the former variety of organising university studies. However, differences still exist. Therefore the historical background of education systems plays a key role and the traditions of school systems and educational concepts cannot be explained without having national histories in mind. In Chapter 12 the authors describe the cooperation between Romanian and Danish researchers and how this cooperation was challenged by different concepts of childhood and wellbeing as well as bringing up children, intermingled with different discourses (adult-orientated versus child-orientated discourse) and paradigms in research (accountability and efficiency-orientated paradigm versus participatory and democratisation-orientated paradigm of research). In Chapter 10 a comparative European research project on assessment had to struggle with differences in the way 'secondary schools' in general and especially 'lower secondary schools' are organised in the involved countries and which purposes they have within their respective education systems. Another example in this chapter is the concept of 'school inspection', which differs significantly between different nations according to the purpose, the organisation and the consequences this might result.

Even though alignment in education systems across Europe is promoted today, one must not forget the historical embeddedness of education. The authors of the chapters mentioned above describe the process of having to accommodate the socio-cultural patterns and research traditions they belong to. In an international project this may become an even more important aspect of the research process. In Chapter 9 the author raises an important question: 'How can sociological gaps as frequent characteristics in an international research project be reflected in the conception phase of a research project?' (p. 196).[7] Her answer is that this can be built into the project in ways that allow all participants, insiders and outsiders, to have some responsibility over the project. This also resonates with the arguments put forward in Chapter 6 about participatory research and Chapter 11 about finding collaborative strategies for social inclusion in Europe. On a meta-level it resonates with what is commonly perceived as an ethical stance in educational research: to give voice to the other – the research participants.

1.5.2 RE-PRESENTATIONS: LANGUAGE MATTERS

What happens when you have four or five different contexts represented by different languages and then have to write up the research in one language (English)? How does one accommodate for all the losses or translation errors this creates? The fact that the language researchers use and the language used by the practice field are sometimes quite different (see Chapters 4, 13 and 14) calls for sensitivity and respect on behalf of the researcher in relation to the research participants so as not to dominate or damage the relationship with the field of practice.

Such a commonality is the problem deriving from language, especially in international projects and international publications, but not only there. According to Giddens (1984/2009) language can be seen as a structure helping us to use the right terms, to think and to express something so that it will be understood by the others. However, structure underlies not only personal ideas, but also cultural and social norms, rules and assumptions based on experiences and/or national history. So, terms and expressions and the use of language in general can differ between countries but also within one country between various groups of people, like researchers and non-researchers.

Bearing this in mind, language was a challenge for almost all of us involved in this book project: most authors and the editors do not use English as their first language. A common experience many of us who work in international contexts and projects have is that you have to get everyone involved in deliberations and discussions. Whether one understands a term or concept in the same way, or one struggles to express what one has in mind so that the other can understand, is a constant challenge when involved in international collaboration. The only means by which this can be addressed is by talking together.

In international projects language becomes a topic due to several reasons. In Chapter 10, the language problem became evident by using English as the *lingua franca*; however, by doing so a hierarchy between the participants was created concerning presentations and publishing of results. Furthermore, the same term did not mean the same in different national contexts, and quite the opposite: different terms were used for the same 'reality'. Also, in Chapter 9, an international research project with Cameroon made it evident that in countries with linguistic diversity the construction of a questionnaire is a tricky job.

Finally, language becomes important when results are presented; we addressed this in a slightly different manner above. Depending on the audience, different formats and expressions are needed. Not being aware of this fact can create pitfalls and might endanger the research project by jeopardising the confidence between researchers and those who accepted the research and opened the field and became informants, allowing researchers to get access to inner worlds, which usually are closed: in kindergartens and schools there is a trust between researchers and informants/participants which can create obstacles, and this must be taken into account. This has to do with the care and respect you have to show in relation to those who chose to participate in research.

1.6 CONCLUSION

For this book 39 educational researchers and social scientists from all over Europe wrote about their experiences and about fundamental challenges they experienced while carrying out research projects. What can we as editors and readers learn from their experiences? Picking up the three perspectives from the beginning of this chapter we try to summarise:

- We learned that education is a multi-faceted research field. Although we can identify a tendency for quantitative educational research with a bias on assessment, there exist so many other ways of defining research questions in the educational field. The large variety of options is encouraging and inspiring.
- We learned that in every stage of a research project, challenges occur. Although the research projects presented in this volume differ greatly concerning the contents, the methods and the contexts they are embedded in, many of the challenges are alike and they are transverse.
- We learned that taking an international perspective is a special challenge for all participants. It provokes irritations, crises and uncertainty concerning the contents, the theoretical and methodological approaches, the idea of cooperation and carrying out a research process. In educational research there exist different national traditions, which have to be kept in mind and these must be negotiated through face-to-face interaction.

The purpose of this volume is to mirror a multiple understanding of educational research as well as a diversity of challenges connected with the three different perspectives addressed at the beginning of the chapter (Figure 1.1). What we contend is that doing educational research is not restricted to one scientific methodology or a given set of methods. One will find educational researchers involved in everything from advanced statistics to those involved in doing ethnomethodology in educational research. As educational researchers we have experienced a lack of internal communication between the different strands of educational research. This at times becomes striking. In light of what we already have stated about educational research as a field representing nearly all disciplines of academia, this is not so surprising. But, given the complexity of the field of education, one could also deem it an asset that so many perspectives and ways of doing research are actualised in educational research. The grand challenge, we contest, is the possible compartmentalisation of the field versus a need for communication between ways of doing educational research and sharing of results from various research endeavours.

NOTES

1 These are just an example of some references, it is obviously not an exhaustive list.

2 We here use school as a broad term designating all forms of formal organisations involved in education from pre-school to university, but we also acknowledge that education takes place in other settings than school.

3 As an example, for such contrast see Schrittesser, Gerhartz and Paseka (2014).

4 See: https://eera-ecer.de/ecer-2018-bolzano/whats-on/keynote-speakers-keynote-panel/susan-l-robertson/ (accessed 20 January 2019).

5 There was little or no funding for educational research in Horizon 2020.

6   For an example of a discussion about reflexivity in qualitative research, see Berger (2015).

7   For further clarification of what is meant by sociological gap, see Chapter 9.

REFERENCES

Arendt, H. (1989) *The Human Condition*. Chicago and London: The University of Chicago Press.

Arfwedson, G. (1984) *Varor är skolar olika?* [Why are schools different?]. Solna: Liber Utbildningsförlaget.

Arthur, J., Waring, M., Coe, R. and Hedges, L. V. (2012) *Research Methods & Methodologies in Education*. London: Sage.

Berger, R. (2015) 'Now I see it, now I don't: researcher's position and reflexivity in qualitative research', *Qualitative Research*, 15(2): 219–234.

Cohen, L., Manion, L. and Morrison, K. (2018) *Research Methods in Education* (8th edn). London and New York: Routledge.

Conrad, F.C. and Serlin R.C. (eds) (2016) *The SAGE Handbook for Research in Education: Engaging Ideas and Enriching Inquiry*. Thousand Oaks, CA: Sage.

Creswell, J. W. (2015) *Education Research: Planning, Conducting, and Evaluating Quantitative and Qualitative Research* (4th edn). Upper Saddle River, NJ: Pearson Education.

Flick, U. (ed.) (2014) *The SAGE Handbook of Qualitative Data Analyses*. London: Sage.

Giddens, A. (1984/2009) *The Constitution of Society: Outline of the Theory of Structuration*. Cambridge and Malden: Polity Press.

Helsper, W. (2008) 'Schulkulturen – die Schule als symbolische Sinnordnung' [School cultures – the school as order of symbolic meanings], *Zeitschrift für Pädagogik*, 54(1): 63–80.

Hoveid, M. and Hoveid, H. (2018) 'Hva er utdanningens kunnskap?' [What is the knowledge of education?], in M. Hoveid, H. Hoveid, K.P. Longva and Ø. Danielsen, *Undervisning som Veiledning* [Teaching as mentoring]. Oslo: Cappelen Damm Akadmisk. pp. 27–80.

Rizvi, F. (2009) 'Globalization and policy research in education', in K. Ryan and B.J. Cousins (eds), *The SAGE International Handbook of Educational Evaluation*. Thousand Oaks, CA: Sage. pp. 3–18.

Robertson, S.L. (2018) 'Setting aside settings: on the contradictory dynamics of "flat earth", "ordinalization" and "cold spot" governing projects shaping education'. Keynote at ECER 2018, Bolzano.

Rutter, M., Maughan, B., Mortimore, P. and Ouston, J. (1982) *Fifteen Thousands Hours: Secondary Schools and Their Effects on Children*. Cambridge, MA: Harvard University Press.

Schrittesser, I., Gerhartz, S. and Paseka, A. (2014) 'Innovative learning environments: about traditional and new patterns of learning', *European Educational Research Journal*, 13(2): 143–155. DOI: 10.2304/eerj.2014.13.2.143.

Silverman, D. (2017) *Doing Qualitative Research* (5th edn). London: Sage.

Willis, P. (1978) *Learning to Labour*. London: Routledge.

PART II

NEGOTIATING RESEARCH CONTEXTS AND DEMANDS FROM THE FIELD

2

ENTERING A FLUID RESEARCH FIELD

Maria P. Figueiredo and Nelson Gonçalves

2.1 INTRODUCTION

Obtaining access to the research field and participants is an essential part of conducting research successfully, particularly in ethnographic and qualitative research. It can vary to a considerable extent and usually requires time and expertise. Even so, it has been noticed that some researchers do not describe their access to the research field in their research reports. This chapter presents challenges regarding access and entrance to the field and how these connected to data collection during a research project about learning in an online community. The study aimed at understanding characteristics and meanings of participation in an existing online community built around a Free/Libre and Open Source Software (F/LOSS): Blender (www.blender.org/). This community was taken as an example of a virtual distributed community of practice in which people voluntarily develop, maintain and contribute to open source software and thereby produce knowledge and learning. The aim was to produce a 'thick description' of the Blender software learning ecosystem through an ethnographic study.

The first challenge to be discussed in the chapter pertains to accessing and interacting with a field that doesn't exist physically, is fluid and intersects online and offline spaces, and has no gatekeepers. A second challenge looks into access to the field in terms of relationships and authenticity. Because the ethnographer was not immersed in a physically delimited field and all the participants were geographically distributed, establishing trust and authenticity were particularly challenging.

Some aspects of the challenges were specific to the community that was studied but most of the decisions and processes that were developed are relevant for any study focusing on existing online communities with distributed participation and leadership.

This chapter was written by the researcher who entered the field and by a second researcher who served as a 'reality check' throughout the process. During the entrance to the field, and the study, weekly discussions were held between the two. This on-going conversation and sharing of the process was important to face several challenges, some of which are part of this chapter. Others had to do with the vulnerability felt in connection to mastery of the software and performance since participating in the community meant comparing oneself to the accomplished software developers and artists. The 'reality check' of discussing what was happening with someone else provided good results in terms of understandings but also wellbeing. This translates to some decisions having been shared while other decisions and actions were authored by only one of us which is reflected in the writing of this text which shifts between a 'we' and a 'he/researcher'. The main voice in this chapter is from the 'reality checker' (she), hence the third person is used for the ethnographer. This is an unusual writing style from an ethnographic perspective justified in this case by the dialogic-reflexive nature of the way we approached writing this text.

2.2 OVERALL DESCRIPTION OF THE STUDY

The chapter is based on a study aimed at understanding characteristics and meanings of participation in an existing online community built around a Free/Libre and Open Source Software – Blender. The research project, developed within a doctoral program in Educational Technology at the University of Minho (Portugal), aimed to build an understanding of learning experiences and trajectories in informal settings. The study focused on the Blender software learning ecosystem as an example of an emerging open participatory learning ecosystem (Brown and Adler, 2008). It was based on the assumption that virtual communities formed within F/LOSS movements can be a relevant landscape to help us uncover some of the nuances of learning in times when the 'Internet has also fostered a new culture of sharing, one in which content is freely contributed and distributed with few restrictions or costs' (Brown and Adler, 2008: 18), and when the 'participatory culture' (Jenkins, 2008) shared by communities of 'homo sapiens digital' (Prensky, 2009) presents new needs and opportunities for education.

The virtual distributed communities of practice in which people voluntarily develop, maintain and contribute to open source software are based on an architecture of participation capable of generating flows, structures and processes that support social learning (Cai and Zhu, 2016; Sack et al., 2006). They present complex boundaries and a rich and diversified nature including unpaid and remunerated participants, from different parts of the world, with very diverse motivations and degrees of involvement: development of the application, sharing of resources related to its use (images, films, models, scripts, etc.), and construction and sharing of educational resources (tutorials, models, etc.). Individuals participate spontaneously through different spaces and tools, learning and teaching skills related to its use, creating and sharing resources, collaborating on artistic projects or developing the tool itself, etc. The expansion of learner-centred opportunities brought by collaboration and social networking applications strengthens the need for an approach to learning as a social process that requires 'learning to be' which involves the learner in building an identity and in participating in a practice and a socially constructed domain (Lave and Wenger, 1991).

By searching for which characteristics and meanings encompass participation in a distributed online community surrounding Blender, we intended to produce a 'thick description' (Geertz, 1973) of the Blender software learning ecosystem, articulating its socio-technical landscape, the components and their interactions, the actors and the networks, based on the trajectories of participation and learning of 'blenderheads' and the researcher's own experience.

2.2.1 METHODOLOGY

The study was ethnographic, characterised by starting with a question (Gregory, 2005) or 'foreshadowed problems' (Schumacher and McMillan, 1993) and the pursuit of the 'emic' perspective. The conception of the research process as inductive, the carrying out of the research in 'natural' settings, and an emergent research design are also ethnographic characteristics (Gregory, 2005). Although this qualitative research approach is commonly associated with data *collection* strategies such as participant observation and interviewing (Schumacher and McMillan, 1993), it is possible to combine these strategies with quantitative data (Gregory, 2005), as was the case here. In this study, the immersion in the context was complemented with social network analysis. Still, the study was field based, inductive and immersive and rested primarily on methods that are common within ethnographic research: observation, in-depth interviews and the analysis of multi-modal cultural artifacts, respecting, therefore, typical elements of ethnography (Hammersley and Atkinson, 2007).

The study's theoretical framework, which guided without constraining the emergent design of the study, encompassed Situated Cognition (Brown, Collins and Duguid, 1989), Communities of Practice (Lave and Wenger, 1991; among others), Connectivism (Downes, 2005), Personal Learning Environment (Attwell, 2007) and Actor-Network Theory (Law, 1992; among others). This should not be interpreted as imposing a conceptual framework or bias to the fieldwork, rather as offering a conceptual lens that facilitated the initial stages of introduction to the community, the access to the field and the exploratory/unstructured data collection and observation.

The observation started before the research project. The main researcher was a user of the software since 2008 and therefore a participant in some of the forums. The study started in 2010 and ended in 2016. The community that was chosen to be studied started online and its main dynamic happened on Internet spaces, like forums, websites, social media platforms. Developing an ethnographic study with a community with such characteristics led to the exploration of concepts and practices such as virtual ethnography, Internet ethnography, online ethnography, digital ethnography and netnography (Hine, 2000; Kozinets, 2010; Landri, 2013; Pink et al., 2016; Webster and Silva, 2013). Like Boellstorff et al. (2012: 4), we started with the assumption that 'ethnographic methodology translates elegantly and fluidly to virtual worlds', and we prepared, therefore, to conduct research considering the specificities of the several spaces that would be included in the study, with their own set of considerations but assuming that 'the ethnographic research paradigm does not undergo fundamental transformation or distortion in its journey to virtual arenas because ethnographic approaches are always modified for each field site, and in real time as the research progresses' (Boellstorff et al., 2012: 5). In doing so, we tackled, as Markham (2017) acknowledges, questions that apply to any contemporary ethnographic or qualitative research project and the peculiar challenges that emerge for digital researchers.

Looking into the tenets of virtual ethnography as described by Hine (2000), some elements of ethnography are recognisable even if adapted to take account of the networked and fluid worlds that the study was interested in: the researcher is understood as being mobile, rather than located in a particular place, and field and boundaries are understood as being discursively constructed, to be explored through the course of the ethnography (Tummons, Macleod and Kits, 2015). These two features are the basis to the first challenge that is described in this chapter: accessing and interacting with a field that doesn't exist physically, is fluid and intersects online and offline spaces, and has no gatekeepers.

The second challenge deals with tenets of ethnography that are more problematised on virtual or digital ethnography: the identity and presence and/or absence of informants and the interstitial and intermittent immersion in the field of the researcher, with a significant impact on the establishment of relationships (Tummons, Macleod and Kits, 2015; Walford, 2018). We focus on authenticity and trust in relationships with participants.

2.2.2 BLENDER, FREE SOFTWARE AND FREE CULTURE

Blender is a multi-platform computer graphics software tool set for the creation of 3D content: animated films, visual effects, art, 3D printed models, interactive 3D applications and video games. It is distributed under a GNU General Public License and developed within an open source model, therefore it is a Free/Libre and Open Source Software. The license grants the following freedoms: to use

Blender for any purpose, to distribute Blender, to study how Blender works and change it, and to distribute changed versions of Blender. These four freedoms are the ones established in 1996 by Richard Stallman for Free Software (2010): the freedom to run the program as you wish, for any purpose (freedom 0); the freedom to study how the program works, and change it so it does your computing as you wish (freedom 1) – access to the source code is a precondition for this; the freedom to redistribute copies so you can help others (freedom 2); the freedom to distribute copies of your modified versions to others (freedom 3). Free is currently accompanied by the word Libre to emphasise that 'Free software is a matter of liberty, not price' and that 'you should think of "free" as in "free speech", not as in "free beer"' (Stallman, 2010: 3).

Blender started as a proprietary software, developed by a Dutch animation studio, NeoGeo, in January 1995 (Roosendaal, 2013). The company was dissolved and the software was further developed by Ton Roosendaal, one of its original authors, as shareware but with poor results for the company involved. Facing the shutting down of the project, in 2002, Roosendaal started the 'Free Blender' campaign, a crowd-funding precursor, which collected enough funds to buy the propriety rights of the application, which allowed its further development and the release of the Blender source code (Blender Foundation, 2013), under the umbrella of the Blender Foundation, an independent non-profit public benefit corporation in the Netherlands. Today, Blender is Free/Libre and Open Source Software largely developed by its community.

Free/Libre and Open Source Software communities have become significant phenomena to consider in the software development domain and beyond. In terms of software development, F/LOSS concepts and values have inspired changes in the mainstream development model, since some of the existing communities have proven economically viable and technically competent options for large-scale development projects and also because the F/LOSS phenomenon is related to the pervasive shift towards increasing distribution of collaborative software development efforts (Sigfridsson and Sheehan, 2011). Incentives for participation in F/LOSS communities are of a socio-cultural nature: a variety of motivations have been identified, such as altruism, career, enjoyment and learning, and desire for reputation (Cai and Zhu, 2016). Due to this nature, qualitative perspectives and methods are useful for studying F/LOSS communities, since they offer means to understand people's activities within social and cultural contexts.

The Blender community is more diverse than other F/LOSS communities because it includes several participants that are not directly involved in the software development. Blender users create several different products with the software and around the software: models, movies, animations, special effects, tutorials, books, t-shirts among others. This close connection between the development of the tool and the growth of a diverse community was suggested from the beginning since the development of the software, by the Blender Foundation, was accompanied by the creation of animated shorts that show-cased and drove the innovation of the soft-ware. Since 2005, several projects have been created and released as open movies: entirely created using open source tools, where the end result and all of the assets used in the studio are published under an open license, the Creative Commons Attribute. Blender contributes, therefore, to a Free and Open Culture in more ways than just developing a software tool.

Inspired by free software, the free culture movement is a social movement that promotes the freedom to distribute and modify the creative works of others in the form of free content or open content without compensation to, or the consent of, the work's original creators, by using the Internet and other forms of media. Akin to open access and open educational resources, it strives to find solutions to dilemmas and conflicts created by intellectual propriety in areas like education, science and culture where it is felt by some that 'The same tool of freedom of yesterday [intellectual propriety] is becoming a tool of control today' (Lessig, 2005: 360). The free culture movement, with its ethos of free exchange of ideas, is aligned with F/LOSS ideas. The importance of the F/LOSS influence is stated by O'Reilly: 'Rather than thinking of open source only as a set of software licenses and associated software development practices, we do better to think of it as a field of scientific and economic inquiry, one with many historical precedents, and part of a broader social and economic story' (2005: 479–480).

The impact of openness as a fundamental concept in digital culture could also be considered for ethnography since 'open source, creative commons and other forms of digital sharing and collaboration become ways of being and relating to others in relation to digital media' (Pink et al., 2016: 11). As the authors suggest, transferring this concept of openness to the digital ethnography research process can help us understand the process of doing digital ethnography in a way that is open: to include different voices, and different sites, to embrace influences as well as needs of other disciplines and external stakeholders.

2.3 MAIN CHALLENGES

2.3.1 CHALLENGE 1: ACCESSING A FIELD WITH NO BOUNDARIES

The first challenge to be discussed pertains to accessing the field. Finding the field was itself a challenge since it did not exist in a physical sense and even in a virtual sense it was fluid and without well-defined boundaries. For any ethnographic study that includes virtual communities, the process of locating and defining sensible boundaries of the field can be convoluted and elusive (Markham, 2005). When field and boundaries don't exist physically, they have to be understood as being discursively constructed, or through connection, interest and flow, rather than geography, nationality or proximity, and to be explored through the course of the ethnography (Markham, 2017).

We started on a central space, the Blender Foundation website, where the software could be downloaded and generic information about the software and its history was available. A forum was also present on the website but it suggested that users who needed help or support should go to a different forum – Blender Artists. This second space was not connected to the Foundation. Browsing through existing threads of discussion and messages on the forum, several references to other spaces could be found – Vimeo or YouTube profiles where users uploaded their work, online tutorials that explained particular features of the software, but also references back to the Blender Foundation website's forum where the developers could be reached. Other forums were also mentioned, as well as several other spaces like repositories for 3D models, the Blender Certified Trainers Program, and a real world space – the Blender Conference that happens every October in Amsterdam.

Other studies of communities connected to F/LOSS have described them as a complex tapestry of heterogeneous actors and components which are geographically dispersed (Sack et al., 2006). The Blender community proved heterogeneous in terms of roles and motivations (developers, users, trainers, artists, among others) and dispersed, both geographically and in different virtual spaces, like website, forums, blogs, social media, video platforms, wiki pages. The website where the observation started gave several leads to investigate as we were trying to follow the process of reading the texts and interactions of interest, much like trail signs, and making defensible decisions about which paths to follow, which paths to disregard, and thereby which boundaries to draw (Markham, 2003).

Some virtual communities have clear membership or boundaries, but that was not the case for the Blender community, which proved to be fluid and complex. In this exploratory phase, some attempts at finding the members were made. There was no list of 'members' anywhere and the different spaces seemed associated with different roles, even if there was some overlap. For example, the developers listed on the website as contributing to the software were mostly not involved in the users' forums, nor were they listed as Certified Trainers. The people who presented in one conference were not together in any other single space. Some participants were present in several places, which meant these were not contained or isolated. The fluidity of the boundaries and of participation, the spread across different platforms, and the loose social organisation with no central gatekeeping, required important decisions for research: on the *conceptual* level and on the *practical* level.

On the *conceptual* level, we deepened the framework with contributions from Gee about affinity spaces (Gee, 2004, 2005; Gee and Hayes, 2012) and from different authors about the field site as a network that incorporates physical, virtual and imagined spaces (boyd, 2008; Burrell, 2009, 2017; Landri, 2013). On the *practical* level, we needed to set criteria to choose when to follow and explore the trail signs and to find a way to connect the different spaces.

2.3.1.1 How the conceptual framework supported the mapping of the field

The characteristics of the Blender community and our focus on the social learning within it suggested looking at how meaning and knowledge were being developed more than the people themselves. The concepts of semiotic social space (Gee, 2005) and affinity spaces (Gee, 2004) were the basis to frame how to approach and include the different spaces where the Blender community spread to: forums, websites, chats, meetings, conferences, games, films, wikis, tutorials, models, repositories among others. 'Affinity spaces' have been defined by Gee (2007: 98) as spaces where 'people "bond" first and foremost to an endeavor or interest and secondarily, if at all, to each other'. Gee proposed the concept as a way to understand how spaces – physical, virtual and blended ones – provide opportunities for individuals, through their communications within groups, to develop affinity for a topic, such as media objects (e.g. software like Blender), and for practices (Hayes and Duncan, 2012). Gee emphasised the metaphor of 'space,' not 'community' (Gee, 2005) not even group (Gee and Hayes, 2012). These distinctions highlight how the forms of social organisation in question and the participation within affinity spaces are much more a fluid endeavour than is typically attributed to membership in a 'community'. The concept of affinity space stresses that the organisation of the space (the online platforms and real world spaces in some cases) is as important as the organisation of the people: using the term group overstresses the people at the expense of the structure of the space, and the way the space and people interact (Gee and Hayes, 2012).

In an affinity space, some participants can see themselves as being part of a community, others will not. The concept of space intends to encompass the differing levels of involvement and participation exhibited by participants and the different routes or trajectories of their participation (Gee, 2004). Because of the shared interest and passion for the semiotic domain it is built around, an affinity space encourages the sharing of knowledge or participation in a specific area, and informal learning is a common outcome.

The Blender Foundation website was the portal into the social semiotic domain of Blender since it gave access to the signs and to ways of interacting with those signs. It also showed some of the affinity spaces that should be looked at, outside the website itself: the forum about the development of Blender, the Blender Certified Trainers Program, the Blender Conference and the Blender Artist Forum. Acknowledging each of these spaces as an affiliation space transformed some of the perceived challenges in features to be studied as part of their identity. For example, these spaces exist because the participants have an affinity for something, not because of some registration or common trait. This means that if someone is there for a moment they are in the affinity space and have the potential to influence it. Routes, forms and intensity of participation will be very diverse among participants. Also, there is no gatekeeping and standards are internal and indigenous; there are no top-down standards and even moderation can be contested and negotiated. More specifically, it was decided that to understand the social learning connected to Blender, the different affinity spaces needed to be explored since an affinity space encourages and enables people to use dispersed knowledge: knowledge that is not actually on the site itself but can be found at other sites or in other spaces (Gee and Hayes, 2012) – which was evident from the initial analysis of the Blender website and its relationship with other spaces.

Our exploration of how to enter a field that only exists as a shifting flow, led to an experience of the field as temporary or momentary assemblages, like Markham (2017) suggested. The author urges us to 'loosen the grip on persistent premises that individuals or groups must comprise the object of analysis; that there is such thing as a whole to be described or explained; or that the boundaries of a situation can be identified' (Markham, 2017: 653).

Our particular assemblage included online and offline spaces, which brought a particular emphasis to a recurrent discussion surrounding virtual ethnography: the relationship between the real and the virtual. Following particular previous studies (boyd, 2008), and the more recent trend of recognising the real and the virtual as a connected and integral part of our contemporary social world (James and Busher, 2015; Webster and Silva, 2013), no privilege was granted to either offline/unmediated nor online/mediated places. The decision was to adopt a network-driven approach (Burrell, 2009, 2017), traversing the different spaces of affinity fluidly, moving along axes of places, artifacts, people and ideas. Meaningful interactions were followed within one setting to another context, whether it was online or offline. Connectivity and mobility became features of the approach. This decision to include several affiliation spaces resembled a multi-site ethnography (Falzon, 2009; Marcus, 1995) in the sense that it meant the study would range across sites, in a spatial (virtual and real spaces) as well as temporal sense (some spaces were explored for past discussions), in order to explore the meanings and artifacts that were of interest but also the relationships between or across these sites, tracing the networks and conjunctions that join them.

Several spaces of affiliation were explored (Table 2.1) and included in the study. The diversity of existing spaces meant considering interactions (forums, conferences) but also artifacts (the software itself, animations, games, models, films, etc.) and systematisations of knowledge (wikis, tutorials, books/handbooks, etc.) as ways to understand the culture and the learning, as part of the semiotic social space of Blender.

In Table 2.1 it is possible to see how some of those different spaces were visited throughout the study but also how some of them only became prominent in certain years. The training courses, the Blender Conference and the national conference and festival were physical or unmediated places of affiliation where the researcher was present and participated. All the others were online or mediated spaces, including blogs, websites, forums, social media, wiki pages, crowdfunding campaigns. Under challenge 2, we will look into how the participation in these different spaces was accomplished.

Table 2.1   Main spaces of affiliation included in the study per year

	2008	2009	2010	2011	2012	2013	2014	2015	2016
Blender Website	■	■	■	■	■	■	■	■	■
Forums	■	■	■	■	■	■	■	■	■
Blender Nation Blog	■	■	■	■	■	■	■	■	■
Tutorials	■	■	■	■	■	■	■	■	■
Mailing Lists	■	■	■	■	■	■	■	■	■
Development platform	■	■	■	■	■	■	■	■	■
Vimeo/YouTube	■	■	■	■	■	■	■	■	■
Training courses	■		■			■	■	■	■
Twitter		■	■	■	■	■	■	■	■
Blender Domain				■	■	■	■	■	■
Support to projects (crowdfunding)			■		■	■		■	■
Blender Cloud							■	■	■
Blender Conference			■	■	■	■			
National Conference/ Cinema Festival					■	■			

In the Blender landscape that was drawn, the several spaces, artifacts, interactions, knowledge, were organised around six axes: education (informal and formal), documentation (user and technical), creative production (movies, video games, 3D models, etc.), software development (trunk, branches, add-ons, etc.), dissemination of information (synchronous and asynchronous) and places to meet others (virtual and physical). The axes are subdivided into different categories that reflect the diversity of experiences that happened in the Blender landscape.

The mapping of the spaces and boundaries was influenced by the theoretical framework in a second way. Debates about virtual ethnographies and multi-sited ethnographies have brought to the forefront the postmodern turn in ethnographic research that foregrounds the co-production of data between the researcher and those whom s/he is researching (Tummons, 2017). The people who move and act within the different sites are seen as best placed to help the researcher to define them (Falzon, 2009). In our case, participants were leaving trail signs to be followed in the different spaces, for example, tagging other users in Twitter, commenting on a tutorial they just finished in a forum discussion, announcing training opportunities in the blog. Informal conversations about some of these signs were used to inform about the relevance of the mentioned space.

More intensively, later in the study, the interviews with some of the participants were used to reflect on the delimitation of the field. Those participants supported the circumscribing of the boundaries of the field. This was also a contribution to the network-driven approach in the sense that different relationships between people and practices were being tracked while trying to make sense of different types of networks and their relation to one another, considering the perspective of the participants themselves.

2.3.1.2 How decisions were made to enter the spaces and how the connections were traced

On the *practical* side, the decision to follow references found in one affiliation space to other spaces (trail signs) required that a set of criteria was defined to support decision-making (or boundary setting).

The *first criteria* was that it had to pertain to Blender, so if the spaces were about animation or modelling without Blender directly involved, they were not included. This also meant that different interests (or passions) around Blender were included: some of the spaces were generic, the website, the blog, Ton Rosendaal's Twitter account, but the developers' platform was relevant for the developers of the software, whereas the forums were more about using Blender for different purposes. The crowdfunding campaigns around the open movies were about supporting the software but the discussions were very much focused on the creative endeavour connected to the films, as well as the concepts of free software and open movies. The mailing lists were focused on particular topics, and the education one was followed more closely. Following the signs, regardless of the facet of the Blender community involved in the particular space, both required and allowed becoming fluent in the semiotic domain and finding ways to participate in it: learning the software, participating in discussions, conferences, training, etc. It also required and allowed learning to use diverse platforms, services and interfaces. This will be discussed under challenge 2.

The *second criteria* stemmed from the non-dualist perspective on the real and virtual: to include affiliation spaces both virtual and physical. The Blender Conference was clearly the most mentioned event that allowed the physical co-presence with participants from the community and so the researcher participated in it, respecting his role as a researcher by presenting a paper about the study to the community itself. Each conference had more than 300 participants who interacted throughout the three days. In one of the conferences, a visit to the Blender Foundation was organised. But other physical spaces were sought after.

The researcher participated in two editions – 2010 and 2011 – of TOSMI (Training with Open Source Multimedia Instruments), a project from InterSpace Association as part of MEDIA (the European Union's support programme for the European audio-visual industry). The geographical dispersion of the community and the financial effort involved in travell-ing suggested that closer physical spaces, like Portuguese affiliation spaces, were considered. This lead to the participation in the Portuguese Blender Conference, for example.

A *third criteria* had to do with language. Only Portuguese and English spaces were included and an intentional effort was made to include the Portuguese community: by being a member and posting in the Portuguese forum, by participating in the first National Blender Conference (2013) and through a master class about free animation (with Blender) at a National Animation Festival (Cinanima, 2012 and 2013), since it allowed access to physical spaces more easily.

A *fourth criteria* was connected to availability of time. When each affiliation space was identified, an estimate of the needed time to explore it and keep track of it (both in the future and for past material) was made. Most of the spaces that were identified had new material being created daily. Extra time was needed to keep records of what was being observed and for the field dairy that was kept. A monthly plan with time allocation for each space was established, which was later checked for accuracy against what had actually been done. Some of the spaces were visited daily, based on their relevance for the community (generic, central) and their frequency of updates – this was the case for Blender Nation, the blog where news was posted daily, and some Twitter accounts. For others, visits were about being alert for updates, like new tutorials, vid-eos on YouTube channels or discussions on new topics, and then scheduling time to participate in it (doing the tutorial, commenting on someone's work, replying in some discussion). Some of the spaces were visited once per month and information was collected then.

Detailed records of which spaces had been visited and when were important and articulated with the monthly plans. Every visit was recorded in Zotero, which allowed screenshots, links, downloaded materials to be combined with tags and notes. Zotero is a F/LOSS references management system that is browser-based, which allowed integration of any web content into an organised database, taggable and searchable.

A *fifth criteria* was later applied, related to the relevance of the spaces for the focus of the study: social learning through participation.

As a way to connect the different spaces and to trace the researcher's path in the field, the first approach to the community was mirrored in his Personal Learning Environment (PLE), which was traced based upon a reflexive account of his own Blender learning experiences (Figure 2.1). A PLE is not an application but rather an approach to the use of technologies for learning, since it 'is comprised of all the different tools we use in our everyday life for learning' (Attwell, 2007: 4).

A diagram was used to represent the personal trajectory.

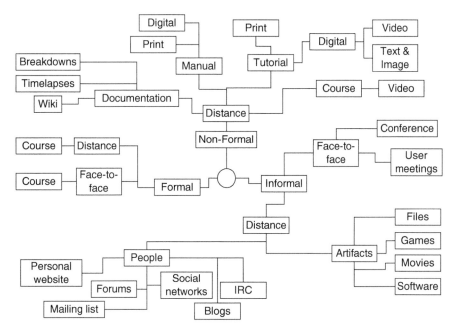

Figure 2.1 Personal Learning Environment

It was an attempt to identify the tools, services and spaces that were used until 2011, grouped according to the European Commission (2001: 32–33) definitions of formal, non-formal and informal learning.

- *Formal*: 'typically provided by an education or training institution, structured (in terms of learning objectives, learning time or learning support) and leading to certification. Formal learning is intentional from the learner's perspective'.
- *Non-formal*: 'is not provided by an education or training institution and typically does not lead to certification. It is, however, structured (in terms of learning objectives, learning time or learning support). Non-formal learning is intentional from the learner's perspective'.
- *Informal*: 'resulting from daily-life activities related to work, family or leisure. It is not structured (in terms of learning objectives, learning time or learning support) and typically does not lead to certification. Informal learning may be intentional, but in most cases it is non-intentional'.

The diagram was used to sum up several of the initiatives, situations and processes that the researcher was involved with, including distance and face-to-face course attendance (i.e. TOSMI), participation in physically 'on site' events (Blender Conference 2010 and informal user meetings), artifact exploration and usage (i.e. official DVD tutorials, magazine tutorials, books, etc.), and communication with others (i.e. lurking in forums, posting/replying, web syndication, IRC chat sessions).

Organising the spaces and artifacts that were being included in the study, and therefore were seen as part of the field, in terms of the researcher's own learning combined the need to show the diversity of elements included while also connecting them to the focus of the study: learning in this particular semiotic domain. It was a way to generate a meaningful scape.

2.3.2 CHALLENGE 2: ESTABLISHING PRESENCE AND RELATIONSHIPS IN A FLUID FIELD

In the study, assembling or mapping the field through the network-driven approach was simultaneous with the processes of access and entrance to the field. Some authors suggest that how a qualitative researcher enters the field is usually taken for granted. More explicit descriptions of the processes through which one gains access and enters the field are therefore necessary to improve research reports. Distinguishing between access and entrance is also suggested as relevant. While access is often a negotiated process, entrance is an engaged practice (Geertz, 1973; Goffman, 1989). Access usually refers to gaining permission to conduct research in a particular field setting, whereas entrance is an engaged practice of 'what you see (and how you are seen) and what you do (and are asked or allowed to do) when you get there after gaining access' (Chughtai and Myers, 2017: 811). Good access, while approaching the field, already requires cooperation from the participants, but entrance or being in the field is about stepping into the practice world of participants (Pole and Hillyard, 2016).

The knowledge that what one says or writes or shares will be available for every participant to scrutinise (Tummons, Macleod and Kits, 2015) was a starting point for choosing the principles of authenticity, coherence and transparency as guides for presenting oneself in the field. Since the field was spread across different spaces and had no formal gatekeeping, access and entrance were multiplied by the number of spaces that were included in the study. Each forum, social media, website, service or platform usually required registration and the creation of a profile. Clarifying the decisions about how to deal with online profiles and registrations was important since online profiles are usually transient and mobile (Driscoll and Gregg, 2010), but a stable, authentic presence across the affiliation spaces was sought after. Coherence was key to that task. The same information was always introduced, using real data and always presenting two important pieces of information: that the user was learning about Blender and that the user was researching how people learned about Blender. This also entailed on some occasions asking for help about how to use or navigate specific services or platforms. Authenticity and transparency were, therefore, basic tenets. But so was passion, an essential ingredient of affinity spaces. Besides clarifying the purposes of participating in the space – learning and researching – the profile or first message also shared the love/respect and commitment regarding the tool's development as F/LOSS. Free software and culture were important drives for the study and therefore the presence of the researcher in each space was always connected to that dimension of himself and the interest in the community. Free/Libre and Open Source Software and free culture are two philosophies or social concerns shared by the vast majority of the people in the Blender community, but not all. Issues related to these topics were common in news or discussions.

Throughout the years, as the researcher moved from a 'newbie' user to a more capable user, the profiles were updated accordingly. Keeping track of the profiles and registrations was important so as to not abandon any space, or potential participant.

Accessing different spaces entailed learning how to register, use and participate in all the services and platforms included. In coherence with the culture of the affinity spaces, this learning was based on available resources in the spaces themselves: either through FAQs, tutorials or asking for someone's help. Affinity spaces are described as encouraging a view of learning where the individual is proactive and engaged with trial and error (Gee and Hayes, 2012). This view of learning does not exclude asking for help, but help from the community is never seen as replacing a person's responsibility for his or her own learning. This vision also meant being available to help others who needed help.

Authenticity, coherence and transparency also drove the decision to maintain a personal website, not directly connected to the study, but that allowed anyone searching for the researcher to find information about him. Finally, in the first participation in the Blender Conference in 2010, the study itself was presented to the audience, already including some data about the community, and suggesting that 'blenderheads', users or developers of the software, would contribute to the research.

The more crucial and complex learning required for entrance into the field was of the software itself. Using and knowing the tool was essential since the conversations were very domain specific (both in terms of technical 3D knowledge, like character anim, motion graph, vfx, game and software development), as were the internal jokes about features and comparison to other 3D software, for example. The option of combining the researcher's own trajectory of learning with the process of mapping and accessing the field worked in the way of articulating both processes and helped establish the presence of the researcher as being 'like us' and being 'one of us' in the Blender affinity spaces.

Access and entrance need to be maintained, by developing relationships in the field, and sustained during the course of the fieldwork (Harrington, 2003). One of the peculiarities of ethnographic fieldwork is the way in which the researcher and his/her interpersonal relationships serve as primary vehicles for eliciting findings and insight and are therefore envisioned as a fundamental medium of investigation (Amit, 2000). For all ethnographic research, this entails poignant ethical dilemmas. For mediated or online spaces, the challenge also involves considering how the ethnographer's presence is differently embodied (Landri, 2013). In our study, the visible presence online included the profiles, registrations, the website and some published papers. There was also unmediated presence in the conferences and in the training. The decisions based on the principles of authenticity, coherence and transparency were important to allow the researcher to participate freely, but consistently, in the discussions, conversations and meetings that happened throughout the years of immersion in the field. Basic guidance for not engaging in heated discussions, not offending participants in forums, not bullying anyone, were strictly followed. But, especially in the physical meetings, issues about F/LOSS versus proprietary software were strongly debated. The possibility of using para-language elements (facial expression, gesture and movement), excluded from the mediated spaces (Markham, 2005), opened opportunities to explore how some participants were more deeply aligned to some of the values that permeate the community – like free culture. Physical meetings made it easier to create complicity and share personal stories about the software and the Blender community. They also helped to clarify how different people connected to the community: even if there was previous interaction online, the physical co-presence induced sharing the connection to Blender, which had brought people together in that place. The diversity was in terms of professional backgrounds, levels and purposes for using the tool, age groups and geographical origin, ideas and valuing of F/LOSS, workflows, interest in programming and code. The diversity could be described as different communities of practice co-existing in a semiotic domain or an imagined community (Anderson, 1983), a socially constructed community, imagined by the people who perceive themselves as part of that group. The researcher recreated himself as one of them.

RESEARCHER CHECKLIST

In the contemporary world, we can consider all communities as imagined and virtual, also acknowledging there are different groupings with different relationships to technology (Shumar and Madison, 2013), therefore field needs to be defined and viewed as a 'network composed of fixed and moving points including spaces, people, and objects' (Burrell, 2009: 189). This approach allows ethnographers to *capture the coherence and fluidity of the different spaces people occupy*, instead of being restricted by artificial boundaries.

- Assembling a field through a network approach requires *time, willingness to learn* and *acceptance of failure*. Finding an entrance point and exploring the different signs requires an openness to the unknown but also the need to establish *criteria* that are coherent with the research questions so that *decisions are not based on accessibility alone.*

- The complexity of following flows, collecting artifacts, observing and recording interactions, even during the delimitation of the field, requires *very good organisation of the research process*, preferably relying on strong support *tools that are flexible and connectable to other tools in a workflow* – for analysis, reporting, etc. The research plan will need to be changed constantly but the structure is needed for recording and keeping track.

- Clear principles and anticipated decisions are essential for an *ethical and trustworthy presence across spaces*. Authenticity is an important aspect and it is connected to *the total online presence* of the researcher, not just the profiles created for the study.

- *Openness* is also a fundamental concept. Not only concerning what *spaces* should be included in the field, or the *diverse participants* to be engaged with the study, but also concerning *collaboration* with the participants. Creatively finding ways of having input from the participants about the field can help better define it.

- Alongside the organisation of the research process, it is also important to *prepare oneself for fieldwork*. Prepare for the need to reformulate the research plan and the timeline, to sometimes have little control over what is happening and when.

- Besides the field diary, having the opportunity to *discuss the ethnographic fieldwork* with someone can prove to be very important. *Voicing* what is happening, questions, doubts, particular episodes, allows the researcher to 'remove the voices in the head' and *find meaning*.

2.4 CONCLUSION

In this chapter, we have addressed the challenges of entering a fluid field in an ethnographic study. The aim of understanding learning trajectories and experiences in a community that exists across different online and offline spaces created the challenge of accessing a field with no physical existence or boundaries. In trying to find a way to construct the field, the concept of affiliation space (Gee, 2005) was crucial to allow connection, interest and flow to locate and define sensible boundaries to the field. Through that process, it was possible to approach the field site as a network that incorporated physical, virtual and imagined spaces (boyd, 2008; Burrell, 2009, 2017; Landri, 2013). A connection to multi-sited ethnography was also useful. Besides the acknowledgement of fluidity in terms of boundaries, the multi-sited approach brought the value of finding ways to allow participants to support the researchers in the mapping of the field. This was accomplished in this study by paying attention to content created by the users, through informal interactions with users about those trail signs left in forums, social media, etc., and in the interviews with some of the participants in the Blender ecosystem that allowed reflection on the field that was mapped, and what was left outside the borders.

From a more practical point of view, the challenge of a fluid field was addressed with systematicity and clarity. We shared the criteria that were needed to make decisions regarding which spaces to include, which trail signs to pursue or let go of. We do not suggest these can be used for other studies, but the necessity of clarifying how decisions are made is important and an on-going endeavour during ethnographic research. Also in practical terms, we valued the use of tools that can help in keeping track of online activity, registering different types of data (websites, visuals, text, sound and video) and commenting on them, facilitating the establishment of connections between artifacts, spaces, people, moments, interactions. The presentation of a Personal Learning Environment was used as an example of how those relationships can be communicated with meaning assigned, in this case, by the study focus on learning.

Both from the conceptual review and our experience, we approached the challenges with the assumption that ethnographic research translates well to fluid fields since it considers the specificities of the spaces where it is developed and is flexible in design, assuming changes as part of the way research progresses. This reliance on the tradition and experience of ethnography while researching an unusual field was also relevant for the second challenge about establishing presence and relationships in a fluid field. For this, we discussed how the principles of authenticity, coherence and transparency guided decisions about how to present oneself, act and react in different spaces, and maintain a collaboration generative relationship with participants.

We hope reading about the challenges lets shine through the wonderful experience of doing ethnography and its relevance for studying emergent phenomena in our world.

ADDITIONAL USEFUL READING

Boellstorff, T., Nardi, B., Pearce, C. and Taylor, T. L. (2012) *Ethnography and Virtual Worlds: A Handbook of Method.* Princeton, NJ: Princeton University Press.

For an introduction to *ethnography in online contexts*, there are several good sources. This one is particularly useful because of the standalone ethnographies the authors produced.

boyd, d. (2008) 'Taken out of context: American teen sociality in networked publics'. PhD Thesis in Information Management and Systems and the Designated Emphasis in New Media, University of California, Berkeley.

Shumar, W. and Madison, N. (2013) 'Ethnography in a virtual world', *Ethnography and Education, 8*(2): 255–272.

These two texts are central for the *discussion between virtual/mediated and real/unmediated spaces.* boyd's work because of its groundbreaking nature and Shumar amd Madison because of its historical perspective and discussion of developments in conceptualisations of the virtual in ethnography.

Gómez Cruz, E. and Ardèvol, E. (2013) 'Ethnography and the field in media(ted)studies: a practice theory approach', *Westminster Papers in Communication & Culture, 9*(3): 27–46.

Tummons, J., Macleod, A. and Kits, O. (2015) 'Ethnographies across virtual and physical spaces: a reflexive commentary on a live Canadian/UK ethnography of distributed medical education', *Ethnography and Education, 10*(1): 107–120.

Both are good examples of reports about *addressing challenges related to accessing the field* in virtual or online ethnographies.

James, N. and Busher, H. (2015) 'Ethical issues in online research', *Educational Research and Evaluation, 21*(2): 89–94.

Walford, G. (2018) 'The impossibility of anonymity in ethnographic research', *Qualitative Research, 18*(5): 516–25.

With different focus and scopes, these two suggestions are important supplements for a discussion on the *ethics of doing ethnographies online.*

REFERENCES

Amit, V. (2000) 'Introduction: constructing the field', in V. Amit (ed.), *Constructing the Field: Ethnographic Fieldwork in the Contemporary World*. London: Routledge. pp. 1–18.

Anderson, B. (1983) *Imagined Communities: Reflections on the Origin and Spread of Nationalism*. London: Verso.

Attwell, G. (2007) 'Personal learning environments – the future of eLearning?', *ELearning Papers, 2*(1): 1–8.

Blender Foundation (2013) History. Available at: www.blender.org/blenderorg/blender-founda tion/history/ (accessed 22 January 2018).

Boellstorff, T., Nardi, B., Pearce, C. and Taylor, T. L. (2012) *Ethnography and Virtual Worlds: A Handbook of Method*. Princeton, NJ: Princeton University Press.

boyd, d. (2008) 'Taken out of context: American teen sociality in networked publics'. PhD Thesis in Information Management and Systems and the Designated Emphasis in New Media, University of California, Berkeley.

Brown, J.S. and Adler, R.P. (2008) 'Minds on fire: open education, the long tail, and Learning 2.0', *EDUCAUSE Review, 43*(1): 16–32.

Brown, J.S., Collins, A. and Duguid, P. (1989) 'Situated cognition and the culture of learning', *Educational Researcher, 18*(1): 32–42.

Burrell, J. (2009) 'The field site as a network: a strategy for locating ethnographic research', *Field Methods, 21*(2): 181–199.

Burrell, J. (2017) 'The field site as a network: a strategy for locating ethnographic research', in L. Hjorth, H.A. Horst, A. Galloway and G. Bell (eds), *The Routledge Companion to Digital Ethnography*. New York: Routledge. pp. 51–60.

Cai, Y. and Zhu, D. (2016) 'Reputation in an open source software community: antecedents and impacts', *Decision Support Systems, 91*: 103–112.

Chughtai, H. and Myers, M.D. (2017) 'Entering the field in qualitative field research: a rite of passage into a complex practice world', *Information Systems Journal, 27*(6): 795–817.

Downes, S. (2005) 'E-learning 2.0', *ELearn Magazine*, October.

Driscoll, C. and Gregg, M. (2010) 'My profile: the ethics of virtual ethnography', *Emotion, Space and Society, 3*(1): 15–20.

European Commission (2001) *Making a European Area of Lifelong Learning a Reality*. Brussels: European Commission.

Falzon, M.-A. (2009) 'Introduction. multi-sited ethnography: theory, praxis and locality in contemporary research', in M.-A. Falzon (ed.), *Multi-Sited Ethnography: Theory, Praxis and Locality in Contemporary Research*. Farnham: Ashgate. pp. 1–23.

Gee, J.P. (2004) *Situated Language and Learning: A Critique of Traditional Schooling*. New York: Routledge.

Gee, J.P. (2005) 'Semiotic social spaces and affinity spaces: from the age of mythology to today's schools', in D. Barton and K. Tusting (eds), *Beyond Communities of Practice: Language, Power and Social Context*. Cambridge: Cambridge University Press. pp. 214–232.

Gee, J.P. (2007) *Good Video Games + Good Learning*. New York: Peter Lang.

Gee, J.P. and Hayes, E. (2012) 'Nurturing affinity spaces and game-based learning', in C. Steinkuehler, K. Squire and S. Barab (eds), *Games, Learning, and Society*. Cambridge: Cambridge University Press. pp. 214–232.

Geertz, C. (1973) *The Interpretation of Cultures*. New York: Basic Books.

Goffman, E. (1989) 'On fieldwork', *Journal of Contemporary Ethnography, 18*: 123–132.

Gregory, E. (2005) 'Introduction: tracing the steps', in J. Conteh, E. Gregory, C. Kearney and A. Mor-Sommerfeld (eds), *On Writing Educational Ethnographies: The Art of Collusion*. Stoke on Trent: Trentham Books. pp. ix–xxiv.

Hammersley, M. and Atkinson, P. (2007) *Ethnography: Principles in Practice* (3rd edn). London: Routledge.

Harrington, B. (2003) 'The social psychology of access in ethnographic research', *Journal of Contemporary Ethnography, 32*: 592–625.

Hayes, E. R. and Duncan, S. C. (2012) *Learning in Video Game Affinity Spaces*. New York: Peter Lang.

Hine, C. (2000) *Virtual Ethnography*. London: Sage.

James, N. and Busher, H. (2015) 'Ethical issues in online research', *Educational Research and Evaluation, 21*(2): 89–94.

Jenkins, H. (2008) *Convergence Culture: Where Old and New Media Collide*. New York: New York University Press.

Kozinets, R. V. (2010) *Netnography: Doing Ethnographic Research Online*. London: Sage.

Landri, P. (2013) 'Mobilising ethnographers investigating technologised learning', *Ethnography and Education, 8*(2): 239–254.

Lave, J. and Wenger, E. (1991) *Situated Learning: Legitimate Peripheral Participation*. New York: Cambridge University Press.

Law, J. (1992) 'Notes on the theory of the actor-network: ordering, strategy, and heterogeneity', *Systems Practice, 5*(4): 379–393.

Lessig, L. (2005) 'Open code and open societies', in J. Feller, B. Fitzgerald, S.A. Hissam and K.R. Lakhani (eds), *Perspectives on Free and Open Source Software*. Cambridge, MA: Massachusetts Institute of Technology. pp. 349–360.

Marcus, G. (1995) 'Ethnography in/of the world system: the emergence of multi-sited ethnography', *Annual Review of Anthropology, 24*: 95–117.

Markham, A. (2003) 'Critical junctures and ethical choices in internet ethnography', in M. Thorseth (ed.), *Applied Ethics in Internet Research*. Trondheim: NTNU University Press. pp. 51–63.

Markham, A. (2005) 'The methods politics and ethics of representation in online ethnography', in N. Denzin and Y. Lincoln (eds), *The Sage Handbook of Qualitative Research* (3rd edn). Thousand Oaks, CA: Sage. pp. 247–284.

Markham, A. (2017) 'Ethnography in the digital internet era: from fields to flows, descriptions to interventions', in N. Denzin and Y. Lincoln (eds), *The Sage Handbook of Qualitative Research* (5th edn). Thousand Oaks, CA: Sage. pp. 650–668.

O'Reilly, T. (2005) 'The open source paradigm shift', in J. Feller, B. Fitzgerald, S.A. Hissam and K.R. Lakhani (eds), *Perspectives on Free and Open Source Software*. Cambridge, MA: Massachusetts Institute of Technology. pp. 461–482

Pink, S., Horst, H., Postill, J., Hjorth, L., Lewis, T. and Tacchi, J. (2016) *Digital Ethnography: Principles and Practice*. Thousand Oaks, CA: Sage.

Pole, C. and Hillyard, S. (2016) *Doing Fieldwork*. London: Sage.

Prensky, M. (2009) 'H. sapiens digital: from digital immigrants and digital natives to digital wisdom', *Innovate, 5*(3): Article 1.

Roosendaal, T. (2013) 'How Blender started, twenty years ago …', 27 December. Available at: http://code.blender.org/index.php/2013/12/how-blender-started-twenty-years-ago/ (accessed 22 January 2019).

Sack, W., Détienne, F., Ducheneaut, N., Burkhardt, J.-M., Mahendran, D. and Barcellini, F. (2006) 'A methodological framework for socio-cognitive analyses of collaborative design of open source software', *Computer Supported Cooperative Work (CSCW): An International Journal, 15*(2–3): 229–250.

Schumacher, S. and McMillan, J. H. (1993) *Research in Education: A Conceptual Introduction*. New York: HarperCollins College Publishers.

Shumar, W. and Madison, N. (2013) 'Ethnography in a virtual world', *Ethnography and Education, 8*(2): 255–272.

Sigfridsson, A. and Sheehan, A. (2011) 'On qualitative methodologies and dispersed communities: reflections on the process of investigating an open source community', *Information and Software Technology, 53*(9): 981–993.

Stallman, R. (2010) *Free Software, Free Society: Selected Essays of Richard M. Stallman*, ed. J. Gay (2nd edn). Boston, MA: Free Software Foundation.

Tummons, J. (2017) 'ICTs and the Internet as a framework and field in ethnographic research', *Acta Paedagogica Vilnensia, 39*: 132–143.

Tummons, J., Macleod, A. and Kits, O. (2015) 'Ethnographies across virtual and physical spaces: a reflexive commentary on a live Canadian/UK ethnography of distributed medical education', *Ethnography and Education, 10*(1): 107–120.

Walford, G. (2018) 'The impossibility of anonymity in ethnographic research', *Qualitative Research, 18*(5): 516–25.

Webster, J. P. and Silva, S.M. (2013) 'Doing educational ethnography in an online world: methodological challenges, choices and innovations', *Ethnography and Education, 8*(2): 123–130.

3

USING PHOTO-ELICITATION INTERVIEWING TO BRIDGE SOCIAL GAPS

Karin Doolan and Linda Liebenberg

3.1 INTRODUCTION

The research study that has inspired this chapter explored how social inequalities shape students' experiences of higher education in Croatia. It theoretically engaged with Bourdieu's conceptual 'toolbox' consisting of cultural, social and economic capital, habitus and field (Bourdieu, 1977, 1984; Bourdieu and Passeron; 1979), within a mixed methods study using survey and interview data. As researchers who explore the lives of young people living in socio-economically marginalised communities through a social justice lens, we are particularly concerned with how research can best capture the experiences and perspectives of these young people. Therefore, the design of the study was guided by an aspiration to provide young people with the opportunity to voice what encourages and discourages their positive studying experiences, with a view of informing policy makers and university leaders interested in advancing socially inclusive educational settings. Additionally, we were aware that the research focused on the everyday, and the taken-for-granted aspects of their lives. As such, the design of the study was further guided by the need to engage in reflective practice on this taken-for-granted lived experience. Auto-driven photo-elicitation interviews (i.e. where participants produce the photographs for the interviews) were therefore used. Specifically, participants produced images for a specified period of time around a pre-determined research focus, after which they engaged in individual interviews with the researcher (Harper, 2002; Liebenberg, 2009). In this chapter we reflect on the experience of using this method, sharing our thoughts on how to enhance the potential of photo-elicitation interviewing in order to better understand the lives of students, particularly socially disadvantaged students, and establish a space for their perspectives to be amplified.

Briefly, photo-elicitation interviews use photographs as reflexive mechanisms within the interview setting. Images can be pre-existing or made specifically for the research; they can be produced by researchers or research participants. Irrespective of the origin of images, they are used within the interview context as a 'can-opener' (Collier and Collier, 1986) to elicit deeper and richer narratives. The intent is to facilitate reflection on the taken-for-granted in people's lives and to use emerging narratives to explore more deeply the structures within which these events and experiences are embedded (Harper, 2002). Consequently, the narrative that is evoked as a result of discussing the image, remains the primary data.

In this chapter we focus on the challenges of how best to use photo-elicitation interviews, particularly in order to encourage and capture the voices of socially disadvantaged students. The first challenge we address is how to use photo-elicitation interviewing so as to avoid theoretical 'blinkers' and make theoretical advances, while simultaneously benefitting from existing social theory in a study. The second overarching challenge we engage with is how to build on the strengths of photo-elicitation interviews, such as reducing the hierarchy between researcher and participant, as well as how to exercise caution with its weaknesses. Finally, we discuss several practical challenges involved in photo-elicitation interviewing: how to encourage participants' narratives about photographs, the financial resources this method requires, as well as ethical considerations specific to photo-elicitation interviews (e.g. how photographs are used by the researcher after the interviews).

After describing the study in more detail, the chapter has three main sections that reflect on the use of photo-elicitation interviews. In the first we discuss the relationship between social theory and photo-elicitation interviewing, emphasising the importance of researchers being alert to insights overlooked by existing social theories. In the second section we highlight some of the strengths of photo-elicitation interviewing, suggesting ways in which these can be enhanced, as well as some cautions to be considered by researchers interested in this method. Finally, in the third section we reflect upon the practical challenges of conducting photo-elicitation interviews, from what guidelines to give to participants to how to observe ethical standards.

3.2 RESEARCHING STUDENTS' EXPERIENCES OF HIGHER EDUCATION

The research study we discuss in this chapter, led by Karin Doolan, explored how students from different social backgrounds experienced their first year of study at a university in Croatia. The general starting point, indicating our commitment to a social justice agenda, was the conviction that 'what creates inequality is the fact that others have differential access to resources, income, wealth and power which enable them to avail of the opportunities presented in education' (Lynch and O'Riordan, 1998: 470). The study's theoretical inspiration was Bourdieu's conceptual 'toolbox' (Bourdieu, 1977, 1984; Bourdieu and Passeron, 1979) – cultural, social and economic capital, habitus and field – as a sociologically encompassing lens for understanding the ways in which students' social backgrounds intersect with characteristics of their past and present educational institutions to shape complex first year student experiences and to reinforce social inequalities.

The study employed a mixed methods design, consisting of questionnaires and interviews, within a broader case study approach. Yin (1984: 23) defines case studies as an empirical strategy by which to examine a phenomenon within its 'real-life context' and which uses 'multiple sources of evidence'. According to Jensen and Rodgers' (2001: 237–239) case study typology, the Croatian study we draw on exemplifies comparative case study research since multiple sites were used for comparison in order to intensively investigate several instances of the researched phenomenon. More specifically, the research was conducted at six faculties within a Croatian university, which were selected as cases of institutions with different completion rates: two faculties had very high retention rates, two moderate and two very low. This selection criteria was informed by the assumption that faculty practices contribute to students' first year experiences and that high retention institutions would have more favourable practices for students than low retention ones. Data provided by the Croatian Bureau of Statistics was used to select case study faculties.

Questionnaire and interview data were collected at these six case study faculties. The study is an example of an 'embedded' mixed methods design, with questionnaire data playing a supplemental role (Creswell and Plano Clark, 2011). Questionnaire data were collected to gain insight into the social profile of first year students at the faculties, to select students for the interviews and to provide a data source for validating conclusions drawn from the interview material. On the other hand, semi-structured interviews were conducted to establish a space for students to share their experiences, while also allowing for systematic comparisons between them. Finally, photo-elicitation interviews were conducted. This approach was used as a means of encouraging participants to direct interview content and reflect on their student experience.

The study consisted of three main phases. In the first phase the study's questionnaire was administered to first year undergraduate students at the selected institutions. The study fields at these institutions included medicine, design, electrical engineering, biotechnology, geology and mathematics. The questionnaire was administered to 642 first year students attending a compulsory lecture in January 2007. The highest response rate was at a department which enrols 35 undergraduates annually (33 students completed the questionnaire), whereas the lowest response rate was at a faculty where 24 per cent of students (86 out of 358 students) completed the questionnaire. The questionnaire reviewed characteristics of the students' secondary school, motivation to study, (dis)satisfaction with their course selection and different aspects of their course provision, assessment of their chances to enrol successfully into their second year of study, their levels of economic, cultural and social capital, and demographic data.

In the second phase, semi-structured interviews were conducted with 28 students, selected on the basis of their questionnaire responses. The selection reflected the social heterogeneity of the student body and included students who had indicated on their questionnaire that they were willing to participate in follow-up interviews. Students were asked to describe why they had enrolled into their particular course, what expectations they had of it, to reflect on their first weeks of studies, what student life looks like for them, their sense of belonging at the university, whether they feel supported by their friends and family, whether they are experiencing any financial difficulties, and whether they have ever considered leaving the course and why.

In the third research phase, photo-elicitation and semi-structured interviews were conducted with 25 of the 28 students initially interviewed. Students were asked to take photographs of their student lives using a disposable camera that was provided to them by the researcher. Out of the 25 students, 10 brought photographs to the interview. Where photographs were not included, a protocol for a semi-structured interview was used containing questions such as how students feel about their course, how they get on with lecturers and colleagues, as well as what they look forward to most and what worries them most about their course. Where photographs were included in the interviews, the focus was on talking about the images.

The challenges involved with photo-elicitation interviewing are manifold (see also Mitchell, 2011; Packard, 2008). For the purposes of this chapter we have singled out three over-arching challenges, whose specificities we elaborate on in the sections that follow: how to benefit from photo-elicitation interviewing in terms of new theoretical insights, how to maximise its methodological strengths, and how to overcome some of the practical challenges specific to this technique.

3.2.1 MAKING THEORETICAL ADVANCES WITH PHOTO-ELICITATION INTERVIEWS

The use of theory in qualitative research is a divisive issue. For researchers working within a phenomenological or grounded theory tradition, the argument is made that working with theory can 'blind' the researcher to the complexity of the phenomena being studied. For others, existing social theory can help uncover complexity. Bourdieu (1988), for instance, advanced the importance of interrelating theory and empirical research. According to Bourdieu, 'Theory without empirical research is empty, empirical research without theory is "blind"' (1988: 774–775). In this section we discuss the relationship between theory and photo-elicitation interviewing. In particular, we address the challenge of how to benefit from photo-elicitation interviews in terms of making theoretical advances.

Most research projects engage with existing theory prior to data collection. Indeed, a consideration of theoretical anchors is often integral to developing research proposals and a key aspect of their assessment. Consequently, we often bring to data collection and analysis our own, pre-existing, theoretical biases. And as Kvale and Brinkmann (2009: 238) have noted, 'Theoretical bias is difficult to counteract'. In the Croatian study this chapter draws on, the theoretical 'baggage' was Bourdieu's conceptual framework: it informed the design of the study's questionnaire and it also informed the design of the protocol for the semi-structured interviews. This is not surprising since in conventional semi-structured interviews, directed by an interview protocol, theoretical commitments are likely to inform questions asked. However, the data collection process with photo-elicitation interviews was theory 'light'. This is because participants had control over the data collection process as a result of making and selecting images to discuss. The only instruction they received was to take photographs that capture their life as students.

On the one hand, the data gathered by both semi-structured and photo-elicitation interviews provided ample evidence in support of Bourdieusian explanations of student experiences. At the risk of oversimplifying an interrelated web of influences shaping student experiences, the narratives of student life were far more wrought with hardship for first generation students from families without economic capital than for second generation students financially supported by their parents. The role of social capital was also evident: students who took photographs of their university friends tended to speak more positively about their higher education experience. Additionally, well-resourced and better organised study programmes, as well as supportive staff, were more conducive to positive experiences. On the other hand, photo-elicitation interviews were key in terms of gaining important insights about the experiences of socially disadvantaged students beyond Bourdieu's concepts. Indeed, photo-elicitation interviewing offered more space for participants to raise issues that were meaningful to them, lessening the impact of theory on the context of the new data (Liebenberg, 2009).

One such issue is the role of residential status in students' experiences: 15 out of the 28 students had relocated to study. In the first interview with students, the role of relocation had not emerged, largely because this question was not asked. Reflecting on the first interview protocol, it was overwhelmingly saturated with questions related to the workings of Bourdieu's capitals and educational fields. In addition, the researcher herself had not moved for study purposes at her own undergraduate course in Croatia. However, the photographs students took for the second interview were overwhelmingly related to the private spaces students occupy. Although it might seem obvious that students' private spaces contribute to their overall student experience, literature on student experiences in higher education often confines students' sense of 'belonging' to educational institutions, overlooking the wider spaces students move in and the impact this can have on their experiences (Doolan, 2010). For example, Bourdieu and Passeron (1979) attributes students' feeling 'at home' or 'out of place' in higher education in terms of their classed habitus and how this habitus reacts to a higher education setting. Photographs taken by students in the discussed research study and their subsequent narratives highlight how emotionally charged broader 'places' are for students and how these 'places' significantly contribute to their overall experience. Indeed, the transition to higher education for students living away from home involves a demanding replacement of familial and familiar spaces with unfamiliar ones, impacting cultural and social capital. Additionally, it means incurring extra living costs, impacting economic capital. Understandably then, adapting to higher education was easier for students who stayed at home as opposed to those who moved. In particular, the move was more challenging for students from families with lower income since financial difficulties weighed on their overall experience.

The ways in which student data moved beyond Bourdieu's theoretical framework are exemplified in the case of Lana, a 19-year-old, first year student who had hopes of becoming a nutritionist and whose parents had completed only primary schooling. She referred to two photographs[1] she took, both of which depicted a rural landscape, as 'home', the place she grew up in and where her family lives. Having relocated for her studies, she explained the financial hardship this involved and how she tries to go 'home' as often as possible.

Similarly, Katarina, a 19-year-old, first year student who was hoping to become a designer and whose parents had completed vocational secondary schooling took photographs of where she grew up. One was of the sea near where her parents live, the other of her with the sea in the background. She entitled the latter 'Me where I belong'. As with Lana, Katarina talked about how much she misses her hometown and how she takes every opportunity to go 'home':

> In the first semester I went home every weekend, every weekend. Every weekend because otherwise I would have gone insane, I wouldn't be able to do anything. Lately, I haven't been that often because I have these tests and things happening on Saturday's, so I couldn't go that much. But I am going this weekend after three weeks and I can't wait, I just can't wait.

Whereas Bourdieu and Passeron (1979) attributed a student's 'sense of belonging' to the characteristics of the education institution, what Lana and Katarina's photographs illustrate is that students' 'insider' and 'outsider' positions relevant for their student experiences are also markedly shaped by other locations. In addition, their experiences, shared by others, point to the 'weight of costs' of studying, particularly for those students from poorer families who have to relocate for study purposes.

Numerous authors have highlighted photo-elicitation interviews as a means of encouraging critical consideration of the taken-for-granted aspects of lived experience (Harper, 2012; Liebenberg, 2009; Thomson, 2008). Furthermore, they have acknowledged that critical reflection of the ways in which daily lived experiences are situated within dominant social narratives provides a space for participants to reposition themselves in relation to dominant knowledge and narratives surrounding their lives (Blackbeard and Lindegger, 2015; Liebenberg, Ungar and Theron, 2015). It is in this way that existing knowledge is uncovered, or new knowledge developed. Our position is that existing theory can both enhance and diminish this potential of photo-elicitation interviews. In the Croatian study, Bourdieusian theory helped the researcher 'notice' how social inequalities were being (re)produced in higher education. However, its focus also risked excluding other issues important to students. In this sense, photo-elicitation interviews, and in particular the very general guidelines given to students with regard to what their photographs should capture, created a space in the study for aspects missed by Bourdieusian theory. As a general remark, if photo-elicitation interviewing is to fulfil its potential as a method which is conducive to theoretical advances, particularly vis-à-vis the experiences of socially disadvantaged young people, the data gathering process needs to remain as open as possible and the researcher needs to intentionally engage with what in the data is new and being overlooked by existing theory.

On a final note, and as with other methodological considerations, photo-elicitation as a data gathering choice needs to be assessed for its compatibility with the social theory informing the research. In the study discussed here, photo-elicitation interviewing is compatible with a Bourdieusian theoretical approach. Bourdieu and Wacquant (1992) was an eclectic methodologist who in his own work combined 'the most standard statistical analysis with a set of in-depth interviews or ethnographic observation' (1992: 227). Furthermore, authors who have taken Bourdieu's project further have worked with qualitative methods more generally and visual research more specifically (e.g. Ingram, 2011; Meo, 2010). In contrast, researchers examining educational choices from a Boudonian (1974) perspective almost exclusively do so using quantitative data.

3.2.2 BUILDING ON STRENGTHS AND ADDRESSING CAUTIONS

The popularity of photo-elicitation interviews has increased substantially in the past three decades (see, for example, Bugos et al., 2014). Much of this is linked to the parallel growth of research areas focused on the new sociology of childhood (James and Prout, 1990), pedagogy of the oppressed (Freire, 2000) and post-colonial studies (Spivak, 1993). Numerous characteristics of especially auto-driven photo-elicitation interviews as a research method have lent themselves to use in these various areas of study. This section reflects on the ways in which the strengths of photo-elicitation interviewing can be enhanced, as well as what cautions researchers should exercise.

According to some authors, images evoke deeper elements of our experiences than words alone are able to (Harper, 2002). Indeed, they can serve as provocative or disruptive mechanisms that stimulate more complex thoughts (Prosser and Schwartz, 1998). Furthermore, through the act of making images and thinking about why these images have been made, together with the significance of the content of images, participants are better able to discuss the taken-for-granted aspects of their lives (Liebenberg, 2009). Similarly, images can serve as reminders to participants of situations or events that furthered their thinking about particular aspects of their lives (Harper, 2002; Loeffler, 2005). Due to these reminders, participants are then better able to elaborate on their experiences and explain their related perceptions (Liebenberg, 2009).

Through the discussion of photographs, photo-elicitation interviews are also seen to reduce the hierarchy between researcher and participant, reducing power imbalances (Harper, 2002). More specifically, the physical focus on the image shifts the researcher's gaze away from the participant (Rollins, 2005). Additionally, the participant is positioned as the expert within the interview, directing and creating content (Blackbeard and Lindegger, 2015; Ford et al., 2017; Liebenberg, 2009). This is because the participant selects the images to be discussed and directs the content of the interview as their interpretive narrative of the image remains the primary source of data. The challenge is then how to enhance the potential of photo-elicitation interviewing to reduce the hierarchy between researcher and participant. In the Croatian study, Doolan (2010), who conducted the interviews, feels she over-controlled the process and disrupted the narrative flow with too many questions too soon, reinforcing the researcher–participant hierarchy. One way to overcome this would have been to let participants talk through their photographs without interruption and then ask follow-up questions about particular photographs. To begin with, a general instruction such as 'Talk me through your photographs' suffices.

As previously stated, one of the main strengths of this method is giving participants the opportunity to reflect on their lives as they take photographs and discuss what they have 'brought to the table'. Importantly, by taking photographs prior to the interview, participants have the opportunity to reflect on the research topic which can facilitate greater experience of personal voice. As Ingram (2011: 292) has noted: 'Allowing participants the time to think about the questions and their response leads to a more considered engagement with the research'. Authors such as Epstein et al. (2006), Ford et al. (2017) and Meo (2010) believe that the use of photographs in their research helped to elicit longer and more comprehensive responses than a traditional interview would have. Indeed, some argue this process of critical reflection can even allow for re-presentation of self. Through this reflective process leading to the interview, participants are able to present new understandings and perspectives of their lives (Blackbeard and Lindegger, 2015; Liebenberg, 2009; Schratz and Steiner-Löffler, 1998). In this sense, photo-elicitation interviews have the capacity to generate new knowledge that has greater validity in terms of representing participants' lives (Liebenberg, 2009). And this is particularly important for studies motivated by the desire to represent the lives of marginalised and often silenced young people.

The challenge then is how to facilitate participants' critical reflection. In practical terms, this involves giving participants enough time to take photographs. In the study of Croatian students' experiences, students were given over a month to take photographs of their student lives. When they were asked whether they would have preferred more or less time for the activity most said that this time frame agreed with them.

There are, however, cautions that should be borne in mind by researchers when considering the use of photo-elicitation interviews. First, the use of photo-elicitation interviews (as with all other methods) requires critical consideration of the relevance of the method to the research question (Liebenberg and Theron, 2015; Pain, 2012). The novelty and allure of providing participants with cameras and then collectively exploring the meaning of the images can belie the fact that this process may not be suited to answering particular questions (Bagnoli, 2009; Liebenberg and Theron, 2015). In other words, as researchers we need to scrutinise the appropriateness of this method for our study, shying away from making such a choice based on how innovative or fun-sounding it may be. In this sense, the choice of photo-elicitation interviewing becomes an ethical issue: we owe it to our research participants to use methods that are most conducive to our research focus and context.

In the study of Croatian students' experiences, the research focus required a mixed methods approach. Photo-elicitation interviews were combined with semi-structured interviews and questionnaires to identify commonalities among students, as well as the uniqueness of their experiences. At times, findings from these different methods strengthened each other, at other times challenged each other. In both cases the study was enriched through a mixed methods approach. As an example of how the study's methods 'worked together', students' photographs and narratives foregrounded the importance of places outside of their faculties and departments to their experiences. The photographs of outdoor places taken by Lana and Katarina discussed in the section above illustrate this. However, students also took photographs of the indoor places they occupy: a room in their parents' house, a room in a student dormitory, the flat that they are renting. In some of these places it was easier to prepare for exams than in others, some of these were described as more comfortable than others. A student who took photographs of her room in a student dormitory talked about how difficult it was for her to get used to a roommate, a small room, a shared bathroom, and general noise coming from the other student rooms. Questionnaire data showed how she is not alone in her dissatisfaction with student accommodation: a significantly higher percentage of students living in their family home or in their own flat were 'extremely satisfied' with their living conditions (53.8 per cent and 68 per cent respectively). In comparison, only 14 per cent of students living in student accommodation reported the same. Whereas photo-elicitation interviews were key in identifying the importance of private indoor spaces for student experiences, questionnaire data demonstrated the extent to which this was shared among students.

In addition to ensuring a 'fit' between one's research focus and method, it is similarly incumbent upon researchers to ensure that the use of photographs aligns with the research population. A growing number of authors are highlighting how their initial choice of medium (e.g. photographs) did not align well with the research group (see, for example, Strack, Magill and McDonagh, 2004; Vigurs and Kara, 2017). In a poignant critique of his own work, Packard (2008), for example, outlines how his assumptions around the use of auto-driven photo-elicitation interviews negated the reality of asking participants in his study to make images. Aspects inherent to the process of sharing cameras with a group of street-involved men and asking them to make images related to their experiences enhanced rather than reduced experiences of disempowerment. In the Croatian study, all the students seemed to have positive reactions to the idea of taking photographs of their student lives. However, in the end only 10 out of the 25 students interviewed made photographs. Most of the students who did not take any photographs explained that they did not know what to take photographs of. Whether or not giving more precise instructions would have resulted in more students engaging in the activity remains open to debate; however, considering instructions provided in other studies suggests this may have been beneficial (see, for example, Ford et al., 2017; Liebenberg and Theron, 2015; Packard, 2008).

3.2.3 PRACTICAL CONSIDERATIONS FOR PHOTO-ELICITATION INTERVIEWS

Photo-elicitation interviews are extremely time intensive, involving multiple meetings with participants to obtain consent, share instructions and review images. We have already touched upon the practical challenges of deciding how much time participants should be given to make photographs and the control they should have to talk about them. In this section we add to this list of practical challenges: how to give instructions to participants regarding what to make photographs of, how many photographs to make, whether to use digital or disposable cameras and how to observe ethical standards related to visual material.

3.2.3.1 Guidelines to participants

The practical challenges of using photo-elicitation interviews with Croatian students began early, when giving them instructions on how to 'produce' photographs for the research. Much thought was put into these instructions. In particular, a consideration was whether they should be given more general guidelines (e.g. please take photographs of your student life) or more precise instructions (e.g. please take photographs of what you experience as the positive and negative aspects of student life). General guidelines were scrutinised for not facilitating the demanding task of visually capturing 'life' at that point in time, whereas precise instructions were scrutinised for framing and possibly restricting students' representations of student life.

Ultimately, a general guidelines approach was taken. Students were asked to 'please take photographs that capture your life as a student'. This decision was made because much of the study already had a 'structured' element to it. Consequently, adding structure to this activity seemed to oppose the general commitment to give students an opportunity to take a lead in the conversation about their student experiences. As was noted earlier, at the time all the students seemed positive about taking photographs; however, less than half took photographs. In the end, giving more precise guidelines may have been helpful. It is therefore worth thinking through the benefits and shortfalls of the generality of instructions in particular studies and possibly following up with the participants prior to the interview, asking them how they are progressing and providing more specific guidelines if they so wish. That can also contribute to a more collaborative research approach.

Regarding how many photographs participants should take, this question is solved for researchers who use disposable cameras since these have a limit on the number of photographs that can be taken. However, for researchers working with digital or phone cameras, the number of possible photographs is endless. On the one hand, having a limit on the number of photographs can help participants cope better with the task: it provides a clear goal to work towards. On the other, it can be restricting for those participants inspired by the activity. If we are committed to 'giving voice' to socially marginalised students, it seems counterintuitive to place limits on the process. Our own position is that one should provide an approximate number of photographs to be made and in the spirit of collaborative design consult with students on how they feel about the number.

In the example Croatian study, disposable cameras were given to students. The choice to use disposable cameras in the study was guided by the concern that socially marginalised students might not have access to a digital camera and at the time of research mobile phones with cameras were not widespread in Croatia. Additionally, limited funding for the study precluded the possibility of providing digital cameras to participants. However, two students came back for the second interview without having used the disposable cameras. Instead, they decided they would use their own, digital cameras. In both cases they did not exceed the limit on photographs in the disposable cameras.

As a final consideration with regard to whether the researcher chooses to use disposable or digital cameras or mobile phones, irrespective of the medium, it is important to ensure that the size and quality of the photographs is satisfactory in case the researcher decides to use them for publications based on their research, provided of course participants agree to this. The absence of images in this chapter illustrates this point.

3.2.3.2 Resources

A further consideration is the resources that a photo-elicitation research project requires. As previously stated, in the study with Croatian students, there was concern that some students may not have access to personal digital cameras (including cameras on phones). Consequently, cameras were provided. Here funding resources became necessary. In addition to availability of cameras, images need to be viewed. In some instances, this may mean having to print images, in others projecting them using a computer and/or data projector (Mitchell, 2011). Again, this requires resources. In the Croatian study, students were asked to bring their photographs to the interview. Although they were refunded for the costs incurred, in hindsight, and in particular thinking about students from socially marginalised backgrounds, it is quite possible that the lack of advance payment placed a strain on these students' budgets. Therefore, such practices should be avoided.

3.2.3.3 Ethical concerns

Finally, ethical concerns and requirements are amplified when using photo-elicitation interviews. While the structure of ethical guidelines pertaining to informed consent, confidentiality and anonymity remain, they are also extended and become more complex due to the use of photographs that may contain images of participants and other people. As a result of this, obtaining institutional ethical approval can become protracted (Phelan and Kinsella, 2013). Delays can be extended by review board members who may not have adequate understanding of image-based methods such as photo-elicitation interviews. However, providing clear statements of how images will be produced, used and stored together with strong justification for the value of including photographs in a study can effectively move the process ahead (Ford et al., 2017; Liebenberg, Wood and Wall, 2018). In developing ethics protocols, careful consideration needs to be given to how participants will be making photographs: what concerns exist regarding participant safety and what measures need to be taken to ensure safety? Also, how will issues of consent be managed when participants are making images that include other people? How will images be used by researchers following the interviews? Will they be reproduced in publications, and if so how? What measures will be taken to ensure that anonymity is maintained? How will images and the related narrative data be stored and for how long? And finally, how will this information be conveyed to participants so that they understand the ways in which their images will be used? Answers to these questions will be driven predominantly by the research focus, context and population of interest.

In the study with Croatian students, at the beginning of each interview students were informed about the purpose of the study, they were informed that the conversation was confidential and that pseudonyms would be used if any of their interview material was used. And indeed, in this chapter pseudonyms are used for the material reported. Students were also told that they did not have to answer any questions they did not feel comfortable with and that they could end the interview whenever they liked. With regard to the photographs, students were asked whether they would mind if their photographs were used for the purposes of academic articles.

All of the students agreed, with a few requests that particular photographs showing them or their friends should not be used.

RESEARCHER CHECKLIST

- Critically assess the relevance of photo-elicitation interviewing to your research questions.

- Reflect on how well this method aligns with your research population.

- Consider whether there is a 'fit' between your study's theoretical framework and photo-elicitation interviewing.

- Be clear in your instructions to participants with regard to what you want them to take photographs of and consider the level of generality or specificity of the instructions.

- Make sure that irrespective of whether you choose to use disposable cameras, digital cameras or mobile phones, your participants have access to them: do not assume everyone has a camera.

- Ensure that participants know how to use the cameras made available: again, do not assume everyone knows how to use a camera.

- Provide guidelines about the number of photographs participants should take with the caveat that they should be free to take more or less, depending on how they feel about the activity.

- If you are using disposable cameras do not expect participants to cover the costs of printing photographs.

- If you plan to use participants' photographs for publications based on your research ensure that the size and quality of the photographs can be used for this purpose.

- Provide enough time to your participants for taking photographs and for reflecting on them prior to the interview.

- Allow your participants to take the lead in the research process: let them talk through their photographs without interruption and then ask follow-up questions.

- Make sure you observe ethical standards: consult with your study participants on how you can use their images.

- Reflect on what new theoretical insights you may have gained from participants' images and their narratives about them which are overlooked by existing theory.

3.3 CONCLUSION

This chapter has focused on the challenge of enhancing the benefits of photo-elicitation interviewing for obtaining richer data on the experiences of socially marginalised youth, using the research approach in ways that amplify reflection and narratives of their experiences. More specific challenges we address include how to gain new theoretical insights about their experiences, as well as how to avoid reinforcing the researcher–participant hierarchy. We advance the position that continuous critical reflection is key to benefitting from existing theoretical insights and identifying important new ones, and that relinquishing control during the interview is necessary to give marginalised youth 'voice'. We acknowledge that both of these efforts on the part of the researcher are difficult, particularly if one's research training has not prioritised them and/or one has strong theoretical commitments. On the level of technical detail, we have discussed the importance of clear and useful guidelines to research participants combined with rigorous observing of ethical standards.

Many of the challenges involved in using photo-elicitation interviews are not unique to socially marginalised young people. How to give clear instructions or how to obtain informed consent pertains to all study participants equally. However, the chapter highlights how certain challenges relating to photo-elicitation interviewing can be particularly problematic for socially marginalised populations. For example, socially marginalised young people may not have cameras to take photographs with nor the funds to print images. Furthermore, the experiences of marginalised communities are more vulnerable to theoretical interpretations developed by those far-removed from their experiences, i.e. by a privileged academic elite. Additionally, over-controlling the photo-elicitation interview on the part of the researcher strengthens the disempowerment of socially marginalised youth. Indeed, despite appearances, photo-elicitation interviews require additional interviewer skill rather than less. As previously discussed, researchers using this method need to have the confidence and ability to let participants assume control of the interview. This relinquishing of control, however, needs to be balanced with the capacity to follow up on what participants have said – sometimes a long while after participants have said something – and to identify what participants are privileging and emphasising (sometimes in unassuming ways) as important.

Collaborative design may be the most effective way to 'relinquish researcher control' and we have concluded that the Croatian study could have benefitted from this approach. For example, participants or community representatives can consult on the design of the study, including instructions regarding photograph-taking. Similarly, researchers can actively involve participants in data analysis, beyond conventional member checks. In the Croatian study, instructions were developed by the researcher herself and participants had the opportunity to comment on the analysis only once it was completed. A more collaborative approach is exemplified by a study with indigenous youth in Canada where service providers were partnered with in order to design a more relevant and impactful study with youth. Furthermore, once youth were engaged in the research process, an active workshop-type process of thematic analysis was engaged in with participants to establish foundational frameworks for findings (see Liebenberg et al., 2017, for more details). Collectively these processes ensured safe, reflective research spaces for youth to engage in critical reflection on their lived-experiences. Similarly, the process ensured that youth voices remained central to the findings and dissemination (see Reich et al., 2017). Photo-elicitation interviewing embedded in such collaborative research contexts has the potential to expose forms of marginality in radically new ways.

Often referred to in terms of their capacity to 'give participants voice', photo-elicitation interviews can provide researchers with a creative and powerful means of working with research participants. Giving critical consideration to this choice of method, and its use, throughout the research process can help develop research findings that are powerfully aligned with participants' lived experience.

ADDITIONAL USEFUL READING

Harper, D. (2002) 'Talking about pictures: a case for photo elicitation', *Visual Studies, 17*(1): 13–26.

Drawing on his extensive experience conducting photo-elicitation studies, Douglas Harper provides a useful introduction and discussion of photo-elicitation as a qualitative method in this article. In particular, the history of this process is provided as is reference to seminal authors in this area.

Liebenberg, L. (2009) 'The visual image as discussion point: increasing validity in boundary crossing research', *Qualitative Research, 9*(4): 441–467.

This article highlights the benefits of using photo-elicitation in qualitative research, especially where it leads to increased validity of research findings when working in marginalised and historically silenced contexts. Using examples from fieldwork, Liebenberg highlights the ways in which the process brings attention to issues of importance and relevance to participants rather than those issues situated within existing academic knowledge structures. Additionally, the article illustrates the ways in which this process adds richness to the data and subsequent findings.

Margolis, E. and Pauwels, L. (2011) *The SAGE Handbook of Visual Research Methods*. Thousand Oaks, CA: Sage.

This seminal volume provides a broad spectrum of discussions around various visual methods, enabling consideration of how photo-elicitation is different from other approaches (including PAR approaches). The volume also provides perspectives on theory and data analysis.

Mitchell, C. (2011) *Doing Visual Research*. Thousand Oaks, CA: Sage.

This publication provides a comprehensive discussion of elicitation methods (including drawings, video and photographs). Professor Mitchell's discussion includes the integration of participatory approaches, and importantly, considerations pertaining to dissemination of findings.

Packard, J. (2008) '"I'm gonna show you what it's really like out here": the power and limitations of participatory visual methods', *Visual Studies, 23*: 63–77.

Packard provides an excellent reflective discussion on his own research, demonstrating the various ways in which limited thought on the technical aspects of photo-elicitation, and the practical implementation thereof, can be both limiting from a research perspective and harmful from an ethical perspective.

NOTE

1   Images have not been included in this chapter as the resolution quality was too poor for publication.

REFERENCES

Bagnoli, A. (2009) 'Beyond the standard interview: the use of graphic elicitation and arts-based methods', *Qualitative Research, 9*: 547–570.

Blackbeard, D. and Lindegger, G. (2015) 'The value of participatory visual methods in young masculinity research', *Procedia – Social and Behavioral Sciences, 165*: 85–93.

Boudon, R. (1974) *Education, Opportunity and Social Equality*. New York: Wiley.

Bourdieu, P. (1977) *Outline of a Theory of Practice*. Cambridge: Cambridge University Press.

Bourdieu, P. (1984) *Distinction: A Social Critique of the Judgement of Taste*. London: Routledge.

Bourdieu, P. (1988) *Homo Academicus*. Stanford, CA: Stanford University Press.

Bourdieu, P. and Passeron, J. C. (1979) *The Inheritors: French Students and their Relations to Culture*. Chicago: University of Chicago Press.

Bourdieu, P. and Wacquant, L (1992) *Invitation to Reflexive Sociology*. Chicago: University of Chicago Press.

Bugos, E., FitzGerald, R., True, E., Adachi-Mejia, A. M. and Cannuscio, C. (2014) 'Practical guidance and ethical considerations for studies using photo-elicitation interviews', *Preventing Chronic Disease, 11*: 14216. DOI: 10.5888/pcd11.140216.

Collier, J. and Collier, M. (1986) *Visual Anthropology: Photography as a Research Method*. New Mexico: University of New Mexico Press.

Creswell, J. W. and Plano Clark, V. L. (2011) *Designing and Conducting Mixed Methods Research* (2nd edn). Thousand Oaks, CA: Sage.

Doolan, K. (2010) '"My dad studied here too": social inequalities and educational (dis)advantage in a Croatian higher education setting'. Unpublished PhD thesis: University of Cambridge.

Epstein, I., Stevens, B., McKeever, P. and Baruchel, S. (2006) 'Photo Elicitation Interview (PEI): using photos to elicit children's perspectives', *International Journal of Qualitative Methods, 5*(3): 1–10.

Ford, K., Bray, L., Water, T., Dickinson, A., Arnott, J. and Carter, B. (2017) 'Auto-driven photo elicitation interviews in research with children: ethical and practical considerations', *Comprehensive Child and Adolescent Nursing, 40*(2): 1–15.

Freire, P. (2000) *Pedagogy of the Oppressed*. New York: Continuum. (Original work published 1970.)

Harper, D. (2002) 'Talking about pictures: a case for photo elicitation', *Visual Studies*, *17*(1): 13–26.

Harper, D. (2012) *Visual Sociology*. Abingdon: Routledge.

Ingram, N. (2011) 'Within school and beyond the gate: the complexities of being educationally successful and working class', *Sociology*, *45*(2): 287–302.

James, A. and Prout, A. (eds) (1990) *Constructing and Reconstructing Childhood: Contemporary Issues in the Sociological Study of Childhood*. Basingstoke: Falmer Press.

Jensen, J.L. and Rodgers, R. (2001) 'Cumulating the intellectual gold of case study research', *Public Administration Review*, *61*(2): 236–246.

Kvale, S. and Brinkmann, S. (2009) *Interviews: Learning the Craft of Qualitative Research Interviewing*. Thousand Oaks, CA: Sage.

Liebenberg, L. (2009) 'The visual image as discussion point: increasing validity in boundary crossing research', *Qualitative Research*, *9*(4): 441–467

Liebenberg, L., Sylliboy, A., Davis-Ward, D. and Vincent, A. (2017) 'Meaningful engagement of Indigenous youth in PAR: the role of community partnerships', *International Journal of Qualitative Methods*, *16*: 1–16.

Liebenberg, L. and Theron, T. (2015) 'Innovative qualitative explorations of culture and resilience', in L. Theron, L. Liebenberg and M. Ungar (eds), *Youth Resilience and Culture: Commonalities and Complexities*. New York: Springer. pp. 203–216.

Liebenberg, L., Ungar, M. and Theron, L. (2015) 'Using video observation and photo elicitation interviews to understand obscured processes in the lives of resilient youth', *Childhood*, *21*(4): 532–547.

Liebenberg, L., Wood, M. and Wall, D. (2018) 'Participatory action research with indigenous youth and their communities', in R. Iphofen and M. Tolich (eds), *Handbook of Qualitative Research Ethics*. London: Sage. pp. 339–353.

Loeffler, T. A. (2005) 'Looking deeply in: using photo-elicitation to explore the meanings of outdoor education experiences', *Journal of Experiential Education*, *27*: 343–346.

Lynch, K. and O'Riordan, C. (1998) 'Inequality in higher education: a study of class barriers', *British Journal of Sociology of Education*, *19*(4): 445–478.

Meo, A. I. (2010) 'Picturing students' habitus: the advantages and limitations of photo elicitation interviewing in a qualitative study in the city of Buenos Aires', *International Journal of Qualitative Methods*, *9*(2): 149–171.

Mitchell, C. (2011) *Doing Visual Research*. Thousand Oaks, CA: Sage.

Packard, J. (2008) '"I'm gonna show you what it's really like out here": the power and limitations of participatory visual methods', *Visual Studies*, *23*: 63–77.

Pain, H. (2012) 'A literature review to evaluate the choice and use of visual methods', *International Journal of Qualitative Methods*, *11*(4): 303–319.

Phelan, S.K. and Kinsella, E.A. (2013) 'Picture this … safety, dignity, and voice – ethical research with children: practical considerations for the reflexive practitioner', *Qualitative Inquiry*, *19*(2): 81–90.

Prosser, J. and Schwartz, D. (1998) 'Photographs within the sociological research process', in J. Prosser (ed.), *Image-based Research: A Sourcebook for Qualitative Researchers*. London: Falmer Press. pp. 115–130.

Reich, J., Liebenberg, L., Denny, M., Battiste, H., Bernard, A., Christmas, K., Dennis, R., Denny, D., Knockwood, I., Nicholas, R. and Paul, H. (2017) 'In this together: relational accountability and meaningful research and dissemination with youth', *International Journal of Qualitative Methods*, *16*: 1–12. DOI: 10.1177/1609406917717345.

Rollins, J. A. (2005) 'Tell me about it: drawing as a communication tool for children with cancer', *Journal of Pediatric Oncology Nursing*, *22*(4): 203–221.

Schratz, M. and Steiner-Löffler, U. (1998) 'Pupils using photographs in school self-evaluation', in J. Prosser (ed.), *Image-Based Research: A Sourcebook for Qualitative Researchers*. London: Falmer Press. pp. 235–251

Spivak, G. (1993) 'Can the subaltern speak?', in P. Williams and L. Chrisman (eds), *Colonial Discourse and Post-Colonial Theory*. New York: Harvester Wheatsheaf. pp. 66–111.

Strack, R., Magill, C. and McDonagh, K. (2004) 'Engaging youth through photovoice', *Health Promotion Practice*, *5*: 49–58.

Thomson, P. (2008) 'Children and young people: voices in visual research', in P. Thomson (ed.), *Doing Visual Research with Children and Young People*. New York: Routledge. pp. 1–19.

Vigurs, K. and Kara, H. (2017) 'Participants' productive disruption of a community photo-elicitation project: improvised methodologies in practice', *International Journal of Social Research Methodology*, *20*(5): 513–523.

Yin, R. K. (1984) *Case Study Research: Design and Methods*. Newbury Park, CA: Sage.

4

PRODUCING AND SHARING KNOWLEDGE WITH A RESEARCH FIELD

Anja Sieber Egger, Gisela Unterweger and Christoph Maeder

4.1 INTRODUCTION

In this chapter we address questions concerning the production and sharing of knowledge in an ethnographic study in the field of education. Since the ethnographic gaze on everyday educational practices and the perceptions of pedagogical actors of their own actions differ systematically, the sharing of ethnographic knowledge runs the risk of provoking irritation and relational dilemmas. The issue is exemplified in a current ethnographic research project in Swiss kindergarten.

Our ethnographic study focuses on how teachers at the kindergarten level try to meet the challenging demands of inclusive education in their everyday practice, while dealing with children of different backgrounds and skills. We do this by exploring the practices of kindergarten staff in addressing, categorising and dealing with the children. During our two-year fieldwork, conducted over three research sites, we began to realise how the practices we observed made our knowledge production about the field problematic in at least two ways. *First*, interpreting their role as being to deal with individual children with treatable, personal, special needs is the prevailing and dominant perspective of the teachers. However, our ethnographic analysis brought to light the interactional and organisational order of 'producing' such children as well. *Second*, we found it very challenging to share this social scientific knowledge with the field, to whom it would be unfamiliar, because their interpretations and our ethnographic interpretations did not match well. Neither the teachers, their principals nor any of the other participants considered themselves to be 'producers' of conspicuous or eye-catching children. Rather, they thought of themselves as individuals who helped the children and their families with their problems and challenges in school. In epistemological terms we can describe it as the pragmatic naturalism of pedagogy that hits theoretical social constructivism in educational research. And since this is not only a practical issue of how to do things in schools as a teacher or researcher, but also a highly theoretical issue concerning different forms of knowledge production, it cannot easily be explained to or negotiated with others in the field but should be dealt with in a methodology paper.

We believe that the challenge of different perspectives and contrasting interpretations (e.g. practical versus academic, and performing versus describing and analysing) are probably inherent in much educational research. Such tensions probably produce relational challenges in the field, sometimes even problems between the research and the field. We further believe this should be anticipated in educational ethnography and beyond, and that ideally everyone doing research involving direct exchanges and interactions with people in the field of education should expect such challenges to arise and be prepared for them.

Consequently, in this chapter we describe and elaborate on selected challenges of this type by using our case as an illustration. We also set out what we have found to be useful ways to handle challenges. The general feature we deal with thus is the tension between familiarity and strangeness in relation to the field, in terms of interpretation and theoretical requirement. This tension necessarily infers relational difficulties between researchers and those being researched arising from their being strangers to each other and with regard to the perspectives each imposes. This topic itself is not new to ethnography. It has already stimulated scientific discussion on the subject (see Atkinson, 2014; Delamont and Atkinson, 1996; Rabinow, 1977; Tedlock, 1987). But we believe that it is relevant to pick this issue up again and present it within the framework of a handbook of research on education. We believe that these tensions are apparent in all research on education in which the researchers and the researched come into personal contact, or where research on education must be fed back to practitioners by the researchers. All this necessarily and foreseeably produces *relational dilemmas*, which must be dealt with if we wish to develop and share our knowledge with practitioners in pedagogy.

4.2 CASE, CONTEXT AND CHALLENGES

Our descriptions of and deliberations on relational dilemmas arising from producing and sharing ethnographic knowledge stem from a research project titled 'Conspicuous

Children: An Ethnography of Processes of Differentiation in the Kindergarten'.[1] The study is being carried out at the Children – Childhood – Schooling research centre at the University of Teacher Education in Zürich. In Switzerland, the kindergarten is mainly part of the public school system and provides inclusive education with the aim of integrating as many children as possible into mainstream education. Pupils considered to have special needs or lacking certain competencies (e.g. linguistic, behavioural, cognitive, social) should receive the support they need as members of mainstream education instead of being taught in separate, special needs environments. To identify children with special needs, teachers are supposed to observe, describe, assess and manage their pupils' everyday behaviour and performance. As we observed in our research, different participating actors are involved in recurrent processes of identifying and defining the special needs of children. Such a definition can mobilise additional resources for teachers and children alike. However, at the same time these processes are linked to the creation of a differentiated social order on the interactional, categorical and organisational level within a kindergarten class, which can itself generate reasons for why some children become 'needy' or 'special'. This second point is somewhat alien to teaching practitioners, but fascinating to the ethnographer's gaze and analysis.

Since 2008, a reform of the first nine years of compulsory school in most of the Swiss Cantons made kindergarten mandatory for all children over the age of four. For two years, teachers are obliged to prepare children for primary school and to foster their individual development as best as possible. Being part of the public school system has consequences for kindergarten on various levels. As well as being compulsory for all children, it also now has a curriculum based on a competency model. Thus kindergarten is on the verge of overcoming its reputation for being 'just a playground' or 'a place to keep little children busy' according to the old stereotypes. The institution of the kindergarten along the lines of its creator, the German pedagogue Friedrich Fröbel, is currently transformed into a place of more targeted focus on integration into schooling under a regime of inclusiveness. Inclusive education, as the current paradigm in Swiss schools today, pays a lot of attention to what is called the 'heterogeneity' of children. The term heterogeneity refers to the individual beliefs and skills of children, as well as differences in language, culture and social background. Although the concept is used widely in both practice and theory, there is no single, broadly accepted definition available (Bailey, 2014). The main goal of inclusive education in practice is to include all children in mainstream schooling instead of separating them into special education settings. From day one at kindergarten, teachers must therefore respond to children's individual characteristics, their possible difficulties in learning and behaviour as well as their various talents and (dis)abilities. And they must include all children every day in their work.

Our research centres on how teachers manage and shape this heterogeneity and differences in class through their pedagogical practices. We are interested in understanding how the social order of the kindergarten is constructed under such a regime.

Additionally, we wish to examine how children are positioned in processes of recognition and how the borders of normality are defined and negotiated. To access such processes from the earliest stage possible, we began our research at the very start of the school career: the first day in kindergarten. The project ran from February 2016 to January 2019. The research team consisted of a total of five persons, one of whom was a doctoral student assigned full time to the project while the others participated between 30 to 50 per cent of the time. It was an ethnographic study. This means that we conducted fieldwork in the form of participant observation, producing field notes, collecting accessible documents, taking photographs and making selective audio-recordings for interviews and other communicative exchanges. This multi-modal data set-up allowed us to capture comprehensive descriptions of what goes on in the kindergarten, our field of research. Plus, it allowed us to obtain minutely detailed protocols, should these be needed for interactional inquiry of, let us say, a verbal exchange between teachers and children or indeed anyone else involved.

For two years our fieldwork was conducted in three kindergartens in an urban area of Switzerland. We visited the kindergartens regularly, for about three to five hours a day, where we participated as visitors and performed our observations at the same time. After every visit, we wrote down our field notes and organised any other data we had recorded. Each kindergarten is assigned to a different school district in the city and serves an average of 24 children and their families. The kindergartens selected for this study were chosen on the basis of their accessibility and the differing socio-economic environments in which they are situated. One is located in a clearly upper-class area, one in a mixed lower-middle-class part of the city with a (nevertheless) considerable proportion of migrants and one in a lower-class area with a mostly migrant population.[2] Officially, all three kindergartens have the same curriculum and are all subject to the same supervision and administration by the city.

Our analytical framework consists of recognition theory (Butler, 1997), which we have combined with the concepts and ideas of Foucault's normalisation (Ball, 2013; Foucault, 1977). We believe that it is through practices of addressing the children that recognition, as per the theory of Judith Butler, is practically performed. Addressing is therefore understood as a pivotal dimension of interactional practice. By addressing somebody in a specific way we express our perception of their social position and social belonging, for example as a child, a male or female, a member of an ethnic group, and so on. This can be observed on the level of interaction as well as on the level of the use of artifacts. We are interested in the construction of those practices of addressing in the everyday life of the kindergarten: To what norms do they refer? What discourses influence them? Which structures of recognition can be seen to be evolving? And finally, what forms of becoming and being a normal or special pupil can be reconstructed from our data?

Thus, we can say that our research contributes to the discussion on how teachers deal with the social and individual differences of their pupils in their everyday practices. And this is exactly where the challenges for our research arise. Whereas the dominant perspective in the field and in pedagogy assumes that their everyday task is to manage and nurture children with different needs, we came to see this differently. What we observed were the activities and actions of teachers and children alike and their accounts thereof, within a quite strict organisational framework of rules and requirements embedded in a wider context. The two perspectives are not completely incommensurable, but the difference is big enough to cause unease on both sides. The normativity of the pedagogical field, with its strong desire to intervene, promote and develop towards integration and an acceptance of the focus on individuals and their characteristics, was difficult for us as ethnographers from the very start. We can register and understand such perspectives as researchers, and as ethnographers we must take them very seriously as examples of native theories belonging to the organisational culture (see Eberle and Maeder, 2016). But we cannot accept an informant's views of the individual traits of the children as given facts or social scientific explanations as a matter of course (see Hammersley, 2006). Through numerous, intensive days of fieldwork, discussions among the research team and applying social theory, we came to another view. As a result, we were confronted with a schism, in terms of looking at the supposedly same situations, actors and interactions but with a very different interpretation. This dichotomy of perspective between the field and its researchers became a major challenge in terms of managing field relations, particularly but not only when reporting back to the field. We view this not as a moral or ethical issue as it is often discussed (Dennis, 2010: 123–127; Iphofen and Tolich, 2018), but as a clearly relational one, inherent and built into this type of research.

With regard to the distribution of knowledge in ethnography, it is widely accepted practice to consider different perspectives when reconstructing knowledge in and about a field. However, it is not only the knowledge of the actors in the field that differs depending on their function and social location; there are also differences between the knowledge of those actors and the researchers, as we have mentioned. While the question of the different perspectives of actors in the field has received a great deal of attention – there is even a name for it: 'thick description' (see Geertz, 1973) – the same cannot be said of the actor–researcher difference, despite the writing culture debate (see Clifford and Marcus, 1986). But at a time when knowledge production in science is intended no longer for use in the scientific domain alone but also for practice in the so-called 'Mode 2' (Gibbons et al., 1994: 3–16), this question is of special relevance. If researchers are to share their knowledge with practitioners, there are particular challenges to overcome: they must present their knowledge, originally formulated for the scientific community, in such a way that it makes sense to practitioners too. This is especially true in a case like ours, where we had regular meetings with the teachers over a period of almost two years. Not only do personal relationships develop, but many questions are raised about what we as scientists do on a daily basis. Teachers rightly ask themselves what the results of such research might be that could be of interest to them too. This claim or interest has turned out to be a major challenge in various respects for us as researchers.

The challenge of feeding back ethnographic findings and interpretations – or 'results' as lay people in the field might say – comes only at the end of a long period of contact with actors in the field. Yet since different perspectives and epistemological interests of the researchers and the practitioners are inherent in this kind of social scientific endeavour, the practical challenges of the encounter between research and field arise from the very beginning. The first contact, which Goffman (1989: 129) describes as 'getting in', is crucial: we as researchers must explain our research goals and questions, making them plausible to local education authorities, teachers and principals. In some way or another, the people we are communicating with will inevitably have their own ideas about the research and what it should mean for their field of work. And very often their expectations regarding research and the usefulness of its findings are quite high, not to say impossible to fulfil.

Another challenge follows on swiftly. Once the field setting has become accessible to the researcher, an ethnographic study necessarily establishes close and ongoing contact between researchers and actors in the field. In our case, it is not only the teachers and educational staff whom we meet on a regular basis, but also the children and their parents. Each has, according to their social location, their own perception of who we are and what we are doing. Many authors have pointed out that the responses of the actors in the field are crucial data to the ethnographers and relevant to the production of knowledge (see Bourgois, 1996; Marcus, 2010). But the main challenge we want to address here is dealing with the educational staff, because being constantly observed is an intrusion for anyone and raises a lot of questions for those under observation: what are they scribbling in their notebooks all the time? What do they think about what I am doing? We make a lot demands on the people in the field, for little return. Questions of power arise here too, with highly skilled academics holding powerful positions. The researcher takes on an odd field position that is hard for the actors in the field to understand: people tend to associate research with numbers and questionnaires, not participant observation. That is why the question, 'What the hell are these researchers doing here in my classroom?', appears to persist. This unstable position can be jolted if the field actor is not willing to let the researcher be part of his/her field. This lack of willingness is subtle and can arise at any moment during the research process, even in situations where initial access to the field is unproblematic and the research gets off to a successful start. To maintain this precarious balance, we as researchers need to give something back and to develop strategies that render relationships stable and (more or less) comfortable for everyone taking part. Furthermore, in our project we were very often confronted with the expectation that we were judging the actions and situations we observed, or at least confirming our judgements, according to a specific normative code of good versus bad practice. Hence, establishing and especially maintaining good field relations around this complex set of expectations and perceptions is a challenge.

Third, we wish to elaborate on the challenge of differing perspectives as mentioned above, in more detail. This problem is one of the underlying causes of the relational dilemma that can occur when feeding back scientific insights. In our study, the practitioners tend to develop a specific view of the problems they encounter in their daily work. In their theory-in-use they see certain children as being unfit or unable to meet without question all the requirements and demands made upon them, often ascribing this lack of competence not only to the children but also to their families and to the style of upbringing at home. We as researchers, on the other hand, develop another theoretical perspective when exploring the role of underlying institutional norms, routines and requirements in the larger context of a societal discourse on education and childhood. To us, from this perspective, it is often the institutional structure, norms and practices that create the frame in which certain children – for whatever reasons – happen not to fit. We want to be able to critically examine these larger-scale circumstances,[3] but very often this is not considered to be our role in the field. This problem of differing perspectives can be described in terms of familiarity and strangeness, or proximity to and distance from the definitions and interpretations of the field respectively.

4.3 RELATIONAL ISSUES: FAMILIARITY, INTERPRETATIONAL AUTHORITY AND FEEDBACK OF FINDINGS TO THE FIELD

In this section we start with what has been discussed as the tension between familiarity and strangeness in relation to a field. By presenting and analysing examples of tensions between the field role and the proximity required for fieldwork versus the scientifically required, theoretical distance from a field, we try to build upon the accepted argument against familiarity in educational research. While familiarity has been rightly accused of obscuring and impeding the sociological gaze in the field of education (see Delamont and Atkinson, 1996), there are other issues linked to this concept too. We wish to extend the notion of familiarity to encompass issues such as proximity and distance between the researcher and researched on different levels, with material from our study. In doing so we oppose the necessary normativity of the pedagogical field and its interests and obligations in education, using the distant gaze of researchers. This leads us to issues of definitional power in such arrangements, where we must ask who has the authority to specify what is really going on (see Clifford, 1983). Finally, we raise a third important issue which is linked to the preceding ones: how to report back social scientific, and in particular ethnographic, interpretations and descriptions to people in the field without offending them or distorting this knowledge?

4.3.1 THE PITFALLS OF MAKING ONESELF KNOWN IN THE FIELD

At the beginning of our fieldwork we were using the title: 'Conspicuous Children: An Ethnography of Processes of Differentiation in the Kindergarten'. Our research focused on how young children at the age of four or five are processed and integrated into a specific institutional structure or regime. Therefore, our interest lay in understanding the processes of differentiating children initiated by the teachers: that is, how are children labelled and categorised, how are they treated (differently) and what are the effects on the local social order and relations of recognition? Under this title, we addressed the processes of singling out then discussing and treating children who – in some way or another – attracted the attention of a teacher. Our scientific concern focused, of course, on the organisational routines and institutional norms within which this singling out happened. For us it was not the individual teacher nor the individual child that mattered, but the local practices and actions within the organisation of the kindergarten. However, the idea of confronting the actors in our three field sites with our original title made us uneasy. First, we were afraid that they would interpret our title against the backdrop of their own experiences and theories, and second, that they would therefore actively present their 'conspicuous children' to us – a reification we wanted to avoid. Furthermore, as Gary Alan Fine mentioned in his famous essay on the ten lies of ethnography, we were worried about sharing our original title with the field because we feared the possibility of not seeing the 'real' daily routines of the teachers: '[It] suggests that there is truth out there that we must be careful not to pollute' (Fine, 1993: 274). Nevertheless, we had to provide a title and tell everyone what we intended to do. This is a routine step in the research process, for which there are certain challenges to manage as Delamont, Atkinson and Pugsley (2010) showed in more detail. Although we were familiar with the difficulties of explaining to others what we were going to do, we had to come up with a way of doing it. We decided that a leaflet would be a good medium for teachers, but there was still the 'problematic' title of the project to resolve. So, we searched for a new one. The result was much less pointed than the original. We renamed the project, 'Everyday Diversity: An Ethnographic Study about Dealing with Heterogeneity in the Kindergarten'. With this title and the corresponding text in the leaflet we not only avoided using the catchword 'conspicuous', we also reacted to the normativity of the field as we had perceived it in earlier projects, as well as to dominant concepts (and therefore theories) on social differences and distinctions in the field. We responded to the normativity with a statement in the leaflet stating that kindergarten teachers are supposed to 'integrate all children into the everyday life of the kindergarten'. This is a dominant normative educational idea that is supported by many practitioners. But we also referred to dominant concepts, namely 'heterogeneity' and 'diversity'. In the pedagogical use of the term, 'heterogeneity' is a given, something that children inevitably carry with them and which includes features such as developmental status, language, competencies and so forth. Our social constructivist approach, in contrast, asks how such differences are created in everyday life, what lines of difference are constructed in interactions and situations, and to what effect.

So even before having spent much time in the field, we found ourselves in a relational dilemma: how much of our theoretical foundations and epistemological interests could we lay bare without confusing or irritating our partners in the field? It was like walking a tightrope, because in contrast with the adjustments mentioned above, we wanted to be open and honest about what we were looking for and what we would be doing in our scientific work. So, we openly described our main goal in the leaflet: to investigate how kindergarten teachers differentiate between children and on what criteria they base their differentiations. When we finally distributed our leaflet in our three sites, it did not appear to irritate or provoke further questions. Although the title and the text provided vague information, the leaflet seamed to fulfil its purpose. This is undoubtedly due to another aspect we have mentioned already: on the leaflet, we were able to identify ourselves as researchers from an established university of teacher education, with a grant from the most prestigious national research funding institution. Thus, we were trustworthy members of the research community, and as such we had the symbolic capital to lay the basis for functioning relationships with actors in the field.

What we had not thought about when starting to discuss a new title for the field, was a challenge that occurred later during the research process: in these times of the Internet and required institutional visibility, we had to inform not only the field of our activities but also the scientific community and funding institutions. We now had the problem of two project titles in circulation: one for the field and one for our scientific and administrative audience. What were we to do with one project and two different titles – one title playing down the provocative question of conspicuous children and the other emphasising it? It became obvious that we were simultaneously located on two different stages – those of the school and of the scientific community – on which we had to represent ourselves and our work.

Here the famous question from Howard Becker popped up: 'Whose side are we on?' (1967). It is not just that we are highly educated researchers from the white middle class; we also wander between the different worlds of public school and science, and between the different perspectives of all the people present in the field. The latter consist first of the kindergarten teachers, but also the special needs teacher, the school principal, the caretaker, the children, the parents, the siblings, and so on. We have to address and manage all these different audiences. In doing so we must draw on different methods of communication, and we must always be aware of playing different roles with different duties to fulfil. Therefore, in the next section we take a closer look at these roles and the question of 'whose side we are on?'

4.3.2 THE QUESTION OF INTERPRETATIONAL AUTHORITY IN THE FIELD OF EDUCATION

As ethnographers we not only address different audiences, but we are also forced to manage different roles and different expectations during fieldwork. Sometimes these have to be fulfilled simultaneously. It is this kind of flexibility in particular that becomes more and more important over time during the research process. The way in which relationships are established at the beginning influences the options for feeding back knowledge later during the research process. To exemplify this, we draw your attention to an example from our field data.

> After having gathered the children in a circle on the second morning of the new school year, the kindergarten teacher starts singing the greeting song. Every child and adult is greeted by his or her name in the song, including me, the researcher. Then, the teacher starts to move the children in a half circle in order to build a little stage. As soon as the teacher is ready, she starts performing a story with mice, an owl and a bear. The bear hides the mice to save them from being eaten by the owl. The children are very focused and intrigued by the play. I am sitting behind the stage to observe the children, but not the play itself. After half an hour, the phone starts ringing. The teacher does not react to this disruption, unlike the children. They start shouting after the third ring: 'The phone! The phone!' It gets loud, but the teacher says she will not answer the phone now and goes on with the story. I am very surprised that the teacher goes on with the story, seemingly unperturbed, while the phone rings for ages. The children on the other hand, cannot concentrate anymore and one after the other is shouting 'The phone, the phone'. Now the teacher gets up to answer it. With a sharp voice, she answers the call with her name. Now suddenly it is very silent in the room. All the children are looking in the direction of the teacher. Meanwhile I take this interruption as an opportunity to note down a few things that I had missed before. I now only hear what the teacher says down the phone and I hear that the children are repeating every answer the teacher gives. Suddenly, the teacher moves in the direction of the door and gives me a sign to take over the class. Everything is going very fast now and I am totally taken by surprise. I get up, leaving my somehow protected place outside the circle, and I move in front of the children to the teacher's chair.

For the next 20 minutes the researcher felt in limbo, as she noted in her field notebook:

> I feel like I am being tested and I am very concerned about the possibility of losing control over the class. I wanted to show the teacher that I can manage the children. Oops. That was a fast change of roles: I changed from being observer to participant, even to manager (we might also say teacher) who tries

to keep things firmly in hand. This was an unwanted change of roles; I was plunged in at the deep end. […] Later, I have a talk with the teacher about the interruption. She mentions that she was very happy to have me around because it was a very important phone call from a doctor concerning the diagnosis of one of the pupils. I reply that it was very stressful for me to take over because I was totally unprepared. Also, I shyly add, she can ask for my support whenever necessary but if possible not to manage the whole class.

We use this scenario as an example for considering another aspect of relational dilemmas and the production of ethnographic knowledge: we call it 'interpretational authority'. The teacher in this excerpt seems happy to rely on the researcher and puts her in front of the class like an assistant teacher. The fact that no chaos resulted gave the researcher a certain degree of credibility in the eyes of the teacher and was an important part of building a trustful relationship at the start. But the scene also makes clear that the teacher probably did not wish to accept the difference between her role and that of the researcher for one understandable reason: the lesson had to go on. That was her main task at that very moment, and so she did not care about their different professional roles. However, we do not believe that this would have happened with a father or a mother in the kindergarten. From a researcher's point of view, this change of roles is a double-edged sword. On one hand, it offered an opportunity to gain experience and knowledge that is of importance to the research. The researcher also gained a better understanding of what the teacher aims to achieve when performing the teaching job. And at the very least it was an important experience for reflecting on the role of a researcher in a school.

On the other hand, not only does the position of observer of the ongoing processes in the classroom get lost, it also establishes a dangerous precedent. The danger can be seen in the possible incorporation of the researcher into the logics and normativity of the field or, more precisely, of the teacher. The teacher knows how to successfully manage a kindergarten, while the researcher takes on the role of novice. We as researchers change in this moment into unskilled beginners, while the teacher is the one who knows how things should run and be. The power game changes here and can turn out to be a tricky thing for the researcher in terms of the ongoing research process, for how do the children react to this situation and perceive the researcher? And how does the teacher perceive the researcher over the following days – as a researcher or an assistant teacher?

Again, the question arises: whose side are we on? Later in the same school year, a boy addressed the same researcher as 'the boss' of the kindergarten. The researcher was very puzzled by this form of address but looking at it from a removed perspective it became clear that the boy saw the researcher as one of the teachers. There were many adults coming and going in the kindergarten and the new children especially saw all unfamiliar adults as teachers, because who else would be working in a kindergarten? We believe that the teachers in our fields hold the same view.

We gain credibility by showing our ability to adapt to the perspective of the field actors, even taking on the role of assistant teacher. But the flipside here is that we also anticipate a certain risk: what happens when the researcher starts feeding back knowledge and she or he suddenly offers a critical interpretation of what goes on in the kindergarten? This must be a very irritating moment for the teacher. Here the only option we see is to counterbalance these different demands at every moment and reflect on what is happening at all times. We need to build trustful relationships and to do so we must juggle different roles. But we should also make sure that the teachers accept us as researchers with a certain role and task.

4.3.3 MASSAGING THE REALITIES – FEEDING BACK DATA TO THE FIELD

After one year of intensive fieldwork, during which the ethnographers and teachers in two of the three kindergartens met nearly every week, each time for several hours, relations between the participants became quite intense. We describe these relations as 'professional friendship', where we knew each other quite well. The ethnographers knew the routines of the teachers with the children and the teachers knew what the ethnographers would do in the kindergarten. The teachers got used to the fact that one or two persons moved around in their kindergarten as friendly, but nevertheless 'professional strangers' (Agar, 1996), constantly taking notes while observing what was going on. A mutual acceptance and intense collaboration were established and worked well. But slowly and constantly the requests on the part of the teachers to know what the ethnographers had found increased. Finally, it became inevitable in two of our three kindergartens that the researchers would have to give feedback on what their research had yielded. In one case this could be done on a small scale, through a personal conversation between two ethnographers and two teachers on the research site itself. In the other, things turned out differently. When the ethnographers accepted the request from the teachers and offered to give them feedback, the teachers asked for a formal presentation in front of a larger audience. For them, as one of the teachers remarked to the ethnographers, this was also a chance to show the work they do to non-kindergarten teachers at the school. The location they chose was at a further education event for the whole school, comprising not only kindergarten teachers but also primary school teachers up to the sixth grade. All in all, about 50 people were anticipated to be in the audience.

At this point we realised that to a certain degree 'our' field had taken over the research agenda. But since we also saw this as a good opportunity to advertise our kind of research, we accepted. In this regard, the relation between field and research was working well. But for the researchers the following question immediately arose: Should we, and how could we, present a perspective on the production of conspicuous children, as formulated theoretically and tracked empirically, to those involved?[24]

Earnest discussion and deliberation on the issue by the research team resulted in the decision not to do so. We foresaw serious danger for the whole research project from a demonstration of such social scientific thinking, which could be misconstrued by our prospective audience as a way of making them feel guilty – which was wrong and something that we obviously wanted to avoid. At this point we were confronted with the unease of not being able to share our scientific knowledge with our field. We could argue that all presentations of research must consider what is called 'recipient design'; that is, the ability of an audience to follow and understand the contents of a presentation. On the one hand, this was 'old wine in new bottles' for anyone in the teaching business: if the audience does not understand what is being said, the presentation makes little sense. On the other hand, there was the matter of not giving a fair, or a fully informed, picture about a researched reality.

The second option, as an exercise of power by withholding knowledge, although unpleasant, was obviously unavoidable for us as a research team. And so, the question immediately arose of what to present instead if we wanted to maintain the image of our research being beneficial to the pedagogical field and for our field persons in particular. It took some considerable effort to find an answer that would work, but eventually we decided to frame the story differently. In our presentation we restricted the social constructive perspective as a theoretical framework. We gave some information on the history of ethnographic research in modern societies, its focus on everyday life and the corresponding need for participant observation. And we pointed to the limitations of such research, such as finding only 'partial truths' (Clifford, 1986) and our representation being only 'blurred genres' (Geertz, 1983). We did everything we could to render our potentially corrosive research approach as harmless as possible. On the content side of the presentation, we emphasised the complexity of the work of the teachers and the children. We provided descriptions at the level of teacher–children interactions, in which generating cooperation was the main issue. Then we considered the teachers' work with the parents and discussed ongoing debates on the salaries of kindergarten teachers. Their salaries are 12.5 per cent lower than those of primary school teachers, a difference that can only be explained historically and politically, and not by the professional requirements of the job. Finally, we also introduced some remarks on the linguistic challenges to be overcome in the kindergarten that we observed: the fact that 12 different first languages were spoken by the children. This fact was used as a resource by the teachers when, for instance, they taught the children how to count in all the different languages or talked about the different birthday customs of the different language groups. But of course, they also knew that this was a major challenge in terms of making sure that every child would be able to follow the school lessons given in the High-German language used in Swiss schools.

By framing our reporting back to the teachers in this way, and by applying the social constructive perspective to ourselves and our research methods instead of towards our work in the kindergarten, we succeeded in gaining the acceptance and respect of our audience. Such adaption of one of the core assumptions of our research was called 'massaging the reality' by one of the members of our research team. As mentioned above, the uneven distribution of knowledge about the creation of a social reality was the price we had to pay; a price we could not avoid paying because we would have lost both access to the field and our reputation as field partners on a personal and general level.

RESEARCHER CHECKLIST

All in all, to summarise, not only were our words to the practitioners to be chosen wisely and appropriately, but our entire research set-up had to be explained differently. The topic structure had to be adapted and researchers' roles in the field had to be negotiated constantly, not only during the fieldwork itself but also when reporting back to the field later on.

If you conduct research where you have to interact with the field personally and intensely, then we recommend that you prepare your work with some questions: is there a strong normative perspective in the field? If so, think about how you can interpret it in relation to your work and your own disciplinary perspective. If you do expect such pitfalls to arise, then prepare yourself by thinking in advance about:

- What to share and commit to in terms of your research upon entering the field.

- How to relate the scientific interpretation of what happens in the field to informants' understanding of what is going on.

- How to communicate back without blurring scientific interpretation but nevertheless meeting the expectations and interpretations of actors in the field.

If your research question comes from a discipline outside of education, e.g. social anthropology or sociology, then this preparation will help you to avoid taking on the field's explanation as a social science explanation – something that happens more easily than expected. Moreover, it is no secret that such considerations take time, so we recommend that you devote a considerable amount of time and energy to working on these three suggestions and prepare your fieldwork and research accordingly. Plan what you want to present and in what form (text, slides, plain talk or a blend of these) well ahead. The true value of all this preparation is the opportunity to establish respectable field relations and solid reporting of your research back to the field, without giving up your theoretical perspective and your scientific reputation.

4.4 CONCLUSION

In our chapter, we started with what we discussed as the tension between familiarity and strangeness in relation to a research field. We presented and analysed the tensions between the field role and the proximity required for ethnography by showing how tricky this can be in terms of issues of (1) identifying oneself, (2) maintaining scientific interpretational authority and (3) the way in which you report back to those being researched. In doing so, we elaborated on the concept of familiarity in educational ethnography. While familiarity has been rightly accused of obscuring and impeding the sociological gaze in the field of education (see Delamont and Atkinson, 1996), these three other issues at least are linked to this concept too. Ethnographic research performed in classrooms is always a joint product between the ethnographers and the people in the field. Therefore, we cannot but adapt to such situations by considering what relational issues might arise. Of course, such customisation of research findings could also be regarded as bending or ceding the truth of what is going on in the field. But since truth is an ideal and not something that one can truly possess or claim independently of the situation, we refer to what has been written long ago: 'It may even be said that the problem is contained *in nuce* in Pascal's famous statement that what is truth on one side of the Pyrenees is error on the other' (Berger and Luckmann, 1991: 17f). Such a removed stance, not only towards the field but also towards research in education, helps to avoid relational problems, which without doubt can themselves impede ethnographic research in education.

ADDITIONAL USEFUL READING

Becker, H. S. (1967) 'Whose side are we on?', *Social Problems, 14* (3): 239–247.

This is a classic and still widely read text on the issue of partisanship in social research in general. Its main argument states that even the choosing of a research topic has relational implications for the researcher and the researched, in ethnography as well. Hence, the answer to the question of taking sides is not straightforward but must be reflected on by the researchers when considering their own position in the research community and the field.

Delamont, S. (ed.) (2016) *Fieldwork in Educational Settings: Methods, Pitfalls and Perspectives* (3rd edn). London and New York: Routledge.

In this book, Sara Delamont gives a comprehensive and thoughtfully written account of how to do educational ethnography. She also mentions possible pitfalls and maintains a useful balance between a more general discussion about the ethnography of education and practical advice. The list of references is well selected and comprehensive. This is a highly recommended book for anyone who wants to engage seriously in the ethnography of education.

Delamont, S., Atkinson, P. and Pugsley, L. (2010) 'The concept smacks of magic: fighting familiarity today', *Teaching and Teacher Education, 26* (1): 3–10.

In this chapter, the authors argue that good educational ethnography should make the familiar strange in order to describe and understand what is going on in education. However, since most researchers are themselves well socialised in classroom settings this goal is hard to achieve for them as observers. Five strategies to overcome inhibitory familiarity for the researcher, also available to all ethnographers focused on teaching and learning, are outlined.

NOTES

1   Swiss National Science Foundation (SNF), Grant No. 100019_159328. Principal investigator: Anja Sieber Egger. For an overview on the current situation of school ethnography, especially in Germany and Switzerland, see Sieber and Unterweger (2018).

2   It is relevant to know that in Switzerland nearly one third of the population was not born there but migrated to the country. This is not the place to describe the complexities of migration and its consequences for the whole country. More comprehensive information in this regard is available elsewhere (Mahnig and Cattacin, 2005; Wanner, 2012; Wicker, 2012).

3   This is not an easy task. As Delamont, Atkinson and Pugsley point out, for a long time there were too many educational ethnographies that took too many aspects of schooling and schooling systems for granted (Delamont, Atkinson and Pugsley, 2010: 4).

4   In ethnographic terms this difference between the insiders' and the observers' perspective is addressed by the distinction between emic versus etic points of view (see Bergman and Lindgren, 2018).

REFERENCES

Agar, M. H. (1996) *The Professional Stranger: An Informal Introduction to Ethnography*. New York: Academic Press.

Atkinson, P. (2014) *For Ethnography*. Thousand Oaks, CA: Sage.

Bailey, S. (2014) *Exploring ADHD: An Ethnography of Disorder in Early Childhood*. London: Routledge, Taylor & Francis Group.

Ball, S. J. (2013) *Foucault, Power, and Education*. London: Routledge.

Becker, H. S. (1967) 'Whose side are we on?', *Social Problems*, 14(3): 239–247.

Berger, P. L. and Luckmann, T. (1991) *The Social Construction of Reality: A Treatise in the Sociology of Knowledge*. London and New York: Penguin Books.

Bergman, Å. and Lindgren, M. (2018) 'Navigating between an emic and an etic approach in ethnographic research: crucial aspects and strategies when communicating critical results to participants', *Ethnography and Education*, 13(4): 477–489. DOI: 10.1080/17457 823.2017.1387066.

Bourgois, P. (1996) *In Search of Respect: Selling Crack in El Barrio*. Structural Analysis in the Social Sciences. Cambridge: Cambridge University Press.

Butler, J. (1997) *The Psychic Life of Power: Theories in Subjection*. Stanford, CA: Stanford University Press.

Clifford, J. (1983) 'On ethnographic authority', *Representations*, *2*(4): 118–146. DOI: 10.2307/2928386.

Clifford, J. (1986) 'Introduction: partial truths', in J. Clifford and G.E. Marcus (eds), *Writing Culture: The Poetics and Politics of Ethnography*. Berkeley, CA: University of California Press. pp. 1–26.

Clifford, J. and Marcus, G.E. (eds) (1986) *Writing Culture: The Poetics and Politics of Ethnography*. Berkeley, CA: University of California Press.

Delamont, S. and Atkinson, P. (1996) *Fighting Familiarity: Essays on Education and Ethnography*. Cresskill, NJ: Hampton Press.

Delamont S., Atkinson, P. and Pugsley, L. (2010) 'The concept smacks of magic: fighting familiarity today', *Teaching and Teacher Education*, *26*(1): 3–10.

Dennis, B. (2010) 'Ethical dilemmas in the field: the complex nature of doing education ethnography', *Ethnography and Education*, *5*(2): 123–127. DOI: 10.1080/17457823.2010.493391.

Eberle, T. S. and Maeder, C. (2016) 'Organizational ethnography', in D. Silverman (ed.), *Qualitative Research* (4th edn). London: Sage. pp. 121–136.

Fine, G.A. (1993) 'Ten lies of ethnography: moral dilemmas of field research', *Journal of Contemporary Ethnography*, *22*: 267–294.

Foucault, M. (1977) *Discipline and Punish: The Birth of the Prison*. New York: Pantheon Books.

Geertz, C. (1973) *The Interpretation of Cultures: Selected Essays*. New York: Basic Books.

Geertz, C. (1983) 'Blurred Genres: "The Refiguration of Social Thought"', in C. Geertz (ed.), *Local Knowledge: Further Essays in Interpretive Anthropology*. New York: Basic Books. pp. 19–35.

Gibbons, M., Limoges, C., Nowotny, H., Schwartzman, S., Scott, P. and Trow, M. (1994) *The New Production of Knowledge: The Dynamics of Science and Research in Contemporary Societies*. London and Thousand Oaks, CA: Sage.

Goffman, E. (1989) 'On fieldwork', *Journal of Contemporary Ethnography*, *18*(2): 123–132. DOI: 10.1177/089124189018002001.

Hammersley, M. (2006) 'Ethnography: problems and prospects', *Ethnography and Education*, *1*(1): 3–14. DOI: 10.1080/17457820500512697.

Iphofen, R. and Tolich, M. (eds) (2018) *The SAGE Handbook of Qualitative Research Ethics*. Thousand Oaks, CA: Sage.

Mahnig, H. and Cattacin, S. (eds) (2005) *Histoire de la politique de migration, d'asile et d'intégration en Suisse depuis 1948*. Zürich: Seismo.

Marcus, G.E. (2010) *Ethnography Through Thick and Thin*. Princeton, NJ: Princeton University Press.

Rabinow, P. (1977) *Reflections on Fieldwork in Morocco*. Berkeley, CA: University of California Press.

Sieber, E.A. and Unterweger, G. (2018) 'Ethnographic research in schools: historical roots and developments with a focus on Germany and Switzerland', in D. Beach, C. Bagley and S. Marquez da Silva (eds), *The Wiley Handbook of the Ethnography of Education*. Hoboken, NJ: John Wiley & Sons. pp. 233–256.

Tedlock, D. (1987) 'Questions concerning dialogical anthropology', *Journal of Anthropological Research*, *43*(4): 325–337. DOI: 10.1086/jar.43.4.3630541.

Wanner, P. (ed.) (2012) *La démographie des étrangers en Suisse*. Zurich: Seismo.

Wicker, H.-R. (2012) *Migration, Differenz, Recht und Schmerz: Sozialanthropologische Essays zu einer sich verflüchtigenden Moderne, 1990–2010*. Sozialer Zusammenhalt und kultureller Pluralismus, Zürich: Seismo.

PART III

EXPLORING OTHER PATHS FOR INTERPRETATION

5

DOING SYSTEMATIC LITERATURE REVIEWS – 'NET FISHING' OR 'WHALE HUNTING'?

Gábor Halász

5.1 INTRODUCTION

This chapter is about exploring existing knowledge before undertaking the adventure of creating new knowledge. Many researchers would agree that one of the most exciting parts of their professional life is penetrating into the world of existing but unexplored knowledge with the hope of discovering evolutionary patterns of thoughts, flows of ideas and hidden connections. Wandering into the boundless web of disciplinary problem communities, in fact, strengthens the feeling that we are not alone with our questions and we can rely on and be connected with others who have similar concerns. We call these expeditions 'literature review' but what we encounter while travelling in this world are not just written words frozen into academic publications or research reports, but real people and communities who communicate and interact with each other while advancing their own knowledge construction projects.

We use the example of two strongly related, consecutive research projects to illustrate the challenges researchers might face when they start their journey into a particularly complex world where the problem is not the lack of maps and navigators but their extreme richness and the often contradictory signals they provide. Both projects were funded by a national research funding agency and both focused on change and improvement in education. The first one (named *ImpAla*) aimed at understanding the impact mechanism of EU funded development interventions targeted at schools. The main research question was: 'What are the conditions for curriculum development interventions to produce deep and lasting changes in the professional behaviour of teachers and schools?' The second project (named *Innova*) aimed at better understanding school and local level innovation processes. The main research question was: 'What are the mechanisms that lead to the emergence of school and local level innovations, how do these innovations spread between schools and teachers, and how do they lead to system level changes?' While *ImpAla* has focused mainly on top-down change processes, the perspective of *Innova* has been bottom-up, and the latter has been a logical follow up of the former.[1]

Both projects have used mixed research methods, combining large-scale surveys (based on the use of electronic questionnaires) with intensive fieldwork (based on case studies and ethnographic observations). From the perspective of this chapter an important component of both projects was a relatively long period devoted to exploring existing knowledge produced by earlier research and the continuation of this activity during the whole life cycle of the projects.

5.2 THE CHALLENGES OF ENTERING A COMPLEX, UNEXPLORED INTERDISCIPLINARY FIELD

In our case, given the complexity of the research questions, exploring existing knowledge through reviewing literature proved to be particularly challenging. It was expected that a large part of the relevant knowledge would be found in a wide range of disciplinary areas such as intervention research, implementation studies, developmental economics, impact assessment, public policy, management and organisational behaviour, communication studies, curriculum theory, research on teacher learning and professional development, innovation studies and some others. All these areas use specific terms, the meaning of which often overlaps those used in other areas. It became clear very early on that if we limit our attention to searching a smaller number of keywords a large part of relevant existing knowledge would remain outside the scope of our 'radar'. This reminded us of the saying attributed to Copernicus: 'To know that we know what we know, and to know that we do not know what we do not know, that is true knowledge'.

The challenges we faced in the case of *ImpAla* and *Innova* have been manifold. First, we had to accept that most of the relevant knowledge has been produced by people with an interest for development interventions and innovation processes, rarely having a specific education focus. These people, belonging to various disciplinary communities, not only use different terms to describe similar phenomena but often they are also isolated from each other. Discovering that they talk about the same thing using different languages requires particularly open and creative thinking. In the case of the *ImpAla* project, for example, one of the most exciting journeys we performed was into the world of the development aid literature produced mainly by development economists, often working for international development agencies or charities, helping the design, implementation and evaluation of aid programmes in poorer countries. Another similarly exciting journey was conducted into the world of teacher professional learning, as the professional beliefs and knowledge of teachers and their learning and sense making play a fundamental role in the success or failure of development interventions. Those who do research in development economics and those who study teacher learning and teacher professional knowledge rarely communicate with each other. It was our task to connect these areas and to reveal those cases where their representatives, using different conceptual frameworks and terminologies, were speaking about problems similar to those we were exploring.

A second related challenge was defining relevant keywords, which is one of the typical stages of doing literature reviews followed by searches in large bibliographic databases. In our case this proved to be practically unfeasible. We discovered relevant and valuable pieces of research, in different disciplinary areas, which were using terms in their titles and abstracts that were not part of our initial repertoire of keywords. What one author might have called 'impact assessment' another might have discussed under the term of measuring 'teacher behavioural change' or 'school improvement'. In this respect, intuition has played a key role in revealing connections between areas originally seen as extremely remote.

The third challenge was the choice between breadth and depth. As we shall see, one of the typical stages of doing a systematic literature review is the selection of sometimes tens of thousands of publications and then filtering them, using pre-established keywords so that a limited number of publications remain in the pool, and then evaluating the quality of them using standard evaluation criteria. A basic requirement is to make this filtering and quality evaluation procedure transparent. At the end, sometimes, only very few publications remain in the pool to be seriously read. This is an effective way to limit breadth and increase depth, which could be described with the metaphor of 'net fishing' as opposed to what we could call 'whale hunting'.

While fishermen who do 'net fishing' throw their net and filter the sea with it, whale hunters direct their boat to places where the chance of encountering these big animals is greater, they wait for them to appear and then they concentrate their efforts on catching them. What we were doing in *ImpAla* and *Innova* could be better described with the second metaphor. We realised that there were a smaller number of great, influential research projects, often consisting of many in-built data collections and combining qualitative and quantitative elements, and it seemed that the most effective strategy was to hunt these big 'whales'. In the case of *ImpAla* the famous 'Rand

Change Agent Study' (see McLaughlin, 1990) was found to be the most valuable piece of research deserving extensive and deep exploration. In the case of *Innova* the 'Minnesota Innovation Research Program' (see Van de Ven, Polley and Garud, 2008) played a similar role. We spent a significant part of our time exploring these valuable 'knowledge mines', exploiting their rich outcomes.

A further, related challenge that merits being mentioned here is the risk of being seduced by intellectually challenging 'attractors' one necessarily meets when doing a reviewing journey. This challenge is not independent from the breadth and depth dilemma but it is different. In the case of our projects, similar to most research undertakings that devote a significant amount of time to exploring existing knowledge, there were traps to avoid: one was exhausting resources before reaching all important unexplored areas, and the other was reaching all of them, but not having enough time to get really acquainted with them. Both are connected with the scarcity of the most valuable resource: time. One way of losing your time is being attracted by a promising path or entering a door that seems to lead to an entirely new word with hundreds of consecutive paths leading again to different directions. You do not have an easy choice: if you enter, you might get lost, if you do not enter, you might miss the chance to discover valuable knowledge. To manage these attractions, the first requirement of the protocols of systematic reviewing is typically the formulation of a clear research question.

Finally, one further challenge is connected with the specific context in which we were studying educational development interventions and innovation processes. The development programmes we were looking at were part of larger national developing strategies, aimed at human resource development and social integration, so their design and implementation was not education specific. Although their (not always explicit) goal was to change the classroom level behaviour of teachers and the way schools design their learning environments, they were not called 'curriculum reform'. Those who designed and implemented them penetrated the 'curriculum policy ecosystem' as powerful actors in possession of resources, which were much larger than those possessed by the traditional players of curriculum regulation and curriculum policy. All these processes unfolded in a specific national context with its unique social, political and cultural dynamics: creating challenges related in general with contextuality – as listed, for example, by Pollitt (2013) – and, in particular, with the specificities of our national context.

'Conducting any type of research project without conducting a literature review can be likened to travelling to a strange and exotic country but never coming out of your hotel room' (Booth, Sutton and Papaioannou, 2012: 1). But reviewing, similarly to travelling, can be done in many ways. At one extreme, every detail can be carefully planned in advance; at the other, we can be led by intuition and by improvisations (without knowing in the morning where we shall pass the next night); but we can also follow various combinations of these extremities. Most travellers do carefully plan before starting their journey in order to avoid the risk of wasting time and money. But there are many, including the author of this article, who think that excluding non-planned and improvised components would impoverish the travel experience and deliberately allow a large open space for unexpected surprises and adventures.

One of the decisions we had to take when we started the exploration of existing knowledge was whether to apply the methodology called 'systematic literature review' (SLR) or to follow the classical approaches, sometimes described as 'narrative reviewing'. In this chapter we use the abbreviation SLR to designate one specific approach of doing systematic literature reviews with the aim of disambiguation. In fact, most methodologists identify SLR with systematic reviewing and often designate other forms of reviewing as 'non-systematic' or 'unsystematic' (Andrews, 2005; Booth, Sutton and Papaioannou, 2012; Gough, Oliver and Thomas, 2017; Hammersley, 2002; Oakley, 2003; Riese, Carlsen and Glenton, 2014). But the exclusive use of the attribute 'systematic' to designate SLRs seems to be rather problematic: in the case of *ImpAla* and *Innova* we have carried out the systematic review of the relevant literature without applying the standard SLR approach, but we do not think that what we were doing was less systematic than what those applying the SLR standards are doing.

We share the view of those who think that the use of word 'systematic' as an attribute of reviewing to designate SLRs hides a conceptual trap. It suggests that reviews using other approaches are 'unsystematic', which, in many cases, certainly is not true. Literature reviews can be systematic without following the SLR standards: they can, for example – if we refer to dictionary definitions of the word 'systematic' – follow a 'fixed plan' and they can be 'methodical in procedure or plan' or 'marked by thoroughness and regularity' without applying SLR protocols.

There are hundreds of publications on the use of systematic reviewing and, in certain disciplinary areas, thousands of published systematic reviews, including SLRs. The reader can easily find manuals on how to do systematic reviewing (some of the most important ones are referred to in this chapter). The aim of this chapter in not to introduce the reader into the methodology of reviewing, applying or not using the SLR approach, but rather to show, using the example of two particular research projects, the challenges and dilemmas researchers face when they decide how to explore existing knowledge related to their research question. But let us first explore what systematic reviewing, including SLR, means.

5.3 THE SYSTEMATIC EXPLORATION OF EXISTING KNOWLEDGE

The emergence of the SLR methodology and the massive production of SLRs is one of the most important trends of modern scientific research. This trend has been supported by a number of converging influences, such as the explosion of scientific production and the need to reconcile contradicting single studies (Cooper and Hedges, 2009; Glass, 1976; Hattie, 2008; Hattie, Rogers and Swaminathan, 2014; Hunt, 1997), the emergence of the 'evidence-based movement' (Davies, 2004; Oakley, 2003; OECD, 2007; Slavin, 2008), and the increasing pressure from funders and users of research (Gough, 2007; Gough, Oliver and Thomas, 2017; Petticrew and Roberts, 2006; Suri, 2013). Those who regularly perform SLRs or do research on SLR, sometimes called 'systematic review methodologists' (Noyes et al., 2013; Snilstveit, 2012; Torgerson, Hall and Light, 2017), can be described as a new quasi profession in the field of scientific research (Garfield, 1977, 1996) belonging to the new academic field of 'science of research synthesis' (Chalmers, Hedges and Cooper, 2002). This emerging profession of systematic reviewing requires a wide range of specific cognitive, personal and social skills (Garfield, 1996; Gough, Oliver and Thomas, 2017; Oakley, 2003), and performing protocol-based systematic reviewing requires significant human, financial, technical and institutional resources (Gough, Oliver and Thomas, 2017; Oakley, 2003).

The fact that with the explosion of the number of original pieces of research it is no longer possible to read all the relevant original reports or publications, an expanding 'synthesis industry' has emerged which, as noted by the authors of a recent article, is 'nearly doubling each year in the social sciences' (Polanin, Maynard and Dell, 2017). The expansion has already led to the emergence of what we can call 'synthesising the syntheses'. The same authors identified 25 reports or publications in the field of education, which could each be described as a 'synthesis of syntheses', that is, using not publications presenting original research outcomes as the unit of analysis but publications presenting syntheses. Perhaps the better known of these is John Hattie's 'meta-meta-analysis' of 800 earlier syntheses, which had covered more than 52,000 original studies (Hattie, 2008).

The major difference between a SLR and other ways of reviewing is that the former follows a strict, pre-defined protocol which is typically established and required by specialised organisations regularly preparing and publishing SLRs. One of these organisations is the UK based EPPI-Centre,[2] which has developed an advanced methodology and a unique culture of SLR in the field of education. In a recent book the leader of this centre and his colleagues distinguished seven consecutive stages of preparing a SLR, each of them being seen as a necessary element of the exercise (see Figure 5.1). As the figure suggests (and the practice of the EPPI-Centre also demonstrates), performing a 'serious' systematic review is a major undertaking which requires significant resources, the collaboration of a well-selected and professionally strong team and also specific skills that can be acquired only through participating in several SLR exercises.

It is important to stress that the EPPI approach is just one of the many competing SLR approaches. A remarkable specificity of EPPI is that it also operates as a platform to discuss the theoretical dilemmas underpinning all efforts to synthesise earlier research. One of these dilemmas – also encountered in our two research projects – is

| **Review Initiation** | |
| Form review team | Engage Stakeholders |

Review question & methodology
Formulate question, conceptual framework & approach

Search strategy
Search & screen for inclusion using eligibility criteria

Description of study characteristics
Code to match or build a conceptual framework

Quality and relevance assessment
Apply quality appraisal criteria

Synthesis
Use conceptual framework, study codes & quality judgments

Using reviews
Interpret & communicate findings with stakeholders

Figure 5.1 The stages of an EPPI systematic literature review

Source: Gough, Oliver and Thomas, 2017

related to the goal or the function of reviewing which has major implications on the review methods we use.

Gough and his colleagues distinguish two basic approaches that they name 'aggregative' and 'configurative'. The former is searching answers to very specific research questions: one example is the famous reviewing exercise initiated by the US congress to synthesise earlier research on the impact of phonic and non-phonic literacy teaching methods on children's reading skills (Ehri et al., 2011; Yatvin, 2002). In 'configurative' reviews research questions might be much less specific and the initial questions might be significantly reshaped by what the reviewed literature reveals. In this case we use our extensive reading of the literature to discover new configurations of ideas or to get inspiration for inventing entirely new configurations, that is, to see something that others have not yet seen. Those who do aggregative types of synthesis of earlier research are typically interested in finding publications or reports focusing on the same or on similar questions. Those whose intention is to discover new configurations are rather interested in looking at different and divergent sources, they tend to cross disciplinary boundaries and to play creatively with keywords when searching for relevant studies.

The distinction between 'aggregative' and 'configurative' reviews is strongly related to the question of who is using the outcomes of the review and how they are using these outcomes. Histories of the 'SLR movement' (see, for example, Chalmers, Hedges and Cooper, 2002; Cooper and Hedges, 2009; Evans and Benefield, 2001; Petrosino, 2013; Suri, 2013) show that when SLR emerged in the field of medical and health sciences clinical practitioners were seen as the main target audience. The primary use of SLR was not to inform future research but to support practitioners or politicians/administrators to make better decisions on specific treatments or interventions based on the best scientific evidence. This is particularly true for the meta-analysis of earlier research which, as Hattie and his colleagues (2014: 197) affirmed, 'has changed the way many researchers review previous literature'. Interestingly SLR has been increasingly seen as the 'gold standard' of reviewing even by those whose research question is not 'what works', that is, whether or not one specific treatment, intervention or method has a positive impact.

While aggregative reviews typically aim at supporting the evaluation of the impact-potential of specific interventions through synthesising the outcomes of earlier research on these interventions, configurative reviews aim at developing new theories and conceptual frameworks or revealing knowledge gaps. While the former is 'exploitative' rather than 'explorative' (March, 1991), the ambition of the latter is to create knew knowledge and to discover unknown relationships. Perhaps the best way to understand the difference between the different types of reviewing is to conceive the activity of reviewing as a specific form of knowledge management (Oakley, 2003; Schryen, Wagner and Benlian, 2015). The choice between the different types or rather the way we combine them has to be determined by what use we want to make of the outcomes of reviewing.

The classical SLR approach might be more appropriate when the method or intervention we study is not too complex and when its impact is less determined by the specific context in which it is implemented. One of the weaknesses of many secondary analyses of primary research is that that they do not identify the complexity of interventions and the contingencies determining their impact. Taking the 'complexity perspective' into account is a major challenge for reviewers doing aggregative reviews. They have to understand the sources and the nature of complexity, which might be related to the method or the intervention (for example, when it cannot be isolated from other factors or when it allows various local applications), to the context (when a high number of interacting agents have impact on the implementation process) or to temporal factors (such as sequences, cycles, feedback loops or the emergence of unexpected outcomes). They also have to understand what evaluation researchers call 'intervention logic', that is, the complex casual relations of impact mechanisms. There is a rich emerging literature on how to cope with the complexity problem in synthesising earlier research (see, for example, Anderson et al., 2013; Cornish, 2015; Greenhalgh et al., 2011; Pawson, 2006; Petticrew, 2015; Petticrew et al., 2015), to be consulted particularly by those who perform SLRs on complex educational interventions.

Within the SLR movement the method called meta-analysis requires special attention. This method, belonging definitely to the aggregative approach, typically addresses relatively simple research questions, and consists of synthesising the conclusions of pieces of primary empirical research aimed at answering this question. In his inspiring book on the history of meta-analysis Hunt (1997), for example, presents in detail the concrete stories of researchers seeking answers to the question of whether putting more money into education and assigning homework lead to higher student outcomes. Meta-analyses typically focus on 'effect-size' measured by a simple standard variable and are less interested in contextual complexity.

5.4 ADDRESSING THE REVIEWING CHALLENGE IN OUR RESEARCH PROJECTS

In our *ImpAla* and *Innova* projects the reviewing process was conceived as a complex knowledge management task. When the projects started we already had a significant amount of knowledge about how development interventions work and about the birth and spread of innovations in education but this knowledge was not appropriately confronted with the knowledge accumulated by others, and we could not really know what we did not know. We were thinking about reviewing (reading and reflecting collectively about our readings) as an exciting and adventurous journey which would support our learning and intellectual development, and – first of all – contribute directly to the creation of a well-grounded theoretical and conceptual framework that would allow the creation of appropriate instruments for the empirical part of our research.

5.4.1 CHOOSING THE RIGHT APPROACH

We wanted to avoid seeing this phase of our research as a formal task, and to escape what one of the editors of a journal of the American Psychological Association described as the 'risk for producing mind-numbing lists of citations and findings that resemble a phone book, impressive cast, lots of numbers, but not much plot' (Bem, 1995: 173). Although there was a clearly defined phase in our project plan devoted to literature review (preceding the data collection phase) our intention was not to close this part at the formally planned deadline (as required by the funding agency) but to continue it during the whole project lifespan. Our earlier experiences told us: a great part of the knowledge hidden in the written words of scientific publications is revealed after re-reading them in the light of other readings and in the light of what we learn from our own data. Our intention was to 'analyse the past to prepare for the future' (Webster and Watson, 2002).

What we were doing in our projects was definitely closer to a configurative approach than to an aggregative one or it was rather a kind of mixture of the two. The most valuable output of the review has not been what appeared in our published reports but a continuously expanding 'reading diary', which has been shared within our researcher community (in September 2017 the length of this reading diary was

3̇08 880 words, including 129 figures and 59 tables). The procedure of reviewing the literature in this case was very similar to what two information systems researchers described as a *hermeneutic literature review* (Boell and Cecez-Kecmanovic, 2014). This approach to reviewing consists of two repeatedly performed complementary cycles: seeking information and clarification/insight (see Figure 5.2). The cognitive mechanisms generated by this approach recall what Argyris (2005) has termed 'double loop learning': goals and rules are modified in the light of experiences and the way problems are defined and solved becomes the source of new problems.

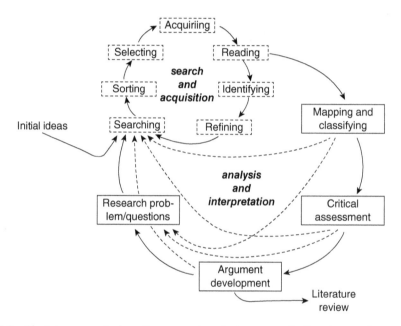

Figure 5.2   The interconnected continuous cycles of a hermeneutic literature review

Source: Excepted from *A Hermeneutic Approach for Conducting Literature Reviews and Literature Searches* by Boell and Cecez-Kecmanovic, © 2014. Used with permission from Association for Information Systems, Atlanta, GA; 404-413-744; www.aisnet.org. All rights reserved

One of the first things one sees when comparing Figure 5.1 and Figure 5.2 is the contrast between the linear and the circular representations. Although the EPPI method supports a certain level of iterativity and flexibility (including the modification of research questions or even changing the criteria of filtering publications during the review process) those who follow this approach would probably say that what is presented here as a 'hermeneutic approach' is not systematic.

As already mentioned, very often the literature on SLRs opposes 'systematic' and 'non-systematic' reviews. However, the borderlines between them are not as sharp as the proponents of the SLR method often pretend, and opposing them can even be questioned (see, particularly, Hammersley, 2002). In fact, instead of contrasting sharply SLRs and other ways of reviewing, it is better to think of them as two sides of a *continuum* where the difference between the chosen approaches is not in being more or less systematic but (1) in the role of pre-defined, typically linear protocols guiding the review process as consecutive phases, and (2) in the purpose of the review. This has been proposed by an author reacting to the approach illustrated by Figure 5.2, who suggested a continuum ranging from 'traditional' or 'interpretative' reviews to SLRs (Schultze, 2015). Those whose aim is to check the validity of a theory are closer to the SLR pole and those whose goal is to develop a new theoretical or conceptual framework are closer to the 'traditional' pole. In the case of *ImpAla* and *Innova* our goal was to develop a theoretical and conceptual framework which would allow not only the elaboration of appropriate tools to be used in the empirical phase of our research, but also to support the analysis and interpretation of data so that our findings could effectively contribute to improving the design of development interventions and the management of innovation processes in education. This latter point deserves special attention because it shows that the intention of providing direct support to practitioners or decision makers is not necessarily less important for those who develop conceptual or theoretical frameworks than for those who test the effectiveness of specific interventions or pedagogical methods.

We conceived the literature review exercise as iterative, taking as a departure point that new insights emerging from the review process should inform further search. We tried to identify those disciplinary areas where we thought we could find relevant research outputs related to development interventions and innovations. This was also conceived as iterative: it was assumed that we would find new, unknown areas of research while progressing with our review. A key feature of our search strategy has earlier been described using the 'whale hunter' metaphor as opposed to the 'net fishing' approach. Our goal was to navigate our 'searching boat' to those places where there was a higher chance of finding relevant research outcomes, more often using 'snowballing' or 'citation searching' (Booth, Sutton and Papaioannou, 2012), that is, exploring chains of references, rather than keyword-based searches. In our case this approach proved to be more productive than searching for keywords in titles and abstracts although we also experienced its limitations related to the reality of isolated, island-like disciplinary communities whose members rarely or never cite each other.

We focused our limited time deliberately on studying the outcomes of those specific research projects that we found to be providing a major contribution to our knowledge, and less on studying those whose contribution was lower. This required the identification of 'key texts regarded as representative of state-of-the-art knowledge' and 'texts that are highly influential' (Schultze, 2015: 182), and we paid special attention to those researchers or researcher communities that seemed to be particularly influential in our area. We were constantly adding new keywords to our repertoire and we were experimenting with new keyword combinations in order to facilitate our penetration into disciplinary areas using different terms than those used in our own disciplinary field. We were very open to reports produced by think tanks or consultancies, not necessarily published in peer-reviewed journals, and a large part of the literature we read was published as book chapters.

5.4.2 INCLUDING PARTNERS AND EXPLOITING DIALOGUE

During the whole review process, we organised regular meetings where we discussed our review findings with various partners. This supported not only the testing of key terms and insights but also generating new ideas, and getting inspiration. Reviewing the literature was combined with a process of collective creation of new knowledge. In this process the lively discussions in a community consisting of both researchers and practitioners (e.g. designers of development interventions or leaders of innovative schools) was as important as our lonely work with texts and databases. Very often new keywords for our literature search emerged from the discussions during these meetings. In the case of *ImpAla*, for example, it was an invited expert performing ex-ante and ex-post evaluations of development programs who called our attention to the notion of 'counterfactual', which later became an important keyword leading us to discover new, relevant pieces of literature.

In fact, what we were doing was more than searching for texts and then reading them. We tried to reconstruct original research projects on the basis of texts and this reconstruction process naturally took much more time than searching and simple reading. In other words, the lower, larger circle of Figure 5.2 (analysis and interpretation) was much more important in our reviewing process than the upper, smaller circle (search and acquisition). This consisted, for example, of regular meetings where one member of our team presented the original research project and these presentations were followed by lively discussions. We also devoted much time to understand the specific context of the research projects being explored, including their antecedents, internal development and after-life. In the case of the 'Rand Change Agent Study', for example, we studied the emergence of the large federal development interventions following the 'Sputnik shock' in the US and we read retrospective studies published one or two decades following the publication of the original study. Similarly, we spent several weeks exploring the famous California maths reform, not only through reading published research reports but also absorbing the 'grey' literature, such as interviews with key players or discussion papers.

In the case of *Innova*, we have conducted a similar deep analysis of the 'Minnesota Innovation Research Program' including the reading of earlier publications of the researchers who realised this project, even if these publications were not directly linked with the core theme of our study (innovation). Studying these publications allowed us to realise how different the perspective of organisational researchers was from that of economists: the second focused mainly on technological innovations while the first focused on how organisational features determine innovation capacities and innovation activities. Going deeper, instead of extending breath, was more important in this process than in a typical SLR, and sometimes extending breath followed going deeper. Expressing this metaphorically: we were 'drilling down' vertically to reach deeper layers and then, when discovering valuable pieces hidden in the depths, we started looking around horizontally to find more, which was exactly the opposite of what those performing a typical SLRs do.

What we were doing was not only searching for publications but also searching for people and their work. We saw publications (the 'literature') as a tool to find the people and their products. In this sense, one could even question whether the term 'literature review' is the best to describe what we were doing. Our assumption was that publications often show only small parts of what research projects produce, and there might be projects where the most significant results have not been published or they were published in a form that is not visible for the most frequently used bibliographic databases.

The role of direct personal contacts could be illustrated by the way we discovered one of our basic readings on complex interventions. This is an inspiring text written by a leading development economist about the tale of a fictional character, 'Ms. Speedy Analyst', presenting the adventurous journey of a young social researcher in a virtual country where she visits people in different positions, having different perspectives, and slowly learns how many factors might influence the impact of an intervention aimed at reducing early school leaving (Ravallion, 2001). This was mentioned by a specialist in development aid affairs during an inspiring conversation at a post-meeting conference dinner. Probably a classical search and paper-selection process, applying SLR protocols, would have never lead to a careful reading of this article which, at the end, has had a major impact on the development of our thinking and conceptual framework. This might also illustrate some of our ethical dilemmas. We started to see our national decision makers designing development interventions hopelessly ignorant when we compared their knowledge with that of Ms. Speedy Analyst at the end of her journey and we had to think about how to use the knowledge generated by literature review in the politically sensitive area of development interventions.

5.4.3 FACING SPECIFIC CHALLENGES IN THE REVIEWING JOURNEY

Probably the greatest challenge we faced was related to resource limitations. As stressed earlier, serious reviewing is extremely resource needy. One of the strengths of SLRs, based on strict protocols, is that they promise a particularly efficient use of researchers' time, although those applying this approach may also pay a high price for this. If they omit important keywords (and the risk of this is very high when you do search in a transdisciplinary environment) or if authors of primary studies do not include important keywords into their titles and abstracts (which is highly probable if what you are searching for is not in the mainstream of their questions and conclusions) the 'fishing net' might be thrown at places far from those where the most valuable 'fish' gather. But there are other, less recognised, scarce resources, such as energy, interest and motivation. If you are using classical SLR protocols, screening, quality assessment and data extraction are three distinct, consecutive stages following each other in a linear way. What we experienced in our projects was that keeping this sequential order reduces one of the most valuable resources: reading motivation.

Coming back to the 'whale hunting' metaphor: one would not expect that hunters continue sailing to promising areas if they notice, unexpectedly, the appearance of a whale before reaching the ideal place. When we discover a valuable piece of research we often stop, and devote our full attention to read the newly discovered item. Doing so, we use, consciously or unconsciously, the energy liberated by the pleasure of discovery to open our mind to the content of the new text and, in this motivated state, we can extract much more content ('data') from it than if we wait for the formal data extraction phase. This happened very often in our review journeys: filtering was stopped and immediate deep reading started, which naturally led to spontaneous quality judging. We learnt to appreciate this state of augmented reading motivation and the related increased openness of our mind, and we did not want to lose this by rigidly respecting the rules of a protocol. This is what in her article, highly critical towards SLRs, MacLure (2007) describes as 'dialogic interaction' between researcher, literature and data or 'slow, careful reading' as opposed to 'regulated reading' or the simple omitting of deep, mindful reading.

Finding valuable pieces might happen even after the search is formally over. We discovered, for example, the existence of an extensive research activity monitoring the impact of development interventions related to the US 'comprehensive school reform' (CSR) movement when the *ImpAla* project was already terminated, and we were working on the literature review of the *Innova* project. Although our focus was no longer on development interventions but on bottom-up innovation processes, we stopped and spent several weeks studying the logic of this particularly interesting form of intervention, including the exploration of the context in which it emerged. This resulted in a much better understanding of the complex relationships between top-down interventions and bottom-up innovation processes and has had a direct impact on the development our conceptual models and frameworks, and, later on, on the design of our data collection instruments.

Looking back on the review process conducted in *ImpAla* and *Innova* one can identify each element of the EPPI model presented in Figure 5.1, but our systematic exploratory work was not led by a 'Cochrane-type protocol' (Higgins and Green, 2011). In our case this would have been inadequate as our goal was not checking whether or not one specific intervention, treatment, solution or method was working but rather to understand the very nature of implementation and innovation processes.

The phases of our reviewing could perhaps be better described by the terms proposed by Suri (2013):

- identifying an appropriate epistemological orientation
- identifying an appropriate purpose
- searching for relevant literature
- evaluating, interpreting and distilling evidence from selected studies
- constructing connected understandings
- communicating with an audience.

Although Suri uses the term 'phases' (as a synonym of 'tasks, decision-points or stages'), which might imply a linear or consecutive chronological order, she also adds: 'these phases are not stages with discreet boundaries where each stage serially follows the previous stage' and 'each phase tends to be revisited and refined several times'. What we were doing could be described using Suri's term as 'an interactively iterative process' where no sequential order was followed and where maintaining a dialogue with partners within and outside academia has remained a priority.

5.4.4 THE IMPLICATIONS OF A PRAGMATIC AND ECLECTIC APPROACH

Our epistemological orientation was defined by our goal to create a conceptual and analytical framework, which would allow us to cope conceptually with the complex phenomena of implementation and innovation and to study these phenomena empirically. This has been a pragmatist orientation without any commitment to specific methodological or epistemological approaches, such as, for example, qualitative or quantitative, positivist or interpretative, realist or idealist, participative or critical. This has been an eclectic approach interested in encountering as many theoretical and conceptual solutions as possible from different problem areas and disciplinary settings. Diversity has been seen as a particularly positive value: we thought the more voices we listen to the higher the chances are to develop a good, applicable, theoretical, conceptual or analytical framework, which was our purpose.

One of the most valuable fruits of reviewing was our increased capability of 'constructing connected understandings', that is, creating a number of analytical models which, subsequently, orientated both the elaboration of data collection instruments (both questionnaires and case study protocols) and the analysis of collected data. These models have been presented in a number of publications, including two in English (Fazekas, 2018; Halász, 2018). In the case of *ImpAla* we developed, among others a micro- and a macro-model to describe the impact mechanisms of education development interventions and these models were guiding both the data collection and the analysis of data. Besides this, a number of specific models have been created.

One of them, for example, made a distinction between receiving units 'in trouble' where the aim of the intervention was to restore a kind of equilibrium and those in a stable state where the aim of the intervention was to trigger change processes, that is, to disturb a state of 'bad' equilibrium. In the case of *Innova* we created a series of models to analyse innovation profiles, the birth process of innovations, the role of agents in innovation processes and the spread or diffusion of innovations, including temporal and spatial dimensions. We would not have been able to create these models without analysing systematically the relevant literature, reading hundreds of publications and research reports, and, on the basis of this, reconstructing the research questions, the hypotheses and the conclusions of the original research projects.

While the EPPI approach defines systematic as 'undertaken according to a fixed plan or system or method', and stresses transparency and reproducibility as key criteria (Gough, Oliver and Thomas, 2017: 261), its critics say that over-stressing planning and documentation of every step of the review process and over-regulating the reading process may lead to artificial 'distortion into clarity' (Sandelowski et al., 2008), to 'suppressing aspects of quality in research' (MacLure, 2007) and may even bring 'risk to scholarship' (Boell and Cecez-Kecmanovic, 2014). In the case of *ImpAla* and *Innova* our reading was systematic but it was not guided by a strict protocol. We have performed a systematic literature review combining the elements of various reviewing approaches.

With both problem areas (implementation and innovation) we found ourselves in a situation similar to what Greenhalgh and her colleagues (2005) described in a paper presenting a case of literature review on the diffusion of health care related innovations. They mentioned three major methodological challenges. First, they had to work with 'fuzzy' terms with contested and competing definitions. Second, they did not know where to search for good research studies in spite of the fact that their team consisted of recognised experts in the given area. Third, they realised that taking a too narrow disciplinary or sectoral focus (health care) they would miss the best sources of original ideas generated in other sectors. This led them to start the review process using 'informal and unstructured methods'. They identified 13 different 'research traditions' connected with several academic disciplines and sectors, from rural sociology and cultural studies through communication, marketing, development or organisational studies to complexity studies.

Earlier in this chapter we enumerated a dozen different disciplinary or sectoral areas where we found relevant studies and this list was far from being exclusive. We also had to face not only the fuzziness of our key terms but also the temporal evolution of their meaning (for example, the current thinking on implementation and the meaning of this term is entirely different from what we found 15–20 years ago). And, not independently from the two previous challenges faced by Greenhalgh's team, we had a very limited knowledge about where to find the relevant publications.

As mentioned earlier we conceived the systematic reviewing of research literature as a knowledge management action. The way we were thinking about this was not far from what we can see in the thinking of some information system researchers. This is well elaborated by Schryen and his colleagues (2015) who – referring to the knowledge dynamics model developed by Nonaka (1994) – classified knowledge in two dimensions: explicit versus tacit and primary versus meta-level, and examined knowledge dynamics using six categories: (1) synthesising, (2) adopting a new perspective, (3) building theories, (4) testing theories, (5) identifying research gaps and (6) providing a new research agenda. The strength of this approach is that it not only includes the tacit dimension but also provides a rich repertoire of using the outcomes of literature reviews for different purposes. The importance of tacit knowledge in scientific research is often stressed by those criticising rigid SLR protocols (Clegg, 2005; Dixon-Woods et al., 2006; Hammersley, 2002; MacLure, 2007).

Performing a systematic literature review based on the combination of the elements of various reviewing approaches naturally implies that making the process transparent becomes more difficult than in cases when you follow a strict protocol. Reconstructing the reviewing process in the case of *ImpAla* and *Innova* is, in fact, a challenging task but not impossible as the whole process has been well documented in the memos of our meetings and also in the long analytical 'reading diaries' we produced.

RESEARCHER CHECKLIST

In this short section we propose a possible checklist for researchers undertaking a systematic literature review before starting new research into a complex problem area. Many items in our list of references present pre-fixed protocols for systematic literature reviews. The checklist below has been constructed on the basis of our own experiences acquired in the two research projects used as examples in this chapter.

- Make an overview of existing approaches to doing literature reviews and assess the strengths and weaknesses of the various approaches in function of your research questions.

- Identify those who might use the outcomes of your research.

- Identify practitioners who might have relevant experience in your field and who might contribute to your exploratory work.

- Identify those research areas that might have produced relevant knowledge in your field of inquiry, paying special attention to areas outside your own disciplinary field.

(Continued)

(Continued)

- Create an initial list of keywords (including their combinations) so that it could later be continuously extended.

- Create an initial list of key authors and research communities or networks which can be seen as key knowledge producers in your research area.

- Create an initial list of 'spaces' or 'platforms' where the members of the communities or networks in your list might regularly meet and communicate, such as regular conferences and specialised journals.

- Identify those bibliographic databases where the chances of finding relevant publications is particularly high.

- Identify those organisations which might produce knowledge in your research field outside the classical academic space (e.g. think tanks, consultancies, knowledge producing government agencies and charities).

- Make a search for existing literature reviews in your research area and start the review process by reading them.

- Organise regular meetings where you can discuss specific research dilemmas, the outcomes of relevant earlier pieces of research and the progress of your literature review.

- Open a virtual communication space where those participating in the literature review process can communicate with each other and can exchange relevant documents.

- Evaluate regularly your progress in your literature review asking repeatedly the question: 'Am I on the right track?', thinking about your literature review project as a self-adapting learning system.

- Regularly record the events of your literature review process, including keeping an annotated 'reading diary' to share within your research community.

5.5 CONCLUSION

When starting a new research project the first thing researchers are typically thinking about is how to explore existing knowledge. One way to do this is reviewing the relevant literature. This is a daunting task, given the growing quantity of former research and the frequent difficulty of drawing clear borderlines between what is within the scope of our research and what is beyond. There are many approaches to doing literature reviews in a systematic way and our choice between these approaches depends on many factors, such as, for example, the nature of our research questions, the potential target audience of our research, and, particularly, the resources we can devote to this activity.

A large part of the literature on systematic literature reviews identify this systematic approach with those protocol-based, highly structured methods we designate in this chapter using the abbreviation SLR. Exploring and synthesising existing knowledge can also be achieved, however, by using more flexible and more open approaches, which are not necessarily less systematic than SLRs. The borderline between these approaches and SLRs are not sharp. As one of the authors quoted in this chapter (Schultze, 2015) has suggested, we can think about SLRs and other, more flexible methods as two poles of a continuum allowing various combinations.

In the case of the two research projects used as illustration in this chapter, a number of challenges had to be faced, including the high-level complexity of the problem areas and their broad interdisciplinary nature. As we could not be entirely sure whether our initial research questions had been appropriately formulated our exploratory work could not be started with what protocols for SLRs typically prescribe: formulating a well-focused research question. Most of the keywords we were using in our searches emerged at a later stage of the project, as we were advancing in our reviewing journey, sometimes several months or even years after the search began. We often found relevant and valuable knowledge and inspiring ideas in those readings, which would have been filtered out if we were using the classical SLR criteria for literature selection. Unlike in most SLRs we selected specific pieces of earlier research and made significant, time-consuming efforts to reconstruct the original research process in our mind, using the methods of workshops and 'discussion days' devoted to these limited number of selected projects.

Research synthesis is part of the work of every researcher, and this part is becoming increasingly important with the explosion of primary research activities around the globe. When we synthesise earlier research the object of our inquiry is not the 'real word' but what other researchers know about it. The methods we use in this type of research are similar to those that we use when we are exploring the phenomena of the 'real word' and we have to use these methods with the same level of rigour as if we were exploring real phenomena. Systematic literature review is the most important way to do this, but when we do it, we always have to keep in mind that reviewing the literature is not an aim in itself: it is just a tool to get closer to the reality reflected in the literature.

ADDITIONAL USEFUL READING

Most relevant readings can be found in the list of references at the end of this chapter. There are, however, a number of further readings which could provide additional inspiring inputs to make well-founded decisions in function of needs and available resources. From the rich repertoire of literature not referred to in this chapter we call the attention of the reader to some further books and articles:

Saini, M. and Shlonsky, A. (2012) *Systematic Synthesis of Qualitative Research*. Oxford: Oxford University Press.

After providing a concise history of doing synthesis reviewing the authors of this book present one specific case to illustrate their own approach. The key element of this approach is the intention to include difficult research questions related to causality, context, personal factors (e.g. 'programme championship') and also ethical and cultural considerations. They offer a wide range of often innovative methods, such as the use of purposive sampling, complex information retrieval strategies, the inclusion of grey literature and the checking, in the articles on primary studies, of specific aspects such as the use of reflexive journaling, quoted words and phrases from participants or inclusion of stakeholder views. The authors put a special emphasis on the applicability of the synthesis review by policy makers, decision makers and social work practitioners.

Snilstveit, B., Oliver, S. and Vojtkova, M. (2012) 'Narrative approaches to systematic review and synthesis of evidence for international development policy and practice', *Journal of Development Effectiveness*, 4(3): 409–429.

This article focuses on international development where contextual factors, like in education, play a particularly important role. It stresses the 'continuum approach' and the need to judge strength and weaknesses. The article emphasises questions raised typically by practitioners concerning the policy relevance of systematic reviews and seeks answers not only to questions of 'what works' but also 'why it works', 'in what context it works', and to questions of feasibility and acceptability. The article offers a detailed analysis of seven methods used in qualitative syntheses (content analysis, thematic summaries, framework synthesis, thematic synthesis, meta-ethnography, realist synthesis and meta-narrative). The article provides illustrations from development interventions in the education sector.

Littell, J. H., Corcoran, J. and Pillai, V. K. (2008) *Systematic Reviews and Meta-Analysis*. Oxford: Oxford University Press.

This is a useful book for those who want to make a meta-analysis of earlier research, using quantitative data and exploring the impact of specific interventions. It helps not only to understand the difference between the broader notion of systematic review and the narrower notion of meta-analysis, but also to confront the typical myths and misunderstandings related with these notions and the risks encountered when performing a meta-analysis. It also examines the notion of effect-size, presenting several ways to calculate it.

Pawson, R. (2006) 'Digging for nuggets: how "bad" research can yield "good" evidence', *International Journal of Social Research Methodology*, 9(2): 127–142.

This is an article recommended to those who are interested in the impact of complex development interventions and have doubts about the dominant forms of systematic review based on the principle of 'appraise-then-analyse sequence'. As the title suggests the author questions the practice of omitting publications from analysis because of their weaknesses of reporting. He argues that 'poor studies', filtered out by a rigorous article selection, may have serious significant explanatory power which might be lost if they are left out of the reviewing process.

NOTES

1   Both ImpAla (project number: OTKA/101579) and Innova (project number: OTKA/115857), led by the author, have been funded by the Hungarian National Research, Development and Innovation Office.

2   See the website of the organisation here: https://eppi.ioe.ac.uk/cms (accessed 22 January 2019).

REFERENCES

Anderson, L. M., Petticrew, M., Chandler, J., Grimshaw, J., Tugwell, P., O'Neill, J. and Shemilt, I. (2013) 'Introducing a series of methodological articles on considering complexity in systematic reviews of interventions', *Journal of Clinical Epidemiology*, *66*(11): 1205–1208.

Andrews, R. (2005) 'The place of systematic reviews in education research', *British Journal of Educational Studies*, *53*(4): 399–416.

Argyris, C. (2005) 'Double-loop learning in organizations: a theory of action perspective', in K.G. Smith and M.A. Hitt (eds), *Great Minds in Management: The Process of Theory Development*. Oxford: Oxford University Press. pp. 261–279.

Bem, D. J. (1995) 'Writing a review article for *Psychological Bulletin*', *Psychological Bulletin*, *118*(2): 172–177.

Boell, S. K. and Cecez-Kecmanovic, D. (2014) 'A hermeneutic approach for conducting literature reviews and literature searches', *CAIS*, *34*: 12.

Booth, A., Sutton, A. and Papaioannou, D. (2012) *Systematic Approaches to a Successful Literature Review*. London: Sage.

Chalmers, I., Hedges, L.V. and Cooper, H. (2002) 'A brief history of research synthesis', *Evaluation & the Health Professions*, *25*(1): 12–37.

Clegg, S. (2005) 'Evidence-based practice in educational research: a critical realist critique of systematic review', *British Journal of Sociology of Education*, *26*(3): 415–428.

Cooper, H. and Hedges, L.V. (2009) 'Research synthesis as a scientific process', in H. Cooper, L.V. Hedges and J.C. Valentine (eds), *The Handbook of Research Synthesis and Meta-Analysis*. New York: Russell Sage Foundation. pp. 3–13.

Cornish, F. (2015) 'Evidence synthesis in international development: a critique of systematic reviews and a pragmatist alternative', *Anthropology & Medicine*, *22*(3): 263–277.

Davies, P. (2004) 'Systematic reviews and the Campbell Collaboration: evidence-based practice in education', in R. Pring and G. Thomas (eds), *Evidence-Based Practice in Education*. Maidenhead: McGraw-Hill Education. pp. 21–33.

Dixon-Woods, M., Bonas, S., Booth, A., Jones, D. R., Miller, T., Sutton, A. J., Shaw, R. L. Smith, J. A. and Young, B. (2006) 'How can systematic reviews incorporate qualitative research? A critical perspective', *Qualitative Research*, *6*(1): 27–44.

Ehri, L. C., Nunes, S. R., Stahl, S. A. and Willows, D. M. (2001) 'Systematic phonics instruction helps students learn to read: evidence from the National Reading Panel's meta-analysis', *Review of Educational Research*, *71*(3): 393–447.

Evans, J. and Benefield, P. (2001) 'Systematic reviews of educational research: does the medical model fit?', *British Educational Research Journal*, *27*(5): 527–541.

Fazekas, A. (2018) 'The impact of EU-funded development interventions on teaching practices in Hungarian schools', *European Journal of Education*, *53*(3): 377–392.

Garfield, E. (1977) 'Proposal for a new profession – scientific reviewer', *Current Contents, 14*: 5–8.

Garfield, E. (1996) 'An old proposal for a new profession: scientific reviewing', *The Scientist, 10*(16): 12–13.

Glass, G. V. (1976) 'Primary, secondary, and meta-analysis of research', *Educational Researcher, 5*(10): 3–8

Gough, D. (2007) 'Weight of evidence: a framework for the appraisal of the quality and relevance of evidence', *Research Papers in Education, 22*(2): 213–228.

Gough, D., Oliver, S. and Thomas, J. (2017) 'Introducing systematic reviews', in D. Gough, S. Oliver and J. Thomas (eds), *An Introduction to Systematic Reviews*. London: Sage. pp. 1–7.

Greenhalgh, T., Robert, G., Macfarlane, F., Bate, P., Kyriakidou, O. and Peacock, R. (2005) 'Storylines of research in diffusion of innovation: a meta-narrative approach to systematic review', *Social Science and Medicine, 61*(2): 417–430.

Greenhalgh, T., Wong, G., Westhorp, G., Pawson, R. (2011) 'Protocol-realist and meta-narrative evidence synthesis: evolving standards (RAMESES)', *BMC Medical Research Methodology, 11*(1): 1–10.

Halász, G, (2018) 'Measuring innovation in education: the outcomes of a national education sector innovation survey', *European Journal of Education, 53*(4). Available at: https://doi.org/10.1111/ejed.12299 (accessed 25 January 2019).

Hammersley, M. (2002) 'Systematic or unsystematic, is that the question? Some reflections on the science, art, and politics of reviewing research evidence'. Text of a talk given to the Public Health Evidence Steering Group of the Health Development Agency, October. Available at: www.researchgate.net/publication/42798662_Systematic_or_unsystematic_is_that_the_question_Reflections_on_the_science_art_and_politics_of_reviewing_research_evidence (accessed 25 January 2019).

Hattie, J. (2008) *Visible Learning: A Synthesis of Over 800 Meta-Analyses Relating to Achievement*. Abingdon: Routledge.

Hattie, J., Rogers, H. J. and Swaminathan, H. (2014) 'The role of meta-analysis in educational research', in A.D. Reid, E.P. Hart and M.A. Peters (eds), *A Companion to Research in Education*. Dordrecht, Heidelberg, New York and London: Springer. pp. 197–207.

Higgins J.P.T. and Green, S. (eds) (2011) *Cochrane Handbook for Systematic Reviews of Interventions*, Version 5.1.0 (updated March 2011). The Cochrane Collaboration. Available at: http://handbook-5-1.cochrane.org (accessed 25 January 2019).

Hunt, M. (1997) *How Science Takes Stock: The Story of Meta-Analysis*. New York: Russell Sage Foundation.

MacLure, M. (2007) '"Clarity bordering on stupidity": where's the quality in systematic review?', *Journal of Education Policy, 20*(4): 393–416.

March, J. G. (1991) 'Exploration and exploitation in organizational learning', *Organization Science, 2*(1): 71–87.

McLaughlin, Milbrey W. (1990) 'The Rand Change Agent Study revisited: macro perspectives and micro realities', *Educational Researcher, 19*(11): 11–16.

Nonaka, I. (1994) 'A dynamic theory of organizational knowledge creation', *Organization Science, 5*(1): 14–37.

Noyes, J., Gough, D., Lewin, S., Mayhew, A., Michie, S., Pantoja, T. and Shepperd, S. (2013) 'A research and development agenda for systematic reviews that ask complex questions about complex interventions', *Journal of Clinical Epidemiology, 66*(11): 1262–1270.

Oakley, A. (2003) 'Research evidence, knowledge management and educational practice: early lessons from a systematic approach', *London Review of Education, 1*(1): 21–33.

OECD (2007) *Evidence in Education: Linking Research and Policy*. Paris: OECD.

Pawson, R. (2006) *Evidence-Based Policy: A Realist Perspective*. London: Sage.

Petrosino, A. (2013) 'Reflections on the genesis of the Campbell Collaboration', *The Experimental Criminologist*, 8(2): 9–12.

Petticrew, M. (2015) 'Time to rethink the systematic review catechism? Moving from "what works" to "what happens"', *Systematic Reviews*, 4(1): 1–9.

Petticrew, M., Anderson, L., Elder, R., Grimshaw, J., Hopkins, D., Hahn, R. and Tugwell, P. (2015) 'Complex interventions and their implications for systematic reviews: a pragmatic approach', *International Journal of Nursing Studies*, 52(7): 1211–1216.

Petticrew, M. and Roberts, H. (2006) *Systematic Reviews in the Social Sciences: A Practical Guide*. Oxford: Blackwell Publishing.

Polanin, J. R., Maynard, B. R. and Dell, N. A. (2017) 'Overviews in education research: a systematic review and analysis', *Review of Educational Research*, 87(1): 172–203.

Pollitt, C. (2013) 'Context: what kind of missing link?', in C. Pollitt (ed.), *Context in Public Policy and Management: The Missing Link?* Cheltenham: Edward Elgar Publishing. pp. 415–422.

Ravallion, M. (2001) 'The mystery of the vanishing benefits: an introduction to impact evaluation', *The World Bank Economic Review*, 15(1): 115–140.

Riese, H., Carlsen, B. and Glenton, C. (2014) 'Qualitative research synthesis: how the whole can be greater than the sum of its parts', *Anthropology in Action*, 21(2): 23–30.

Sandelowski, M., Voils, C. I., Barroso, J. and Lee, E. J. (2008) '"Distorted into clarity": a methodological case study illustrating the paradox of systematic review', *Research in Nursing & Health*, 31(5): 454–465.

Schryen, G., Wagner, G. and Benlian, A. (2015) 'Theory of knowledge for literature reviews: an epistemological model, taxonomy and empirical analysis of IS literature'. Completed Research Paper. Thirty Sixth International Conference on Information Systems, Fort Worth, 13–16 December.

Schultze, U. (2015) 'Skirting SLR's language trap: reframing the "systematic" vs "traditional" literature review opposition as a continuum', *Journal of Information Technology*, 30: 180–184.

Slavin, R. E. (2008) 'Perspectives on evidence-based research in education – what works? Issues in synthesizing educational program evaluations', *Educational Researcher*, 37(1): 5–14.

Snilstveit, B. (2012) 'Systematic reviews: from "bare bones" reviews to policy relevance', *Journal of Development Effectiveness*, 4(3): 388–408.

Suri, H. (2013) *Towards Methodologically Inclusive Research Syntheses: Expanding Possibilities*. Abingdon: Routledge.

Torgerson, C., Hall, J. and Light, K. (2017) 'Systematic reviews', in R. Coe, M. Waring, L.V. Hedges and J. Arthur (eds), *Research Methods and Methodologies in Education*. London: Sage. pp. 166–180.

Van de Ven, A. H., Polley, D. and Garud, R. (2008) *The Innovation Journey*. Oxford: Oxford University Press.

Webster, J. and Watson, R.T. (2002) 'Analyzing the past to prepare for the future: writing a literature review', *MIS Quarterly*, 26(2): xiii–xxiii.

Yatvin, J. (2002) 'Babes in the woods: the wanderings of the National Reading Panel', *Phi Delta Kappan*, 83(5): 364–369.

6

DOING PARTICIPATORY STORIES RESEARCH – DETOXING NARRATIVES

Sabine Krause, Gertraud Kremsner, Michelle Proyer and Raphael Zahnd

6.1 INTRODUCTION

This chapter deals with challenges of participatory approaches to storytelling used to learn about deep-rooted cultural understandings in order to establish a common and accessible ground for learning about each other. Listening to and sharing stories – traditional (myths, legends, wonder tales and fables), fictional, personal experiences and stories made up to suit the occasion (Grove, 2013) – shape our individual but also our social and cultural identities: we use stories to share our experiences in, of and with individuals every day. We tell and listen to stories to link to others, to (be) entertain(ed) or to be noticed but also to present, defend or underpin our positions. Moreover, the educational potential of stories becomes clear while taking into account that '[t]hrough stories we find out about new experiences and ideas, we develop empathy and imagination, and we learn how to face challenges and solve problems' (Grove, 2013: 3). Additionally, stories are fundamental parts of the process of 'doing culture' (Hörning and Reuter, 2004; Schatzki, Knorr and von Savigny, 2001) and thereby crucial to shaping community, work on self (storified self, Zingaro, 2009), and communal identity, which again connects to educational processes. Despite its contribution to decoding and understanding shared individual, social and cultural norms, and giving orientation to communal living (Davis, 2002; Weisser, 2017), storytelling – except for life history research (e.g. Atkinson, 2004; 2010) or biographical research/narration analysis (Dausien and Kelle, 2009; Schütze, 1983/2012) – is not subsequently (being) utilised in educational research.

Against this backdrop, we aim to explore both educational potential and the vital role of storytelling in navigating, acquainting and coming to terms with rules and commons of living together via focusing on stories. Our research project 'Detoxing Narratives' aims to open the floor to multi-faceted narrations with free choice of presentation mode as these are introduced, performed and inspired by various narrators in order to widen the oftentimes narrow perspective on accepted narrations with experimental approaches to storytelling (Crehan, 2016; Grove, 2007; Jackson, 2013). By doing so, we focus particularly on socio-cultural dynamics of self and 'other' which can be found within the act of storytelling, defined as mutual dependency between teller(s) and listener(s). Therefore, our aim is not (only) to focus on content, but primarily on social interactions in the act and interpretation of storytelling, turning it into an act of participation. This is of particular importance under consideration of wider societal contexts, because '[s]ocial movements are dominated by stories and storytelling, the narrative goes to the heart of the very cultural and ideational processes' (Davis, 2002: 4). Linked to our interest in the stories told, our research is targeting the question of how open spaces or inclusive arenas (inspired by Situational Analysis, see Clarke, 2012) can be established to widen the field of accepted stories within a group of people.

The aim of this chapter is to reflect critically on three challenges in our own research. These challenges are summarised in the following questions: (1) Which narrators and which stories are taken into account and whose voices are being heard? (2) Which forms of narrations/stories are (being) accepted? (3) How do we overcome limitations in understanding stories that are less familiar or even contradict common understandings?

6.2 OVERALL DESCRIPTION OF THE RESEARCH PROJECT

In stories, a narrator pursues a plan in narrating, bringing to life a chain of events, and simultaneously presenting an interpretation of those events. Thus narrations are used to inform; but they might as well be used to put forward a certain understanding by purposefully misleading the audience. Therefore, 'Detoxing Narratives' takes researching stories one step further in critically questioning the emergence of stories and underlying concepts within. In supporting certain interpretations of events, a story can no longer be considered 'neutral' but as a product of narrative (Lamarque, 2004). Many attempts have been made to defining narrative, we follow Ryan (2007: 24) here and 'agree that narrative consists of material signs, the discourse, which convey a certain meaning (or content), the story, and fulfill a certain social function'. The ambivalence of the terms 'stories' and 'narratives', and the many ways to make use of them, calls for careful deconstructions of what is told in which way and how the story is performed. Thus 'Detoxing Narratives' investigates structural features of narratives, the stories told, and their use in collaboration with storytellers and listeners. Next to exploring the theoretical impact stories can have, the research entails so-called storytelling workshops joined by diverse storytellers and -sharers. Their stories serve as sources of empirical data. Stemming from this shared research interest in stories and narratives, the four authors join parts of their research efforts in the participatory projects network 'Detoxing Narratives'. In our individual research undertakings, we delve into single aspects connected to narratives that in turn help to develop shared approaches; as research projects network we not only discuss and develop our individual projects, but also develop and conduct the workshops. In this chapter, however, we will focus on stories and the challenges named above that come with narrating stories.

The impact stories can have in shaping current societal developments led to the idea to employ a participatory approach to storytelling – framed as Participatory Stories Research (PSR). In participatory research 'the emphasis is on a "bottom-up" approach with a focus on locally defined priorities and local perspectives' (Cornwall and Jewkes, 1995: 1667), which in our case meant that we invited a diverse range of people from differing cultural backgrounds to present their stories or listen to stories in experimental workshop settings that embrace the different approaches the storytellers bring with them, trying not to narrow it down to closed theoretical approaches or framings but actively and collectively creating common grounds of understanding. In short PSR combines stories shared by (a)typical people in (a)typical contexts in (a)typical modes to (a)typical audiences, analysed in collaborative ways. In this, we aim to not exclude certain groups and to broaden classic approaches to storytelling often limited to specific oral or written modes. Those workshops are a first step to creating an inclusive arena for all kinds of storytellers, in which we enable and encourage different modes of telling and understanding stories including oral narrations accompanied by alternative and augmentative communication techniques such as sign language and technical aids, video with commentary, and pictures.

The epistemological stance we take in this approach is to undertake a shift from stories and storytellers as objects of interest in rationally outlined and theoretical thick research processes to enable engagement with the storytellers as experts in their field, subjects, and therefore equal partners in the process of narrating: since stories are formed and (re-)produced by all of us, research on narrations should be conducted collaboratively with all people who want to, try to, have to or prefer not to tell stories – no matter what formal education one has or which label one has to bear. This is of particular importance when persons struggle for words (and consequently also for narrations) due to biographical experiences linked to exclusion and classification. Borrowing from arts (education), we understand every performance as performing the alien with and for others that transgresses boundaries to be experienced by a responsive subject that in turn co-produces the narration (Waldenfels, Stähler and Kozin, 2011). This understanding outlines the turn from 'persona to be' to 'persona in practice' (Alkemeyer, 2015) and enacts the theoretical position of unthinking categories. This shift in research philosophy is closely linked to shifts in conceptualising research and the research persona: as a consequent conclusion of these considerations we take into account Gramsci's (1999) 'Philosophy of Praxis', with which every person is considered to be knowing and therefore a potential contributor to the process of knowledge production. Thus our research project refers to approaches which aim at also involving non-academic persons in research – particularly persons who are classified and considered as persons at the margins, such as people with (learning) disabilities, migrants or refugees. This stance is related to social engagements that strive for de-marginalising people by creating inclusive communities.

Stemming from these considerations, participatory research approaches aim at involving particularly marginalised persons in research processes – associated with the new role to contribute to research as 'active participants, not only as subjects but also as initiators, doers, writers and disseminators of research' (Walmsley and Johnson, 2003: 9), and therefore this seems to be a promising approach to researching storytelling. Participatory approaches can be found in differing variations such as Participatory Action Research (PAR), Participatory Research, Emancipatory Research, Feminist Research and others (Flieger, 2003; Nind, 2014; Walmsley and Johnson, 2003). Particularly Walmsley and Johnson (2003) propose to view all of these diverse, though familiar approaches under one umbrella, since all of them involve 'users', 'non academics' or 'persons concerned' in research, albeit at varying degrees. 'Detoxing Narratives' refers to this broad notion of participatory research by placing collaborative methodological challenges and creative approaches centre stage: continuously analysing and reflecting our own role as researchers and that of co-researchers (those who might typically not be considered researchers outside participatory enabling research settings). The research process itself as well as (creative) strategies to generate data and to disseminate outcomes and results are important and serve as independent research questions. The ongoing reflections include weighting theoretical understandings of knowledge and what can be considered as knowledge in the academic world. The challenge in pursuing this kind of open research approach is that presuppositions on what is traditionally considered academic or worthy scientific knowledge is eroded. Opening the floor to all kinds of people and stories and, simultaneously, minimising phases of abstract theoretical input during the workshop sessions, enables participation to all kinds of listeners. Furthermore accessible support measures such as simultaneous interpreters can be provided in order to enhance chances to participate – knowing and reflecting the fact that translations already are interpretations. Additionally, participatory approaches have to be critically reflected against a 'jack of all traits' research approach. It does have its boundaries when it comes to provision of costly support devices or a reflected approach to persons who simply refrain from being part of research efforts.

With these short theoretical remarks on the shared background of our research project network, in the following we focus on the presentation of the workshops conducted so far and the three challenges identified during further reflections. So far we conducted three workshops with participants from a variety of backgrounds (among them persons labelled as people with refugee background, people with disabilities, researchers, teachers and students) on storytelling and Storysharing® (Grove, 2014). Although all three workshops serve as a database for our research, only selected examples can be subject to detailed accounts here. The workshops were planned by us by identifying potential storytellers and advertising the workshops within and outside of the University of Vienna's social media and other channels. The storytellers were chosen in accordance with availability (due to the pre-funding/pending in application status of the project, international guests had to be available through other means) and presumed diversity. Up to four storytellers were invited to share up to an hour of a story with the possibility for the audience to pose questions. All of these workshops pointed to the potential of (non-)verbal narrations along with the application of creative methods such as pictures, audio-files, sign language and live translation of non-English or German video material (simultaneous translation was provided between these two languages as participants spoke either one or both of these languages). These were used to engage with the audience and to raise curiosity in others' stories, but also pointed to limitations, e.g. in accessibility and cultural understanding as well as in being translatable to others.

In order to give insights into our work, we describe in detail one of the stories shared during the second workshop – the story of Mae Nak (Thai: 'Mother Ghost'), told by Siriparn Sriwanyong from Srinakharinwirot University Bangkok. We chose this one because it is a story used for pedagogical purposes in Thai culture (e.g. Dharma teachings), which indicates that the structure of the story is easily accessible and allows for cultural understanding despite depicting an alien culture to most people in the audience. Also this example emphasises different forms of translations that are essential during storytelling. In this very popular folk tale that – according to the narrator – shapes a lot of Thai spiritual beliefs, ghostly appearances give lessons about bonds in life, letting go and the impermanence of life. In brief the story retells a love story of ancient times. Nak and her husband Mak were in love and expecting a baby, when Mak was called to war and had to leave Nak behind. She missed him so badly that she could not cope with the stillbirth of their child alone and died in grief. In traditional Thai belief, souls of the dead are transferred to their next lives but those having some unfinished business stay behind as lost souls if they fail to comply with one of the most important Buddhist commandments, to let go of all worldly matters. These lost souls remain around their loved ones as ghosts to guard them or haunt those who hurt them. Nak was not ready to leave Mak behind and appeared to him in her 'normal' shape upon his arrival. Mak was very happy to find her and the baby both well when he returned from the warfront and ignored all his neighbours' warnings, who could see Nak and her baby's real shapes. Only by chance was he confronted with the truth, when something was dropped on the floor and while picking it up, Mak could see the true horror of an untidy house and his marital ghost. During a complex farewell process and with the help of a popular strong monk, Nak was convinced of the need to let go and transgress to her next stage on the way to Nirvana.

To bring this story to life, Siriparn Sriwanyong used a widely available film version of this tale with scenes chosen and cut with the help of his nephew. He showed the movie and halted at certain moments to summarise and explain the context – despite English subtitles. In a permanent interplay between reality and illusion, the movie was used to visualise the story, not only to tell the tale of Mae Nak but to present essential insights into Buddhism, too. Siriparn Sriwanyong emphasised the importance of his example as it is a key story for children to learn to read cultural codes and symbols and to gain knowledge about and understandings of Buddhism. This tale is told in various ways and it is implicitly and explicitly referred to in many different ways and contexts in Thailand. Everyone is said to know the story of 'Mother Ghost'. Thus, it can be stated that it serves an educational purpose and was presented as an essential base for an interpretive understanding of Thai culture.

In listening to Siriparn Sriwanyong's story, different styles of and approaches to taking the participant's viewpoint in the workshop became obvious. For one, he stopped the movie several times to highlight a specific detail such as a spider tapping its body against the wall of Mae Nak's hut, which most participants didn't even notice. In Thailand, on the other hand, this occasion marks the onset of bad luck. On a semantic level the comprehension of the film's message presented quite a struggle for almost everybody in the audience since its plot and many of the symbols used are rooted in a culture which most people had little access to and no common understanding of. Re-telling the story of Mae Nak in the setting of the workshop indicated the value of this story for Thai people and evoked curiosity in the audience. This became apparent through the many questions asked during and after the performance of the story. This story clearly highlighted the different socialisations represented in the room; the different concepts of loss/letting go and the acknowledgment of ghostly appearances pointed to boundaries in 'Western' thinking that can be seen as a challenge for understanding stories.

6.3 MAIN CHALLENGES

In discussing the stories shared by our storytellers, we were searching for narrations reflecting cultural heritage and traditions considering their influence on normative

and formative elements of the social and cultural life (for detailed information see
http://detox.univie.ac.at). Summarising the challenges associated with 'Detoxing
Narratives' relates to different layers as both the subject (stories) and the research
approach (participatory) depart from 'regulated', academically verified research paths
at times. Taking into account the socio-political agenda that unites our research network this comes as little surprise. Nevertheless, by remaining true to ourselves, we
have to question our own selection process for inviting storytellers, to name one of
the many unanswered challenges introduced in the beginning of this chapter. Out of
numerous challenges, three will be subject to detailed accounts: (un)heard voices,
that is whose voices are taken into account; accepted stories and modes of storytelling;
and understanding stories.

6.3.1 (UN)HEARD VOICES

Which narrators and which stories are taken into account and whose voices are being
heard?

Inviting Siriparn Sriwanyong was not only easy in terms of his availability (the
workshop took place during a teaching exchange between Bangkok and Vienna) but
also served as the exotic touch to our second workshop. Next to the well known
and more or less – at least geographically – close contexts of Switzerland, the UK and
Poland, Thailand proved to be the cherry on top of our workshop. On the one hand
this is due to the fact that it shows the irritations and disruptions stories can cause
to our comfort zones of knowledge. We can no longer associate Thailand only with
nice food and islands (or maybe prostitution, so as to not sound to superficial) but
we are suddenly confronted with the magic of Thailand's celluloid spiritual side. The
questions raised during and after the storyteller's presentation proved us right.

Everybody seemed to have fallen in love with but at the same time feared Mae Nak,
which is the reaction the story intends. Siriparn Sriwanyong, on the other hand, serves
as an example of the perfect navigator to tell such a story, as he had been studying
in both Thailand and the US. He has learned to understand different types of questions and make himself understood in languages other than his mother tongue. He
knew which parts of the story to translate, and which ones to charmingly omit so as
not to cause the audience a headache, as one has to be Thai in order to understand.
His most important task was probably the transliteration and translation of symbols
and concepts inherent in the film, offering a simultaneous translation not on the level
of language but directed towards understanding the cultural aspects of the story. The
performance, which involved stopping the video at previously chosen points, summarising what was on screen and then explaining cultural aspects to the audience, is
part of a didactic, informed translation of his story.

Taking Siriparn Sriwanyong's case as an example for storytelling and confronting
the audience with 'other', alien social and cultural settings, the situated emergence of

the story of Mae Nak may cause some irritations but Siriparn – with his knowledge on navigating the situation and his standing as a researcher and teacher – cannot be considered as unheard voice in a narrow sense. Telling stories to an audience, which is willing to listen – as during the workshops – usually is 'a preserve that remains largely for the rich and famous' (Atkinson, 2010: 7). Against this backdrop, many people not only become excluded from telling and listening to stories but are also deprived of ownership of their own stories; the latter because many of them have 'none of the usual "stock of stories" – from family, friends and community – nor the everyday documents, photographs and memorabilia of family life, from which to draw in order to make sense of their lives' (Atkinson, 2004: 692). This may be the case for persons at the very margins who are often at a loss for ways to express and/or describe who they are (in socio-cultural terms) and what they have been through; refugees might be considered as belonging to this group (Jackson, 2013). To regain these stories, enabling alternatives to the predominant way of storytelling, is essential (Atkinson, 2010) – this can be considered as the heart of PSR. This poses the question of how to empower those unheard voices – how to make them visible as individuals with a personal history.

Getting access to storytellers and their stories from various ethnic backgrounds is a challenge in educational science in general. Since our attempt was to find out whether it would be possible to widen the common grounds of narrating, we aimed to invite people living at the very margins. According to Nussbaum (2011) these people can be found among communities of people with a refugee background and groups of people with disabilities. Even though this appears to be the onset of a good explanation for the choice of the people we invited, it does not serve the same purpose for solving the question of whether we managed to invite people who usually don't have the opportunity to speak up. It remains a difficult question where to find people who are normally not being heard. Despite our struggle with this issue, we tried to establish an inclusive arena by inviting people from diverse (non-/formal) academic backgrounds with differing life histories. By opening an inclusive stage we wanted to challenge cultural borders and widen the space of acceptance as far as possible because the potential of storytelling is that '[it] reworks and remodels subject–object relations in ways that subtly alter the balance between actor and acted upon, thus allowing us to feel that we actively participate in a world' (Jackson, 2013: 35). However, the challenge we faced at this stage was the danger of reproducing classifications: deliberately inviting both narrators and audience on the basis of 'maximum' heterogeneity, attributions such as persons with 'refugee' or 'migrant' background as well as '(non-)academic' people were taken into account. Further on, 'refugees' and 'people with disabilities' proved to be diffuse concepts both of which include a varied group of human beings. Therefore, our main struggle with the process of setting up a group was the question of how we could academically justify such a process. Additionally, we had to ask ourselves whose voices remain (un)heard because none of us has any connection to them. Thus (un)heard voices are unknown/unconsidered voices that we do not turn to when getting curious, also voices that we do not care about or we turn down for any reason. Not every person could have been accommodated in the contexts provided so far. For example, simple measures such as translations so far remain limited to German, English and sign language if inquired. Dealing with language issues led us to consider not only the question of whose voices are being heard and the challenge this presents in the context of research ethics but also the methodological issues which we tried to approach with creative solutions. In breaking up the traditional forms we point to recent practices of, for example, refugees and/or people with (learning) disabilities sharing (life) stories via smart phones, which point out sophisticated and easily accessible methods of sharing stories. More accessible modes of communication may help to communicate and share personal issues more easily. Wider communication networks and a growing number of shared experiences may also help in gaining attention and re-enabling different kinds of stories.

6.3.2 ACCEPTED STORIES AND MODES OF STORYTELLING

Stories play a vital role in making sense of individual and communal life and are embodied through practices in everyday life but are also connected to the past, where 'narratives define historical identity and self-understanding' and therefore point to what is valued (Carr, 2006: 231). When looking into heritage, traditions and cultural experiences in research settings, we often focus on formed and normed (Rabinow, 1989) oral tradition and written sources or reflective practices to gain text-based data for further analysis. However, rational verbal reflection limits the perspective on diversity of heritage considering the variety of narrations and traditions in storytelling and flexible forms of sharing and narrating stories among some groups. Thus, the challenge here lies in breaking up the traditional modes of narrating.

The basic condition of all forms of narrating is a 'reportable' or 'tellable' story and that the story is worth telling: 'A would-be narrator must be able to defend the story as relevant … to get and hold the floor and escape censure at its conclusion' (Norrick, 2004: 79). This puts the narrator, and his or her ability to share a story with the audience, in a prominent place.

Narrating comprises choosing a familiar subject, shaping the content, structuring it in such a way that it constructs knowledge and finally 'verbalising' the story in temporal order. Storyteller and audience then work collaboratively on the situated emergence of (known) stories: 'by constructing, relating, and sharing stories, people contrive to restore viability to their relationship with others' (Jackson, 2013: 37), within the story and within the social interaction of storysharing. But which stories and which modes of storytelling are (being) accepted? What are the conditions to accept narrations and force their re-iteration? And what is perpetuated in stories? These are vital questions concerning the structural element of narrating and the story itself, because 'although the stories that are approved or made canonical in any society tend to reinforce extant boundaries, storytelling also questions, blurs, transgresses, and even abolishes these boundaries' (Jackson, 2013: 43). Blurriness allows for listeners to understand and accept narrations that are unfamiliar because fuzzy boundaries provide access points to connect with the unfamiliar. The 'Detoxing Narratives' project aims to enable space for alternative modes of performance, to help open up self-contained stories and allow for fuzzy boundaries and different modes of storytelling. Nevertheless, so far most of the storytellers invited continued to choose classical tools such as talking while presenting slides. The demand for accessibility was met by being open to questions and by giving the impression of curiosity on all sides. Interestingly only a few storytellers trusted the audience to follow the story presented without any technical aide, having faith in the imagination of their audience.

But in dealing with stories as social and cultural utterances where form follows the creative attempts of narrators, and bearing in mind the performative aspect of sharing narrations with a live audience, flexible modes of narrating emerge that might include fragmentation, stumbling or non-linearity in narrating, all of which we experienced during our workshops. Borrowing from literary studies (for an overview see Rivkin and Ryan, 2017) where the variety of textual forms is acknowledged and celebrated, and relying on functional pragmatics in linguistics (for example Detges and Waltereit, 2002), we take storytelling as situated praxis which is moved by the immediate interaction of narrator and listener that re-frames familiar subjects and knowledge(s), possibly going beyond closed narrations. Considering the problems of a rational approach towards stories, one focus of the 'Detoxing Narratives' project is to find alternative non-verbal, or not solely/primarily verbal, ways of presenting stories and sharing cultural heritage. Hence the scholarly approach to this kind of knowledge is to head along new paths through, for example, considering art-based expressions, photovoice, role play, video-clips, etc. (Collier, 2003; Gee, 1999; Harper, 2002; Hymes, 1981). This implies turning our backs on the idea of limited reference to scholarly celebrated, academic written achievements and solely audible voice-based and academically elaborated traditions. Therefore, the 'Detoxing Narratives' project is about educating the audience on the one hand but on the other hand we clearly focus on the creative process of re-telling stories with the audience in order to find new common grounds.

When talking about storytelling, we should differentiate possible occasions of stories: those told for their own sake from those told for a specific purpose (Norrick, 2000). As far as this looks like a useful analytical distinction, the performative turn we suggest with the act of storytelling overcomes this dichotomy: the story is valued as knowledge that has its own dignity while performances serve a specific purpose. Coming back to Siriparn Sriwanyong, this might become clearer: he had chosen the story of Mae Nak when invited to share a 'typical' Thai story and he interpreted 'typical' as essential for understanding Buddhist concepts. He valued this story over others and decided to visualise it for the audience. His commenting on the visual translation of the story (he stopped the video at several points, summarised and explained) helped the audience to 'read' and connect to cultural elements represented here; the audience on the other hand questioned the certainty of his interpretation at some points, leaving him puzzled with 'misunderstandings'. Siriparn Sriwanyong stumbled on words, and even lost words when trying to explain what he intended to show; at the same time his presence, gestures and mimic expressions played a crucial role in a nevertheless interpretive understanding of the situated sharing process. The double translation (Buddhist/non-Buddhist, Thai/English and English/German respectively) and parallel transformation of the story helped negotiations on meaning and bridged gaps in cultural understanding. Translation in the context of deconstructing storytelling consists of de-familiarising oneself from taken-for-granted understandings expressed in the stumble of words; the irritation or wonder upon unexpected cultural codes and values in the audience turned into an attitude of appreciation of the other. What we observed was a fragmentation of (factual) knowledge that was complemented by the situated performance, which in the end led to an interpretive understanding of Thai culture and Buddhism that finally helped to re-examine one's own cultural settings.

Growing up means not only learning about stories, modes of narrating and the history of the social group that is fundamental for the understanding of a specific group but also gaining chances to participate in this group. To keep stories negotiable and to open up the floor for other viewpoints or for critical response brings negativity into the picture: it 'raises questions about the validity of narratives and by implication about the values they reflect and the soundness of the lessons derived from them' (Carr, 2006: 232). In terms of education this kind of negativity must be met in preparing people to deal with failure and uncertainty and to see and think beyond their very own settings.

6.3.3 UNDERSTANDING STORIES

When talking about stories told and the process of collaborative production of meanings, the third challenge is the one most reflected upon: how do we overcome limitations in understanding stories that are less familiar or even contradict shared understandings? We all, even in doing research, take part in narrations and perpetuate interpreted understandings of stories. The question is, is it possible to step back from this involvement, and ask ourselves how can we find a way to overcome both narrow styles of reasoning in doing research, and pre-formed styles that limit what we might endeavour in our workshops?

To open up the floor to all kinds of stories from all possible (social and cultural) backgrounds leads to different questions attached to the task of understanding stories. Firstly, it points to the different conceptualisations of 'knowledge' and 'styles of thinking'

(Fleck, 1979), especially with regards to our own conceptualisations as researchers. What do we recognise as an act of storytelling, and what do we 'understand' as an alternative story? Which persons do we regard as being without a voice and which forms of narrating do we consider as challenging? As researchers socialised in a specific context, we carry a specific, biographically formed pattern of understanding with us reflecting the different contexts we have been living in during our life. Thus, framing stories as 'alternative stories', categorising people as being 'voiceless' is not only a theoretical problem but one rooted in our personal (hi)stories. Secondly, it leads to the problem of understanding the content. How is it possible to understand stories rooted in a context that is strange for oneself (see the case of Siriparn Sriwanyong's story)? Both aspects are basically rooted in cultural norms and a certain understanding of scholarly knowledge, affecting the audience, the researcher and the research process as a whole. In making sense of stories, we build on our own patterns of thinking – a result of our collected experiences (Feuser, 2011). The processes of sorting and categorising but also of understanding are therefore not only rooted in the person telling the story or the story itself but emerge in the process of listening.

The only path towards a mutual understanding of shared stories is to leave the dominating patterns of interpretation behind and participatively create (new) ways of understanding the stories told. Those potentially decolonised understandings of knowledge that are no longer oriented along binary patterns call for different modes of knowledge production, understanding and presentation and are likely to challenge the audience as well as the researchers. Siriparn Sriwanyong's at times humorous approach to what he considered to be clumsy questions from 'Westerners' caged in their understanding of what a story is laid out to be, challenged everyone present. The invitation to share a story is to evoke with it images, connotations and (re-)presentations; the storyteller is the one to choose his*her form of presentation according to her*his intentions. This results in a variety of possible presentations and interpretations. Thus, to make it all work, a key challenge is to sensitise the auditorium to the possibly diverse modes of 'telling stories', which includes some preparation and introduction to the multitude of possible forms of narrating and in situ obstacles to understanding, such as giving an overview of unfamiliar Thai names and the interrelations of the various characters in the story. Further on, the process of understanding necessitates listening, talking, asking questions, giving answers, trying to understand the answers and asking again, steadily pondering the story, its structure and background, regardless of the problem that a final understanding can never be reached. One of the main features of an inclusive arena would be feeling safe to ask any question, regardless of the way it is posed or the language used, without fear that it would be considered a 'stupid' question, as everyone would be considered a learner.

All aspects of our third challenge carried important consequences: firstly, (personal and shared) knowledge and understanding can no longer be considered as factual, encapsulated and final but as fluid and flexible. Secondly, knowledge and understanding not only are rational but also refer to embodied forms of knowledge that are shared during storytelling, too, and to 'silent' knowledge in artifacts. Thirdly, other than rational explanations of the world as (valuable) knowledge have to be considered, e.g. spiritual. In our view, it is only possible to create an inclusive arena if these consequences are taken into account and if the process of sharing narrations is combined with a steadily reflection of the personal life.

6.4 FURTHER CHALLENGES

A rather concrete challenge of practical methodological relevance is that of translation, interpretation, transfer into different understandings, socialisations and explanations of cultural contexts. One issue is that of mere translation from one language to another, which is governed through available networks and is therefore limited. Another need arises if people not only do not speak the same language (dialects should be considered especially) but also come from very different cultural contexts, for example on the one hand our long-standing research partner Siriparn Sriwanyong acting as head of a research department in Bangkok and on the other hand a grandmother living in the Austrian countryside. Though representing extreme poles, this example stands for many issues related to cultural transfers. Interestingly, at other points and much to our surprise, an encounter between the Austrian grandmother and a woman with a forced migration background from Chechnya in our third workshop proved that similarities often come unexpectedly.

Respect for research ethics and the involved parties is of the utmost relevance. As we decided to apply a participatory approach, the project had to consider the needs of involved participants. Additional time must be made available in order to prepare and reflect on stories and modes of storytelling that guests share or that involve content that might be difficult to digest. Additionally, an invitation to share a story implies the necessity to respect personal spaces. Also, a common ground has to be negotiated that enables a space for understanding (translations) of distant tales, unknown modes of narration or different languages being used.

Our research project was motivated by personal involvement, social engagement and a rather unreflected urge to change the world through what one is doing, methodologically anchored in action research. This might often affect the choice of storytellers as well as the radius in which our workshops were being advertised. Thorough reflection of these aspects is still lacking among the research team. Applying an uncommon research approach – including elements of participation of non-academics – meant being at the mercy of other researchers' or participants' questions concerning whether what we were doing still constitutes research and in what way. The unconventional agenda of our research project makes it hard to fit it into given application and publication guidelines. Explaining a rather complex research idea in easy terms and for differently socialised colleagues is something that should not be underestimated, leading to the next heading of this chapter.

RESEARCHER CHECKLIST

- Closely consider and reflect on the choice of storytellers for workshops as well as the general line of events: gender balance, equity in time slots allocated and periods of Q&A allowing discussions on most if not all questions in the room. Additionally, it is essential to accept that some people prefer not to share their stories. Regardless of their motivation, no one should be talked into it.

- Unleash creative potential that challenges both the storytellers themselves, the audiences' imagination as well as what academic spaces are generally used for. As mentioned earlier, more often than not, storytellers remain within what appears to be expected of them: e.g. orally tell a story accompanied by slides. PSR takes courage to unearth creative potential among all involved parties: the researchers, the storyteller, the audience and processes of data analysis.

- Enable safe spaces for storytellers, listeners and developers of the research process: feeling safe, acknowledged and understood is crucial for enabling the sharing of stories as this can be an intimate process.

- Employ communication aids (interpreter, technical) and measures to enhance accessibility in general: some communication aids are empowering as they provide the ability to take part in the communication process or help to emphasise certain aspects. Interpreters, translators and different kinds of media help in research, whether to gather information or to make it more comprehensive; as researchers we should keep in mind that interpretations, translations and media representations are trans-lations and trans-formations inducing shifts in meaning. Considering diverse speakers and listeners, special attention has to be given to universal design settings.

- Be prepared to engage in self-reflection. As mentioned before, researchers are part of a given academic tradition and carry specific, academically and biographically formed rationales in thinking. In giving thought to this, we realised that our research can only work in connection with an ongoing biographical reflection concerning the personal and professional position of ourselves. This is a challenging task since it concerns the researcher's – our – identity, and therefore is not only a rational but also emotional process. Particularly the emotional part should not be underestimated because the reflection about one's own biography can reveal difficult patterns in one's own life and the life of one's family (e.g. racism, connections to historical facts such as colonisation or national socialism).

6.5 CONCLUSION

Our project idea enables inclusive arenas for generating and performing narrations and narratives as well as exchanging experiences beyond spoken language and its 'basic cultural tools' of listening, reading and writing, in a safe setting; thus challenging narration (research) settings, one-sided analysis of oral traditions of people beyond the mainstream, and well-established anthropological accounts.

The 'Detoxing Narratives' projects network is based on a circular process of workshops and further theoretical elaboration under the premises of PSR: (1) designing a space of mutual exchange, (2) inviting storytellers with various experiences and backgrounds, (3) telling, discussing and reflecting on stories in a set-up space, (4) jointly evaluating with all participants the process of telling and sharing stories (especially concerned with widening narrow perspectives), (5) reflecting profoundly on what has worked, (6) reflecting and evaluating the results and returning to the start. With this approach, we are aware of and rely on the fact that 'research will be complexified rather than simplified; dialogue should further enrich our reflexivity and criticality in ways that make us better researchers' (Nind, 2015: 196).

Main challenges encountered during the implementation of our approach touched upon the following three areas: (1) the choice of and access to non-mainstream narrators or stakeholders as well as their accessibility, (2) the broadening of perceptions of what is an academically recognised narration practice (Rabinow, 1989), and (3) the acknowledgement of qualities of knowledge and ways of thinking beyond traditional convention. We aim not only to invite others to tell a story but to shape the space in which it is conveyed, and take ownership of the choice of narration mode by thinking beyond and challenging conventions. We assume that a broader approach is of use to everyone; not only for people facing multi-faceted problems in utilising the 'basic cultural tools'. As a consequence, we understand sharing socio-cultural knowledge, involvement in cultural heritage and traditions and the production of knowledge as situated practices that go far beyond rational or complex verbalised utterances. These result from processes of interaction which is why we want to enable and encourage spaces. In telling different stories in other ways we seek to underline representations of knowledge in practices and performances and reframe these as 'doing narrations'. The stories invented and shared intend to detox common narratives of many of the marginalised groups we are working with: we refer to these as counter-narratives or detoxing narratives.

ADDITIONAL USEFUL READING

Our project website:[1] it explains the overall aim, presents us as a team and reports past and planned events. There are numerous websites that provide insights into the benefits and capabilities of storytelling, we recommend the TED Talk by Chimamanda Adichie: 'The Danger of a Single Story'.[2]

Bührig, K. and ten Thije, J. D. (eds) (2006) *Beyond Misunderstanding: Linguistic Analyses of Intercultural Communication.* Amsterdam, PA: John Benjamins Publishing.

This edited volume gathers a variety of examples for linguistic analysis that might help in learning to 'see' and 'get a feeling' for analyses of speech acts. The notion of culture/intercultural in this volume highlights the creative aspects inherent in cultural translations and shows how different means can contribute to inter/cultural understandings.

Glaser, B. G. and Strauss, A. L. (1966) *Awareness of Dying.* New Brunswick, NJ: Transaction Publishers.

A classic in the development of one of the most flexible and open approaches to data, which continues to influence and empower generations of qualitative researchers. This book sets the scene for the basic understanding of our research approach. Glaser and Strauss patiently observed, respected what they saw and took time (and could afford to take the time), and only then started to develop an understanding of the right questions to ask of the competent people available and the corresponding answers to be sought.

Grove, N. (2014) *The Big Book of Storysharing: A Handbook for Personal Storytelling with Children and Young People Who Have Severe Communication Difficulties.* London: Routledge.

Nicola Grove is an important source concerning the concept of storysharing. Our research is partially based on her concept and tries to develop it further.

Hartog, J. (1996) *Das genetische Beratungsgespräch: Institutionalisierte Kommunikation zwischen Experten und Nicht-Experten* [Genetic counselling: institutionalised communication between experts and non-experts]. Tübingen: Narr.

It might look counter-intuitive to read about a biological understanding of human beings when analysing cultures. But Jennifer Hartog analyses dialogues between experts and non-experts and stresses the translational aspect between these two groups in terms of a cultural translation and fragmentation of knowledge. Science and everyday life appear as two modes of thinking in specific, non-interchangeable fields with certain dignity.

Morin, E. (2014) *Für ein Denken des Südens* [Engaging with southern thinking]. Berlin: Matthes & Seitz.

One aim in our project is to 'unthink' accustomed structures in order to overcome categorisations and hence to take a first step to overcome the social divide we observe (and think) today. One way to achieve this is to merge the predominant rationale, and highly structured thinking of the 'West' with styles of thinking that recognise the poetry, complexity and quality of life – thinking that can be found in 'non-Western' contexts and also in stories of people with learning disabilities.

Rheinberger, H.-J. and Bulucz, A. (2015) *Hans-Jörg Rheinberger – Die Farben des Tastens* [The colors of groping]. Frankfurt: Edition Faust.

A small book, mainly based on an interview with Rheinberger. Among other topics, Bulucz and Rheinberger are arguing about the question of how research can be conducted. Referring to what Rheinberger calls 'Forschungsexperiment' (research experiment), they see research as a steadily ongoing and dynamic process switching between theoretical reflection and working in the field.

NOTES

1   http://detox.univie.ac.at (accessed 28 January 2019).

2   www.ted.com/talks/chimamanda_adichie_the_danger_of_a_single_story (accessed 28 January 2019).

REFERENCES

Alkemeyer, T. (2015) '"Was man ist und was man tut": Die Konstitution des Subjekts in der Praxis', *Berliner Debatte Initial*, *26*(3): 105–115.

Atkinson, D. (2004) 'Research and empowerment: involving people with learning difficulties in oral and life history research', *Disability & Society*, *19*(7): 691–702.

Atkinson, D. (2010) 'Narratives and people with learning disabilities', in G. Grant, P. Ramcharan, M. Flynn and M. Richardson (eds), *Learning Disability: A Life Cycle Approach* (2nd edn). Maidenhead: Open University Press. pp. 7–18.

Carr, D. (2006) 'Review of history: narration, interpretation, orientation by Jörn Rüsen', *History and Theory*, *45*(2): 229–243.

Clarke, A. (2012) *Situationsanalyse: Grounded Theory nach dem Postmodern Turn*. Wiesbaden: VS Verlag für Sozialwissenschaften.

Collier, J. (2003) 'Photography and visual anthropology', in P. Hockings (ed.), *Principles of Visual Anthropology* (3rd edn). Berlin and New York: Mouton de Gruyter. pp. 235–254.

Cornwall, A. and Jewkes, R. (1995) 'What is participatory research?' *Social Science & Medicine*, *41*(12): 1667–1676.

Crehan, K. (2016) *Gramsci's Common Sense: Inequality and its Narratives*. Durham, NC and London: Duke University Press.

Dausien, B. and Kelle, H. (2009) 'Biographie und kulturelle Praxis: Methodologische Überlegungen zur Verknüpfung von Ethnographie und Biographieforschung', in B. Völter, B. Dausien, H. Lutz and G. Rosenthal (eds), *Biographieforschung im Diskurs*, 2. Auflage. Wiesbaden: VS Verlag. pp. 189–212.

Davis, J. E. (2002). 'Narrative and social movements. Stories of change: narrative and social movements', in J. E. Davis (ed.), *Stories of Change: Narrative and Social Movements*. Albany, NY: State University of New York Press. pp. 3–29.

Detges, U. and Waltereit, R. (2002) 'Grammaticalization vs. reanalysis: a semantic-pragmatic account of functional change in grammar', *Zeitschrift für Sprachwissenschaft*, *21*(2): 151–195.

Feuser, G. (2011) 'Entwicklungslogische Didaktik', in A. Kaiser, D. Schmetz, P. Wachtel and B. Werner (eds), *Didaktik und Unterricht*. Stuttgart: Kohlhammer. pp. 86–100.

Fleck, L. (1979) *Genesis and Development of a Scientific Fact*. Chicago: University of Chicago Press.

Flieger, P. (2003) 'Partizipative Forschungsmethoden und ihre konkrete Umsetzung', in G. Hermes and S. Köbsell (eds), *Disability Studies in Deutschland – Behinderung neu Denken. Dokumentation der Sommeruni*. Kassel: bifos. pp. 200–204.

Gee, J. P. (1999) *An Introduction to Discourse Analysis: Theory and Method*. London and New York: Routledge.

Gramsci, A. (1999) *Selections from the Prison Notebooks*, ed. and trans. Q. Hoare and G. Nowell Smith. London: Elec Book.

Grove, N. (2007) 'Exploring the absence of high points in story reminiscence with carers of people with profound disabilities', *Journal of Policy and Practice in Intellectual Disabilities*, 4(4): 252–260.

Grove, N. (ed.) (2013) *Using Storytelling to Support Children and Adults with Special Needs. Transforming Lives through Telling Tales*. London and New York: Routledge.

Grove, N. (2014) *The Big Book of Storysharing: A Handbook for Personal Storytelling with Children and Young People Who Have Severe Communication Difficulties*. London: Routledge.

Harper, D. (2002) 'Talking about pictures: a case for photo elicitation', *Visual Studies*, 17(1): 13–26.

Hörning, K. H. and Reuter, J. (2004) 'Doing Culture: Kultur als Praxis', in K.H. Hörning and J. Reuter (eds), *Doing Culture: Neue Positionen zum Verhältnis von Kultur und sozialer Praxis*. Bielefeld: transcript. pp. 9–15.

Hymes, D. (1981) *In Vain I Tried to Tell You: Essays in Native American Ethnopoetics*. Philadelphia: University of Pennsylvania Press.

Jackson, M. (2013) *The Politics of Storytelling: Variations on a Theme by Hannah Arendt* (2nd edn). Copenhagen: Museum Musculanum Press.

Lamarque, P. (2004) 'On not expecting too much from narrative', *Mind & Language*, 19(4): 393–408.

Nind, M. (2014) *What Is Inclusive Research?* London, New Delhi, New York and Sydney: Bloomsbury.

Nind, M. (2015) 'Toward a second generation of inclusive research', in T. Buchner, O. Koenig and S. Schuppener (eds), *Inklusive Forschung*. Bad Heilbrunn: Verlag Julius Klinkhardt. pp. 186–198.

Norrick, N. (2000) *Conversational Narrative: Storytelling in Everyday Talk*. Amsterdam, PA: John Benjamins Publishing.

Norrick, N. R. (2004) 'Humor, tellability, and conarration in conversational storytelling', *Text – Interdisciplinary Journal for the Study of Discourse*, 24 (1): 79–111.

Nussbaum, M. C. (2010) *Die Grenzen der Gerechtigkeit: Behinderung, Nationalität und Spezieszugehörigkeit*. Berlin: Suhrkamp.

Rabinow, P. (1989) *French Modern: Norms and Forms of the Social Environment*. Chicago and London: The University of Chicago Press.

Rivkin, J. and Ryan, M. (eds) (2017) *Literary Theory: An Anthology* (3rd edn). Hoboken, NJ: John Wiley & Sons.

Ryan, M. L. (2007) 'Toward a definition of narrative', in D. Herman (ed.), *The Cambridge Companion to Narrative*. Cambridge: Cambridge University Press. pp. 22–35.

Schatzki, T. R., Knorr C. K. and von Savigny, E. (eds) (2001) *The Practice Turn in Contemporary Theory*. London and New York: Routledge.

Schütze, F. (1983/2012) 'Biographieforschung und narratives Interview', in J. Obertreis (ed.), *Oral History: Basistexte*. Stuttgart: Franz Steiner Verlag. pp. 99–112.

Waldenfels, B., Stähler, T. and Kozin, A. (2011) *Phenomenology of the Alien: Basic Concepts*. Evanston: Northwestern University Press.

Walmsley, J. and Johnson, K. (2003) *Inclusive Research with People with Learning Disabilities: Past, Present and Futures*. London and Philadelphia: Jessica Kingsley Publishers.

Weisser, J. (2017) *Konfliktfelder schulischer Inklusion und Exklusion im 20. Jahrhundert: Eine Diskursgeschichte*. Weinheim and Basel: Beltz Juventa.

Zingaro, L. (2009) *Speaking Out: Storytelling for Social Change*. Walnut Creek, CA: Left Coast Press.

7

DOING MULTI-LEVEL STATISTICAL MODELLING WITH HIERARCHICALLY NESTED SAMPLES

Tim Mainhard, Theo Wubbels and Perry den Brok

7.1 INTRODUCTION

If a student indicates his or her level of enjoyment during class, it is likely that his/her answer is more similar to that of classmates than to the enjoyment of students in other classes with other teachers. Hence, student's responses are not independent and statistical and conceptual problems will arise if this characteristic of the data is ignored in statistical analyses. The challenge we discuss in this chapter is that if researchers are not taking this problem of non-independent data into account they are much more likely to report something as 'being significant', while in fact results are spurious (i.e. a type 1 error). Multi-level modelling (or hierarchal linear modelling) is the most commonly used approach to overcome this challenge. In this chapter we offer a gentle primer to multi-level analysis.

This chapter describes, based on our own research and data, conceptually and technically how researchers can deal with data that originates from, for example, students who are nested in groups. In educational settings, the data one uses can often be viewed as a 'multi-stage sample': first you may find some schools willing to help with your study, and a number of teachers from these schools volunteer to participate, which then defines the population of students that can be involved in your study. The multi-level slang used here is: students are nested in teachers, which in their turn are nested in schools (i.e. a hierarchically nested sample). In this chapter, we are describing how we approached such a nested dataset and how results of a multilevel analysis can be interpreted.

7.2 THE CASE: STUDENT ENJOYMENT OF CLASS AND TEACHER FRIENDLINESS

In this chapter we discuss the challenges and possibilities of multi-level modelling on the basis of a dataset that was collected to answer the question how interpersonal teaching practices (teacher friendliness or interpersonal communion) are connected to students' enjoyment in class (based on Mainhard et al., 2018).

The social environment is considered to be a major source of emotions in academic settings (Pekrun, Elliot and Maier, 2006). In classrooms, interpersonal processes are therefore a potentially important predictor of students' emotional experiences. Because teachers are the focal point of many social exchanges, and they are the professionals whose task is to organise the (social) classroom environment, our study focused on the role of the teacher in student emotions. More specifically, in the current chapter we focus on the question to what degree teachers' friendliness, or in terms of the meta-label used in interpersonal theory, teacher communion (Horowitz and Strack, 2010), is associated with the enjoyment students experience in class. Because earlier studies have indicated that student gender and age are also associated with student enjoyment, we wanted to include them as well in our study. For the ease of explanation we have used in this chapter a subsample of the original study (Mainhard et al., 2018) to highlight the challenges a dataset poses that consists of students that are grouped in classes.

The *data* we are using consists of 87 teachers of one large secondary school. For each teacher one class was selected and on average there were 20 students in a class (min. 10; max. 34). In total we included data of 1716 students clustered in 87 classrooms. There were about as many girls as boys involved in the study.

The *measures* used were a short questionnaire that assessed *student enjoyment*, representing the dependent variable. Enjoyment was measured with four items consisting of a five-point Likert scale bounded by 'strongly disagree' and 'strongly agree'. The stem for the items was, 'During the lesson of this teacher …'. An example item for enjoyment was, '… I enjoy myself'. The items were adapted from the Academic Emotions Questionnaire (AEQ; Pekrun et al., 2011). The first two predictors we consider here are *student gender* and *student age*. Teacher *friendliness* or communion is the third predictor. It was assessed with the Questionnaire on Teacher Interaction (QTI; Wubbels,

Créton, and Hooymayers, 1985) which students completed. The QTI assesses both teacher social influence or agency, as well as teacher interpersonal communion or friendliness. In this chapter we focus only on communion or friendliness. Because we were interested in teacher friendliness as a general teacher characteristic, we viewed the students in a classroom as multiple observers of a teacher. We therefore calculated the mean of all student perceptions of a single teacher to derive a single measure per teacher representing teacher friendliness (also see Lüdtke et al., 2009).

7.3 MAIN CHALLENGES AND HOW THEY WERE ADDRESSED

7.3.1 CHALLENGES

The aim was to determine to what degree teacher friendliness in class and student gender and age would help to understand to what degree students experienced enjoyment during class. The main challenge was to avoid spurious findings, that is to avoid claims regarding the association between teacher friendliness and student enjoyment that are in fact not true. This was a real challenge as students were grouped (i.e. nested or clustered) in classes and therefore students in the same class were likely to be more similar in their enjoyment and their perception of the teacher than students in different classes (see Figure 7.1, where we take three classes as an example for the clustering of student enjoyment and Figure 7.2 with the clustering of both student enjoyment and student perception of teacher friendliness). In situations like this, when student answers are not independent, normal ANOVA or regression analysis are no longer adequate as they need independent data. Disregarding this heightens the chance of finding significant associations between teacher friendliness and student enjoyment that are in fact not there (i.e. a type 1 error).

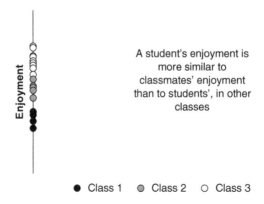

Figure 7.1   Student enjoyment in three classes

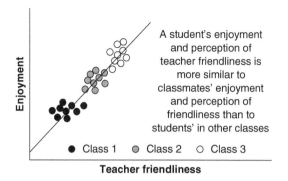

Figure 7.2   Student enjoyment and teacher friendliness in three classes

A related challenge was to assess the degree to which independence plays a role in the current data – with other words: to what degree is student enjoyment more similar when students share the same classroom? Yet another way to frame this question is: to what degree is there consensus among students that lessons of a specific teacher are enjoyable? To overcome these challenges, researchers commonly use multi-level analysis.

7.3.2 ADDRESSING THE CHALLENGES

7.3.2.1 When and why to use multi-level analysis?

Dependence in, for example, perceptions of students (e.g. enjoyment of class) occurs because students are influenced by their class environment in similar ways. On the other hand, there are many class characteristics that can be framed as being influenced by students as well (e.g. the general achievement level in a class or the average socio-economic status). Classes are hierarchical systems which can be described at these different levels: enjoyment or gender of a specific student (i.e. the individual level), or group size or number of females at the group level (Hox, Moerbeek and van de Schoot, 2017). Just like these group characteristics, teacher characteristics can function like a group level variable. For example, teacher experience or gender are the same for all students in the same class. In educational research questions may arise that connect the group and individual level. In our case: to what degree do interpersonal teaching practices (i.e. teacher friendliness) affect students' enjoyment of class?

As we discussed earlier, the data we used can be viewed as a 'multi-stage sample' and students were nested in teachers, which in their turn were nested in one school (i.e. a hierarchically nested sample). Students represented the level 1 units, and teachers the level 2 units. Because all teachers came from the same school and not many different schools, we disregarded the school level. Note that for generalisability of our findings it might have been nicer to sample teachers from many different schools. At each level there may be several variables of interest. In our study, there was enjoyment of class, age and gender. At level 2, variables of interest might be teacher experience or gender of the teacher. We used the average teacher friendliness the students of a class perceived. At the school level, variables like school size, location or the existence of special educational programmes may be relevant in some studies.

7.3.2.2 Why do we need to take this nesting into account when we do a statistical analysis?

In our example, we have 87 teachers that teach classes of about 20 students each. We could do our analysis with 87 teachers, that is, we could summarise students' enjoyment and perception of teacher friendliness data as an average value per teacher (see Figure 7.3 for the three classes example). However, we would lose much statistical power and including all of the 1716 students would be much more attractive.

On the other hand, if we would use student enjoyment and predict it with teacher friendliness on the individual student level, the level 2 variable 'friendliness' would be 'blown up': we would act as if we had 1716 different and independent observations of teacher friendliness, although in fact we only have 87 teachers (see Figure 7.4).

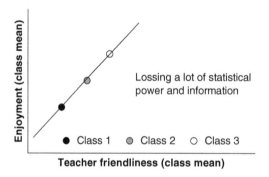

Figure 7.3   Student enjoyment (class mean) and teacher friendliness (class mean) in three classes

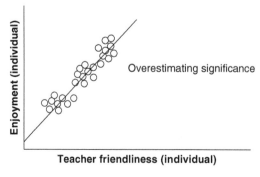

Figure 7.4   Student enjoyment (individual) and teacher friendliness (individual) in three classes

The problem here is that almost all commonly used methods for analysis (regression, ANOVA and so on) assume that data are independent (i.e. not nested). Not taking the nesting into account leads to significance tests that will indicate statistical significance far more often, that is, researchers are much more likely to report something as 'being significant', while in fact results are spurious (i.e. a type 1 error). If in our case, teacher friendliness would be strongly connected to student enjoyment, and on top of this in very similar ways for all students in a class, we might be prone to conclude that this is true for all teachers. It is, however, possible that this connection is different in different classes. The association between teacher friendliness and enjoyment may be weaker in some classes or, in some cases, effects may even be reversed (see Figure 7.5). So then even results could be reported that are the opposite of when the nesting of the data is considered.

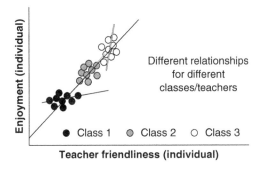

Figure 7.5   Relationship of student enjoyment (individual) and teacher friendliness (individual) in three classes

The strength of the relationship within a class could be explained by teacher characteristics, for example the average friendliness in class or teacher gender (see Figures 7.6 and 7.7).

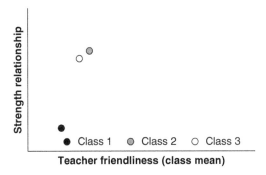

Figure 7.6   Strength of relationship between enjoyment and teacher friendliness and mean teacher friendliness in three classes

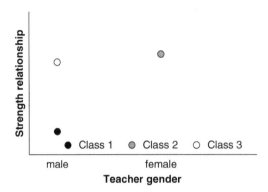

Figure 7.7   Strength of relationship between enjoyment and teacher friendliness and teacher gender in three classes

7.3.3 THE ANALYSIS STRATEGY

In our approach we follow several steps that are common in multi-level modelling:

1. In step one, we assessed the degree of nesting or, in our case, the students' consensus in a class on their enjoyment of class. Technically, we *decompose the variance* in our dependent variable in two parts: variance in student enjoyment due to the teacher (level 2) and variance in enjoyment due to individual students (level 1). It is important to note that the lowest level also includes variance due to measurement uncertainties (i.e. the so-called residual or error). To frame it differently, the question here is which part of student enjoyment can be accounted for by differences between teachers or classes (between variance) and how much of the variance in enjoyment can be accounted for by differences between students within the same class (within variance).
2. In step two, we added predictor variables. Once we have decomposed the variance into a student and a teacher part, we can try to *explain variance* in student enjoyment at both levels separately. We have a predictor at the teacher level (*teacher friendliness*) and two predictors at the student level (*student gender* and *student age*).

For each analysis step we provide SPSS® 24 (IBM Corp., 2016) syntax and the output tables generated by IBM SPSS Statistics software ('SPSS'), along with our interpretation of the results. There are several programs that are able to perform multi-level analysis, specialised multi-level software like HLM (Raudenbush, Bryk and Congdon, 2017) or MlwiN (Charlton et al., 2017), but also more general statistical programs like SPSS can perform multi-level analysis. For a more comprehensive and advanced description of multi-level analysis strategies please consult, for example, Hox, Moerbeek and van de Schoot (2017) or Snijders and Bosker (2012).

Before we analyse the data it is important to think about how our data file should be organised. Most software needs a so-called long data format. Unlike the wide data format, where all responses belonging to one teacher are arranged in one row in SPSS, in the long data format each response (in our case each student) represents one row or case. Thus, in the long format each teacher has several rows in the dataset, equalling the number of students that rated a teacher, see Figure 7.8 below. SPSS needs this format to identify the way the data are organised: which students rated which teacher? In Figure 7.8 the data are arranged with so-called slow running variables (they only change per teacher, e.g. 'Teacher' and 'Communion_teacher') towards the left (the teacher number) and fast running variables (they can change every row) towards the right (like student number and enjoyment). This very much helps to navigate through your dataset.

	Teacher	COMMUNION_teacher	Student	Enjoyment	Communion	gender	age_c	var
1	1001	,69	1	4,25	1,44	0	-,16	
2	1001	,69	2	3,00	1,18	0	-1,06	
3	1001	,69	3	3,75	1,48	1	-1,36	
4	1001	,69	4	2,75	,51	1	-,46	
5	1001	,69	5	3,75	1,19	1	-,06	
6	1001	,69	6	2,50	,44	1	-1,36	
7	1001	,69	7	3,75	,72	1	-1,26	
8	1001	,69	8	1,25	-,97	1	-,96	
9	1001	,69	9	3,00	,63	1	-,66	
10	1001	,69	10	3,00	-,12	1	-,36	
11	1001	,69	11	2,75	1,00	1	,24	
12	1001	,69	12	2,00	,01	0	-,66	
13	1001	,69	13	1,75	,12	0	-,86	
14	1001	,69	14	2,50	1,18	0	-,16	
15	1001	,69	15	3,50	1,12	0	-,96	
16	1001	,69	16	1,75	,84	0	-,16	
17	1001	,69	17	3,00	,76	0	-1,26	
18	1001	,69	18	3,75	,72	0	-,06	
19	1001	,69	19	2,75	1,26	0	,44	
20	1001	,69	20	2,75	,72	0	-1,46	
21	1001	,69	21	2,50	,63	1	-,66	
22	1001	,69	22	4,75	1,31	1	-,16	
23	1001	,69	23	2,50	-,39	1	-1,36	
24	1002	,37	24	3,50	,79	1	,04	
25	1002	,37	25	3,25	,79	1	-,16	
26	1002	,37	26	3,00	,46	1	2,04	
27	1002	,37	27	2,25	,05	0	,64	

Figure 7.8 Screenshot of a part of the data file used in this chapter

7.3.4 THE ACTUAL ANALYSES

7.3.4.1 Variance decomposition (step one): is there consensus among students?

As a first step, we decomposed the variance in student enjoyment in two parts: a student part including measurement error (level 1) and a teacher part (level 2). This model helps to identify the degree of consensus between students or, put differently, the degree to which student enjoyment is affected by the teacher. More technically, this can also be understood as assessing the nesting effect due to the higher level (i.e. the teacher). The syntax for this model is:

SPSS syntax:[1]

```
Mixed Enjoyment
/PRINT = solution testcov
/Random = intercept | subject (Teacher).
```

The 'Mixed' statement tells SPSS that we want to perform a multi-level analysis, that is, that we deal with non-independent data. The '/PRINT' statement asks SPSS to generate certain output tables (see below). The '/Random' statement tells SPSS that we want to take into account that the average enjoyment (i.e. the intercept) may differ per teacher (i.e. 'subject (teacher)'). It indicates the nesting variable in our dataset. The 'Random' in the '/Random' statement also refers to the fact that in multi-level analysis the sampling units, here teachers, are considered to be a random sample of all possible teachers in the population we are interested in (e.g. Dutch or Western European teachers). Just as in non-nested samples (i.e. normal regression), the intercept reflects the general average of the dependent variable in the sample. However, in multi-level analysis there is variance over this mean value (i.e. the intercept is random). Thus, we ask with this statement to calculate how much the teachers vary in their intercepts of student perceived enjoyment. Let us now consider the output tables. Note that these SPSS tables follow European notation and use commas as a decimal indicator.

Mixed Model Analysis

Information Criteria[a]	
-2 Restricted Log Likelihood	4210,105
Akaike's Information Criterion (AIC)	4214,105
Hurvich and Tsai's Criterion (AICC)	4214,112

Bozdogan's Criterion (CAIC)	4227,000
Schwarz's Bayesian Criterion (BIC)	4225,000
The information criteria are displayed in smaller-is-better form.	

a. Dependent Variable: Enjoyment.

Fixed Effects

Type III Tests of Fixed Effects[a]

Source	Numerator df	Denominator df	F	Sig.
Intercept	1	86,478	2719,106	,000

a. Dependent Variable: Enjoyment.

Estimates of Fixed Effects[a]

						95% Confidence Interval	
Parameter	Estimate	Std. Error	df	t	Sig.	Lower Bound	Upper Bound
Intercept	3,036101	,058224	86,478	52,145	,000	2,920364	3,151838

a. Dependent Variable: Enjoyment.

Covariance Parameters

Estimates of Covariance Parameters[a]

						95% Confidence Interval	
Parameter		Estimate	Std. Error	Wald Z	Sig.	Lower Bound	Upper Bound
Residual		,607145	,021270	28,545	,000	,566856	,650298
Intercept [subject = Teacher]	Variance	,262237	,044826	5,850	,000	,187582	,366604

a. Dependent Variable: Enjoyment.

Reprint Courtesy of International Business Machines Corporation, © International Business Machines Corporation.

The first interesting thing is the 'Estimate of Fixed Effects' table. The estimate for the average intercept is 3.036, which resembles the average enjoyment in our sample (which is also called 'the grand mean'). To assess the degree of consensus between students of a class, or put differently, the degree of nesting in our sample, we need to look at the 'Estimates of Covariance Parameters' table. The 'Residual' row represents the variance between students at the lower level (.607; variance in student responses including error) and the intercept row represents variance at second level (.262; variance in student enjoyment between teachers). The Wald test (a version of the t-test) for the intercept variance is significant, indicating that the differences in student enjoyment between teachers is statistically significant (i.e. there is a nesting effect). This means that, apparently, part of the difference in enjoyment the students in our sample reported was due to the teachers that were involved. If this was not the case, it would be questionable whether carrying on with multi-level analysis is worthwhile. To assess the magnitude of the nesting effect, we calculated the percentage (i.e. the relative amount) of variance at the second level:

level 2 variance / total variance = (.262 / (.607 + .262) = .30

This tells us that 30% of the variance in student enjoyment resides at the teacher level (i.e. is due to the teacher). In educational studies, this can be considered a rather substantial nesting effect (c.f. Lüdtke et al., 2009). This figure (i.e. .30) is also called the intraclass correlation (ICC). Conceptually, the ICC describes the average agreement between two, within one class of randomly selected students. Therefore, it can also be considered a measure of consensus between students in a class, because the ICC describes to what degree two random students in a class can be considered similar in their response.

7.3.4.2 Adding predictors to the multi-level model (step two): do student gender and age, and teacher friendliness explain differences in student enjoyment?

As a second step, now that we had *decomposed* the variance in student enjoyment into a teacher and a student part, we wanted to *explain* variance. As is advised by Hox, Moerbeek and van de Schoot (2017) and Snijders and Bosker (2012), we first added predictors at the lower level (student gender and age):

SPSS syntax:

```
Mixed Enjoyment with gender age
/PRINT = solution testcov
/FIXED = gender age
/RANDOM = intercept | subject (Teacher).
```

We have now extended the 'Mixed' statement with the predictor variables gender and age. Also, we have asked SPSS to estimate these predictors as so-called fixed variables (see the third row of the SPSS syntax starting with '/FIXED'). Thus, we want to examine the association of student gender and age with student emotion as being similar (i.e. fixed) in all of the classrooms. For the rest, the syntax remains unchanged.

These are the output tables SPSS produces:

Mixed Model Analysis

Information Criteria[a]

-2 Restricted Log Likelihood	4215,351
Akaike's Information Criterion (AIC)	4219,351
Hurvich and Tsai's Criterion (AICC)	4219,358
Bozdogan's Criterion (CAIC)	4232,243
Schwarz's Bayesian Criterion (BIC)	4230,243
The information criteria are displayed in smaller-is-better form.	

a. Dependent Variable: Enjoyment.

Fixed Effects

Type III Tests of Fixed Effects[a]

Source	Numerator df	Denominator df	F	Sig.
Intercept	1	108,151	2594,285	,000
gender	1	1671,868	7,685	,006
age	1	516,872	2,513	,114

a. Dependent Variable: Enjoyment.

Estimates of Fixed Effects[a]

						95% Confidence Interval	
Parameter	Estimate	Std. Error	df	t	Sig.	Lower Bound	Upper Bound
Intercept	3,100951	,060882	108,151	50,934	,000	2,980275	3,221627
gender	-,109453	,039483	1671,868	-2,772	,006	-,186895	-,032012
age	-,003477	,002194	516,872	-1,585	,114	-,007787	,000832

a. Dependent Variable: Enjoyment.

Covariance Parameters

Estimates of Covariance Parameters[a]

Parameter		Estimate	Std. Error	Wald Z	Sig.	95% Confidence Interval	
						Lower Bound	Upper Bound
Residual		,605432	,021224	28,526	,000	,565231	,648492
Intercept [subject = Teacher]	Variance	,251603	,043439	5,792	,000	,179373	,352920

a. Dependent Variable: Enjoyment.

Reprint Courtesy of International Business Machines Corporation, © International Business Machines Corporation.

If we look at the 'Estimates of Fixed Effects' table, we see that now estimates for gender and age are also included. Note that the average intercept for student enjoyment is somewhat adjusted due to adding predictor variables. While gender has a statistically significant effect on the enjoyment students report ($p = .006$), age is not a significant predictor ($p = .114$). The average effect of gender on student emotions is estimated with $B = -.109$ (see 'Estimate' column). Gender was coded 0 for boys and 1 for girls. Thus, on average, girls reported somewhat lower enjoyment in class than boys. Next, we assessed how much variance the predictor variables explained in student enjoyment. In the 'Estimates of Covariance Parameters' table it can be seen that the teacher (i.e. 'Intercept [subject = Teacher] Variance') and student level (i.e. 'Residual') variances are now estimated as .251 and .605. Thus, both estimates are somewhat lower. Although we expected that gender would explain differences between students, some variance at the teacher level was also explained. This is because of unequal distributions of gender in classrooms. A simple way to calculate the amount of explained variance is to calculate the ratio of the amount of reduction in variance per level. For the student level this was: .607–.605 = .002; .002/.607 = .003. Thus, only a very small amount of between student variance, 0.03%, was explained. For more sophisticated ways of calculating the amount of explained variance please refer to either Hox, Moerbeek and van de Schoot (2017) or Snijders and Bosker (2012).

As a next step, we added our predictor at the second or teacher level. We wanted to assess whether teacher friendliness could explain why classrooms differ in their average reported enjoyment (i.e. the intercept of enjoyment in our model). Remember that we calculated the mean friendliness per teacher by averaging the friendliness perceptions of all students in a class (i.e. the student data were aggregated). Thus, students were viewed as multiple observers of the teacher. Doing so makes sense, however, only if students agree in their estimates of teacher friendliness to a certain degree. In our study consensus between students in a class on teacher friendliness was substantial, as was indicated by an ICC of .52. Please refer to Lüdtke et al. (2009) for a discussion and examples of how to assess the reliability of aggregated variables.

SPSS syntax:

```
Mixed Enjoyment with gender friendliness
/PRINT = solution testcov
/FIXED = gender friendliness
/RANDOM = intercept | subject (Teacher).
```

The SPSS syntax was extended accordingly by adding 'friendliness' to the 'Mixed' statement in the first row as a predictor and by asking for the estimation of a fixed effect for friendliness in the third row in the SPSS syntax. Because age was not significant it was deleted from our model. If our question had been not an explorative one we could also have chosen to leave age in our model. However, especially if samples are small, it is better to include fewer predictors.

The syntax produces the following output tables:

Mixed Model Analysis

Information Criteria[a]

-2 Restricted Log Likelihood	4098,993
Akaike's Information Criterion (AIC)	4102,993
Hurvich and Tsai's Criterion (AICC)	4103,000
Bozdogan's Criterion (CAIC)	4115,885
Schwarz's Bayesian Criterion (BIC)	4113,885
The information criteria are displayed in smaller-is-better form.	

a. Dependent Variable: Enjoyment.

Fixed Effects

Type III Tests of Fixed Effects[a]

Source	Numerator df	Denominator df	F	Sig.
Intercept	1	157,252	7575,918	,000
gender	1	1712,567	8,673	,003
Communion_Teacher_cen	1	78,853	238,774	,000

a. Dependent Variable: Enjoyment.

Estimates of Fixed Effects[a]

Parameter	Estimate	Std. Error	df	t	Sig.	95% Confidence Interval Lower Bound	Upper Bound
Intercept	3,097544	,035588	157,252	87,040	,000	3,027253	3,167836
gender	−,114182	,038771	1712,567	−2,945	,003	−,190226	−,038137
friendliness	,721654	,046702	78,853	15,452	,000	, 628693	,814614

a. Dependent Variable: Enjoyment.

Covariance Parameters

Estimates of Covariance Parameters[a]

Parameter		Estimate	Std. Error	Wald Z	Sig.	95% Confidence Interval Lower Bound	Upper Bound
Residual		,605848	,021252	28,508	,000	,565595	,648965
Intercept [subject = Teacher]	Variance	,045444	,012119	3,750	,000	,026945	,076643

a. Dependent Variable: Enjoyment.

Reprint Courtesy of International Business Machines Corporation, © International Business Machines Corporation.

The 'Estimates of Fixed Effects' table indicates that teacher friendliness is highly significant ($p < .001$) and its effect is estimated with $B = .72$. Thus, the more friendly a teacher is, the more enjoyment students report on average in a given classroom. The 'Estimates of Covariance Parameters' table indicates that adding teacher friendliness reduced the variance in student enjoyment at the teacher level from .251 to .045, which equals as much as 82% of explained variance at the teacher level. The variance at the student level (i.e. the residual variance) was hardly affected by adding this second-level predictor, small changes can be considered unimportant. Thus, so far the overall conclusion would be that teacher friendliness is an important predictor of *average* student enjoyment in class. Until now, we used teacher friendliness only to predict average class levels of enjoyment, but how about individual students' enjoyment? What if a student thinks the teacher is more or less friendly than the average class perception of teacher friendliness? To find out, we calculated how much a specific student differed from his/her classroom average of teacher friendliness:

friendliness – classroom average friendliness = friendliness_student

This variable represents an additional level 1 predictor and it was added as a final step to our model:

SPSS syntax:

```
Mixed Enjoyment with gender friendliness friendliness_student
/PRINT = solution testcov
/FIXED = gender friendliness friendliness_student
/Random = intercept | subject (Teacher).
```

Mixed Model Analysis

Information Criteria[a]

-2 Restricted Log Likelihood	3596,749
Akaike's Information Criterion (AIC)	3600,749
Hurvich and Tsai's Criterion (AICC)	3600,756
Bozdogan's Criterion (CAIC)	3613,638
Schwarz's Bayesian Criterion (BIC)	3611,638
The information criteria are displayed in smaller-is-better form.	

a. Dependent Variable: Enjoyment.

Fixed Effects

Type III Tests of Fixed Effects[a]

Source	Numerator df	Denominator df	F	Sig.
Intercept	1	136,507	8008,098	,000
gender	1	1702,444	6,412	,011
friendliness	1	79,860	232,971	,000
friendliness_student	1	1623,492	592,982	,000

a. Dependent Variable: Enjoyment.

Estimates of Fixed Effects[a]

						95% Confidence Interval	
Parameter	Estimate	Std. Error	df	t	Sig.	Lower Bound	Upper Bound
Intercept	3,083176	,034454	136,507	89,488	,000	3,015044	3,151308
gender	-,084659	,033433	1702,444	-2,532	,011	-,150233	-,019085

(Continued)

(Continued)

Estimates of Fixed Effects[a]

| | | | | | | 95% Confidence Interval | |
Parameter	Estimate	Std. Error	df	t	Sig.	Lower Bound	Upper Bound
friendliness	,720938	,047233	79,860	15,263	,000	,626939	,814938
friendliness_ student	,673920	,027675	1623,492	24,351	,000	,619638	,728203

a. Dependent Variable: Enjoyment.

Covariance Parameters

Estimates of Covariance Parameters[a]

| | | | | | | 95% Confidence Interval | |
Parameter		Estimate	Std. Error	Wald Z	Sig.	Lower Bound	Upper Bound
Residual		,444025	,015585	28,490	,000	,414506	,475647
Intercept [subject = Teacher]	Variance	,055310	,012336	4,484	,000	,035723	,085634

a. Dependent Variable: Enjoyment.

Reprint Courtesy of International Business Machines Corporation, © International Business Machines Corporation.

The 'Estimates of Fixed Effects' table indicates that teacher friendliness_student (i.e. the deviation of a student from the classroom mean of teacher friendliness) is highly significant ($p < .001$) and its effect is estimated with $B = .67$. Thus, the more friendly a student thinks a teacher is as compared to the classroom average, the more enjoyment this student is likely to report. The 'Estimates of Covariance Parameters' table indicates that adding teacher friendliness_student reduced the variance in student enjoyment at the student level from .605 to .444. This equals about 26% of explained variance at the student level, which can be considered a large effect.

Overall, by applying multi-level analysis, we were able to achieve a reliable estimate of the association between teacher friendliness, which did not overestimate the statistical significance of teacher friendliness. Teacher friendliness can be considered an important factor in student enjoyment of class, which can be seen in the amount of variance explained.

RESEARCHER CHECKLIST

Below, a general outline of the process of doing a multi-level analysis is provided by highlighting some of the crucial questions.

- *Is the data clustered in nature?* Think of several measurements within one participant, several students rating their experience in the same class, several teachers providing perceptions about the same teacher team, an intervention study that allocated entire classes or teams to experimental conditions.

- *How many higher level units (i.e. clusters, groups, classes) are there?* If your analysis includes, let's say for example, five or less units (e.g. classes), it is worthwhile to think about an alternative approach. For example, it is possible to add class as a dummy to the analysis instead of viewing class as a truly random factor (i.e. representing a random sample of the entire population of classes). Ideally you have at least 20–30 higher level units (i.e. teachers).

- *Organise your data file.* Create what is called a 'long data file'. That is, make sure that there is a separate row or case in your data file for every data point of your dependent variable (see Figure 7.8 for an example). This means that if you have 87 classrooms with 20 different measures of enjoyment per class, because there are 20 students in a class, your data file should have 87 × 20 rows of data (instead of only 87 or one row per class).

- *To what degree is the clustering of the data affecting my study?* That is, to what degree has the grouping of participants an effect on the data you have collected? This can be examined with the intraclass correlation of the dependent variable and by checking whether the variance at the grouping level (e.g. the class or team level) is statistically significant (see 'the variance component model' discussed above).

- *To which level do your predictors belong?* Make sure you have a good idea whether your predictor belongs to, for example, the student level or the class level. Variables like student gender or age belong to the student level because they are potentially different for each student. Class size or subject taught belong to the class level (i.e. the clustering variable).

- *Think about centring your predictors.* More often than not it is worthwhile to centre your predictor, because it makes the interpretation of your

(Continued)

(Continued)

results easier. For example, if you centre class-size around the grand-mean of class-size in your sample (i.e. calculate 'Class-Size' – 'Average Class-size' for every classroom), the resulting Beta in your analysis represents the effect for the average classroom in your sample.

- *Check the assumptions.* One of the most important assumptions in multi-level analysis is that the residuals (errors) are normally distributed. This means, if your predictor (e.g. gender) helps to understand only differences at relatively high levels of student enjoyment, but not at lower levels of enjoyment, your predictor means different things at different levels of the dependent variable (e.g. enjoyment). This will make it hard to interpret your results.

- *Have fun!* In our experience, preparing your data and figuring out what model is best suited to answer your research question is very time consuming. If you accept this, figuring out the analysis will be much more fun. Also, try to find someone you can work on the analysis with. Approach more experienced researchers every now and then for advice.

7.4 CONCLUSION

7.4.1 THE CURRENT CASE

For the problem as we have described, multi-level modelling is the most suited solution. If regression analysis or ANOVA are used with data from nested samples, results are likely to be untrustworthy. This depends of course on the size of the nesting effect (e.g. in this case how much do classes differ in the enjoyment students report). If this effect is small, results from an ordinary regression will resemble those of a multi-level analysis rather closely.

An alternative approach to the data would be to calculate class means for enjoyment and proceed with an analysis at the teacher level ($N = 87$ instead of $N = 1716$ in our sample), that is, a normal regression or ANOVA. Such an analysis would, however, have a reduced power to detect statistical effects and it would only be possible to study associations at the level of the class not for individual students.

Sometimes, with smaller samples, it is also possible, and with very small samples like five teachers even advisable, to add teacher-IDs as dummy variables to the analysis. Doing so, the regression weight per teacher shows how much a teacher (or class) diverts from the effect found for the teacher chosen as reference for the other dummies.

A third alternative is to select only one student per class and teacher and proceed with normal regression or ANOVA. In this case, all ratings of enjoyment included in the dataset stem from different classroom environments and can therefore be considered independent. The drawback is that, to achieve a similarly sized dataset, such a data collection is very likely to be much more tedious than sampling an entire class.

7.4.2 MORE CHALLENGES AND OPPORTUNITIES IN MULTI-LEVEL MODELLING

In order to provide the reader with a more comprehensive idea of what features multi-level models have, we briefly discuss some of them. Please refer to multi-level textbooks like Hox, Moerbeek and van de Schoot (2017) or Snijders and Bosker (2012) for an elaborate discussion and for examples.

7.4.2.1 Random slopes

In multi-level models it is possible investigate random slopes. For example, to what degree is the effect of student gender the same or different in all of the classrooms we have included in our study? Thus, unlike in ordinary regression analysis, we can investigate whether the average effect of gender as we have discussed it above is an adequate description for all classrooms. Actually, our sample classrooms differed in the magnitude that gender affected enjoyment (i.e. a significant random slope).

7.4.2.2 Model fit

An additional feature in multi-level modelling, as compared to ordinary regression or ANOVA, is that the improvement of the fit of a multi-level model with the underlying data can be tested. That is, we can assess whether our model better describes the data with every change we make (e.g. adding predictors). Model fit refers to the degree that the multi-level model is in accordance with the underlying structure of the data we collected (i.e. the variance–covariance matrix of our variables). In multi-level modelling the –2 Restricted Log Likelihood is commonly used to asses model fit, and a lower value indicates an increased fit (see the first table in each of the SPSS outputs provided above called 'Information Criteria'). The –2 Restricted Log Likelihood is a relative fit index, that is, it is not possible to compare it across models for different dependent variables or for models that do not directly build on each other. For the last model in our example this value was 3596.749 (see the 'Information Criteria' table) and for the model without predictors this value was 4210.05. We can now assess with a x^2-difference test whether this reduction (mostly referred to as deviance) in –2 Restricted Log Likelihood of about 613 equals a statistically significant improvement of our model. The degrees of freedom needed for this test equal the number of parameters that have been added to the model, in our case this is = 3 (i.e. three fixed effects). The calculation indicates that $\Delta-2$ Restricted Log Likelihood (3) = 613, $p < .001$, thus our model fit improved significantly. Although this test is informative and often applied, Hox, Moerbeek and van de Schoot (2017) advise to use the Wald test for evaluating the significance of fixed effects (i.e. the significance test provided by SPSS in the 'Estimates of Fixed Effects' table) and the x^2-difference test to evaluate the significance of random effects like a random slope.

7.4.2.3 Sample size

As in all statistical analyses, sample size is an important issue. In multi-level models the ratio between the level 2 and level 1 units is important too. For a simple model, like the one we presented, 30 teachers with each about 10–20 students may be sufficient (Hox, Moerbeek and van de Schoot, 2017).

7.4.2.4 Longitudinal data

Multi-level analysis is well suited for longitudinal data. In fact, longitudinal data represents a special case of nesting. If we had asked students repeatedly to rate their teacher's friendliness and their enjoyment, these measures would have been nested within students. Thus, we would have needed to add an additional level: level 1 occasions, level 2 students, level 3 teachers. Also, unlike repeated measures ANOVA, multi-level models can handle missing values at the lowest level. So, if some of the students would not have rated their enjoyment every time we asked them to, it would still be possible to include their data.

ADDITIONAL USEFUL READING

Hox, J. J., Moerbeek, M. and van de Schoot, R. (2017) *Multilevel Analysis: Techniques and Applications*. London: Routledge.

Snijders, T. A. and Bosker, R. J. (2012) *Multilevel Analysis: An Introduction to Basic and Advanced Multilevel Modelling*. London: Sage.

Two well-known, thorough introductions to multi-level analysis. For both books, syntax (i.e. computer code) is available for the examples they use for a number of statistical programs (like SPSS, SAS, MlWin and so on). You can find them on the website of the Institute for Digital Research and Education of the University of California Los Angeles (UCLA; https://stats.idre.ucla.edu/other/examples) or on the websites of the authors.

Heck, R. H., Thomas, S. L. and Tabata, L. N. (2013) *Multilevel and Longitudinal Modeling with IBM SPSS*. London: Routledge.

Field, A. (2013) *Discovering Statistics Using IBM SPSS Statistics*. London: Sage.

These two books focus on multi-level modelling in SPSS (also referred to as Mixed Models in SPSS).

Lüdtke, O., Robitzsch, A., Trautwein, U. and Kunter, M. (2009) 'Assessing the impact of learning environments: how to use student ratings of classroom or school characteristics in multilevel modeling', *Contemporary Educational Psychology, 34*(2): 120–131.

Den Brok, P., Brekelmans, M. and Wubbels, T. (2006) 'Multilevel issues in research using students' perceptions of learning environments: the case of the Questionnaire on Teacher Interaction', *Learning Environments Research, 9*(3): 199.

Lüdtke et al. provide a primer on doing research on classroom environments and how to use student ratings. They also focus on issues regarding reliability of aggregated measures and centring of predictor variables. Also placed in the context of learning environments is the paper by den Brok, Brekelmans and Wubbels, which spcifically focuses on the impact of decisions about what level is studied using students' perceptions of the teacher–student relationship as assessed with the Questionnaire on Teacher Interaction (QTI).

NOTE

1   If you are not familiar with the use of code or syntax in SPSS, please consult one of the many instructional videos available on the web.

REFERENCES

Charlton, C., Rasbash, J., Browne, W.J., Healy, M. and Cameron, B. (2017) MLwiN Version 3.00. Centre for Multilevel Modelling, University of Bristol.

Horowitz, L.M. and Strack, S. (2010) *Handbook of Interpersonal Psychology: Theory, Research, Assessment, and Therapeutic Interventions*. Hoboken, NJ: John Wiley & Sons.

Hox, J.J., Moerbeek, M. and van de Schoot, R. (2017) *Multilevel Analysis: Techniques and Applications*. London: Routledge.

IBM Corp. (2016) IBM SPSS Statistics for Windows, Version 24.0. Armonk, NY: IBM Corp.

Lüdtke, O., Robitzsch, A., Trautwein, U. and Kunter, M. (2009) 'Assessing the impact of learning environments: how to use student ratings of classroom or school characteristics in multilevel modeling', *Contemporary Educational Psychology, 34*(2): 120–131.

Mainhard, T., Oudman, S., Hornstra, L., Bosker, R. J. and Goetz, T. (2018) 'Student emotions in class: the relative importance of teachers and their interpersonal relations with students', *Learning and Instruction, 53*(2): 109–119.

Pekrun, R., Elliot, A.J. and Maier, M.A. (2006) 'Achievement goals and discrete achievement emotions: a theoretical model and prospective test', *Journal of Educational Psychology, 98*(3): 583.

Pekrun, R., Goetz, T., Frenzel, A.C., Barchfeld, P. and Perry, R.P. (2011) 'Measuring emotions in students' learning and performance: the Achievement Emotions Questionnaire (AEQ)', *Contemporary Educational Psychology, 36*(1): 36–48.

Raudenbush, S. W., Bryk, A. S, and Congdon, R. (2017) HLM 7.03 for Windows [Computer software]. Skokie, IL: Scientific Software International, Inc.

Snijders, T.A. and Bosker, R.J. (2012) *Multilevel Analysis: An Introduction to Basic and Advanced Multilevel Modelling*. London: Sage.

Wubbels, T., Créton, H.A. and Hooymayers, H.P. (1985) 'Discipline problems of beginning teachers: interactional behaviour mapped out'. Paper presented at the annual meeting of the American Educational Research Association, Chicago (ERIC Document Reproduction Service Np. Ed. 260040).

8

DOING DATA ANALYSIS – COLLABORATION, CREATIVITY AND CRITIQUE

Liselott Aarsand and Pål Aarsand[1]

8.1 INTRODUCTION

In everyday talk among researchers there is no doubt that they find research to be an exciting, meaningful and joyful experience. One of the main aspects of research, however, is also to encounter and learn how to deal with demanding challenges that require much effort, thus at times leaving the researcher feeling disoriented, exhausted and even overwhelmed. Furthermore, in contrast to the more or less sequential and logical presentations of the research process appearing in many journal articles, monographs and research reports, quite often free from feelings of despair or other dramas as experienced by the researcher or research team, it has convincingly been claimed that 'real research is often confusing, messy, intensely frustrating, and fundamentally nonlinear' (Marshall and Rossman, 1999: 21). As aptly captured in this quote, the research process may appear to be a bumpy road, and to engage in research may also mean placing yourself in challenging situations where there seldom is a standard solution to facilitate your work.

Taking that as the point of departure, there is of course a wide range of challenges that researchers might face in the various research projects in which they are involved. Drawing upon our own experiences from more than 20 years each within various research fields and university contexts, we have participated in a myriad of daily discourses and conversations in research groups, seminar groups, workshops and international conferences. Not surprisingly, across distinct research topics, research projects and methodological designs, there is one aspect of the research process that seemingly preoccupies scholars: the analytical work. Just as important, this perhaps anecdotal insight also highlights another main aspect of the research process: it appears to be a dynamic interplay of individual and collaborative work, where receiving critical and creative input from colleagues within various forums is an integral part of the process. Such collaborative activities may have the potential to contribute to the sole researcher, the dyad or the research team, better equipping us all to reflect on, revise and cope with challenges that we face during the research process.

In this chapter we will address analytical research work as a challenge and further suggest a particular practice of collaboration as one way of managing this. However, even though collaborating on analytical work may seem valuable or self-evident in some research contexts, it may also create tensions and perhaps even appear as slightly naïve. In contemporary academic life it cannot be denied that such phenomena as the competition rationale are also highly prevalent (e.g. Naidoo, 2016; Olssen, 2016), and it should not be taken for granted that researchers find themselves within environments where organisational structures and cultures support all forms of collaborative work. Bearing this in mind, we would still argue that there are several reasons why we in particular should recognise and encourage collaboration on analytical work. On the one hand, such activities may follow a competition rationale revealing a desire for success, first and foremost in relation to getting published or funded. On the other hand, such initiatives may rather question that stance and instead stimulate an alternative rationale that highlights the crafting of knowledge in itself. And most likely, in their everyday work, researchers or a research team are guided by a combination of both rationales. Nevertheless, it is crucial to highlight the collaborative activities that appear as fruitful for researchers themselves when engaging in knowledge production.

8.2 COLLABORATIVE DATA ANALYSIS SESSIONS AS A RESOURCE

In focusing on analytical research work, instead of providing yet another recipe for successful educational research, we rather wish to contribute to this body of knowledge by highlighting one such practice that we have found to be significantly beneficial: *collaborative data analysis sessions* (Hindmarsh and Tutt, 2012: 58; Tutt and Hindmarsh, 2011). These can be described as focused gatherings where social, educational or other scientists actively seek input from colleagues and in this way collaborate on analytical work. A main aspect inherent in these activities is to view, read and discuss together empirical material, for example, video- or audio-recordings and transcripts, which may open many opportunities and contribute to the emerging analysis in any research project (Derry et al., 2010).

Given the importance of reflexivity in the practice of qualitative research (e.g. Collier, Moffatt and Perry, 2015; Finlay, 2012; Kvale and Brinkmann, 2009; Roulston, 2010) scholars are persistently encouraged to examine how theoretical and methodological lenses colour the kinds of analyses that they produce, and it could easily be argued that reflective enactments are seldom carried out in isolation. Hence, the emerging knowledge may be understood according to how individual and collaborative efforts are undertaken in and through the various social forums where we as scholars participate, and this shapes how we learn the trade of crafting research. How we approach the analysis task, how we encounter, agree and disagree among a diversity of perspectives, and not least how we examine, challenge and judge our own and each other's analysis is in fact fundamental to the construction of knowledge. By putting ourselves, as researchers, under the magnifying glass to further explore what happens when we engage in analytical work, the aim in this chapter is to provide some key lessons for how to initiate, develop and establish one example of what may be considered a sustainable research practice.

8.3 KNOWLEDGE PRODUCTION IN AND THROUGH SOCIAL PRACTICE

Novice researchers may find that the process of analysing data is more than challenging, which is probably a familiar experience for anyone working in teaching and supervision within qualitative research and qualitative methods in higher education (e.g. Bryman, 2001; Coffey and Atkinson, 1996; Heath, Hindmarsh and Luff, 2010; Silverman, 2011). For Master degree and PhD students who put themselves in the position of trying to learn the trade, analysis is sometimes even considered to be 'something of a mystery' (Silverman, 2011: 57). In opening up the black box and trying to demystify what analysis is all about, or at least better equip the novice researcher to make further progress, the literature presents many 'lists' for how to work through particular procedures or undertake a stepwise process, which of course may be very helpful.

For more experienced researchers, however, the situation is somewhat different even though there is no doubt that struggling with analytical shortcomings is a common dilemma. Despite having successful experiences, high ambitions, and having expended an enormous amount of time on writing the manuscript, in the hands of reviewers, editors and other scholars the work may still show signs of analytical weaknesses evoking such responses as 'poor', 'not convincing', 'unclear', 'mismatched to theoretical framework' or 'lacking sophistication', which often leads to rejection from the journals where researchers want to publish their work (e.g. Sarangi, 2017). Some analytical shortcomings seem to appear regularly, for instance, when the aim is to conduct substantial discourse analysis it has been noted that 'writers are not doing analysis if they summarise, if they take sides, if they parade quotes, or if they simply spot in their data features of talk or text that are already well-known' (Antaki et al., 2003: 29).

To engage in and continue professional development and learning in research work, social networks and research communities are necessary, not least because they can offer critical and transparent conversations that may improve the analysis. Most likely many of us within the research community, in the widest sense, would agree that good data analysis is first and foremost about the necessity to 'develop a working, hands-on, empirical, tacit knowledge of analysis' (Rapley, 2011: 274), which rather points to research and analysis as work and practice. Exaggerating slightly, we can say that analysing data is literally about rolling up one's sleeves and letting the real business of research begin, whether you are a novice, well-experienced, on your own or a team researcher. Hence the question – how do we deal with analytical trials, tribulations and shortcomings wisely?

There is of course no single or standard response to such a complex question, and probably this is far from expected. On the contrary, it could be argued that 'social science tries to describe things that are complex, diffuse and messy' (Law, 2004: 2), and the same is definitely also true if we are to describe in detail how to undertake analytical work. However, in trying to avoid a situation where the metaphors become overwhelming rather than helpful, some simplicity will be added if we at least could agree that research and analysis are activities, something people *do*. Such a stance contributes to depicting knowledge production as social and constructive, which several classic studies clearly illustrate with respect to what has been called 'science in the making'. It has been argued convincingly that scientific knowledge and technologies evolve in social context, or put differently, 'they participate in the social world, being shaped *by* it, and simultaneously *shaping* it' (Law, 2004: 12). Within that realm, empirical explorations of research practices have elucidated various features of the research process in terms of what scientists do when they engage in research (e.g. Hindmarsh and Tutt, 2012; Latour and Woolgar, 1986; Tutt and Hindmarsh, 2011). As such, knowledge production is located within the frame of everyday work, where scholars' ways to act, think and talk are highlighted, which brings the social, collaborative and interactive aspects of research to the forefront.

8.4 ANALYTICAL EXPLORERS, CARTOGRAPHERS AND DETECTIVES

Embracing the idea of knowledge production as social practice directs our focus onto *how* research activities are organised and undertaken, where it is also important to describe how scholars engage in various tasks, settings and activities to address particular problems, generate new understandings and knowledge and examine how they interact and collaborate on making sense of whatever their research is about.

When addressing the analytical work in the research process, some metaphors are used to describe what analysis is really about: acting as the explorer, cartographer and detective (e.g. Sidnell, 2014: 97). The metaphor of the analyst as an explorer or cartographer points to what appears to be an unmotivated gaze by revealing the importance of discovering, mapping and describing new or unknown practices or phenomena. The metaphor of the analyst as a detective, on the other hand, refers to a motivated gaze, where initial subtle impressions or ideas may systematically be followed up, perhaps turning out to be substantial. Sometimes this metaphor comes with a well-known fictional character where the research process is characterised as 'not unlike the detective work of Sherlock Holmes or the best traditions in investigative reporting' (Marshall and Rossman, 1999: 22).

The metaphors used to describe analytical work are useful because they all illustrate what qualitative research and researchers are striving to do. However, they still tend to depict the researcher, as well as the research process, as a lonely figure and an isolated practice and could perhaps easily be confused with the image of the great genius, or the brilliance of just one person's work. Moreover, by ascribing metaphors like 'being an adventure' to research work, thus intimating excitement, exploration and creativity, attracting and piquing our interest as researchers, the image may even be strengthened, probably also making it feel slightly different from the hard and time-consuming everyday grind, the struggle with looming deadlines and the lack of financial support that we also have to deal with. Running the risk of cracking the perhaps extravagant aura of research once and for all, there is also another side to any adventure, wisely captured in how 'everybody knows that walking in unfamiliar areas can be dangerous and can result in getting lost' (Larsson, 2004: 100). To continue to explore new areas, to keep on track, to improve and to deliver great research results, researchers, research teams and research communities need to maintain a dynamic interplay between the individual and collaborative work.

By drawing loosely upon the case of the famous fictional character Sherlock Holmes to illustrate and discuss challenges and contributions to analysis in the research process, rather than celebrate one person's work, we aim to highlight the interplay between individual and collaborative aspects of such investigations. While there is no doubt that detective work, as well as research work, involves much individual effort, there are still parts of the process that are or may become more collaborative in nature. A main aspect of Mr Holmes's detective work is the social interaction between him and Dr Watson, how they talk, discuss and confront each other, constantly considering alternative interpretations and preparing to suddenly alter their course. Hence, the dialectics of open agreement and disagreement is highly prevalent in their exploration to successfully solve yet another intriguing case.

We will therefore, in the next sections, unpack one such practice and reveal what happens when researchers engage in analytical work, where they share and test their emerging analysis and seek collaborative assistance in and through conversation. A prominent feature is how the researchers assume the role of being each other's *critical friend*, defined as 'a trusted person who asks provocative questions, provides data to be examined through another lens, and offers critiques of a person's work as a friend' (Costa and Kallick, 1993: 50), which highlights the dynamics of an inherent tension between intimacy and distance. In outlining the nature of critical friendships, the mutual and trusting relationship between active participants engaged in dialogue with the aim of making stronger research cases is a key factor (van Manen, 1990). Bearing in mind these aspects of collaborative work, we hope to illustrate the potential of such activities by describing the way in which they may be inspiring, valuable and supportive of substantial analysis in the making, in and through the context of social interaction. Perhaps such encounters are also necessary if we are to create and establish even better research practices in educational science.

8.5 COLLABORATING ON ANALYTICAL WORK

The data sessions we have looked into – appearing as three empirical examples in the next sections – have been organised by a group of researchers who have met regularly in monthly sessions for five years. The data session is multi-disciplinary, where the researchers are involved in distinct research fields, have varied experiences from research and are in various positions, including professors and PhD students. All the participants are expected to do research as part of their work at the university, yet the amount of time available differs. The members of the group share a similar research interest in social interaction and draw upon such traditions as ethnomethodology, discourse analysis and applied linguistics. The sessions are data driven in the sense that transcripts, video-recordings and audio-recordings constitute the types of empirical material that the researchers are focused on in their meetings.

The structure of the collaborative data analysis session is similar from one session to the next. Usually it starts with the *presenting researcher(s)* giving a brief overview of a particular research project. The purpose is to help the other participants at the data session, the *co-participating researchers*, to gain a sense of the aim of the research project, for instance, by describing the research questions, the context, the participants and so on. The presentation of the research project is often completed rather quickly, followed by questions from the co-participating researchers who want to clarify any points they are not sure about. Next, extracts from the empirical material are introduced, which may be done by watching video-recordings, listening to audio-recordings and/or reading transcriptions of selected data. Often video-/audio-recordings and transcripts of the same example of social interaction are used simultaneously. It is worth noting that the presenting researchers are at various stages in their analytical work. Some of them have a specific theoretical, empirical and analytical interest and thus base substantial analytical claims on the data material being presented, while others present data where the analysis is at an early stage and largely in the making.

To investigate how collaborative data analysis sessions may contribute to analytical work in research, we have chosen three examples from the same data session where different challenges were made relevant and addressed. The selected data session, which lasted for two hours and consisted of nine researchers, has been video-recorded and transcribed following a modified convention developed within conversation analysis (Jefferson, 2004) (see Appendix) and translated into English. All the participants gave their informed consent and, in accordance with research ethical standards, they have been given pseudonyms.

The three examples show how the dialogue in the data session refers to well-known challenges and questions that qualitative scholars from time to time struggle with and have to solve in their analytical work. Does the presented data material 'answer' the research questions? Do the transcripts display the analytical points? Do the analytical tools work? We do not claim that all the challenges researchers may encounter in analytical work are easily solved in and through collaborative data analysis sessions, our aim is rather to point out the ways in which such sessions can be valuable.

8.6 THREE EMPIRICAL EXAMPLES

In the upcoming sections we will focus on how the researchers in the data session jointly identify, work on and discuss different challenges related to analysis. In scrutinising this session we take a social interactional approach to highlight the collaborative work undertaken by the participants (Goffman, 1974). Such an approach offers opportunities to investigate *how* people organise their participation as they communicate with, confront and support one another through sharing knowledge and displaying their expertise (Goodwin, 2013).

In the three excerpts that follow, the researchers Molly and Kevin present selected transcriptions of video-recorded data from an on-going research project on social service practices. Initially they inform the data session group that they are working on an article where their focus is on the use of screens and documents in encounters with the social services. In the first excerpt we will see how the data session addresses challenges related to *the data*: is the selected data material significant in relation to the research questions? In the second excerpt we will illustrate how the data session addresses *the transcript*: do the transcripts display the analytical points accurately? Finally, in the third excerpt we show how the data session addresses *the analytical tools*: are the analytical tools precise and good enough to lead to fruitful and interesting analysis?

8.6.1 FOCUSING ON THE DATA

A challenge that qualitative researchers may face when writing texts or making presentations is to select instances or examples that convincingly display the relevance of the data and, ultimately, the findings. In the analytical process, the researcher often finds a wide range of aspects in the empirical material interesting, and may well be tempted to follow a myriad of various threads in the dataset. Frankly speaking, at least in the qualitative genre, a researcher can easily find him/herself swimming in a large pond of data making multiple suggestions as to what appears to be relevant. Therefore, analytical work is much about organising, choosing and sorting the data in suitable ways (e.g. Derry et al., 2010). Furthermore, to equip oneself to take the next step in the analysis, it may be necessary to decide what seems to stand out as worthy and valuable to study in detail and which examples are the best ones when taking a particular body of research into account. Data sessions may serve as an arena where it is possible to calibrate, examine and perhaps also agree with colleagues on what seems reasonable to continue working on.

The relevance of the selected data may be confirmed in various ways. This may be expressed explicitly when a participant tells you that he or she finds the data interesting, but relevance may also be displayed implicitly through emerging discussions in the group. In excerpt 1, we will illustrate how the data session addresses the relevance of the data:

Excerpt 1: Focusing on the data

Presenting researchers: Molly and Kevin

Co-participating researchers: Tina, Sander, Signe, Gina, Ann, Liam and Peter

1	Gina	Hrm yea↑ ou:: I think it's a very interesting example and very rich
2	Liam	Um:h ((nods))
3	Sander	((Nods))
4	Gina	E:::m: and when it comes to u:sing this document as an <u>opening</u> to the first conversation
5		(0.5) the::n it see::ms this utterance in three well utterances one and three from the
6		counsellor seem to have a kind of <u>double func</u>tion (0.3) related <to:> <u>both</u> getting to
7		know each other
8		(0.8)
9	Liam	Uhm
10	Gina	Or getting to know you and getting to kno[w your c[ompetence, both are parts in
11	Liam	[Uhm [uhm

12	Gina	o:pen [ing (0.3) to potential participation and we see:: I think in twenty-three (0.4) that
13	Sander	[((Nods))
14	Gina	e:: the user reacts by elaborating on (.) his own competence e:: and it's interesting I think
15		because a CV can possibly be a sensitive thing also in the way that it's, the way it's
16		framed with such [hedging disclaimers with 'ju:st' (0.2) can 'ju:st read through your CV'
17	Liam	[Uhm
18	Gina	just to get to know it' [((lifts pointing finger)) and it switches from it (0.4) well I mean
19	xxx	[Uhm:: ((several of the participants in the seminar))
20	Gina	from yours to it [I think this illustrates that double functionality
21	Liam	[Um:h

When we enter the episode, Molly and Kevin present a transcript from a social service encounter where a client's CV is being discussed. At the very beginning it can be seen how one of the co-participating researchers, Gina, tells the group that this is not only an interesting example of selected data, it is a 'very interesting example and very rich' (line 1). The co-participating researchers Liam and Sander show through minimal responses and by nodding that they agree with Gina (lines 2 and 3). However, telling someone that they have interesting and rich data is not enough in this setting, convincing arguments of why this is the case have to be provided. The relevance of the data is shown in how Gina presents a possible way to start the analysis as she suggests that the presenting researchers should focus on how the counsellor and the client react to and use the documents – for instance the CV – placed in front of them (lines 4–21). Gina also points to the importance of paying attention to *the way in which* this document is treated and talked about (lines 14–16), and even strengthens this claim by making use of the analytical notion 'hedging disclaimers'. The introduction of the concept is followed by a demonstration of how the analysis may be conducted (lines 16–20).

Even though Gina is the one who is doing the talking, she is not alone in the analytical work. Liam and others support her suggestion, which is shown through such minimal responses as 'uhm' and nods (see lines 2, 3, 9, 11, 13, 17, 19 and 21). Hence, it could be argued that the relevance and the analytical accessibility of the data are displayed by Gina and confirmed by the co-participants in the group. However, Gina's proposal is not to be seen as a full analysis, rather it is an analytical enactment that points to a possible way to approach the data, a suggestion of *where* to start and *what* to look for.

8.6.1.1 Challenges and contributions

Making content logs is one way of organising the data and of sorting and initially selecting episodes (e.g. Jordan and Henderson, 1995). However, finding good examples that have the potential to display and explain the studied phenomenon in presentations and texts is still a challenge in research. Presenting empirical material at data sessions provides an opportunity for researchers to show how they enter their data to investigate the research topic/questions and to receive feedback on the relevance of the presented episodes. Excerpt 1 shows how the co-participating researchers not only confirm the relevance of the selected data, but also offer a possible way to analyse the particular transcript. If the co-participating researchers do not see how the examples are suitable for answering the research questions in a convincing way, then this may be because the chosen episodes lack relevance, or because the presenting researchers have not framed, explained and pointed out how the selected episodes are relevant. It could then be argued that the data analysis session gives the presenting researcher(s) reasons to elaborate on the significance of the selected data in relation to the research topic/questions.

8.6.2 FOCUSING ON THE TRANSCRIPT

Another challenge that qualitative researchers have to deal with is to attain high-quality descriptions that are robust, thus revealing the nuances, variations and complexities needed to accomplish a particular kind of analysis (e.g. Tracy, 2010). Bearing this in mind, making adequate representations of social data is a key issue for any researcher, and perhaps in particular for those who are studying social interaction. Data sessions may contribute to this work as several researchers are looking closely and carefully into the same transcripts. When video-/audio-recordings are displayed together with transcripts there is an opportunity to explore and examine how interactional data are being transformed into transcripts, which in turn may generate discussions on details that are present, or indeed absent. When transcripts are presented without audio-/video-recordings, they may still be a topic of discussion, for instance, if they are found easy to follow and understand, or in the way in which they support the emerging analysis. Such dialogues indicate that something may be fuzzy or missing, or needs to be adjusted and perhaps even double-checked by returning to the recorded data once again.

In collaborative data analysis sessions, the co-participating researchers are invited to provide their interpretations of the representations to the presenting researcher(s) data, which also involves commenting on the transcripts. In excerpt 2, we will show how suggestions on how to improve the transcripts are initiated and established as a joint focus of attention:

Excerpt 2: Focusing on the transcript

Presenting researchers: Molly and Kevin

Co-participating researchers: Tina, Sander, Signe, Gina, Ann, Liam and Peter

1	Liam	I ((takes up the transcription and looks at it)) became very curious about these <u>pictures</u>
2		[how have you been discussing (.) would they look like this?
3	Molly	[Ye::s
4	Liam	((Turns the sheet toward Molly and slides over with his hand)) how have you been
5		discussing this I'm just curious?
...	...	((Left out 46:15–47:28: talks about how they have made the transcripts))
7	Peter	As Tina said one has to be very exact wit[h regard to where the images are placed so that
8	Liam	[Yes
9	Peter	one knows where the image comes in if the point is to use it as an analytical
10		[object and not just as an illustration
11	Liam	[U:hm
12	Molly	[Uhm ((nodding))
13	Peter	As it's now it works as an illustration=
14	Molly	=Yes
15	Gina	Good point
16	Peter	If it's turned into part of the data then [it needs to have a <u>function</u> [I think into the
17	Gina	[Yes ((nods)) yes [yes
18	Peter	sequence a::=
19	Liam	=into the sequential
20	Molly	What do you think then, does it need to be (0.2) mo[re
21	Peter	[Yea I think=
22	Gina	=exactly placed?

When we enter the episode, the data session group has already been working on the emerging analysis for a while. One of the co-participating researchers, Liam, picks up the transcript, holds it up in front of the group and states that he is curious about how the presenting researchers, Molly and Kevin, argue in favour of the pictures in the transcript (lines 1–2). Molly overlaps with an extended 'ye::s' (line 3) indicating that she is noting what is being said, before Liam completes his utterance and asks if the images in the transcript in fact should look like they do (line 2). He turns the transcript towards Molly and slides his hand over it as he repeats the question 'how have you been discussing this' (lines 4–5). Liam indicates that he does not necessarily understand the use of the pictures in the transcript. In fact, he asks for the idea, or more precisely, the reasons for choosing and using the particular pictures in the transcript. The focus is then on the transcript and how pictures together with text are used to display the interactional episode that they are analysing.

Next, the presenting researchers, Molly and Kevin, explain how they have crafted the transcript. After this, the co-participating researcher Peter points back to what Tina said earlier (line 7), that one has to be very exact with regard to *where* to put the images into the transcript. Thus Peter aligns with Tina and rhetorically strengthens the upcoming argument by emphasising how other members of the group already have pointed out the same type of weakness. He then explains that the details about how to locate pictures in transcripts are important, not least if they are to be seen as 'analytical objects' as opposed to 'illustrations' (lines 7–13). Molly agrees with this (lines 12 and 14); however, Peter does not seem satisfied with how they previously talked about the distinction between pictures as an illustration and pictures as an analytical object. This can be seen when he specifies what 'exact' means when it comes to the transcriptions (line 16): the picture 'needs to have a <u>function</u>' (line 16) and it should be placed exactly within the 'sequential' organisation of the unfolding activity (line 19). Gina and Liam align with Peter's explanation (lines 17, 19 and 22). It could then be argued that there is general agreement on the importance of paying attention to *how* pictures are used and function in transcripts, and that pictures have to be placed exactly where whatever happens that is being illustrated occurs in the communicative flow.

8.6.2.1 Challenges and contributions

Detailed transcriptions of a social activity may be considered as a way to create transparency in the analysis (e.g. Potter, 2012). For researchers, an important aspect is to obtain feedback on how the transcripts work when they are read, interpreted and understood by others. This concerns what is included and what is omitted, what is required and what is considered unnecessary to display (e.g. Ochs, 1999 [1979]), and also how, for instance, images, bodily placements, movements, objects, words that are hard to hear and intonation may be part of the transcript. Excerpt 2 shows how the co-participating researchers direct their critical gaze onto the use of pictures in the transcript. In the discussion, the data session points out what is considered to be a weakness in the transcript before the participants suggest how to deal with this challenge so the transcript can be improved. Hence, data sessions may generate valuable suggestions as to how to develop the transcripts. If this act of testing the transcripts merely leads to confirmation, this can also be valuable as it can encourage the presenting researcher(s) to proceed.

8.6.3 FOCUSING ON THE ANALYTICAL TOOLS

Selecting and systematically using a fruitful analytical framework that helps research-ers to make an adequate and robust analysis is a well-known challenge for qualitative researchers. To novice researchers, it may even be a challenge to read the empirical material with the chosen theoretical lens at all, which otherwise may appear as a lack of fit between the analytical tools, the data and the analysis. Sometimes the focus in the analysis needs be sharpened, at other times the analytical concepts have to be changed to convincingly craft and display interesting findings. To more experienced researchers, the challenge is usually related to cultivating an analytical gaze (e.g. Sarangi, 2017). At stake is the challenge of choosing and using analytical tools to craft data in a convincing way. When researchers meet across disciplines and research fields in collaborative data analysis sessions, there is often a struggle between various theoretical and analytical approaches where, for instance, the same analytical concept is defined, understood and used differently. How the researchers interpret and apply the theoretical approach and analytical concepts is critically scrutinised to find out the way in which they can contribute to a fruitful and interesting analysis.

The collaborative data analysis session provides a site where the participants can enter into a discovery mode, and where multiple or competing analytical concepts may be suggested for dealing with the empirical material in potentially suitable ways. In excerpt 3, we return to the data session group as they investigate the second tran-script of the day and this will show how alternative theoretical notions are suggested for further work:

Excerpt 3: Focusing on the analytical tools

Presenting researchers: Molly and Kevin

Co-participating researchers: Tina, Sander, Signe, Gina, Ann, Liam and Peter

1	Sander	Then I will continue (.) I think (0.5) m:: what we recently saw what we maybe saw to
2		a larger degree was like an interactional invitation [of and it's about what is said (0.2)
3	Gina	[Umh ((nods))
4	Kevin	[((Nods))
5	Sander	here it's about (0.5) well (.) what's on the table he:re i::t's (0.2) a huge po:wer
6		a:::symmetry so this is a li:fe [threatening situation where a lot is on the table (0.2)
7	Liam	[Um:h exactly
8	Sander	and then it's as you ((gazes at Gina)) correctly pointed out a good counsellor that in

9		fact is::::: gives (.) so it gi::ves >room for participation< in this <u>process</u> that's life
10		threatening to:: this person (.) not exactly in the conversation but it's something about
11		this as a pro<u>cess </u>[that the talk is part of a process that's important to this person and
12	Gina	[Uhm
13	Sander	gives participation within the process um: its own process in a way (0.5) yeah it's
14		[in a sense on different lev[els
15	Gina	[Yes [yes it is
16	Liam	[u:hm
17	Kevin	Yeah maybe that's what it is yeah °that was good° xxx ((turns to Gina))
18	Gina	Xxx
19		(2.0)
20	Peter	E:: I think you have to decide what's meant by participation [here and think if one
21	Gina	[Yes
22	Peter	is thinking of using an interactional perspective on participation then I don't think it
23		<u>fits</u> with respect to the data <u>material</u> that you <u>have</u> here rather I think that you
24		should talk about 'common ground' [or 'joint focus of attention' (.) something [like
25	Liam	[Um:h [Um:h
26	Peter	that instead of seeing how one establishes and sustains the conversation

When we enter the episode, the co-participating researcher Sander takes the floor and starts by telling the data session group how he understands the previously discussed transcript (line 1). Thus, he indicates that what they are looking at now is something slightly different. Gina and Kevin agree with this interpretation (lines 3–4). Sander then turns to the present transcript, also from a social service encounter, and claims that what the data session group sees here is a 'huge po:wer a:::symmetry' (lines 5–6). By emphasising 'huge' and prolonging the 'o' in power and the 'a' in asymmetry, he underlines the episode as something spectacular. In fact, he claims that the client in the excerpt is in what emerges as, at least symbolically, 'a li:fe threatening situation' (line 6). Liam supports this initial description of what happens in the transcript (line 7). Then Sander claims that Gina's categorisation of the counsellor as clearly professional, a discussion that took place earlier, was correct. He thus aligns with Gina's understanding of the counsellor's behaviour while also signalling to the other participants that several of them share this interpretation (line 8). This statement is followed by an account where Sander argues that the counsellor appearing in the transcription makes room for participation.

Liam, Gina and also Kevin, one of the presenting researchers, show that they agree with this interpretation (lines 15–17).

However, the co-participating researcher Peter takes a critical stance to this line of reasoning (line 20). In particular, he questions the way that the data session group suddenly seems to use the notion 'participation', indicating that the way it is used now differs from how the same concept was used earlier during the same session (lines 20 and 22). More precisely, Peter suggests that it has to be decided how to understand this notion while at the same time he seems to assume that the ethnomethodological definition is preferred, which, moreover, is in line with the theoretical framework that was claimed by the presenting researchers. When Peter directs the focus to the theoretical framework, he also points out that the suggested analysis in fact breaks with the initially declared theoretical approach. Thus, how to select, understand and stringently use analytical concepts is a key issue related to coherence and thus to the quality of the study.

8.6.3.1 Challenges and contributions

The theoretical framework that researchers choose colours how a phenomenon is to be understood and described (e.g. Silverman, 2011). The practice of co-analysing data necessarily means that distinct and probably also competing interpretations are brought to the table. Sometimes the selected analytical tools are confirmed as suitable, at other times alternative ways of thinking that may improve the conditions for making adequate decisions about analytical concepts will be provided. As such, the analytical work may be extended as well as enriched, thus recognising the implications of theoretical and methodological choices. Excerpt 3 illustrates how the use of an analytical tool is problematised. Finding and using relevant analytical tools is a challenge that is often placed on the agenda in data sessions, mainly because in this context it suddenly becomes clear whether or not the analytical concepts in fact work. This generates various scenarios, for instance, either one has to explain and use the analytical concepts more precisely and convincingly, or one has to find other analytical concepts. No matter what way the presenting researcher(s) then chooses to proceed, the discussion in the data session contributes to moving the research work one step forward.

RESEARCHER CHECKLIST

Following the discussion above, we will provide some recommendations aimed at creating and establishing a good research practice with a particular interest in dealing with challenges in analytical work by organising collaborative data

(Continued)

(Continued)

analysis sessions. Data sessions may of course be organised in many different ways, for instance, when it comes to deciding the appropriate number of participants, the session length, session regularity, kinds of data and so on.

Recommendations to the presenting researcher:

- Be well prepared for the data session so you will obtain useful comments, suggestions and critiques from the co-participants:

  o Bring video-/audio-clips and transcripts that you find relevant for the research question(s) in your project. Remember that relevance is not self-evident, but rather something you have to create to convince your audience how your emerging analysis is to be seen within the realm of the research questions.

  o Bring a nuanced and precise representation of the data. This refers to good quality transcripts as well as audio- and/or video-recordings. Remember that the co-participants' contributions depend on what is said and presented at the data session, and this only. The representations of data are thus important in how they condition what may be seen and said at the data session.

  o Bring a preliminary analysis of the data. If you already have an idea of what you 'see' in the data, this will be a helpful starting point for the co-participants. It will reveal what you are aiming for when conducting the analysis, and it will also be easier for others to relate to the particular research questions that your project is addressing.

- Keep an open mind when it comes to alternative approaches, interpretations and suggestions about your data. It may be easy to immediately reject alternative interpretations or quickly turn down other suggestions for how to develop the analysis. Rather try to listen carefully and take some time to critically consider the suggestions as valuable or not to your work, even though you may well take another analytical path.

- Do not rush through the data during the data session, but let the co-participants spend time on each recording and/or transcript. Read and re-read for a while. Getting into unknown social data from a complex research project requires much effort on the part of your co-participants, so make sure that they have enough time to get a grip on your selected data. In the data session discussed in this chapter, the seminar group used two hours to discuss two transcripts.

- Be mindful of research ethics when you prepare the empirical material and work with the data during the data session. Make sure that you follow procedural as well as practical research ethics at all times. Remember to collect and shred transcripts, or other hardcopy data that has been handed out, at the end of each session.

Recommendations to the co-participating researcher:

- Try to approach, understand and make further suggestions about the data from the presenter's theoretical, methodological and analytical point of view. Remember that the project might not mirror your own research interest or methodological preferences, so that providing quite far-fetched suggestions is not very helpful for the presenting researcher(s).

- Try to encourage the creation of a meaningful, reflexive and critical practice. Often it is necessary to pose tricky questions, unravel the taken-for-granted assumptions and work through one's own and other's blind spots, which requires a major effort. Remember to articulate this in a language that is accessible to all involved participants.

- Participate genuinely, and do not assume the role of an eavesdropper. Try your best to contribute to the research project whether you are a novice or a well-experienced researcher. Therefore, get involved in the dialogue so you can provide fruitful comments to the analysis and the emerging discussion to the best of your ability.

- Do not evaluate the presenters or the other participants' contributions during the data session. Rather try to contribute to shaping and establishing an inclusive research practice and dialogue. At this point, there are no wrong answers, and, quite frankly, it is not up to you but rather to the presenting researcher(s) to decide what is valuable or irrelevant in the session.

8.7 CONCLUSION

In this chapter we have situated the research process within the theoretical framework of social interplay, practices and activities to elucidate the interactive work undertaken by the participants (e.g. Goffman, 1974). Furthermore, by using the particular case of collaborative data analysis sessions (Hindmarsh and Tutt, 2012; Tutt and Hindmarsh, 2011) we have highlighted how researchers are involved in the dynamics of what may be called 'science in the making' (e.g. Latour and Woolgar, 1986; Law, 2004). Even though the appearance of collaborative data analysis sessions and similar practices across research groups in the Western world indicates that there is a broad acceptance of the value of such work, only a few scholars have looked into the details of these activities *in situ*. To gain better knowledge, we have used a rather detailed analysis of glimpses from a data session to unpack this setting with a particular interest in the potential value when coping with challenges in analytical work.

By drawing loosely on the idea of critical friendship (Costa and Kallick, 1993; van Manen, 1990) we can see in the three examples how this appears to be a prominent feature of the enactment: critique, questioning and provocation are coupled with mutuality, trustiness and genuineness. To demonstrate the concept in practice in the context of collaborative data analysis sessions, we have in particular highlighted how through these activities the researchers help each other to make sound decisions and develop substantial research cases. Moreover, by assuming the role of the presenting researcher one is expected to respond to difficult questions that are raised by colleagues on, for instance, what it means to select, represent and bring accuracy into the data and analysis. By assuming the role of a co-participating researcher in data sessions, one is expected to carefully, empathically and critically listen, observe and be engaged in a dialogue aimed at supporting other people's research by introducing various skills and multiple perspectives to the process. In these dialogues, some taken-for-granted assumptions may be unravelled, examined and discussed, and probably alternative possibilities that add something new or enrich the analytical work may also emerge.

The empirical examples clearly illustrate how the presenting researchers and the co-participating researchers are equally important for maintaining the practice and also for developing it in and through social interplay. For all researchers participating in such collaborative work, this practice can be educative in itself in terms of it being an available space where novices as well as experts gain access to how analytical challenges may be identified, discussed and sometimes also successfully coped with. It is a great opportunity for us, as researchers, to enrich our own scholarship in terms of sharpening our analytical awareness and skills, letting ourselves be inspired and – not least – to learn from creative and critical colleagues while sharing, wrestling with and questioning each other's analytical practices.

From a slightly different angle, collaborative data analysis sessions may also be seen as an arena where scholars have the opportunity to address, debate and elaborate on prevailing demands on high-quality qualitative research (e.g. Tracy, 2010). Across the three examples it has been illustrated how key issues relating to quality are recurrently discussed. For instance, the dialogue reveals critical and reflexive awareness on such quality concerns as (1) how the research topic was examined through the interplay between the research questions and the data, and how this relationship preferably could be refined to appear in a more convincing way; (2) what kinds of data were collected, and to what extent the data are useful for developing substantial knowledge about the selected phenomenon chosen for study; (3) how the data have been created, the context of the presented transcript and/or video-/audio-recordings, and how this could be represented sufficiently, and; (4) in what way the pieces of data are to be seen as part of an emerging pattern, or if they rather appear as single cases.

Within this realm, what are held to be adequate ways of dealing with data and analysis is a highly prevalent concern, which points to the fact that researchers – in the investigated sessions as well as in general – are part of similar and distinct research communities. Therefore, what may be taken for granted, appearing as implicit, needs to be made explicit, transparent and accessible in and through dialogue if we are to create and establish fruitful and inclusive settings. In and through public display, the quality standards and normative assumptions of how to craft data and analysis are then unravelled, scrutinised and negotiated, probably also guiding and challenging junior as well as senior researchers in their everyday work.

All in all, collaborative data analysis sessions may be considered a site for learning that has the potential of influencing analysis in the making. By introducing elements from critical friendship it should be clear that these settings do not necessarily mean that the participants have to agree, confirm or merely reproduce dominant views. Instead, such data sessions may rather be seen as sites of diversity, contestation and argumentation, which we would claim are key issues in what may be called 'the pedagogies of research'. Data sessions are just one out of several relevant practices that may be initiated and established in social and educational research, thus giving primacy to the commonplace interactions of everyday life among scholars engaged in the production of knowledge. Such sessions are not a standard solution for every problem that the researcher may encounter, nor are they a 'one-size-fits-all' way to deal with analytical work. We would, however, argue that they can be a significant resource and remarkably useful in the delicate work of doing analysis, which essentially is about how to craft substantial and excellent research.

ADDITIONAL USEFUL READING

Collier, D. R., Moffatt, L. and Perry, M. (2015) 'Talking, wrestling, and recycling: an investigation of three analytical approaches to qualitative data in education research', *Qualitative Research, 15* (3): 389–404.

This article draws on the idea of collaborating on analysis among critical friends. It illustrates how researchers may use diverse methodologies to work on the same data, which reveals different analytical foci and understandings. Some important details of theoretical and methodological implications are highlighted. The text reminds the reader of the value of cross-paradigm conversations to promote reflexivity and enrich scholarship.

Derry, S. J., Pea, R. D., Barron, B., Engle, R. A., Erickson, F., Goldman, R., Hall, R., Koschmann, T., Lemke, J. L., Sherin, M. G. and Sherin, B. L. (2010) 'Conducting video research in the learning sciences: guidance on selection, analysis, technology, and ethics', *Journal of the Learning Sciences, 19* (1): 3–53.

This text focuses on four challenges that social researchers, regardless of theoretical and methodological backgrounds, face when collecting and using video-recordings to conduct research in learning environments. It discusses and suggests how to handle 'selection in video research', 'analysis of data from video-recordings', 'technology for video research' and 'ethical concerns in video data collection'. The text gives the reader valuable tools for reflecting on the use of video-recordings and how to improve quality in research.

Gibbs, P. and Angelides, P. (2008) 'Understanding friendship between critical friends', *Improving Schools, 11* (3): 213–225.

This article explores the concept 'critical friend' and in particular discusses the meaning of friendship within such relationships. It highlights distinct roles, skills and qualities of critical friendships, and also clarifies the notion 'friend' compared to 'companion' or 'acquaintance'. The text gives the reader a problematisation of contemporary ideas on how collaboration and networking may contribute to improvement, which may be valuable for researchers assuming various roles inside and outside of academia.

Hindmarsh, J. and Tutt, D. (2012) 'Video in analytic practice', in S. Pink (ed.), *Advances in Visual Methodology*. London: Sage. pp. 57–73.

This text highlights data sessions as a common practice in the social sciences, where researchers collaboratively share, view and analyse recorded social activities. By unpacking data sessions, it describes how analysis is accomplished as practical research work. The text gives the reader valuable insights into how collaboration on data may open up rather than shut down analytical possibilities. It also illustrates how challenges the researcher may face, as well as concerns for research quality, are negotiated in and through social interaction.

Law, J. and Urry, J. (2004) 'Enacting the social', *Economy and Society, 33* (3): 390–410.

The text draws attention to knowledge production as social, interactive and cultural practice, and in particular highlights the power of social science and its research methods. It discusses how social research methods are never innocent, but rather political, by contributing to the production of social realities and worlds. This excellent text relates to a wider debate on research, encouraging the reader to mindfully reflect on what social research is and what it does.

Tracy, S. J. (2010) 'Qualitative quality: eight "big-tent" criteria for excellent qualitative research', *Qualitative Inquiry, 16*: 837–851.

This article is a valuable contribution to the debate on quality in the qualitative research genre. It presents a model consisting of eight key markers of quality in qualitative research. The text gives the reader a useful pedagogical compass, and also demonstrates how excellent research is not a simple or straightforward process. Accordingly, it promotes dialogue, debate and reflexivity among qualitative scholars.

NOTE

1   The authors, presented alphabetically, are co-equally responsible for the text.

REFERENCES

Antaki, C., Billig, M. G., Edwards, D. and Potter, J. A. (2003) 'Discourse analysis means doing analysis: a critique of six analytical shortcomings', *Discourse Analysis Online*, 1.

Bryman, A. (2001) *Social Research Methods*. Oxford: Oxford University Press.

Coffey, A. and Atkinson, P. (1996) *Making Sense of Qualitative Data: Complementary Research Strategies*. Thousand Oaks, CA: Sage.

Collier, D. R., Moffatt, L. and Perry, M. (2015) 'Talking, wrestling, and recycling: an investigation of three analytical approaches to qualitative data in education research', *Qualitative Research*, *15*(3): 389–404.

Costa, A. and Kallick, B. (1993) 'Through the lens of a critical friend', *Educational Leadership*, *51*(2): 49–51.

Derry, S. J., Pea, R. D., Barron, B., Engle, R. A., Erickson, F., Goldman, R., Hall, R., Koschmann, T., Lemke, J. L., Sherin, M. G. and Sherin, B. L. (2010) 'Conducting video research in the learning sciences: guidance on selection, analysis, technology, and ethics', *Journal of the Learning Sciences*, *19*(1): 3–53.

Finlay, L. (2012) 'Five lenses for the reflexive interviewer', in J.F. Gubrium, J.A. Holstein, A.B. Marvasti and K. McKinney (eds), *The SAGE Handbook of Interview Research: The Complexity of the Craft* (2nd edn). Thousand Oaks, CA: Sage. pp. 317–331.

Goffman, E. (1974) *Frame Analysis: An Essay on the Organization of Experience* (new edn). New York: Harper & Row.

Goodwin, C. (2013) 'The co-operative, transformative organization of human action and knowledge', *Journal of Pragmatics*, *46*: 8–23.

Heath, C., Hindmarsh, J. and Luff, P. (2010) *Video in Qualitative Research: Analysing Social Interaction in Everyday Life*. Thousand Oaks, CA: Sage.

Hindmarsh, J. and Tutt, D. (2012) 'Video in analytic practice', in S. Pink (ed.), *Advances in Visual Methodology*. London: Sage. pp. 57–73.

Jefferson, G. (2004) 'Glossary of transcript symbols with an introduction', in G. Lerner (ed.), *Conversation Analysis. Studies from the First Generation*. Amsterdam, PA: John Benjamins Publishing. pp. 13–31.

Jordan, B. and Henderson, A. (1995) 'Interaction analysis: foundations and practice', *Journal of the Learning Sciences*, *4*(1): 39–103.

Kvale, S. and Brinkmann, S. (2009) *Interviews: Learning the Craft of Qualitative Interviewing*. Thousand Oaks, CA: Sage.

Larsson, S. (2004) 'The joy and despair of writing', *Nordic Studies in Education*, *24*(2): 97–112.

Latour, B. and Woolgar, S. (1986) *Laboratory Life: The Construction of Scientific Facts* (2nd edn). Princeton, NJ: Princeton University Press.

Law, J. (2004) *After Method: Mess in Social Science Research*. London: Routledge.

Marshall, C. and Rossman, G.B. (1999) *Designing Qualitative Research* (3rd edn). London: Sage.

Naidoo, R. (2016) 'The competition fetish in higher education: varieties, animators and consequences', *British Journal of Sociology of Education*, *37*(1): 1–10.

Ochs, E. (1999 [1979]) 'Transcription as theory', in A. Jaworski and N. Coupland (eds), *The Discourse Reader*. London and New York: Routledge. pp. 167–182.

Olssen, M. (2016) 'Neoliberal competition in higher education today: research, accountability and impact', *British Journal of Sociology of Education*, *37*(1): 129–148.

Potter, J. (2012) 'Discourse analysis and discursive psychology', in H. Cooper (Editor–in–Chief), *APA Handbook of Research Methods in Psychology (vol. 2). Quantitative, Qualitative, Neuropsychological, and Biological.* Washington, DC: American Psychological Association Press. pp. 111–130.

Rapley, T. (2011) 'Some pragmatics of qualitative data analysis', in D. Silverman (ed.), *Qualitative Research* (3rd edn). London: Sage. pp. 273–290.

Roulston, K. (2010) 'Considering quality in qualitative interviewing', *Qualitative Research*, *10*(2): 199–228.

Sarangi, S. (2017) 'Editorial: En'gaze'ment with text and talk', *Text & Talk, 37*(1):1–23.

Sidnell, J. (2014) 'Basic conversation analytical methods', in J. Sidnell and T. Stivers (eds), *The Handbook of Conversation Analysis.* Chichester: Blackwell Publishing. pp. 77–99.

Silverman, D. (2011) *Interpreting Qualitative Data* (4th edn). London: Sage.

Tracy, S. J. (2010) 'Qualitative quality: eight 'big-tent' criteria for excellent qualitative research', *Qualitative Inquiry, 16*: 837–851.

Tutt, D. and Hindmarsh, J. (2011) 'Reenactments at work: demonstrating conduct in data sessions', *Research on Language and Social Interaction, 44*(3): 211–236.

van Manen, M. (1990) *Researching Lived Experience: Human Science for an Action Sensitive Pedagogy.* London and Ontario: The Althouse Press.

APPENDIX: TRANSCRIPT CONVENTIONS

Symbol	Meaning
?	Inquiring intonation
=	Contiguous utterances
:	Prolongation of preceding vowel
[…]	Lines left out
(2.0)	Pause 2 seconds
(.)	Pause shorter than 0.2 second
Xxx	Something was said but the transcriber could not discern its content
Wo[rd [Word	The brackets indicate the onset of overlapping speech
Word	Underlined means stressed word (or part of it)
WORD	Loud speech
°Word° ((laughing))	The degree signs indicate that the talk between them was quieter than the surrounding talk
>Word<	Comments made by the researcher
Hehe	Embeds faster speech than surrounding speech
	Laughter

PART IV

BUILDING A COMMON GROUND FOR UNDERSTANDING

9

DISCUSSING SOCIOLOGICAL GAPS AND POWER RELATIONS IN AN INTERNATIONAL SETTING

Sarah Désirée Lange

9.1 INTRODUCTION

How can quality criteria for scientific work be met under the terms of the specific challenges of glocal asymmetries and transformations in the course of globalisation processes? This question arises when observing the rising internationalisation of the research landscape in educational science. For transnational and international research projects there are specific challenges which influence the research process. The aim of this contribution is to discuss sociological gaps and power relations as two methodological challenges that researchers may encounter, when conducting research in an international context.

The socialisation in the research field context is not a condition for research, yet if not present, it requires even more reflective handling of this 'socialisation gap'. In addition, power relations can be challenging for research in international education. Their omnipresent impact can only be damned if they are reflected, revealed and enter the consciousness of the researcher. What kind of reflection efforts? 'Reflecting competence' can be described as a necessary core competence for research in international education and serves for this contribution as 'red thread'. With reflection we refer to Dewey's 'reflective thinking' (Dewey, 1933). According to Rodgers (2002) the following four criteria characterise Dewey's concept of reflective thinking: (1) reflection as a meaning-making process, (2) reflection as a rigorous way of thinking, (3) reflection in community, and 4) reflection as a set of attitudes.

The discussion in the main part of this contribution focuses on answering how challenges in research in international education may be handled. The discussion is based on the research-methodical discourse on the classical quality criteria, which Lienert and Raatz (1998) differentiate into primary and secondary quality criteria. Primary criteria are objectivity, reliability and validity and secondary quality criteria are economic efficiency, usefulness, standardisation and comparability. To quantify analysis features with data collection instruments such as a questionnaire, the comparability of data needs to be ensured. The basic idea is the assumption that higher standardisation of research content, research process and research situation lead to higher compliance with quality criteria.

Why can the compliance with quality criteria for research be a specific challenge for educational research in an international setting? For example, to meet the criterion of objectivity, the conducting, analysis as well as interpretation need to be independent from the test coordinator. One could think of the independency from the cultural context of the test coordinator in a questionnaire survey. Related to possible situations in research in international education, this means, for example, ensuring that the results of a questionnaire survey are independent from the cultural context of the test coordinator.

One of the main messages of this contribution is to argue that there exists no objective or 'correct' research approach. However, it can be the aim of researchers to reflect options for action, from which consciously an adequate action strategy is derived. Criteria for such a decision can be (1) a certain research question, (2) the specific situation of a certain research project and (3) a certain research team. It is hoped that this contribution can provide a basis for intensive methodological reflections. The chapter is based on a quantitative study on teaching quality in sub-Saharan Africa. This exemplary research project was conducted in a development cooperation country; the context of the study is schools in the Northwest and Southwest regions in Cameroon. The chapter discusses two methodological challenges and possible solution strategies and reasons for using them in the research process. The discussed challenges were selected according to two main criteria. On the one hand, challenges were selected which are dominantly described in the discourse on research methods for international educational research. On the other hand, challenges were chosen from the authors' research experience. The following Section 9.2 will give insight into the design, methodological approach and the empirical results of the case study. This lays the groundwork for Section 9.3, in which the two focused challenges – power relations and socialisation gaps – will be discussed. After the research checklist encompassing reflective questions in

Section 9.4, Section 9.5 will summarise the main points and discuss in what way the portrayed challenges are specific for the African context or generalisable towards an international context.

9.2 THE CASE STUDY: A QUANTITATIVE STUDY ON TEACHING QUALITY IN SUB-SAHARAN AFRICA

The case study is a quantitative study on the effectiveness of cascade training implemented in professional development in Cameroon (detailed in Lange, 2016). This completed PhD research was financially supported by the Elite Network Bavaria and conducted from 2010 to 2015 in the Northwest and Southwest regions of Cameroon. This study draws on data collected in the context of a scientific evaluation survey commissioned by the Protestant Development Service (Bread for the World) and conducted by a researcher team from the Institute of Education at the University of Erlangen-Nuremberg (later University of Bamberg). First, the research context and second, the research process is described. This chapter aims to set the frame for the discussion of the methodological challenges and of possible strategies in dealing with these challenges.

9.2.1 RESEARCH CONTEXT

In the discussion on educational quality, teachers play a central role and the qualification level of teachers is seen as closely related to teaching quality. The general question that underlies the study is the global challenge of effective and qualitative teacher training (Lange, 2014). In the international discourse it is widely acknowledged that continuing professional development programmes are a relevant determining factor for teaching quality (Tatto, 2006). This leads to the question: what training model is effective for professional development of teachers? For development cooperation countries, the low baseline of teaching quality and limited financial and personal resources reinforce the need for cost-effective professional development strategies. A frequently implemented professional development model for on-the-job training of teachers is cascade training. The core idea of this training model is that selected individuals participate in further training with the objective that these act as multipliers to pass on their newly acquired knowledge in school-based training to a larger group of individuals (Hayes, 2000). Due to its 'snowball system', cascade training is expected to be an effective means to train many teachers within a short period. Yet, a general critique is that cascade training may lead to a dilution of the training content (McDevitt, 1998). Despite its frequent and widespread implementation, the question of the effectiveness of cascade training is a research desideratum.

The specific context of this study are countries in sub-Saharan Africa, which are often characterised by limited personal and financial resources in teacher training. The context of countries in sub-Saharan Africa is used as a reference group, but it is acknowledged that the African countries in Southern Africa are diverse and heterogeneous. Due to a high lack of teachers in Cameroon, often teachers are recruited who only have academic qualifications in their subjects, but no teaching certification. Tambo (1995: 61–62) called this the 'non-formal model' of teacher training, as these teachers are expected to qualify for teaching on-the-job. This lack of qualified teaching staff underlines the relevance of professional development activities.

The Republic of Cameroon, often referred to as 'Africa in miniature', is a dominant-party presidential state, which is ruled by the authoritarian ruler Paul Biya and his party, the Cameroon People's Democratic Movement (CPDM) since 1982. Biya succeeded his incumbency throughout various election periods until today – also by means of constitutional changes to enable his re-election (DeLancey and Mokeba, 1990). Corruption is also a major problem in Cameroon.

Anchimbe (2012: 3) states that there are over 270 indigenous languages spoken in Cameroon – in addition to the two official languages of French and English. This number shows that Cameroon is a multi-lingual country – a situation which takes extra consideration for research. The multi-lingual background is an integral characteristic describing the plurality of the Cameroonian students and teachers. Besides the autochthonous languages, the linguistic heritage of the former colonial powers is associated with various problems (Webb, 1994). Furthermore, there is the specific situation in Cameroon that there exist two former colonial languages (English and French), which are both official languages. The presented study was conducted in the Anglophone part of the country, which takes on an underdog position versus the political strength and the geographical span of the dominant Francophone part of the country (Konings and Nyamnjoh, 1997). The differentiation into an Anglophone and a Francophone part of the country reflects the deep division of the society in Cameron, which since October 2016 has led to bloody clashes and even closed schools in Anglophone Cameroon.[1] Beginning as an Anglophone demand for more say in the government of President Paul Biya, that movement evolved at the end of 2016 into strikes, demonstrations and an uprising. The English speakers claim to be discriminated by government policies – especially in the education and judicial systems.[2] The English speakers in Cameroon make up about 20 per cent of the population of 24 million.[3] A number of Anglophone activists are calling for secession and the creation of a new country, which they want to call Ambazonia. The confrontations led to heavily militarised areas and killings on both sides. The so-called 'Anglophone crisis' appears to be not only about language, but about economic imbalances, marginalisation and exclusion from top civil service jobs. According to the UN, the fighting has forced an estimated 40,000 Cameroonians to flee to Nigeria[4] – in addition to the hundreds of thousands of internally displaced persons.[5]

9.2.2 RESEARCH PROCESS

The following section provides details on the research question, the design, the pilot testing, the data collection and the results of the research project on teaching quality in Cameroon.

9.2.2.1 Research questions

The study focuses on the empirical analysis of the effects of a professional development programme, which is implemented in Anglophone Cameroon as cascade training. Thus, the study aims to answer the following research questions: what effects of the cascade training can be estimated (1) on the self-reported teaching practice of the teachers, (2) on the actual teaching practice of the teachers and (3) on the students' achievement?

9.2.2.2 Design

The process-product paradigm further developed by Helmke (2012) as an offer-use model is used as the theoretical foundation for the research design and the development of the data collection instruments. Lipowsky (2010) adapted the offer-use model for the effectiveness of professional development of teachers. This model depicts how complex and sensitive to failure effective professional development is. It comprises factors that are related to the training, the context and the teachers. According to the model, data were collected on the background variables of the students, the teachers and the schools to control for the comparability of the programme and control group and to handle possible confounding variables. The study was conceptualised as a quasi-experimental control group design. The intervention programme is ongoing since 1997; therefore, a pre-post design was not possible. Yet, the method combinations used in the survey allowed more differentiated empirical access to the research object.

9.2.2.3 Pilot testing

For the questionnaire survey of this study, predominantly internationally tested scales were chosen, which have been tested in different cultures (although not in the context of the study at hand, in Cameroon). Much effort has been put into the multiple revisions of scales, in which the local cooperation partners in Cameroon played a crucial supervisory part. The local experts in Cameroon were involved intensively in the preparation of the data collection instruments for the selection of the scales, for the comprehensive choice of formulations and for the choice of individual words or fixed terms. In a few cases, scales or items were translated from German into English. The translation was double-checked according to the common back translation procedure (Cha, Kim and Erlen, 2007). In addition, to use the pilot phase most effectively, interactive phases were integrated, in which the research subjects could voice themselves in regards to the comprehensibility of the instruments. In the presented study, people who had filled out the questionnaire in the pilot study were interviewed on a voluntary basis about the comprehensibility and the usage of terms in the questionnaire. In addition, the participants were encouraged to give written comments to the questions and the wordings used in the questionnaires.

9.2.2.4 Data collection

The study is conceptualised as a control group design. Data were collected in 13 schools in Anglophone Cameroon. Profound knowledge of the school context is needed for the selection of suitable control schools, so that the control schools and the programme schools resemble each other. Thus, a local expert did the selection in accordance with the following requirements: school performance, location of the schools (city or rural area), composition of the student bodies (from economically dis-/advantaged homes) and school size. In addition, the entire research process was accompanied by numerous expert workshops and expert interviews and the collection of school context data was based on a school principal questionnaire. The research was conducted with instruments in English. The test instrumentation consisted of a questionnaire survey (a teacher questionnaire, a student questionnaire and a principal questionnaire), a video study and a student achievement test.

The sample comprised $N = 292$ secondary teachers, $N = 15$ video-taped lessons and $N = 1.095$ students. The data collection of the video study included 15 lessons of multipliers and trained teachers in programme schools as well as lessons from teachers in control schools. The lessons were analysed by a high-inferent rating from two independent raters. The rating system was developed based on the criteria of teaching quality by Helmke (2012). The aim of the video survey was to gain insight into everyday classroom practice, so the lessons to be video-taped were selected randomly within each sample school. The students' academic achievement was measured by means of a competence-based standardised test that consists of a reduced number of items taken from the item pool of the Third International Mathematics and Science Study (TIMSS) in natural sciences (Martin et al., 2000). Due to this reduction, the question of the construct validity was important, in particular for the students' achievement test. The item difficulty of the used TIMSS test was correlated with the original tests and an extremely high correlation (.99) emerged. This suggests that the shortened test assesses the same context as the original test, namely, the student competencies in natural science.

9.2.2.5 Results

The results suggest that the analysed intervention has an impact on the teachers' self-reported and actual teaching practice and that there is a mediated effect of the trained teachers on their students' achievement.

Effects of the cascade training on the self-reported teaching practice of the teachers

The minor differences between the multipliers and the trained teachers in the programme schools showed that the quality of the training has not become diluted and thus has not lost its effect on the lower ends. In the comparison of multipliers in programme schools and teachers trained by the multipliers, there is a difference in favour of the multipliers in programme schools. The results also pointed out the difference between trained teachers that remained in programme schools and trained teachers that migrated to other schools. From research on the professional development of schools, it is known that it is essential for the success of school development that the whole school participates in the training – including the school management and all staff members. The investigated sample showed that trained teachers in control schools did not report of any significant effects of the in-service activities on their classroom practice. This result underlines that change in school development processes depends not on individuals alone, but on the school culture and thus on all staff members.

Effects of the cascade training on the actual teaching practice of the teachers

The results of the high-inferent ratings of videotaped lessons from teachers in programme and in control schools offered insight into the actual teaching practice of the teachers. The analyses showed that there are significant differences between the three teacher groups (trained multipliers from programme schools, trained teachers from programme schools, untrained teachers from control schools). Teachers from programme schools show in their teaching practice a significantly higher degree of professionalism than untrained teachers in control schools. This indicates the effectiveness of the professional development programme. In terms of the effects of the cascade training, there are only slight and not significant differences between the group of trained multipliers and trained teachers in programme schools. This means that the professional development programme does not have a higher effect on teachers that were trained intensely as multipliers than on teachers trained in the school-based trainings. Both cascade tiers show elements of teaching quality in their classroom practice. These results underline the outcomes of the self-reported data from the questionnaire survey.

Effects of the cascade training on the students' achievement

The results suggest that the cascade training has an effect on the students' achievement. The results showed that if students had a trained teacher in natural sciences, this has a positive effect on their achievement. Also, in the student achievement data, no significant difference between the group of multipliers and the group of trained teachers was found. This supports the assumption that the cascade training implemented in the professional development programme analysed in the study at hand was effective.

9.3 MAIN CHALLENGES AND HOW THEY CAN BE ADDRESSED

Based on the described methodological approach and research process of the presented case study, methodological challenges for research in international education are discussed. The focus will be on the challenges relating to the sociological gap and to power relations in research. These methodological challenges are, in both cases, (1) first described and located within the international research discourse, and (2) possible strategies for reflecting and dealing with the challenge are presented.

9.3.1 SOCIOLOGICAL GAPS IN RESEARCH

9.3.1.1 Social positioning within the educational research discourse

The first challenge to discuss in more detail for research in international education is the question of the social positioning of the researcher. In social science, there is the structural necessity that researchers move within a social framework and thus need to position themselves towards the research object and the research context. In the context of research in development corporation countries, the specific challenge is that the 'sociological gap' can be rather large. With the term 'sociological gap' I refer to disparate spaces of experiences which may be described with a gap – between context known and familiar to a researcher through primary and secondary socialisation experiences and an unknown and unfamiliar research context. This 'gap' is likely to apply especially to young scholars from the 'global north' conducting their PhD research in 'the global south'.

The challenges can be described theoretically with insider-outsider questions, located at different levels. Thereby, 'insider' means the ascription of experiential spaces, which are acquired, for example, through socialisation. The tension in relation between insider-outsider borders is an inherent topic for social science research. However, the urgency of these questions arises in relation to the differences of the site-dependency between researcher and 'researched' (cf. Irvine, Roberts and Bradbury-Jones, 2008). On the one hand, insider-outsider questions determine methodological decisions taken during the conception phase – such as the choice of the research problem and of the research design – and, on the other hand, they determine methodical decisions taken during the data collection phase. In the current discourse the ascription as 'insider' or 'outsider' is no more understood to be dichotomous, but relational (Kelly, 2016).

It is assumed in the discourse that the 'insider-outsider challenge' can be reflected in the methodological groundwork of a study (Milligan, 2016). This reflection refers, for example, to the self-reflective analysis of the researcher's own socialisation and relation to the research project. This can be seen as a condition to recognise the researcher's own blind spots, which can be explained by not belonging to certain minority or majority groups in society. In such reflection processes, affiliations can reveal themselves as advantages or as disadvantages – according to research context and research situation. Thus, an 'insider' may have the advantage of specific context knowledge and knowledge gained from experience concerning a specific cultural context; however, this advantage may diminish the more objective perspective of the outsider. An unambiguously positive or negative connotation for the role allocation of an 'insider' or an 'outsider' seems inadequate; on the one hand, from a sociological perspective, all individuals belong to several and different groups and, on the other hand, these ascriptions (as insiders and outsiders) can be described as contingent identity constructions (Kelly, 2016: 59).

The 'insider-outsider model' is a dynamic model that describes the positions of power depending on the context of the power positions. The critical self-reflection of the social positioning seems important for the research processes – in particular, in demarcation to categorisations and essentialisations of individuals concerning their role as insider or outsider (Robinson-Pant, 2016).

9.3.1.2 Reflecting sociological gaps in the research process

The following questions aim to guide possible ways to reflect sociological gaps in the research process. How can I supplement my limited perspective on the object of research within the research process? How can I show my awareness for ethical research guidelines in dealing with research subjects who are unfamiliar with the notion of research?

Multiple perspectives

Research is a knowledge process, which is always limited to the subjective perspective of the researcher. This limitation is even more apparent in the complex contexts of dependencies and relationships influencing research in the 'global south'. How can this challenge be dealt with? It appears advantageous to establish structural exchange between multiple perspectives within the research team. Such structures can support the exchange about the process of knowledge development – also reflecting consciously the social positioning of the researcher. On the one hand, the possibility is discussed to compensate for possible 'blind spots' from individuals by forming an international and/or interdisciplinary research team. 'Such collaborations make it possible to investigate phenomena across national and cultural boundaries, addressing issues of conceptual and linguistic significance from both the insider and the outside and, in so doing, seek to enhance contextual relevance' (McNess, Arthur and Crossely, 2016: 22). It is hoped that people with different perspectives and knowledge gained from experience can enrich the analysis process. Another strategy to reflectively organise the epistemological process is to incorporate local experts into the research process (Liamputtong, 2008: 6). For example, during the communicative or the proce-dural validation of interpretations, this can lead to an exchange of multiple perspectives as well as to the contextualisation of individual steps. Robinson-Pant (2016: 45) encourages the use of questions on insider-outsider positions in the analysis process, to gain culture-related knowledge about the research object by means of a dialectic analysis process; thereby, she stresses that the focus should be on the dialectic process and not on the emphasis of fictional insider and outsider extreme poles. In the study in Cameroon, this challenge was dealt with by close cooperation with local experts. In addition, the insider knowledge was of particular importance for how data were collected during the whole research process; for example, data were collected by means of workshops and interviews and, in addition to questionnaires, context data were also analysed. The focus was on the main stakeholders of the analysed interven-tion (the multipliers and the advisor team of the intervention), to fulfil the objectivity of application in the research process.

Research ethics

Research processes imply constant decisions – for example, concerning the choice of the research question or the choice of the methodical design. Each of these markings has social practices as a result, which influence the way in which researchers and researched are related to each other. Social science research also depends on the relationship level. Whether a basis of trust is established is mainly influenced by the communication and the degree of openness in the communication process – and also the expectations towards the conducted research. Respectful and responsible dealings with each other implies an orientation towards research ethical guidelines.

In some countries, ethical guidelines are formalised and controlled through University Research Ethics Committees (e.g. in Australia) (Gillam, 2013), in other countries the researchers themselves have the major responsibility for adhering to ethical guidelines (DGS and BDS, 1992). On the basis of the ethical codex of the German Society for Sociology (DGS) and the Professional Organisation of German Sociologists (BDS), Unger (2014: 88–89) formulated the following as research ethical principles: the striving towards scientific integrity and objectivity, the voluntariness of the participation in research, the principle of informed consent, the principle of non-damage and with it the guarantee of confidentiality and anonymity. In reference to the ethical code of the Nationwide Health and Medical Research Council, Drake (2014: 308) stresses 'anonymity, privacy and confidentiality, voluntary participation, informed consent, duty of care, and storage and security of information'.

What may challenge the research process conducted in an international context? Especially for research in international education conducted in development coopera-tion countries, adequately informing research participants and ensuring that they fully understand the process and the functions of research as well as the distribution of research results are two challenging aspects in regards to research ethical guidelines.

In the data collection, particular measures need to be undertaken if the 'researched' are a group of persons from whom one can assume a basic understanding of research, research aims, the function of data collection instruments as well as the way in which collected data continues to be used (Shamim and Qureshi, 2013). Prerequisites for research in the context of development cooperation countries is therefore ensuring the greatest possible transparency and thoroughly informing participants about the processes of a research project and the relevance and further usage of empirical data (Lange, 2015). In the Cameroon study, this responsibility was met by establishing contact, for example, with the school principals through the local partners well ahead of time and by scheduling appropriate times and phases for clarifications during the data collection. Specific for research in development cooperation countries are also questions on how research results can be used for capacity development of regional or national research structures. The research results of the study in Cameroon were used to conduct specific workshops for target groups, such as with the principals from the sample schools or with local education policy stakeholders.

9.3.2 POWER RELATIONS IN RESEARCH

9.3.2.1 Power relations within the educational research discourse

The second challenge to discuss is power relations in educational research. Educational processes and teaching-learning settings are in a complex way embedded on multi-levelled asymmetrical tension. Concerning the role of researchers a 'double asymmetry' (as active and passive partner) can be described. On the one hand, researchers, who want to analyse these educational processes, inevitably move into these complicated webs of relationships. On the other hand, researchers are also active creators of these asymmetries. For example, on a passive note a researcher is confronted with expectations, for example in regard to possible research outcomes, and on an active note a researcher is the project organiser responsible for deciding, for example, who collects the data and how the test leaders are trained. The challenge is that these power-theoretical relations are usually not disclosed. Hence, the question arises in which situations and how these power-theoretical relations can be reflected in the research process – especially concerning the positioning of the researcher *in relation* to contextual asymmetries. It is assumed that the accumulation of these diverse asymmetries leads to increased complexity of a research situation. This complexity should be reflected in the conceptualisation and realisation of a study in international education – even more so if carried out in a development cooperation country. The challenge with power relations and ruling relations in the research process is theoretically located in the discourse on post- and neo-colonial theory. A starting point for post-colonial studies is the awareness that the effects of colonialism (1) are sustainable, (2) that they impact the 'global north' to the same extent as the 'global south' and (3) that they constitute themselves in all areas of society. Currently the focus of post-colonial perspectives is directed on a critical discussion of globalisation theories. Representatives of post-colonial theory want to point to the global dimension of the colonial past and colonial power to avoid a historiography reduced to European parameters (Hall, 1992).

In the international discourse on international and comparative education, post-colonial theory approaches are only strongly present in the last few years (Tikly and Bind, 2013). Questions on the relationship between different world regions and comparisons and analyses of different world regions are themes that occupy the discipline of international and comparative educational research inherently. Takayama, Sriprakash and Connell (2017) make the case for a long overdue discussion on the question: on which knowledge base does the discipline of international and comparative education rely? The authors criticise that the disciplinary knowledge is produced based only on traditions and methods from English-speaking countries; they favour making non-European approaches for international and comparative education also visible. Raewyn Connell (2011) uses in this respect the term 'Southern Theory' and describes it as a body of thought from the global south. She refers to many major thinkers from sub-Saharan Africa, Latin America, Iran, India, Australia, and criticises the stock of 'classical' theory as well as globalisation theory, which are based exclusively on a 'global north' perspective.

To break down the Eurocentric worldview, which is dominating the international and comparative education discourse, a few authors try to integrate knowledge systems of local and indigenous minorities into the mainstream discourse. Assié-Lumumba (2016: 1) sees for example in the 'Ubuntu' worldview potential to renew international and comparative education – also in regards to epistemological challenges: 'The Ubuntu paradigm is articulated as an alternative framework for defining relations within and across the borders of local and global spaces, as a permanent corrective measure that can offer possibilities of growth and renewal to the field of comparative and international education'.

Beside questions regarding the knowledge base and worldview that underpin international education, power relations and dependencies in the research field can be even more evident. International educational research runs the risk of being politically instrumentalised. Nóvoa and Yariv-Mashal (2003) describe, for example, the danger that international and comparative research degenerates to a 'mode of governance'. These questions were and are also discussed in regards to the political usage of results from international large-scale assessments or rather how these results are directly or indirectly translated into educational policy measures (Meyer and Benavot, 2013). The aim of research is to produce new knowledge. In particular, if international research is carried out in development cooperation countries, neo-colonial power relations also become evident in the dependency of local organisations or projects on development cooperation money. Often their existence or continued project funding depends on the outcome of project evaluations. If researchers work in the highly politicised field of development cooperation, such instrumentalisation can only be counteracted by intensive reflection on the role and the expectations of the different actors towards the conducted research. This involves consciousness of the structural dependence of organisations on money from development cooperation funding. In addition, with respect to the possible political agenda of third-party donors, it is the task of researchers to make sure that research results are not controlled or driven by political players, but instead are guided by the aim of knowledge profit. Research cannot be apolitical, but the question is, who decides how research results are presented?

9.3.2.2 Reflecting power relations in the research process

The following questions aim to guide possible ways to reflect power relations in the research process. Is there non-Western theoretical and empirical knowledge, which I can include to the knowledge base of my research? Do the categories I use to operationalise my research focus mirror my awareness that categories can reiterate social injustice? What methods do I use for my research and what power-related premises underlie those decisions? What effect can language-related decisions within my research have on the research participants and on the outcomes?

Knowledge base

From a power-structural and post-colonial perspective, it seems important for research in international and comparative education to question critically on which knowledge base researchers refer to for the theoretical location, the description of the research state, the interpretation of the results, etc. (Aman, 2017). For decisions in the research process, it is not only about the choice of the knowledge base, but also about the assessment and the hierarchical structuring of knowledge supplies. The German as well as English-speaking discourse in international and comparative education is mainly limited to products of thinkers from the 'global north'. Thus, the yields of non-English-speaking researchers do not – or only marginally – appear in the self-description of the history of the discipline in the main introduction books for international and comparative education (Takayama, Sriprakash and Connell, 2017). This limited access to alternative non-Western schools of thought makes it difficult for researchers to consider a knowledge base from the 'global south' (a pool of authors is presented, for example, in Connell, 2011). Especially for the conceptualisation of a research project, it requires from a post-colonial perspective intensive reflection on whose knowledge is incorporated, according to which criteria the knowledge base is selected and whether there exist possible alternative schools of thought (cf. Assié-Lumumba, 2016: 9).

Categories

For an adequate understanding of power structures and ruling relations, which can be evident in social relations in the research process, social categories also need to be reflected. Especially for the test instrumentation in quantitative research projects, often nationally coded differentiations are then determined and used as fixed categories (cf. Klees, 2017). Diehm, Kuhn and Machold (2010: 79) point out that the research object is also generated by the analysis itself, thus, by the labels used in the research process. Particularly in the use of socially constructed categories of difference, the authors issue a warning against the reification of social constructs. In this context, the criticism of Dale and Robertson (2009) can also be added. They criticise the over-interpretation of the category 'nation', which can become powerful through the ascription of differences due to national affiliation (Bhabha, 2012). Despite this criticism and the appeal for the reflected choice of categories on the one hand, it needs to be acknowledged on the other hand that researchers cannot renounce the use of categories and that this leads to indissoluble tensions.

Use of methods

In regard to the collection process, three aspects are relevant – the selection of the population to be surveyed, the selection of the data collection method and the data analysis method. To avoid a one-sided perspective of research objective, multi-level case studies (Eschenbacher, 2012) or mixed methods designs (Schoonenboom and Johnson, 2017), which are characterised by the combination of accesses with different methods and different data collection instruments, are suitable. In the study of Lange (2016), for example, data were collected using different data collection instruments (questionnaires, achievement test, videography) and the perspective of all involved groups of persons was measured empirically with the aim to receive a full picture of the research object (the analysed multiplier training) (continuing on case studies in international and comparative education: Bartlett and Vavrus, 2017). Looking at the data analysis process, on the one hand the choice of analysis methods can be discussed as well as, on the other hand, the way the results are published. As the empirical results of international and comparative studies can be of interest to a variety of different target groups – groups which differ in interests and concerns – a target group specific presentation of empirical results is necessary. These target group specific communication strategies need to be planned during the conceptualisation of the research (Lange, 2015).

Test language

The question of the language in which data are collected can be an indicator for the distribution of power relations. The chosen language(s) can in itself challenge or support regional power relations. Firstly, researchers need to analyse the local language situation by differentiating autochthone languages of regional tradition and allochthone non-local languages. In many world regions, especially if multi-lingualism is a common everyday life phenomenon, the language situation is rather complex. The choice of language for data collection should be a reflected and reasoned decision to make sure that the sample population is reached and that language is not distorting the results.

The language decision is always dependent on both the research interest and the research context. Thus, for example, in a country like Rwanda, as one of the very few countries in Africa in which virtually the whole population speaks one language (Kinyarwanda), research is best carried out using this language (cf. Krogull, Scheunpflug and Rwambonera, 2014). In a context that is characterised by linguistic diversity, an assessment conducted in various languages would be an option. For example, South Africa conducted a national assessment in 12 different languages (Benavot and Köseleci, 2015: 18). Whether more than one language is used may also be related to the resource question regarding the organisation and translation services. Hennink (2008: 21) warns that 'failure to recognise and acknowledge the role of language and communication issues in cross-cultural research may impact on the rigour and reliability of the research'.

Among the 20 million people who live in Cameroon a high plurality of native languages exists (Kouega, 1999) (cf. Section 9.2.1). As the research focus of the Cameroon study is directed towards the analysis of a school development measure, all data were collected in the language of instruction of the Northwest and Southwest regions in Cameroon – English. Our decision in favour of English mirrored awareness of the local dominant power structures in Cameroon – with Anglophone Cameroon being in a marginalised situation. Both the decision of which language to use in the tests as well as the language usage are relevant. In our study, it occurred that some current concepts in English are not common in the English used in the Cameroonian context. Further, it needs to be considered that if a language is used in research that is not the mother tongue of the interviewees, often the test lengths must be adapted. To deal with language-related challenges the pre-test and several revisions were conducted in close cooperation with the local partners in Cameroon were crucial.

RESEARCHER CHECKLIST

From the preceding discussion of the methodological challenges, reflection questions were derived, which can serve young scholars as reflection aid for their self-reflection of the research phase. These questions can only be a guiding orientation and have to be adapted according to the research interest and design of the individual research project. Discussion of these questions with the supervisor, colleagues or mentors can support the development of a self-reflective attitude towards the researcher's own research project.

(Continued)

(Continued)

REFLECTIVE QUESTIONS FOR THE PREPARATION PHASE

- What do I need to know about the research context to match research interest and sampling strategy?

- Which groups of persons are questioned? Which perspectives on the research object do they include in the research process?

- Do I reflectively deal with my normality concepts and (if appropriate) reflect the social category 'whiteness' in the research process?

- How can I organise exchange on or about the knowledge profit during the research process while also reflecting the social positioning of the researchers?

REFLECTIVE QUESTIONS FOR THE DATA COLLECTION PHASE

- Do I adequately deal with the complexity of the research object by the methods of historicising, contextualising and pluralising?

- Are the selected research methods adequate for the research object and are the research processes and results presented in a clear and understandable way, in particular for those with less research experience?

REFLECTIVE QUESTIONS FOR THE PUBLICATION PHASE

- How can it be ensured that the research process is of benefit for the research subjects?

- How are the empirical results made available to all groups of persons who could gain an increase in knowledge from the empirical results (also the local practice partners)?

9.4 CONCLUSION

The concluding section will highlight two aspects. Firstly, other possible ways of handling the two methodological challenges highlighted in this section will be discussed.

Secondly, a summarising conclusion aims to classify the discussed statements concerning their potential to be generalised.

9.4.1 STRATEGIES TO DEAL CONSTRUCTIVELY WITH THE DISCUSSED CHALLENGES

In what ways can the discussed two challenges – the sociological gap and power relations – be dealt with constructively? The following paragraphs will outline two strategies – one for each challenge – which can be helpful to demonstrate awareness of the discussed challenges. These strategies may be helpful especially for young scholars in the conception phase of their research.

9.4.1.1 Dealing with power relations: intensifying active involvement of the 'researched'

How can existing power relations within the relational structures of a research project be reflected in regards to the role of the 'researched'? One possible answer is to prevent research subjects being pushed into the role of research objects. This danger seems particularly pressing, if research focuses on persons who are specifically in need of protection, due to age, living situation or experience (Knight, Roosa and Umaña-Taylor, 2009). From their research practice with refugee children, Kaukko, Dunwoodie and Riggs (2017) suggest, instead of 'fixed' ethical guidelines, the application of 'relational ethics' to stress flexibility, which is needed to adapt to the changing needs and context conditions of the 'researched'. The approach of participative research practice shows how the 'researched' can be included as active designers in the research process. Thereby, it always focuses on the question: how can it be ensured that the research process (in any possible way) benefits the researched persons? In this respect, Nind (2008: 4) poses the question 'research for, with or on'?

The demand for reflective discussions about invisible norms and perhaps dominant normality images linked with the social category of 'whiteness' in the research process can be seen as an answer to post-colonial criticism. The idea of a decolonising research practice (Smith, 2002), for example community-based or tribal research projects, which are organised and conducted bottom-up, can contribute to the strengthening of researched indigenous population groups (cf. Kovach, 2010). To follow the claim that before the utilisation of the collected data both mutual understanding and deferential contact should dominate the research situation, interview methods are discussed in which the researched assume a high degree of responsibility for knowledge production. As examples for decolonial methods, Vannini and Gladue (2008) mention 'talking circles' or 'reflective dyadic interviewing'.

9.4.1.2 Dealing with sociological gaps: strengthening the development of local research structures

How can sociological gaps as frequent characteristics in an international research project be reflected in the conception phase of a research project? One possible answer is that this challenge can be used as a strategy, meaning that from the outset local experts carry responsibility for the research project. The involvement of local experts within a balanced partnership of equals can on the one hand help to prevent sociological gaps and on the other hand contribute to the capacity development in favour of local research structures. In many development cooperation countries there is a lack of research structures (Adair, 1995). To explicitly aim for local capacity development offers the chance for all phases in the research process to include local researchers (cf. SACMEQ: Murimba, 2005). Within the scope of the PISA for Development project in each participating country, this is tackled by analysing the local capacities, which are still needed and why, and in which time frame these need to be built up as a fixed part of the conceptualisation phase (cf. OECD and World Bank Group, 2014).

This implies of course that on site people are found who, for example, want to be trained as test coordinators and that on site trainings for test coordinators can be carried out. An alternative is that the data collection is completely and independently conducted by local researchers. This could lead, perhaps, to the decrease or to the avoidance of the described challenges (insider-outsider or transmission of power relations). Yet, this requires an already established local research network with trained people or an extensive budget, which allows the expansion of the local institutional capacities in the fore field of a study (Lockheed, 2013).

9.4.2 SUMMARISING CONCLUSION

The research process is essentially characterised by multi-layered contingencies. How can young scholars prepare for unpredictable and unplanned challenges? This chapter has tried to describe challenges, which can appear in studies that are conducted in the context of international education. The challenges in regards to power relations and to sociological gaps – also relating to the research experiences in the case study reported from Cameroon – were described from a methodological perspective with the aim to carve out the underlying theoretical questions.

How specific are the discussed challenges for the non-European research context? Are sociological gaps and power relations challenges that only appear in the African context, in the context of sub-Saharan Africa, in Cameroon or in Anglophone Cameroon? The preceding sequence shows already the onion-like contextualisation, which is necessary to take into consideration the scope of empirical results. For such contemplations the 'cube model' of Bray and Thomas (1995) can be a helpful instrument for analysis to avoid a one-dimensional approach towards a research object. This model illustrates in cube-format different types and levels for comparative and multi-level analysis. Are the described challenges transferable to the European context? *Yes* and *no*. *Yes*: the discussion of the challenges in the core part of this chapter shows that both challenges (power relations und sociological gaps) underlie basic methodological questions, which are always crucial and inevitable for reflection. These questions on power structures and on possible sociological gaps depend on the researcher's epistemological positioning in relation to the research object. *No*: the manner in which the challenges arose in the case study showed a few characteristics of research undertaken by researchers from the 'global north' in the 'global south' – a research situation typical for international education research.

Connected with this is the hope that the described challenges stimulate reflection about research and that the suggested possible strategies can give orientation for the research process. Self-reflectiveness is of crucial relevance in the research process in threefold terms – with an epistemological perspective, with a power-theoretical reflection of asymmetrical relationships as well as with a view to research ethical questions. Yet, the described challenges can also occur completely differently or not at all in the research process in a study in international education. Especially for young scholars it seems to be relevant to reflect not only on practical and methodical research questions, but also on what kind of research they want to conduct and how thereby to comply with research ethical guidelines. The aim can be the shaping of a research-reflective attitude, which orientates at the following fundamental guidelines: concepts of transparency, subjectivity and reflectivity as indicators of methodological rigour and of high-quality research (Lange and Parreira do Amaral, 2018). In the attempt to comply with these criteria, one is confronted with challenges, which are not insurmountable, but which require special attention and sensibility in the form of personal and financial resources. Important methods for the analysis of complex phenomena are historising, contextualising and pluralising (cf. Farah and Steiner-Khamsi, 2014; Hantrais, 1999). For this purpose, through all phases of the research process it is necessary (1) to adopt a critical-reflective attitude towards one's own research interest and research context and towards the role as researcher, (2) to maintain a sensibility for all people participating in the research ('researched' and colleagues), and (3) to take into account the complexity of the social reality with dynamic and multi-dimensional models (e.g. insider-outsider, intersectionality, mechanisms of reproduction).

ADDITIONAL USEFUL READING

Connell, R. (2011) *Southern Theory: The Global Dynamics of Knowledge in Social Science*. Cambridge: Polity Press.

Raewyn Connell's focuses in her analysis on schemes of domination. This monograph provides a critical juxtaposition of theoretical northern and southern accomplishments and thereby gives voice to often disregarded theoretical achievements in mainstream social science. She especially highlights social theorising in the recent past in Africa, Iran, Latin America and India and emphasises the need to learn from, not only about, these texts.

Crossley, M., Arthur, L. and McNess, E. (eds) *Revisiting Insider-Outsider Research in Comparative and International Education*. Oxford: Symposium Books.

With this book, the editors make an overdue contribution to the discussion on methods and methodologies within international and comparative education. The long unquestioned use of the terms 'insider' and 'outsider' is discussed from various viewpoints. As a whole, this edited collection is dominated by representatives of the British discourse on the theme, nevertheless, the necessary critical stance for an appropriate reinvestigation of the topic is the common theme throughout the book.

Dale, R. and Robertson, S. (2009) 'Beyond methodological "isms" in comparative education in an era of globalisation', in R. Cowen and A. M. Kazamias (eds), *International Handbook of Comparative Education*. Dordrecht: Springer Netherlands. pp. 1113–1127.

This chapter is a must-read for scholars doing research in international and comparative education. With their fundamental but simple differentiation into three methodological 'isms' (i.e. nationalism, statism, educationalism), the authors pinpoint methodological problems, which need to be reflected for the design of international and comparative educational research within a globalised world. Recently, the authors added 'spatial fetishism' – referring to the complex attachment of a research object to the spatial sphere – as a fourth methodological 'ism' (Robertson and Dale, 2017).

Lange, S. (2016) *Achieving Teaching Quality in Sub-Saharan Africa: Empirical Results from Cascade Training*. Wiesbaden: Springer.

This publication gives detailed insight into the conception, data collection and data analysis phase of a good-practice example of empirical research conducted in Cameroon. The research is used as reference to outline and illustrate the methodological challenges addressed in this chapter. Conducted in the context of development cooperation countries, the effects of cascade training in professional development in Anglophone Cameroon are analysed with a mixed method design.

Takayama, K., Sriprakash, A. and Connell, R. (2017) 'Toward a postcolonial comparative and international education', *Comparative Education Review, 61* (S1): 1–24.

With this special issue, the authors offer a critical confrontation on how the discipline of international and comparative education until now deals and reflects coloniality. In addition, the issue reveals and thereby problematises how, in the past, knowledge production and also the self-description of the history of the discipline of international and comparative education was often narrowed to Eurocentric and Western perspectives. The authors claim the need for stronger non-European theoretical and methodological approaches.

NOTES

1   www.voanews.com/a/english-speaking-students-do-not-return-to-school-in-came roon/4014474.html (accessed 1 November 2018).

2   https://edition.cnn.com/2017/10/07/africa/cameroon-torn-by-deadly-clashes/index.html (accessed 1 November 2018).

3 https://mg.co.za/article/2018-08-10-00-cameroons-crisis-deepens (accessed 1 November 2018).

4 www.reuters.com/article/us-cameroon-separatists-exclusive/exclusive-we-are-in-a-war-cameroon-unrest-confronted-by-army-offensive-idUSKBN1FS1Y8 (accessed 1 November 2018).

5 https://reliefweb.int/report/cameroon/unicef-cameroon-humanitarian-situation-report-may-2018 (accessed 1 November 2018).

REFERENCES

Adair, J. G. (1995) 'The research environment in developing countries: contributions to the national development of the discipline', *International Journal of Psychology*, *30*(6): 643–662.

Aman, R. (2017) 'Colonial differences in intercultural education: on interculturality in the Andes and the decolonization of intercultural dialogue', *Comparative Education Review*, *61*(1): 103–120.

Anchimbe, E. A. (ed.) (2012) *Language Contact in a Postcolonial Setting: The Linguistic and Social Context of English and Pidgin in Cameroon*. Berlin and Boston: De Gruyter.

Assié-Lumumba, N'D. T. (2016) 'The Ubunto paradigm and comparative and international education: epistemological challenges and opportunities in out field', *Comparative Education Review*, *61*(1): 1–21.

Bartlett, L. and Vavrus, F. (2017) *Rethinking Case Study Research: A Comparative Approach*. Florence: Routledge.

Benavot, A. and Köseleci, N. (2015) *Seeking Quality in Education: The Growth of National Learning Assessments, 1990–2013: Background Paper Prepared for the Education for All Global Monitoring Report 2015, Education for All 2000–2015: Achievements and Challenges*. Paris: UNESCO.

Bhabha, H. K. (2012) *The Location of Culture*. Hoboken, NJ: Taylor & Francis.

Bray, M. and Thomas, R. M. (1995) 'Levels of comparison in educational studies: different insights from different literatures and the value of multilevel analyses', *Harvard Educational Review*, *65*(3): 472–491.

Cha, E.-S., Kim, K.H. and Erlen, J.A. (2007) 'Translation of scales in cross-cultural research: issues and techniques', *Journal of Advanced Nursing*, *58*(4): 386–395.

Connell, R. (2011) *Southern Theory: The Global Dynamics of Knowledge in Social Science*. Cambridge: Polity Press.

Dale, R. and Robertson, S. (2009) 'Beyond methodological "isms" in comparative education in an era of globalisation', in R. Cowen and A. M. Kazamias (eds), *International Handbook of Comparative Education*. Dordrecht: Springer. pp. 1113–1127.

DeLancey, M. W. and Mokeba, H. M. (1990) *Historical Dictionary of the Republic of Cameroon*. Metuchen, NJ, and London: The Scarecrow Press.

Dewey, J. (1933) *How We Think* (original work published 1910). Buffalo, NY: Prometheus Books.

DGS and BDS (1992) *Ethik-kodex der Deutsche Gesellschaft für Soziologie (DGS) und des Berufsverbandes Deutscher Soziologen (BDS)*. Available at: www.soz.univie.ac.at/fileadmin/user_upload/inst_soziologie/DGS_Ethik.pdf (accessed 11 November 2017).

Diehm, I., Kuhn, M. and Machold, C. (2010) 'Die Schwierigkeit, ethnische Differenz durch Forschung nicht zu reifizieren – Ethnographie im Kindergarten', in F. Heinzel and A. Panagiotopoulou (eds), *Qualitative Bildungsforschung im Elementar- und Primarbereich: Bedingungen und Kontexte kindlicher Lern- und Entwicklungsprozesse*. Baltmannsweiler: Schneider-Verl. pp. 78–92.

Drake, G. (2014) 'The ethical and methodological challenges of social work research with participants who fear retribution: to "do no harm"', *Qualitative Social Work: Research and Practice*, *13*(2): 304–319.

Eschenbacher, H. (2012) 'The research process in a multi-level mixed-methods case study: international organization headquarters and field employee perspectives of a program in Southern Sudan', *Research in Comparative and International Education*, *7*(2): 176–191.

Farah, S. and Steiner-Khamsi, G. (2014) 'Rethinking culture, context, and comparison in education and development', *Current Issues in Comparative Education (CICE)*, *16*(2): 3–5.

Gillam, L. (2013) 'Ethical considerations in refugee research: what guidance do formal research ethics documents offer?', in K. Block (ed.), *Values and Vulnerabilities: The Ethics of Research with Refugees and Asylum Seekers*. Bowen Hills: Australian Academic Press. pp. 21–39.

Hall, S. (1992) 'The west and the rest: discourse and power', in S. Hall (ed.), *Formations of Modernity*. Oxford: Polity Press. pp. 184–227.

Hantrais, L. (1999) 'Contextualization in cross-national comparative research', *International Journal for Social Research Methodology*, *2*(2): 93–108.

Hayes, D. (2000) 'Cascade training and teachers' professional development', *ELT Journal*, *54*(2): 135–145.

Helmke, A. (2012) *Unterrichtsqualität und Lehrerprofessionalität: Diagnose, Evaluation und Verbesserung des Unterrichts*. Seelze-Velber: Klett/Kallmeyer.

Hennink, M. M. (2008) 'Language and communication in cross-cultural qualitative research', in P. Liamputtong (ed.), *Doing Cross-Cultural Research: Ethical and Methodological Perspectives*. Dordrecht: Springer. pp. 21–34.

Irvine, F., Roberts, G. and Bradbury-Jones, C. (2008) 'The researcher as insider versus the researcher as outsider: enhancing rigour through language and cultural sensitivity', in P. Liamputtong (ed.), *Doing Cross-Cultural Research: Ethical and Methodological Perspectives*. Dordrecht: Springer. pp. 35–48.

Kaukko, M., Dunwoodie, K. and Riggs, E. (2017) 'Rethinking the ethical and methodological dimensions of research with refugee children', *Zeitschrift für internationale Bildungsforschung und Entwicklungspädagogik*, *40*(1): 16–21.

Kelly, P. (2016) 'Constructing the insider and outsider in comparative research', in M. Crossley, L. Arthur and E. McNess (eds), *Revisiting Insider-Outsider Research in Comparative and International Education*. Oxford: Symposium Books. pp. 57–71.

Klees, S. J. (2017) 'Quantitative methods in comparative education and other disciplines: are they valid?', *Educação & Realidade*, *42*(3): 841–858.

Knight, G. P., Roosa, M. W. and Umaña-Taylor, A. J. (2009) *Studying Ethnic Minority and Economically Disadvantaged Populations: Methodological Challenges and Best Practices*. Washington, DC: American Psychological Association.

Konings, P. and Nyamnjoh, F. B. (1997) 'The Anglophone problem in Cameroon', *The Journal of Modern African Studies*, *35*(2): 207–229.

Kouega, J.-P. (1999) 'Forty years of official bilingualism in Cameroon', *English Today*, *15*(4): 38–43.

Kovach, M. (2010) *Indigenous Methodologies: Characteristics, Conversations, and Contexts*. Toronto: University of Toronto Press.

Krogull, S., Scheunpflug, A. and Rwambonera, F. (2014) *Teaching Social Competencies in Post-Conflict Societies: A Contribution to Peace in Society and Quality in Learner-Centred Education*. Münster: Waxmann.

Lange, S. (2014) 'Learner orientation through professional development of teachers? Empirical results from cascade training in Anglophone Cameroon', *Compare: A Journal of Comparative and International Education*, *44*(4): 587–612.

Lange, S. (2015) 'Methodische Reflexionen zur Teilnahme von Ländern der Entwicklungszu-sammenarbeit an internationalen Vergleichsstudien', *Zeitschrift für internationale Bildungs-forschung und Entwicklungspädagogik (ZEP)*, *38*(4): 16–24.

Lange, S. (2016) *Achieving Teaching Quality in Sub-Saharan Africa: Empirical Results from Cascade Training*. Wiesbaden: Springer.

Lange, S. and Parreira do Amaral, M. (2018) 'Leistungen und Grenzen internationaler und ver-gleichender Forschung – "Regulative Ideen" für die methodologische Reflexion?', *Tertium Comparationis*, *24*(1): 5–31.

Liamputtong, P. (2008) 'Doing research in a cross-cultural context: methodological and ethical challenges', in P. Liamputtong (ed.), *Doing Cross-Cultural Research: Ethical and Methodological Perspectives*. Dordrecht: Springer. pp. 3–20.

Lienert, G. A. and Raatz, U. (1998) *Testaufbau und Testanalyse*. Weinheim: Beltz.

Lipowsky, F. (2010) 'Lernen im Beruf – Empirische Befunde zur Wirksamkeit von Lehrerfortbildung', in F. Müller, A. Eichenberger, M. Lüders and J. Mayr (eds), *Lehrerinnen und Lehrer lernen – Konzepte und Befunde zur Lehrerfortbildung*. Münster: Waxmann. pp. 51–72.

Lockheed, M. (2013) 'Causes and consequences of international assessments in developing coun-tries', in H.-D. Meyer and A. Benavot (eds), *PISA, Power, and Policy. The Emergence of Global Educational Governance*. Oxford: Oxford Studies in Comparative Education. pp. 163–184.

Martin, M.O., Gregory, K.D., O'Connor, K.M. and Stemler, S.E. (eds) (2000) *TIMSS 1999 Technical Report*. Chestnut Hill, MA: International Study Center, Lynch School of Education, Boston College.

McDevitt, D. (1998) 'How effective is the cascade as a method for disseminating ideas? A case study in Botswana', *International Journal of Educational Development*, *18*(5): 425–428.

McNess, E., Arthur, L. and Crossely, M. (2016) '"Ethnographic dazzle" and the construction of the "other": shifting boundaries between the insider and the outsider', in M. Crossley, L. Arthur and E. McNess (eds), *Revisiting Insider-Outsider Research in Comparative and International Education*. Oxford: Symposium Books. pp. 21–38.

Meyer, H.-D. and Benavot, A. (eds) (2013) *PISA, Power, and Policy: The Emergence of Global Educational Governance*. Oxford: Oxford Studies in Comparative Education.

Milligan, L. (2016) 'Insider-outsider-inbetweener? Researcher positioning, participative methods and cross-cultural educational research', in M. Crossley, L. Arthur and E. McNess (eds), *Revisiting Insider-Outsider Research in Comparative and International Education*. Oxford: Symposium Books. pp. 131–144.

Murimba, S. (2005) 'The impact of the Southern and Eastern Africa Consortium for monitoring educational quality (SACMEQ)', *Prospects*, *35*(1): 91–108.

Nind, M. (2008) *Conducting Qualitative Research with People with Learning, Communication and Other Disabilities: Methodological Challenges*. ESRC National Centre for Research Methods Review Paper.

Nóvoa, A. and Yariv-Mashal, T. (2003) 'Comparative research education: a mode of governance or a historical journey?', *Comparative Education*, *39*(4): 423–438.

OECD and World Bank Group (2014) *PISA for Development. Capacity Needs Assessment: Zambia*. Available at: www.oecd.org/pisa/aboutpisa/NEW_Pisa%20for%20Development_Zambia_FINAL_revised.pdf (accessed 1 February 2019).

Robertson, S. and Dale, R. (2017) 'Comparing policies in a globalizing world: methodological reflections', *Educação & Realidade*, *42*(3): 859–876.

Robinson-Pant, A. (2016) 'Exploring the concept of insider-outsider in comparative and interna-tional research: essentialising culture or culturally essential?', in M. Crossley, L. Arthur and E. McNess (eds), *Revisiting Insider-Outsider Research in Comparative and International Education*. Oxford: Symposium Books. pp. 39–56.

Rodgers, C. (2002) 'Dewey reflective thinking', *Teachers College Record, 104*(4): 842–866.

Schoonenboom, J. and Johnson, R.B. (2017) 'How to construct a mixed methods research design', *Kölner Zeitschrift fur Soziologie und Sozialpsychologie, 69*(2): 107–131.

Shamim, F. and Qureshi, R. (2013) 'Informed consent in educational research in the South: tensions and accomodations', *Compare: A Journal of Comparative and International Education, 43*(4): 464–482.

Smith, L. T. (2002) *Decolonizing Methodologies: Research and Indigenous Peoples*. London: Zed Books.

Takayama, K., Sriprakash, A. and Connell, R. (2017) 'Toward a postcolonial comparative and international education', *Comparative Education Review, 61*(1): 1–24.

Tambo, L. (1995) 'Models and practice in initial secondary teacher education in Cameroon', *Teacher Education Quarterly, 22*(1): 59–67.

Tatto, M. T. (2006) 'Education reform and the global regulation of teachers' education, development and work: a cross-cultural analysis', *International Journal of Educational Research, 45*(4–5): 231–241.

Tikly, L. and Bind, T. (2013) 'Towards a postcolonial research ethics in comparative and international education', *Compare: A Journal of Comparative and International Education, 43*(4): 422–442.

Unger, H. V. (2014) *Partizipative Forschung: Einführung in die Forschungspraxis*. Wiesbaden: Springer.

Vannini, A. and Gladue, C. (2008) 'Decolonised methodologies in cross-cultural research', in P. Liamputtong (ed.), *Doing Cross-Cultural Research: Ethical and Methodological Perspectives*. Dordrecht: Springer. pp. 137–160.

Webb, V. (1994) 'Revalorizing the autochthonous languages of Africa', in M. Pütz (ed.), *Language Contact and Language Conflict*. Amsterdam, PA: John Benjamins Publishing. pp. 181–204.

10

ADDRESSING THE CONTEXT IN CROSS-NATIONAL COMPARATIVE RESEARCH

Herbert Altrichter, Miriam Galvin,
Gerry McNamara and Joe O'Hara

10.1 INTRODUCTION

This chapter discusses some of the challenges of cross-national educational research. Several interrelated terms, including 'cross-national research', 'international cross-cultural research', 'cross-national comparative research' and 'international research', are used to describe these types of studies and the challenges they face. Although there may be subtle differences between these terms, all describe research aimed at examining and comparing a particular issue or phenomena across two or more countries where culture, either explicitly or implicitly, plays a role (Gardner et al., 2012).

The following paragraphs consider the experiences of the authors in the EU-funded research project 'Impact of School Inspections on Teaching and Learning (ISI-TL)' in which research groups from six European countries collaborated to study the work procedures of new school inspections and how these procedures affected schools in their countries. In this project a range of issues arose, related specifically to the international nature of the research. For example, central concepts and relevant features of the research context were perceived differently in participating countries (e.g. what do we mean by 'secondary schools'? Is the 'inspection unit' independent from the administrative authorities or associated with them?). Access, return rates and pressure to return questionnaires greatly differed between countries due to the support a study received from the educational authorities and due to other contextual features. Questionnaires – even if meticulously translated – may be interpreted differently due to the special context of the respondents, who hence attend to the questionnaires with different understandings and mental maps. Each of these challenges and indeed others arose in this project and are likely to arise and require active attention in all cross-national research undertakings.

We begin by outlining a brief description of the project and how it was conducted. We will focus on the key challenges that emerged and indicate approaches taken to solve them. For clarity we have systematised these challenges as follows: sampling and access, the meaning of concepts and instruments in cross-national contexts, communication through formalised teams and collaborative structures, epistemology and methodology and publishing and dissemination of outcomes. Each will be considered below followed by a guide or checklist designed to make researchers aware of the likely problems and suggesting ways of reducing or eliminating them.

This systemisation of the issues for the sake of clarity should not mask the fact that they are interrelated and interdependent. A central argument of the chapter is that 'organisational/practical', 'epistemological/conceptual' and 'ethical' decisions made over the course of a research project influence each other. A seemingly 'organisational/practical' decision (e.g. how is access to the respondents organised and who is to be included in the sample?) may have 'epistemological' implications, that is, it may open up or limit specific roads to understanding, thereby shaping the potential results to some degree. And it may also have 'ethical' implications, that is, it organises the potential role and voice of the participants of the research, thereby also influencing whether knowledge, views and interests are fairly recorded and taken into consideration.

10.2 OVERALL DESCRIPTION OF CASE

Our experiences in cross-national comparative research originate from – at least for the purposes of this chapter – our participation in the EU-funded research project 'Impact of School Inspections on Teaching and Learning (ISI-TL)'. In this study, research teams from six European countries (i.e. Austria, Czech Republic, England, Ireland, Netherlands, and Sweden) – who were also joined in some phases by researchers from Norway and Switzerland – collaborated to better understand the processes and effects of school inspections in different European countries. The project was led and coordinated by Melanie C. M. Ehren, then working at the University of Twente, Netherlands, and later on at the University of London Institute of Education.[1] In summary, the study pursued the following two lines of research:

1 The identification of the main processes by which school inspections impact school improvement. This involved an in-depth documentary analysis.
2 The study of the processes by which schools cope with and react to school inspections. This phase saw the distribution of a questionnaire to school principals.

10.2.1 IDENTIFYING THE PROCESSES BY WHICH SCHOOL INSPECTIONS CAN BE EFFECTIVE FOR SCHOOL IMPROVEMENT

In the first phase, the research teams wanted to identify the logic of school inspections and their elements and goals in the project's respective countries. This was important for several reasons: first, it is necessary for researchers to acquire a good initial understanding of the object of their research before doing fieldwork. Second, the cross-national setting of the research made meticulously clarifying what school inspections consist of and aspire to in the different countries a requirement; this was essential to find out in what respects school inspections were doing the 'same thing' in different countries, to what degree they were comparable and in what respects they differed.

Table 10.1 summarises this comparison, spelling out what features are considered important for the operation of school inspections and in what way countries differ with respect to these features. If the differences between countries are hypothesised to be relevant with respect to the research questions and the underlying theories, they can be used for empirical analyses. Table 10.1 includes assumptions about the amount of 'accountability pressure' that national inspections have on individual schools. Altrichter and Kemethofer (2015) took these assumptions as hypotheses and found in their questionnaire data (which will be explained in the next section in greater detail) that schools in countries with more 'accountability pressure' show more improvement activities in the wake of school inspections; however, there are also more unintended consequences, such as narrowing of the curriculum and discouraging new teaching strategies (see Ehren et al., 2015).

There is a third reason for these initial analyses. An important goal of the first research phase was to formulate one or more conceptual models of school inspections that could identify the processes by which school inspections in different countries seek to be effective and stimulate school improvement. Given the lack of a 'theory of school inspection', this conceptual model was to be taken as a guideline that would

Table 10.1 Summary of inspections characteristics (from Altrichter and Kemethofer, 2015: 38)

	The Nether- lands (NL)	England (ENG)	Sweden (SE)	Ireland (IE)	Czech Republic (CZ)	Austria (AT; Styria)	Swit- zerland (CH)
Types of inspection							
Cyclical inspections of all schools	Every 4 years	Every 5 years	Every 4–5 years	Every 5 years	Every 3 years	Every 2–4 years	Every 4–5 years
Differentiated inspections	x	x	x	-	-	-	-
Thematic school inspections	x	x	x	x	x	-	x
Standards							
Legal aspects	x	x	x	x	x	x	x
Context and process quality	x	x	x	x	x	x	x
Outcomes	x	x	-	-	x	-	[x][a]
Thresholds for distinguishing failing schools	x	x	-	-	x	-	
Consequences							
(Advising on) sanctions	x	x	x		x	-	-
Interventions	x	x	x	x	x	x	x
Reporting							
General/thematic reports	x	x	x	x	-	-	-
Reports on individual schools to the general public	x	x	-	x	-	-	-
Scores on 'pressure scale'	**5**	**5**	**2**	**2**	**3**	**0**	**0–1**

Note: 'x' indicates the presence of characteristics/mechanisms in each country. Dimensions printed in italics are assumed to add to 'pressure' on individual schools. The hits on these dimensions add up to the score on the 'pressure scale' in the last line of the table.

a Student outcomes are only used in some Swiss cantons which have introduced standardised testing.

Source: Does accountability pressure through school inspections promote school improvement? Herbert Altrichter and David Kernethofer, *School Effectiveness and School Improvement*, 2015, Taylor & Francis Ltd, reprinted by permission of the publisher (Taylor & Francis Ltd, http://www.tandfonline.com)

organise the research. Because it spelt out the normative aspirations (what results do the inspections aim to achieve?) and the functional ideas (by what processes are these results to be achieved?) of the proponents of school inspections, empirical research can test these assumptions and contribute to a better understanding of the effective and non-effective processes of school inspections.

How were these 'normative models' of school inspection identified? In each of the participating countries, an analysis of the relevant documents (e.g. inspection frameworks, legal papers and the documents describing the rationales behind the inspection methods) was used to reconstruct assumptions on the causal mechanisms underlying the intended effects of school inspections (see Leeuw, 2003, for the procedure). Additional interviews with the inspection officials and policy makers were scheduled in each country to validate and clarify the reconstructed assumptions. For this purpose, inspection officials and policy makers were asked to indicate whether the assumptions in the reconstructed inspection model provided an accurate description of the current inspection methods, their intended effects and the intermediate mechanisms explaining these effects. Their comments and clarifications were used to revise the reconstructed assumptions.

The assumptions were summarised in country-specific 'programme theories' (see Jones and Tymms, 2014 for an example). A 'programme theory' (Leeuw, 2003) served to describe and organise the intended effects of inspections in each country, the characteristics of the inspection and the mechanisms through which the effects were expected to occur.

In another step, the six countries' programme theories were compared to distinguish commonalities and differences in their assumptions regarding the causal mechanisms of their respective inspection systems (see Ehren et al., 2013). The assumptions that were similar in most programme theories were considered the 'conceptual core of inspection', representing those potential causal mechanisms that could explain how school inspections may lead to school improvement, something that all national inspection systems in the study seemed to subscribe to. However, there were also differences between the national inspection systems that the research team identified as areas that the empirical research needed to attend to.

The conceptual model identifies three overarching 'effective mechanisms' attributed to school inspections (printed in bold in Figure 10.1). By 'Setting expectations' and 'Giving feedback' (if feedback is accepted and understood by the schools), the inspections aim to stimulate and drive improvement and self-evaluative actions by the evaluated school. The school's stakeholders are also expected to react to inspection standards and reports and provide additional stimulation to the school, hence helping (or urging) the school to improve. These improvement actions result in an increase in the school's improvement capacity and lead to effective school and teaching conditions, which are expected to improve student results (Ehren et al., 2013).

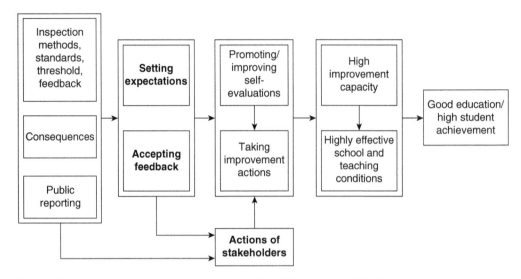

Figure 10.1   Conceptual model of school inspections (Ehren et al., 2013: 14)

Source: reprinted by permission from Copyright Clearance Center: Springer Nature, Impact of school inspections on improvements of schools – describing assumptions on causal mechanisms in six European countries, M.C. M. Ehren, H. Altrichter, G. McNamara © 2013

10.2.2 STUDYING PROCESSES BY WHICH SCHOOLS COPE WITH SCHOOL INSPECTIONS

The 'conceptual model' of the processes and effects of the school inspection was to be empirically tested in the second stage of this international project. Approximately 2300 primary and secondary school principals in seven European countries (Netherlands (NL), England (ENG), Sweden (SE), Ireland (IE), Austria (AT; Region Styria), Czech Republic (CZ) and Switzerland (CH; five German-speaking cantons Aargau, Appenzell Ausserhoden, Graubünden, Schwyz and Zug) participated in the autumn of 2011 in an online survey, of which the goal was to collect comparative data on the mechanisms and processes of school inspections in different accountability systems. Data collection was repeated with a slightly amended instrument in autumn 2012 and 2013 to collect longitudinal data.

The sampling procedure differed between the countries: in smaller inspection systems, all schools were included (Ireland, Austria/Region Styria and Switzerland/five cantons), while other countries used a random sampling strategy (Sweden and Czech Republic). In England and the Netherlands, the sampling originally followed a regression-discontinuity design based on the inspection results. Because the response rate initially did not meet the expected figures, the sampling strategy was changed in England to a random sampling of a larger target group. In the Netherlands, three groups of schools were part of the target sample: 'high risk', 'risk' and 'no risk' schools. Because of oversampling of the 'risk' and 'high risk' schools, schools experiencing above-average pressure may be over-represented. Because of this, Dutch data were not included in the analyses comparing countries. Table 10.2 gives an example that represents the different sampling strategies and response rates.

Table 10.2 Summary of sample characteristics in each country

Country	Sampling strategy	Target Sample		Actual Sample		Response rate	
		Prim.	Sec.	Prim.	Sec.	Prim.	Sec.
Netherlands (NL)	purposive[b]	408	359	73	15	18%	4%
England (ENG)	random	1422	637	189	101	13%	16%
Sweden (SE)	random	1167	987	567	464	49%	47%
Ireland (IE)	full	3200	729	123	42	4%	6%
Czech Republic (CZ)	random	150	170	56	69	37%	41%
Austria (AT)	full	503	194	345	149	69%	77%
Switzerland (CH)[a]	full	465		132		28%	

a In Switzerland, no information about school type in the target sample is available. Three principals responded that they work in a special school and four did not respond to this question.

b See text for details.

The questionnaire of the first data collection round included 73 questions that were based on the 'conceptual model' presented above. On a 5-point scale ranging from 'much less time' (= 1) to 'much more time' (= 5), school principals scored items for the amount of time used for (improvement) actions the school had taken before, during or after school inspections. A 5-point scale ranging from 'strongly disagree' (= 1) to 'strongly agree' (= 5) was used when asking for intermediate processes, effective school conditions and unintended consequences (see Gustafsson et al., 2015, for more details on the research procedure). Table 10.3 gives an example of the main concepts and variables used in the questionnaire.

Data were collected country by country and inspected for plausibility and missing data. Country data files were collated in a shared data file that was used for the cross-country analyses.

Throughout the three-year funding period of the project, the international project team organised their work in four two-day face-to-face meetings, several Skype conferences and numerous email exchanges moderated by the project leader. Even before the start of the project, a plan was created for national and international publications, associated research

Table 10.3 Overview of latent variables

Latent construct	Example item	Number of items	Scale	Cronbach's Alpha	N
Setting expectations	The inspection standards affect the evaluation and supervision of teachers.	7	strongly agree (1) – strongly disagree (5)	.84	1109
Stakeholders sensitive to reports	The school's Board of Management/ Board of Governors is very aware of the contents of the school inspection report.	3		.71	1112
Accepting feedback	The feedback received from the inspectors was useful.	5		.81	1218
Promoting/ improving self-evaluation	Compared to last academic year, I spent less/more time on the self-evaluation process as a whole.	3	much less (1) - much more (5)	.87	2316
Improvement in capacity building	Compared to last academic year, I spent less/more time involving teachers in making decisions about using new teaching methods.	7		.80	2203
Improvement in teacher participation in decision-making*	Compared to last academic year, I spent less/more time involving teachers in making decisions about using new teaching methods.	2		.63	2280
Improvement in teacher cooperation*	Compared to last academic year, I spent less/more time on improving teachers' collaboration in discussing assessment results of students with each other.	2		.68	2364
Improvement in transformational leadership*	Compared to last academic year, I spent less/more time in my leadership role communicating the school's vision to the staff, pupils, parents and others.	2		.63	2316

Note: * denotes a subset of items representing a narrow latent variable in the nested-factor 'Improvement in capacity building'.

questions and lead and co-authors for these publications. Although this plan was not put into practice in all aspects, being changed according to new analytic questions and publication opportunities, the original plan may have helped the different project partners (some of them who had not collaborated before) find their place in the project, assuring them that their interests and capacities would be taken care of in the project.

Some publications were written in the researchers' national languages; however, the main scientific yield of the project was to be published in English. Again, an international project team can take advantage of the language competencies and knowledge of the publishing field of native (and close-to-native) English speakers; however, there must be some measures in place to ensure that these capacities are not translated in a way that would give too little credit to the contributions of other national research teams.

10.3 MAIN CHALLENGES AND HOW THEY WERE ADDRESSED

Over the course of a research project, many decisions must be made; in sum, these decisions shape the specific form, or 'Gestalt', of the project and open up (and limit) specific opportunities of knowing and understanding. We will discuss some of the decisions that we felt were relevant for the development of our cross-national project on school inspections, including sampling and access, the meaning of concepts and instruments in cross-national contexts, analysis and publishing and group dynamics and formalised collaborative structures. This section moves from the specific to the general – addressing in its latter part some general conceptual issues that need to be considered when undertaking research in cross-national contexts.

10.3.1 SAMPLING AND ACCESS

Sampling, the process of selecting those elements (persons, documents, instances, cases, etc.) from a population of interest that will be taken as data sources, involves crucial decisions for the research process. For example, all researchers need to consider issues of sample representativeness, types of sample, sample frame, rates of response among other things. This brings up issues that are relevant to both cross-national and comparative research. From a project perspective, the challenge was to find an approach for sampling that was sensitive to the different contextual conditions faced by all the research partners while at the same time producing findings that were methodologically robust. It became clear during the research that the ability of each participating research group to generate useful, comparative data depended in many cases on the complex interrelationship between their research context and organisational capacity.

In practice, sampling depends on and is partly shaped by access, i.e. by the ways researchers can come into contact with their respondents and cases; by the 'gatekeepers' that may help with organising or observing or commenting on this contact; and by the 'atmosphere', which is attached to the contact by the specific way and context in which the communication takes place. In our project, for some of the researchers, for example, the Austrian and the Swedish researchers, the research context was relatively benign; they received positive collaboration at a national and regional level from relevant administrative stakeholders. For other researchers, for example, the Irish, there was little formal collaboration with the centralised authorities. One of the practical outcomes of this difference was the fact that response rates between these three partners varied significantly. This was a situation that the English researchers also faced in the original round of surveys. However, for the English researchers, their organisational capacity resulted in a significantly different research narrative emerging; they were a large, nationally embedded and independent research group with ready access to a significant cohort of school leaders, resulting in the refining of their sampling strategy in the second and subsequent rounds of the survey distribution; this in turn led to a significantly enhanced response rate.

If researchers seek access to schools, support from the regional or national school administration may be very useful from an organisational perspective (and, ultimately, results in a 77 per cent response rate such as in the Austrian case). However, the respondents, in this case the school leaders in an Austrian administrative area, may perceive researchers as not independent. Because of this organisational association between researchers and administrators (which need not necessarily taint the research interests and data interpretation), the respondents might feel pressure to give 'socially desirable' answers.

Ultimately, the different sampling strategies and the diverse types of access resulted in different response rates (seen in Table 10.2) and in the data collected under (hypothetically) different circumstances. In the final analysis, the type of data generated and the claims made from it had to be tailored to the different realities encountered. Thus, the final report included a range of findings – some of which were applicable across all partners and others that were relevant to a subset. Ultimately, this was viewed as a strength by the project team; however, it was also a compromise that was not envisaged in the original study and emerged organically from the different experiences of the researchers.

Drawing on our experience of cross-national research projects – including the previously mentioned ISI-TL project – we can distinguish three broad aspects of research decisions: epistemological, organisational/practical and ethical. We have argued that the three types of decisions mutually influence each other. 'Sampling and access' provide excellent examples for substantiating this claim. Sampling clearly has epistemological implications: which actors are included or excluded, for example, in a group discussion may influence what we can know and understand in a field and what kind of knowledge our research generates. Increasing the number of respondents is usually good for epistemological reasons, but it also has practical implications: it may drive costs up and put pressure on the time of the research team. A questionnaire in a country's dominant language may be cheaper, but it may effectively exclude language minorities. This may result in epistemological flaws (because the research object is selectively represented by the sampling strategy), but it also has ethical implications because different parts of the society do not have an equal chance of being heard. As a consequence, the findings and recommendations for action and further research may be based on an incomplete concept of the situation. Special measures to account for the diversity of respondents and to include language minorities (e.g. by doing additional oral interviews in particular respondent groups; see for example Altrichter et al., 2011) may mitigate these problems but may also be connected to additional epistemological challenges when data from different sources are compared; and they may also give rise to additional ethical considerations because the protection and anonymity of the respondents are more difficult to ensure in face-to-face interviews.

In many cases, there is no one best solution when making research design decisions; rather trade-offs of various alternatives must be taken into account before deciding on a way forward. We suggest that considering the epistemological, ethical and practical implications of design decisions is an appropriate heuristic device for enhancing the quality of a research project (Feldman et al., 2018: 172).

Such decisions must be made in every research project, not only in cross-national comparative projects. It follows that most of the research problems we will discuss in the following paragraphs are not limited to cross-national studies. However, some of these 'perennial' research problems seem to become more visible in cross-national projects – and certainly emerged in the course of the ISI-TL project – because different understandings and meanings are more difficult to detect between subcultures within a single language group (in which the researchers usually represent a more privileged part of society) than between different language groups represented by researchers of (more or less) equal status.

10.3.2 MEANING OF CONCEPTS AND INSTRUMENTS IN THE ERA OF 'TRAVELLING POLICIES'

Cross-national projects usually come to an agreement on a working language (which in most cases is English) that will be used for the shared conceptual and methodological design of the project, for the main concepts, for the original versions of the instruments and for the shared core of analysis and interpretation. Again, this gives rise to a range of issues that must be considered.

10.3.2.1 Equivalent instruments

The most straightforward and plausible issue relates to the instruments used. The original version of a research instrument – be it a questionnaire as in our case, a list of questions for interviews or a set of categories with which to analyse texts and documents – will usually be developed in the working language of the project.

Because European cross-national projects usually contain a range of different languages in the participating countries, it is necessary to translate the instruments into the participants' national languages. The issue of language is further complicated by the existence of regional linguistic variations. An example of this arose during the ISI-TL project. Austria and the participating Swiss cantons used German as their main language yet it could not be taken for granted that an identical questionnaire would be 'equivalent' in terms of meaning. Our experience would suggest that regional variations in semantics and differences in the school systems must be taken into account when developing instruments. The goal, therefore, is to achieve more than just a literal translation; rather, there should be an equivalence of meaning and commonality in understanding the survey instrument (Buil, de Chernatony and Martínez, 2012). Semantic equivalence relates to which terms in the translation connote the same meaning in the translation as they do in the source language. A challenge of functionally equivalent questionnaires is the lack of equivalent markers or terms for words or concepts that do not exist in the target language or culture.

In addition to being shaped by the translation process, a cross-national survey instrument can be influenced by cultural and political sensitivities. It is necessary to consider policy and different administrative and political structures in the study, along with an understanding of the societal context within which the phenomena are located (Lynn, 2003). There are differences in legislation, norms and guidelines (Iwarsson, Wahl and Nygren, 2004) and various notions of education, inspection, autonomy and the value of research.

As we have already seen, translating the instruments is a multi-step process, throughout which researchers should strive for questions that are comparable at the level of meaning, not simply literal translations of the original versions. A common procedure includes (1) the translation of the English original into a national language and then (2) a retranslation of the national version back into English. Differences between the two English versions may indicate possible problems of translation equivalence. (3) The researchers then pilot the national version using a small sample of people who are prepared to use the 'thinking aloud' method to voice all ideas that come to mind when filling out the questionnaires; this is another way of detecting problems of translation equivalence (Behling and Law, 2000).

10.3.2.2 Conceptual equivalence

Developing on and expanding the language theme addressed in the previous section, cross-national and comparative research must not take for granted that concepts on the educational practices using the same or similar words have the same meaning in different languages and in different countries.

As we have already stated, it is important to beware of English concepts used in different languages. This is a real challenge for multi-national and multi-lingual research groups. Given that many researchers use English as the lingua franca at conferences and in their publications, there is a tendency to use English words to quickly communicate phenomena from a national setting to an international audience, even though the meaning in different national contexts may not be identical.

An interesting example of the challenge of finding a common understanding of frequently used terms can be seen in the description of the various stages of school systems in cross-national research projects. These overviews often use what seem to be relatively uncontested terms such as primary or secondary school – however, our experience across a range of projects would suggest that the proper interrogation of what exactly is meant by these terms is essential. For example the term 'lower secondary school' is often used when researchers from different countries talk about their school systems. The use of this term can be linked to a sampling strategy which is often seen as being central to the validity of the study as a whole. The problem of course is that the term 'lower secondary' has no universal meaning. For a person from Ireland it may refer to students who are between 12 and 15 years of age, for an Austrian it speaks about students from 10 to 14 years of age, a Norwegian sees it as referring to students from 13 to 16 years of age, and a Turkish researcher considers that it is speaking about students of 10 to 13 years of age. Although such 'factual problems' can be solved by looking at reference books (e.g. Eurydice, 2017), it is sometimes more difficult regarding the more complex terms that are at the centre of the research focus. Often, more complex terms carry a richer and potentially more diverse meaning. We can be sure that issues of meaning and conceptual clarity will be elaborated on throughout the research process and that we will understand the concept at the end of the research better than at the beginning. This brings some comfort in the initial phases of a cross-national project (where there is designing, sampling and data collection) because at this point, having a common understanding of the central concepts is necessary. A pertinent example is the concept of 'school inspection', which is a trickier conceptual challenge (Altrichter and Kemethofer, 2016). In Austria, officers of the centralised school administration are traditionally called 'inspectors' while the administrators in many school systems of the German Bundesländer are called 'Schulaufsicht' (a term also used in Austria as a synonym for 'inspectors'). When some of the German states introduced new 'inspectorates', their mission and work procedures reproduced the inspection procedures in the Netherlands and England to some degree. Although the identical word 'inspector' is used in Austria and in the German states, this term describes two functionally distinct groups of people in the different countries.

But then comes another question: can German 'inspectors' be identified with Dutch, English or Irish ones (Brown et al., 2017; Ehren et al., 2013)? Certainly, they have been modelled according to these examples in some respects. In other respects, there are profound differences: German inspectors are emissaries of the state who evaluate schools, which are state institutions, while Dutch inspectors inspect comparatively autonomous school boards on behalf of the central state (and Swedish inspectors inspect schools maintained by communities.

One aspect of our era of 'globalisation' is that legislators and school reformers look to other countries when searching for models for school improvement. 'School inspection' is certainly a good example for a 'travelling policy' because inspection systems have been modernised or newly implemented in many European education systems. Although several building blocks of inspection systems seem to reappear at various places, one should keep in mind the warning by Ozga and Jones (2006) when making comparisons: the embedding of supposedly similar policies into different national contexts may lead to a broad variation of results because different contextual constellations may transform the processes and results. In our empirical work, we have shown that inspection systems seem to work differently in high-stake and low-stake systems (Altrichter and Kemethofer, 2015).

There can be significant diversity in the language and concepts employed in research, policy dialogue and everyday societal discourse between countries. Certain terms can be commonly used in one setting and yet have no conceptual equivalent in others (Salway et al., 2011). Language is not simply a medium for conveying concepts. We cannot assume that the same word has the same meaning when used in distinct cultural contexts.

The careless use of 'culturally loaded' meanings (Mangen, 1999) can severely limit comparative understanding. However, the need for explicitly 'translating' and conveying more complex meanings of concepts may also serve as a stimulus for conceptual clarity and the further development of underlying theoretical assumptions.

10.3.2.3 Communication and collaboration of research teams

Language may also be an issue when it comes to communication within cross-national research teams. Again, the native speakers of the project's working language are more likely to have a dominant position when making decisions about the design, interpretations and publishing of the research. Sometimes, there are numerous pragmatic reasons to have the English native speaker be the lead researcher, presenter of the results and lead author of the main publications to be published in competitive (English language) journals. Sometimes, however, this does not do justice to the energy and ideas that the research members of smaller language communities invest.

There is an even deeper issue in international collaboration. Researchers in a cross-national project may come from different institutional and national cultures that emphasise different values and styles of acting. This may result in differences in interpreting both everyday actions and research decisions, possibly culminating in misunderstandings.

'Culture' is a difficult term to define because cultural groups are always internally heterogeneous and contain individuals who adhere to a range of diverse beliefs and practices. Furthermore, the core cultural beliefs and practices that are most typically associated with any given group are also constantly changing and evolving over time. (OECD, 2016: 7)

Pointing to possible 'cultural differences' does not mean that research teams have to 'know' all the 'cultures' to do justice to all the variations of judgement and life styles that may occur. Rather, researchers need a 'reflective stance' with respect to their interactions in the research team and to the distribution of duties and tasks. This will most likely lead to adjustments during a project to increase compatibility towards different work styles and make best use of the researchers' various competencies. In this perspective, the capacity for team-based reflection and further development of research practice is one of the success factors for cross-national research.

In conclusion, it is crucial in cross-national research to develop a transparent organisational project structure and organise clear channels of communication. Within such a project structure it is usual to assign leading roles for different parts and aspects of the project to team members from different participating countries. It is also important to reflect on the project structure from time to time, and to adjust the types and channels of communication and the distribution of tasks and duties according to the developing experience of collaboration.

10.3.2.4 Publishing and dissemination

Particularly important decisions arise when it comes to reaping the results of the project. Who is publishing what research results and in what journals is a tricky question when one wants to do justice to the different workloads, research expertise and language competencies. In most social science projects, project teams do not name all project participants as authors of the papers as is sometimes the case in natural science settings. Even if this were to be done, all the participants who have invested work and expertise should have the chance to publish in a way that is conducive for their further research and careers. Our experience with the following strategy has been so far quite good: plan papers and authors and contributors in the early phases of project design. This will give project members from different countries some sense of belonging to the project and what they can potentially gain from it. This had proved helpful, even if some changes were deemed necessary during the course of the project when it was found that the results could be bundled in another way than anticipated or additional ways of publishing in conferences and journals materialised.

10.3.2.5 Equivalence and context

To summarise the preceding paragraphs, in cross-national research, using one language in multi-lingual research environments as a common working language brings with it a range of issues that must be coped with: it necessitates the translation of instruments, striving for the equivalence of meanings. It may conceal 'culturally loaded' meanings (Mangen, 1999), and English concepts may be too easily understood in other languages although they still convey different meanings.

Additionally, in cross-national research teams, English as the working language tends to establish a hierarchy when it comes to decisions on the design and publishing of the research. In the following sections we explore the implications of these insights moving beyond the confines of individual projects to a more general overview of their implications when engaging in cross-national research.

One way to control possible epistemological, organisational and ethical biases is to explicitly strive for equivalence and attend to the specific context. Translation equivalence aspires to semantically and contextually reach equivalent concepts and instruments. Data equivalence or comparability refers to data that have, as far as possible, the same meaning or interpretation and the same level of accuracy, precision of measurement, validity and reliability in all countries and cultures (Buil, de Chernatony and Martínez, 2012).

Functional equivalence deals with whether the concepts, objects or behaviours being studied are equivalent across cultures or countries in terms of their function or role. Conceptual equivalence is concerned with whether the same constructs, objects and other stimuli exist in different cultures or countries and are expressed in similar ways. Category equivalence relates to the question of whether the same classification scheme can be employed across the different contexts of analysis (Buil, de Chernatony and Martínez, 2012). Exploratory and qualitative research are the best options for establishing whether the constructs, products and objects investigated are conceptual and functionally equivalent.

Hantrais (1999) maintains that contextualisation is central to all the possible approaches that can be used for comparative social research. Approaches to cross-national comparative research may be seen as context free, context bound or context dependant. Hantrais's (1999) schematisation outlines three possible approaches: the universalist, culturalist and societal approach.

- Universalist approaches are grounded in the assumption that independent from a specific context, universal characteristics are identified in social phenomena. The search for similarity and convergence is emphasised, often as a means of testing the wider applicability of a theory developed at national level.
- Culturalist approaches focus on national uniqueness and particularism and cross-cultural contrasts or differences. For proponents of culture boundedness or relativism, contextualisation is at the nexus of comparative research, and the existence of truly universal concepts and values is rejected.
- Societal approaches look at how members of organisations import values, norms and roles from external subcultures, such as family, education and community, thus influencing how these subcultures organise internally. By treating social phenomena as components of systems, it follows that explanations of behaviour must be examined with reference to the factors intrinsic to the system in question.

All research is influenced by the political climate in which it is generated and conducted (Doiron and Asselin, 2015), which is generally reflected in obtaining financial resources and research funding priorities. Regulations, policies and ethical guidelines affect the national research context and may differ at international levels.

10.3.2.6 Epistemology and methodology

All researchers carry a series of core presuppositions about the nature of reality and their place within it. These core beliefs influence how they approach the theory and practice of research and are influenced in turn by the cultural context within which they live and work. This has been a central argument of the chapter, one that can be extended to linked conceptual areas of epistemology and methodology (Lincoln and Guba, 1985). Epistemological orientations shape and determine a particular view of the world and 'reality', and they determine the methodological approaches taken in a research project. Much cross-cultural research is based on a realist perspective, both at the ontological and epistemological levels (Yeganeh, Su and Chrysostome, 2004). Earlier sections of this chapter have demonstrated how these orientations can impact on the conduct of research at both a practical and ethical level. In this section, we explore some of the more theoretical challenges that can emerge in a research project. A number of theoretical and methodological debates are evident in comparative cross-national research, including the following:

- Construct equivalence: the research instrument measures the same traits across groups or cultures to ensure the same phenomenon is being investigated.
- Concept equivalence: the meaning of the research concepts and materials should be equivalent across populations.
- Operational equivalence: comparable operational methods are employed (e.g. standard operating procedures).
- Translation procedures.
- Recognition of and creating structures to account for different contexts

Although many quality criteria for cross-country comparisons are like those established for undertaking rigorous research in more general terms, certain aspects are particularly salient in defining quality when comparing large 'macro-social' units, for example, the need to pay explicit attention to the importance of contextual differences and related complexity arising from differences in the political, cultural and institutional arrangements in which systems sit (Cacace et al., 2013). These challenges also arose for the research team working on the ISI-TL project. An awareness of the impact of context on discussions relating to the meaning of concepts such as quality, impact, governance and system became central to attempts to make sense of emerging datasets from across the participating countries.

Both case-oriented and variable-oriented research designs (Ragin, 1989) address the complexity associated with comparing large macro-social units in cross-country comparisons. Variable-oriented comparisons select variables that appropriately reflect all the factors that are relevant to the phenomenon compared while demonstrating an awareness of the limitations of the comparability of the data gathered in different national contexts. Case-oriented comparisons provide a contextual description adequate enough to meet the aims of the comparison. For both types of comparisons, the strengths and weaknesses of the data and analysis should be critically discussed. By way of example, the vertical case study approach recasts the considerations of context to engage multiple scales simultaneously while foregrounding the empirical benefits of systematic comparison in educational research. In this way, they allow for reconceptualising the dilemmas of culture, context and comparison (Bartlett, 2014).

Hantrais (2014) suggests that methodological pluralism, or 'multi-strategy' research, can be exploited to extend the scope of comparative studies, test and reinforce validity, explore new insights and offer differing or complementary explanations for observed similarities and differences.

The philosophical and methodological assumptions underlying much of the current discourse that involve what learning is (the ontology of learning) and how we come to know what learning is (the epistemology of learning) are rarely made explicit. Even though these assumptions have profound implications for education policy and practice (Tikly, 2015), it is important, therefore, not to reduce methodological issues in comparative education to a discussion of the harmonisation of statistical data (Belfiore, 2004). However, it is also important to recognise that the impetus for doing this often comes from a position of pragmatism, one which seeks to ensure that the research is completed within an agreed time frame and in a manner that meets the requirement of external funders. This push to the pragmatic is common in all research projects but is perhaps more explicitly referenced in multi-national research contexts and hence needs to be considered by the research team at all stages of the research.

The experience of working in international teams can act as a spur for theoretical and methodological developments (Brannen, 2003). This was the experience of the team working on the ISI-TL project. There is an opportunity to build alliances between qualitative and quantitative researchers and integrate qualitative features into quantitative research (Ragin, 2006). The research project discussed in this chapter was an excellent example of this. It contained researchers from both qualitative and quantitative backgrounds who were required to develop an agreed conceptual framework to explain both the meaning and the impact of the data emerging from the various stages of the project. Over the course of the three years of engagement researchers moved from a position that might be characterised as being one where methodological 'purity' was considered paramount to one where the relative contributions of different approaches to data collection and analysis were seen as contributing equally to the phenomenon under investigation. This is important as quite often the choice of research methodology is embedded in the national or disciplinary context of the research team. In other words, there can often be an expectation regarding what high-quality or impactful research will result from a qualitative or quantitative methodological approach. Although it can be challenging to move beyond these perspectives for research teams, there is often a significant learning opportunity for individuals and groups when they are challenged to examine their methodological stances by others who are equally as embedded in their own conceptions of quality research.

From a methodological perspective, the opportunities offered by the multiple lenses of a cross-national research team are significant. From the perspective of the ISI-TL project team the engagement with researchers representing different cultural, linguistic, pedagogical and philosophical perspectives resulted in initial confusion but ultimately greater methodological rigour and insight. It led to a series of discoveries in areas that had been considered, for many, unproblematic and accepted. For example, unit non-response and item non-response is a feature of virtually all surveys. However, there is a lack of attention paid to the non-response error rate in cross-cultural research. Most of the focus is on measurement equivalence while operational equivalence (sampling, coverage, non-response, data collection procedures, etc.) is rarely mentioned. Response rates that appear similar across countries or cultures may in fact mask differences in the composition of the non-response rate (Couper and Leeuw, 2003).

In summary then, when attempting to develop research with new colleagues, researchers need to be cognizant that they may be coming from a different paradigm and that negotiation will help ensure each worldview is recognised, respected and employed in a way that can achieve a balance in the relationship (Doiron and Asselin, 2015).

RESEARCHER CHECKLIST

Based on the above we have tried to put together a researcher checklist for those starting out on cross-national research projects. Many key issues will only arise as the research progresses of course but it is advisable to address the following as early as possible. Giving consideration to some of these issues both at the grant writing phase and then at the first consortium meeting will greatly help the project to progress smoothly.

- Meaning of concepts: don't take for granted that concepts using the same or similar words in different languages have the same meaning in the educational practice in different countries. Beware of English concepts used in different languages: many researchers use English as the lingua franca at conferences and in their publications. They often turn to English words to quickly communicate phenomena of their own national setting to an international audience, even though the meaning in different national contexts may not be identical.

(Continued)

(Continued)

- Work towards conceptual equivalence: use conceptual differences between national research teams as springboards for conceptual development. Differences in understanding and theoretical underpinnings may show paths for clarification and the further development of a concept.

- Epistemological and methodological development: be aware of the challenge of pragmatism. Often, the challenges of successfully operating a research environment with colleagues from other national contexts leads to the adoption of a lowest common denominator approach. In other words, the research team seeks to iron out difficulties and complexities by focusing on a limited range of universal outcomes. Although practical, this can often result in real epistemological and methodological insights being lost.

- Sampling and access: beware of varying conditions regarding access to research sites and respondents in different countries, and plan for access and sampling as early as possible. Be transparent regarding the access and sampling strategies used in your research reports, even if this may open some starting points for criticism.

- Communication and collaboration: give the project a transparent organisational structure and organise clear channels of communication. Assign leading roles with respect to various parts and aspects of the project to team members from different participating countries. Reflect on the project structure from time to time to adjust the types and channels of communication and the distribution of tasks and duties according to the developing experience of collaboration.

- Publishing and dissemination: plan papers and authors and contributors in advance (even if some changes will be necessary during the course of the project) to give participant members from different countries some sense of belonging to the project and its potential gains.

10.4 CONCLUSION

In the above we have set out to extrapolate from the experience of an international research project the major challenges that this type of work is likely to create. We have characterised these challenges under a number of main headings: sampling and access, meaning and equivalence of concepts, language and instruments and team working and collaboration. We have used the project experience to indicate ways of dealing with these problems and produced a simple checklist to alert future researchers to such pitfalls.

It might appear from the above account that the project in question was very problematic and perhaps a failure. Nothing could be further from the truth. All of the partners had considerable experience of similar projects and few of the issues that arose were new or came as a surprise. As in many areas of work, experience, good leadership and relaxed and positive personal relationships overcame problems and the project outputs and outcomes not only satisfied the funding agency but added to the theory and practice of school inspection in Europe.

There are personal and organisational challenges associated with any group conducting cross-national work, and this is especially true for research teams (Livingstone, 2003). Establishing an effective operational structure is important. In common with many complex international projects involving several partners, the numerous differences across countries present operational challenges that can become barriers to effective working (Salway et al., 2011).

Cross-national comparative research demands compromise among research teams and the need to build and manage the research team. Studies that include more than one national context and involve researchers with different disciplinary affiliations, based at disparate institutions and operating within contrasting academic environments, imply significant additional conceptual, methodological and logistical complexity, as well as increased costs, when compared to national studies (Salway et al., 2011).

Nevertheless, these challenges in international research contexts should be viewed as opportunities for reflecting on uncontested norms of truth, methodologies and positions of power (Doiron and Asselin, 2015). Cross-national comparative research encourages conceptual and methodological development through the exchange of ideas and experience between diverse research teams. It is premised on the understanding that we have much to learn from each other and also in terms of providing greater insight and awareness into our own research processes and procedures (Gardner et al., 2012).

ADDITIONAL USEFUL READING

Feldman, A., Altrichter, H., Posch, P. and Somekh, B. (2018) *Teachers Investigate Their Work: An Introduction to Action Research Across the Professions* (3rd edn). London and New York: Routledge.

This book introduces a type of research by which practitioners and researchers collaborate to develop educational practices. Several strategies for designing research plans and collecting, analysing and reporting data are explained using research examples from Great Britain, Continental Europe and North America.

Jørgensen, C. R. (2015) 'Three advantages of cross-national comparative ethnography: methodological reflections from a study of migrants and minority ethnic youth in English and Spanish schools', *Ethnography and Education, 10* (1): 1–16. DOI: 10.1080/17457823.2014.922891.

By linking findings and methodological reflections from a research study into the schooling experiences and life projects of migrants and minority ethnic youth in England and Spain, this paper shows how cross-national comparative ethnographies enable researchers to (1) contextualise and compare topics identified by research participants in the course of the fieldwork, (2) analyse topics, which only appear in one research setting, and (3) explore and challenge how concepts and categories are employed by research participants in different settings.

Livingstone, S. (2003) 'On the challenges of cross-national comparative media research', *European Journal of Communication, 18* (4): 477–500. DOI: 10.1177/0267323103184003.

This article examines the rationale for comparative research and the challenges and contradictions that it poses. Using a four-fold typology of models for comparative research, a range of epistemological debates regarding cross-national comparison are juxtaposed with the practical experiences of media and communications researchers.

Robinson-Pant, A. and Singal, N. (2013) 'Research ethics in comparative and international education: reflections from anthropology and health', *Compare: A Journal of Comparative and International Education, 43* (4): 443–463. DOI: 10.1080/03057925.2013.797725.

Within methodological debates on comparative and international education, issues around research ethics have rarely been directly interrogated. By bringing together insights from discussions in the fields of anthropology and health research, this paper aims to develop a 'situated' approach for exploring educational research ethics across cultures and institutions. It begins with a critique of the legalistic starting point on educational research ethics existing in many northern institutions, which have often been imposed on other cultural contexts, with a particular focus on examining issues of consent, anonymisation and harm.

Vulliamy, G. and Webb, R. (2009) 'Using qualitative research strategies in cross-national projects: the English–Finnish experience', *Education 3–13, 37* (4): 399–411. DOI: 10.1080/03004270903099868.

Describing the qualitative research methods used in two comparative research projects that were conducted in England and Finland, this article discusses the specific issues encountered in researching in two countries with different languages and different cultures. The research findings reveal not only the ways in which qualitative data can portray teachers' experiences and perceptions of government reform and identify the differences between government rhetoric and lived reality, but also the value of such data for comparative purposes. The power of global trends in education to affect fundamentally the lives and work of teachers internationally is demonstrated.

NOTE

1   The research teams included (in addition to the authors of this paper) Melanie Ehren, Gerry Conyngham, David Greger, Jan-Eric Gustafsson, Stephan Gerhard Huber, Karen Jones, David Kemethofer, Eva Myrberg, Guri Skedsmo and Peter Tymms.

REFERENCES

Altrichter, H., Bacher, J., Beham, M., Nagy, G. and Wetzelhütter, D. (2011) 'The effects of a free school choice policy on parents' school choice behaviour', *Studies in Educational Evaluation*, *37*(4): 230–238.

Altrichter, H. and Kemethofer, D. (2015) 'Does accountability pressure through school inspections promote school improvement?', *School Effectiveness and School Improvement 26*(1): 32–56.

Altrichter, H. and Kemethofer, D. (2016) 'Stichwort: Schulinspektion', *Zeitschrift für Erziehungswissenschaft, 19*(3): 487–508.

Bartlett, L. (2014) 'Vertical case studies and the challenges of culture, context and comparison', *Current Issues in Comparative Education, 16*(2): 30–33.

Behling, O. and Law, K. S. (2000) *Translating Questionnaires and Other Research Instruments*. Thousand Oaks, CA: Sage.

Belfiore, E. (2004) 'The methodological challenge of cross-national research: comparing cultural policy in Britain and Italy', Centre for Cultural Policy Studies University of Warwick Research Papers, Coventry, 2004 wrap: 52357, No. 8. Available at: http://wrap.warwick.ac.uk/52357/ (accessed 21 May 2018).

Brannen, J. (2003) 'Towards a typology of intergenerational relations: continuities and change in families', *Sociological Research Online, 8* (2): 1–11.

Brown, M., McNamara, G., O'Hara, J. and O'Brien, S. (2017) 'Striking a balance? The continuing evolution of Inspection and school self-evaluation in Ireland', in J. Baxter (ed.), *School Inspectors: Operational Challenges in National Policy Contexts*. London: Springer. pp. 71–96.

Buil, I., de Chernatony, L. and Martínez, E. (2012) 'Methodological issues in cross-cultural research: an overview and recommendations', *Journal of Targeting, Measurement and Analysis for Marketing, 20*(3): 223–234. DOI: 10.1057/jt.2012.18.

Cacace, M., Ettelt, S., Mays, N. and Nolte, E. (2013) 'Assessing quality in cross-country comparisons of health systems and policies: towards a set of generic quality criteria', *Health Policy, 112*(1): 156–162. DOI: 10.1016/j.healthpol.2013.03.020.

Couper, M. P. and Leeuw, E.D. (2003) 'Nonresponse in cross-cultural and cross-national surveys', in J.A. Harkness, F.J.R. van de Vijver, and P. Mohler (eds), *Cross-Cultural Survey Methods*. New York: Wiley. pp. 157–177.

Doiron, R. and Asselin, M. (2015) 'Ethical dilemmas for researchers working in international contexts', *School Libraries Worldwide, 21*(2): 1–10. DOI: 10.14265.21.2.001.

Ehren, M. C. M., Altrichter, H., McNamara, G. and O'Hara, J. (2013) 'Impact of school inspections on teaching and learning: describing assumptions on causal mechanisms in six European countries', *Educational Assessment, Evaluation and Accountability, 25*(1): 3–43.

Ehren, M. C. M., Gustafsson, J.-E., Altrichter, H., Skedsmo, G., Kemethofer, D. and Huber, S. G. (2015) 'Comparing effects and side effects of different school inspection systems across Europe', *Comparative Education, 51*(3): 375–400.

Eurydice (2017) *The Structure of the European Education Systems 2017/18: Schematic Diagrams. Eurydice Facts and Figures*. Luxembourg: European Commission/EACEA/Publications Office of the European Union. Available at https://eacea.ec.europa.eu/national-policies/eurydice/content/structure-european-education-systems-201718-schematic-diagrams_en (accessed 21 May 2018).

Feldman, A., Altrichter, H., Posch, P. and Somekh, B. (2018) *Teachers Investigate Their Work: An Introduction to Action Research Across the Professions* (3rd edn). London and New York: Routledge.

Gardner, P., Katagiri, K., Parsons, J., Lee, J. and Thevannoor, R. (2012) '"Not for the fainthearted": engaging in cross-national comparative research', *Journal of Aging Studies*, 26(3): 253–261. DOI: 10.1016/j.jaging.2012.02.004.

Gustafsson, J.-E., Ehren, M. C. M., Conyngham, G., McNamara, G., Altrichter, H. and O'Hara, J. (2015) 'From inspection to quality: ways in which school inspection influences change in schools', *Studies in Educational Evaluation*, 47: 47–57.

Hantrais, L. (1999) 'Contextualization in cross-national comparative research', *International Journal of Social Research Methodology*, 2(2): 93–108. DOI: 10.1080/136455799295078.

Hantrais, L. (2014) 'Methodological pluralism in international comparative research', *International Journal of Social Research Methodology*, 17(2): 133–145. DOI: 10.1080/13645579.2014.892656.

Iwarsson, S., Wahl, H.-W. and Nygren, C. (2004) 'Challenges of cross-national housing research with older persons: lessons from the ENABLE-AGE project', *European Journal of Ageing*, 1(1): 79–88. DOI: 10.1007/s10433-004-0010-5.

Jones, K. L. and Tymms, P. B. (2014) 'Ofsted's role in promoting school improvement: the mechanisms of the school inspection system in England', *Oxford Review of Education*, 40(3): 315–330.

Leeuw, F. L. (2003) 'Reconstructing program theories: methods available and problems to be solved', *American Journal of Evaluation*, 24(1): 5–20.

Lincoln, Y. S. and Guba, E. G. (1985) *Naturalistic Inquiry*. Newbury Park, CA: Sage.

Livingstone, S. (2003) 'On the challenges of cross-national comparative media research', *European Journal of Communication*, 18(4): 477–500. DOI: 10.1177/0267323103184003.

Lynn, P. (2003) 'Developing quality standards for cross-national survey research: five approaches', *International Journal of Social Research Methodology*, 6(4): 323–337.

Mangen, S. (1999) 'Qualitative research methods in cross-national settings', *International Journal of Social Research Methodology*, 2(2): 109–124.

OECD (Organisation for Economic Co-operation and Development) (2016) *Global Competency for an Inclusive World*. Paris: OECD.

Ozga, J. and Jones, R. (2006) 'Travelling and embedded policy: the case of knowledge transfer', *Journal of Education Policy*, 21(1): 1–17.

Ragin, C. C. (1989) *The Comparative Method: Moving Beyond Qualitative and Quantitative Strategies*. Berkeley, CA: University of California Press.

Ragin, C. C. (2006) 'How to lure analytic social science out of the doldrums: some lessons from comparative research', *International Sociology*, 21(5): 633–646. DOI: 10.1177/0268580906067834.

Salway, S. M., Higginbottom, G., Reime, B., Bharj, K. K., Chowbey, P., Foster, C. and O'Brien, B. (2011) 'Contributions and challenges of cross-national comparative research in migration, ethnicity and health: insights from a preliminary study of maternal health in Germany, Canada and the UK', *BMC Public Health*, 11(1): 514. DOI: 10.1186/1471-2458-11-514.

Tikly, L. (2015) 'What works, for whom, and in what circumstances? Towards a critical realist understanding of learning in international and comparative education', *International Journal of Educational Development*, 40(Supplement C): 237–249. DOI: 10.1016/j.ijedudev.2014.11.008.

Yeganeh, H., Su, Z. and Chrysostome, E. (2004) 'A critical review of epistemological and methodological issues in cross-cultural research', *Journal of Comparative International Management*, 8(1). Available at: https://journals.lib.unb.ca/index.php/JCIM/article/view/459 (accessed 21 May 2018).

11

ORGANISING INTERNATIONAL COLLABORATIVE RESEARCH FOR SOCIAL INCLUSION

Rocío García-Carrión, Aitor Gómez González
and Javier Díez-Palomar

11.1 INTRODUCTION

Conducting international collaborative research provides a unique opportunity for generating knowledge that goes beyond the local or national existing research knowledge. Scholars working together across national borders can advance knowledge that contributes to solving global problems. However, conducting collaborative research between different teams in different countries and cultural contexts is challenging. Researchers belong to different traditions, histories and cultures and they bring their own paradigms and worldviews into the collaborative research process. When doing European collaborative research, scholars must address common research questions and concerns that have to be relevant across national and cultural boundaries. In this context, the methodologies used to deal with such a complex task play a crucial role when we aim not only to describe or explain an educational or social reality, but to transform it. This is particularly important if we aim to demonstrate how educational research contributes to improve individuals' lives providing concrete benefits to improve educational practices and policies in Europe.

Particularly, this chapter presents a case of international collaborative research conducted within the EU-funded project, *INCLUD-ED Strategies for Inclusion and Social Cohesion in Europe from Education* (Flecha, 2006–2011). This was an integrated project that involved research centres and higher education institutions located in 14 European countries. Overall, more than 50 researchers from different disciplines, including education, sociology, psychology, economy, among others, aimed at addressing the main research question of the study: which educational strategies contribute to social cohesion and which lead to social exclusion? Tackling this complex question required an interdisciplinary and international research team who could not be limited to a description of the components of the educational systems, nor to a comparison between European countries; rather it focused on explaining elements that influence school failure or success and their relationship with other areas of society, particularly focusing on social groups that are vulnerable to being socially excluded.

In the context of conducting this five-year EU-funded project, the challenge we discuss in this chapter is related to how researchers may address the tension between *local* particularities and needs (i.e. cultural features) when conducting international collaborative research. This tension emerged across the lifespan of the project, from the organisation and implementation to the analysis and dissemination and it is particularly relevant in the case we discussed because its emphasis moved beyond comparative studies into a European dimension of research.

The methodological approach used in this study played a crucial role in dealing with the challenges encountered. This chapter presents some of the main features of the communicative methodology, which involved maintaining an ongoing dialogue with major stakeholders in the field of education, throughout the five years of the project's development, contrasting and including their contributions into the process of knowledge creation. This methodological approach resulted in a useful tool to address the challenge of doing international collaborative research in the INCLUD-ED project (Flecha, 2017).

11.2 COLLABORATIVE RESEARCH TO FIND STRATEGIES FOR SOCIAL INCLUSION IN EUROPE

Over the last decades the European Research Framework has given priority to building a critical mass and solid foundations for combating social exclusion. In the context of the Lisbon Strategy (2010), developing high-quality education systems was a crucial issue to guarantee the long-term competitiveness of the European Union. Aiming to address such a complex challenge, the European Commission funded the INCLUD-ED project: *Strategies for Inclusion and Social Cohesion in Europe from Education* (Flecha, 2006–2011).

The main objective of this project was to analyse educational strategies that contributed to social cohesion and those that led to social exclusion, in the context of the European knowledge-based society, providing key elements and action lines to improve educational and social policy. Overall, the research focused on the study of the interactions between educational systems, agents and policies, up to the compulsory level (see Figure 11.1). As represented below, the project did not only cover educational structures (educational systems, reforms and policies), but also individuals' agency (teachers, students and communities, focusing on socially vulnerable groups), taking into consideration the impact of diverse educational strategies and practices at the European, state and local level. The five different social groups targeted – because of their special condition of being socially vulnerable – in the INCLUD-ED project were: women, youth, cultural groups, migrants and people with disabilities. A specific rationale underlying this choice was discussed among the consortium and described in detail in the project.

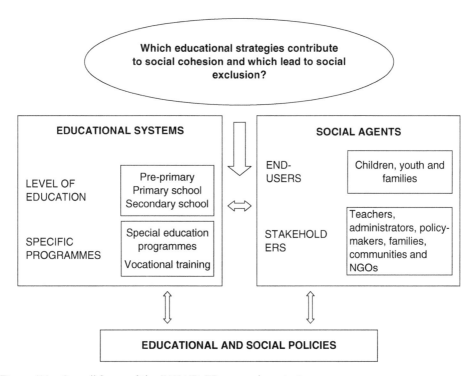

Figure 11.1 Overall focus of the INCLUD-ED research project

The project started in November 2006 and lasted five years, until December 2011. For five years the INCLUD-ED consortium provided plausible answers to the questions related to social inclusion and social cohesion highlighted in the midterm review of the Lisbon Strategy, by focusing on the process of endowing the young generation with the skills needed in a dynamic knowledge-based economy and society. Such a complex task was led by the Community of Research on Excellence for All (CREA), University of Barcelona. This research group, which we are part of, designed the project and established a consortium with 14 higher education institutions across Europe: Danube University Krems (Austria); Center for European Policy Studies (Belgium); Dublin City University (Ireland); University of Cyprus (Cyprus); University of Helsinki (Finland); Eötvös Loránd University (Hungary); University of Florence (Italy); Vytautas Magnus University (Lithuania); University of Malta (Malta); Baltic Institute of Social Sciences (Latvia); University of Timisoara (Romania); Slovenian Institute for Adult Education (Slovenia); Autonomous University of Barcelona (Spain); and University of Nottingham (United Kingdom). This consortium stands out for its interdisciplinary character and for an extensive expertise in the analysis of social exclusion and inclusion in the different areas of society (i.e. education, labour market and social policy).

The efforts of this interdisciplinary team were focused on advancing knowledge in the field of social cohesion in Europe by conducting a multi-level study that looks into theories, policies, practices and outcomes across European educational systems. To address this ambitious goal, the project was designed through six studies grouped in

Table 11.1   Structure and research questions of the INCLUD-ED project

Clusters		Research Questions
Educational systems in Europe	**Study 1**	Which school systems and educational reforms have generated high rates of school failure and which ones generated low rates?
	Study 2	Which educational practices (at the level of system, school and classroom) increase school failure and which ones lead to school success?
Connections between education and social exclusion and inclusion	**Study 3**	How does educational inclusion/exclusion impact inclusion/exclusion from diverse areas of society such as employment, housing, health and political participation?
	Study 4	How is educational inclusion/exclusion affecting the most vulnerable social groups, particularly women, youth, migrants, cultural groups and people with disabilities?
	Study 5	Which mixed interventions between education and other areas of social policy contribute to overcome exclusion and foster social cohesion in Europe?
Social cohesion	**Study 6**	How does community involvement in education contribute to strengthen connections between education and diverse areas of society?
		How do these mixed interventions contribute to social cohesion?

three research clusters that analysed in depth European educational systems, the role of social agents in them, and the coordination of educational and social policies (see Table 11.1). In Table 11.1 we capture the structure of this integrated project and the research questions corresponding to each of the studies carried out.

The methodological design of this project followed a transformative mixed methods approach (Mertens, 2018), using and combining qualitative and quantitative data (Creswell and Clark, 2007) under a communicative orientation (Flecha, 2014). Overall, all the studies combined different types of data collection according to the operational objectives established to answer the research questions properly (see Table 11.2). Particularly relevant for the main goal of the INCLUD-ED project were Study 2 and Study 6, as they provided sound empirical data for advancing knowledge in educational actions that achieved better academic results and social cohesion in schools and communities. Specifically, in Study 2 we conducted 20 case studies (five in each educational stage: pre-primary, primary, secondary, special education programmes and vocational training) to analyse effective educational practices that were decreasing the rates of school failure. These case studies were conducted in Cyprus, Finland, Hungary, Latvia, Spain and United Kingdom in 2009. Similarly, in Study 6 we conducted six four-year longitudinal case studies to examine the role of the communities involved in schools that contributed to reduce inequalities and marginalisation, and to foster social inclusion and empowerment. These longitudinal case studies were conducted in Finland, Lithuania, Malta, Spain and United Kingdom from 2007 to 2011. In both projects, quantitative and qualitative data were collected and analysed (see Table 11.2).

Table 11.2   Data collection and analysis

	Data Collection	**Data Analysis**
Quantitative	Questionnaire	Statistical analysis
	Secondary analysis of existing datasets	
	(e.g. OECD, EUROSTAT, UNESCO, PISA, PIRLS, TIMSS)	
Qualitative	Literature review	
	(e.g. ERIC, SOCIOFILE, JSTOR, ACADEMIC PREMIERE SEARCH)	
	Policy analysis	
	(e.g. Directives, policies, EURYDICE, LEXIS-NEXIS)	
	Documents	Content analysis
	Standardised open-ended interviews	Communicative data analysis (exclusionary and transformative dimensions)

Whereas different methods and techniques were conducted in the studies listed in Table 11.1, the communicative methodology was used throughout the project. The communicative methodology seeks to move beyond traditional theoretical dualisms in social sciences, such as structure/individual, subject/object, relativism/universalism, by assuming a series of postulates: universality of language and action, people as transformative social agents, communicative rationality, disappearance of the interpretative hierarchy, and dialogic knowledge (Gómez, 2017). This methodology requires creating the conditions that enable intersubjective dialogue between participants and establishing clear criteria and consensus to identify emerging categories and to contrast interpretations (Padrós et al., 2011).

For our case, the analysis of educational strategies that contribute to social cohesion and educational strategies that lead to social exclusion required the inclusion of the maximum diversity of voices (i.e. all related stakeholders and end-users) and to draw from a wide range of sources. While the voices of vulnerable groups have been traditionally excluded from research, the communicative methodology relies on the direct and active participation of the people whose reality is being studied throughout the whole research process.

The communicative approach used in this international collaborative research was operationalised through a particular organisation of the research, management, data analysis and dissemination of the results. This approach has emerged as particularly useful to deal with the challenges encountered throughout the project, as it is presented in detail in the next section.

Working effectively with partners from different countries, cultural backgrounds and disciplines cannot be taken for granted. The different educational contexts and countries in which the studies were conducted had different discourses and meanings around some of the key approaches – conceptual and methodological – underpinning the research.

In addition, the magnitude of this project required a particular organisational structure to deal with the challenges that emerged when (1) planning and organising the studies, (2) designing and collecting the data, (3) analysing the data collected and (4) guaranteeing the ethical requirements. This chapter discusses the ways in which the INCLUD-ED project and the researchers involved dealt with those challenges and the extent to which the communicative methodology (Gómez, Puigvert and Flecha, 2011) served as a useful tool to enhance a collective dialogue among the researchers, stakeholders and end-users, including those belonging to vulnerable populations.

11.3 FROM THE LOCAL TO THE GLOBAL: MAIN CHALLENGES ENCOUNTERED IN THE RESEARCH PROCESS

11.3.1 PLANNING AND ORGANISING THE STUDIES: REACHING CONSENSUS

One of the first challenges we faced in this research was establishing a common ground for understanding the main problems this project aimed to address.

Particularly, defining key concepts, such as 'community' or 'social inclusion' or 'social exclusion', was essential for all the partners to move in the same direction in future phases of the project. Researchers' understandings of those concepts might not be the same in Spain or in Finland. Therefore, the first step was to agree on a common definition of a set of key concepts so that the collection of data may allow a comparative analysis. The consortium agreed on the need to define key concepts. In fact, we discussed the key concepts for each of the six studies, and the partners involved on those had specific virtual meetings for that purpose. As a result, a glossary of key concepts became a very useful tool for the project. Definitions were derived from a systematic review building on the interdisciplinary background of the researchers. The concepts used in and derived from the different studies were progressively incorporated into the glossary throughout the entire duration of the project. However, the process for agreeing on these key concepts was not straightforward, and required several discussions and dialogues. Engaging in dialogue with others allowed us to use the powerful cultural and symbolic tool – language – to make meaning and understand other people's minds (Vygotsky, 1978; Wertsch, 1990). But not all forms of dialogue and communication are productive to co-construct knowledge.

Only a dialogue based on validity claims instead of power claims (Habermas, 1984) could be successful, where final decisions are taken following the force of arguments and not the argument of the force, breaking with the interpretative hierarchy. Communicative methodology is based in an egalitarian and intersubjective dialogue among all participants that follows this orientation. Everyone has the capacity of language and action (Habermas, 1984), and for this reason, using a communicative rationality, social agents can contribute to transform social reality. The research work in INCLUD-ED was organised following these common postulates of the communicative methodology, assuring that all participants could argue in an equal position, looking for wide consensus and agreements, which were the basis of all research actions.

Similarly, sharing and developing in a coherent and consistent way a common methodological framework is also a challenge when doing international collaborative research. In any international collaboration, as in the case presented here, the methodology has to be established and agreed upon by all the partners before the beginning of the project. In the INCLUD-ED project, the communicative methodology was part of the proposal submitted, and actually, it was one of the strengths in the project evaluation as it was recognised as a 'research perspective which has shown to have a significant social and political impact on the European educational and social systems' (Ministerio de Ciencia e Innovación, 2010). Anyhow, an additional effort was required to ensure that all the partners used and implemented the methodology according to its postulates and principles throughout the project.

Particularly, one of the most frequent tensions referred to how we can incorporate participants into the research process from the very beginning until the end of the process without losing rigour and validity. The inclusion of the participant voices during the whole research process, interacting always with the researchers in an egalitarian way, assured the rigour and validity of the research process. Researchers contributed to dialogue with participants with the theoretical background on social cohesion and educational systems and participants could use this academic knowledge to link to or contrast with their impressions, feelings and opinions. The final interpretation is co-created between both researcher and participant. The diversity of the participants, in terms of culture, ethnicity, age and social conditions, also enhanced this dialogue and produced a better understanding of reality as well as an enrichment of the theorising process, because the theory is improved directly through the participant voices.

The communicative methodology, which assumes that reality is a product of a social construction in which everyone participates from his/her own point of view, contributes to overcome this debate offering methodological instruments to solve the traditional dichotomy between objectivism and subjectivism.

INCLUD-ED illustrates this statement because we created a research structure that integrated several research bodies, to assure precisely the participation of researchers and social actors representing different vulnerable groups in equal terms, looking forward to a better understanding of reality. This structure was composed of: the *Panel of Experts* with representatives from the five vulnerable groups mentioned above; the *Advisory Board* also containing a wide range of representatives of vulnerable groups to guarantee the presence of the targeted vulnerable groups in the project; the *Working Groups* aiming at particular aspects or dimensions of the research work; and the *Free-Task Oriented Groups*, comprised of voluntary collaborators in the project providing their prior knowledge on a certain topic together with their own expertise on the matter. Table 11.3 summarises this structure to address the challenge of including the voices of end-users with the research team in an egalitarian way.

Table 11.3 Communicative research organisation in INCLUD-ED

Body of research	Aim	Participants
Advisory Board (AB)	The AB is a consultancy body containing a wide range of representatives of vulnerable groups. The purpose of this committee is to guarantee the presence of the vulnerable groups in the project and that the consortium provides recommendations that are meaningful to them.	Members from NGOs including an organisation working with blind people, an association of participants in adult education, an Arab and Muslim socio-cultural association, a cultural association of Roma people, volunteers in schools, members from foundations working with migrants or ethnic minorities, members of multi-cultural groups, members of women organisations.

Body of research	Aim	Participants
Panel of Experts (PoE)	The PoE is a scientific consultancy body, which is formed by members who contribute with their expertise on subjects that are relevant to the project aims. This panel assesses the scientific relevance of the results and provides input regarding policy recommendations.	Professors from different universities, members of the educational authorities in different European countries, members of organisations working with people from ethnic minorities (such Roma people), migrants, women, etc., members of European lobbies of women, researchers in other institutes of research other than the ones engaged in the partnership of the project, and members of the head units of different European governments.
Working Groups (WG)	The WGs carry out different tasks on the specific fields they have been assigned according to their areas of expertise.	Members of the research team (partnership consortium).
Free-Task Oriented Groups (FTOG)	The FTOGs include voluntary collaborators in the project that provide their knowledge on particular topics. These FTOGs channel the participation of different stakeholders interested in the project, offering them the opportunity to participate in a very flexible and open way.	Voluntary experts, including professors from the university, researchers, etc.

All these bodies of research created inclusive spaces for dialogue, hence the analysis of the data collected, as well as the design of the instruments to collect these data, were discussed by dozens of persons who provided their expertise to identify and clarify the evidence to fulfil the project's aims. This is called *communicative organisation* of the research process, and it is one of the main features of the communicative methodology. Communicative organisation is a standardised procedure conferring rigorousness and reliability both to the data collected and their interpretation, because it contributes to universalise the analysis since it includes many different voices and perspectives in the dialogue. Using communicative organisation, through all these research bodies described in Table 11.3, unveils the tensions of including different sources of knowledge resulting in a deeper analysis and reliable findings.

11.3.2 CHOOSING INSTRUMENTS AND REACHING VULNERABLE GROUPS, SCHOOLS AND COMMUNITIES

The decision about choosing the instruments mainly depends on the forms of data that are available for the researchers to collect. Usually, the most common types of data include qualitative data such as observations, interviews, documents or audio-visual materials (now we can also include digital materials), and/or quantitative data such as surveys, scores and other quantitative data sources, etc. (Creswell, 1998).

The case studies conducted in this project, specifically within the Study 2 and the Study 6 as described above, included both quantitative and qualitative data (see Table 11.2). Therefore, the research team discussed which instruments were the most appropriate to collect evidence from students' achievements and teachers and families' engagement in each European country. Instruments had to be useful to work in different locations, implemented by researchers with different backgrounds, with people using different languages, with different cultural references, which make it very difficult to cope with a common set of research instruments. This process again entailed several phases of discussion among the researchers, translation of the tools and validation through a piloting with diverse populations. Once again, an egalitarian dialogue becomes a key tool to address the possible difficulties that emerge from this process. In the case of the research presented here, the communicative methodology provided procedures and criteria to deal with cultural and conceptual differences to ultimately reach consensus on the tools, which ones and how to use them.

In this process of designing tools for data collection and during the fieldwork, it is particularly relevant for all members of the research team to get acquainted with the postulates and theoretical foundations on which the communicative methodology is grounded. Its interdisciplinary theoretical bases include Habermas's theory of communicative action (1984), which argues that there is no hierarchy between the interpretations of the researcher and the subject, and their relation should be based on the arguments they provide and not on their social or academic position. In the same vein, Garfinkel's ethno-methodological framework (Garfinkel, 1967) is also taken into account for a better understanding of the subjects' insights in their contexts. These principles were particularly relevant when piloting the questionnaires, for example, in the Study 4, when doing research with vulnerable groups, and including their views and voices to achieve culturally relevant tools. Having the universal capacity to argue and the importance of the interactions in mind, we used virtual and face-to-face meetings with all consortium members to design the research instruments to collect the data. Through these meetings, we concreted a first version of all data collection techniques and later, we met with the Advisory Board in order to validate these techniques. Overall, these theoretical foundations and their operationalisation in the research align with the transformative paradigm to provide a framework for addressing and overcoming educational and social inequalities and injustice through the research methods used (Mertens, 2007).

Measuring students' achievement emerged as one of the critical issues to deal with when doing research in different educational systems. In the case discussed here, schools were located in different European countries for Study 2 and Study 6. One of the selection criteria for the participant schools referred to provide evidence of students achieving higher than other schools with similar socio-economic conditions. Schools were located in different European countries, as described before in this chapter, which increased the diversity of the educational systems involved. In order to address these challenges, the international research team focused on finding evidence of educational actions that would work best in many different contexts. 'Evidence' is an important word here and played a crucial role in tackling the methodological difficulties of having highly heterogeneous case studies among them.

After many discussions drawing on validity claims (Habermas, 1984), the international research team reached a consensus on defining 'evidence' as any data source external to the school involved in the study, such as standardised tests, socio-economic descriptions of the families attending the school based on standard measures, etc. Because every case study was a complex unit of analysis, we decided to use a multi-method approach using both quantitative and qualitative data, since mixed methods usually provide a more complex, holistic picture of the reality (Creswell, 1998). Particularly, for the case studies conducted in the Study 2 and Study 6, statistical data related to students' achievement, school reports, policy and administrative documents, such as curriculum plans, were collected.

Agreeing on a questionnaire to be used with vulnerable groups living in different countries raised several challenges when conducting Study 4. The questionnaire served the objective of exploring how educational exclusion affects the vulnerable groups defined in our research, and what kind of educational provision contributes to overcoming their respective discrimination. The researchers used previous questionnaires already validated internationally as a starting point. We selected batteries of questions, and we came up with several drafts. Each one was discussed by the different bodies of research (see Figure 11.2). In doing so, we included the voices of the relevant stakeholders and vulnerable groups in the design of a useful instrument to collect the data. This is highly relevant for researchers who may work with cultural or ethnic minorities who have their specific cultural backgrounds. Enabling direct interactions with members of the Roma community, migrants or people with disabilities, is critical to develop an in-depth understanding of their life experiences and cultural values. This was critical to understanding how to approach these groups and to gaining a deeper understanding of their trajectories of inclusion/exclusion and the role of educational provision within these trajectories.

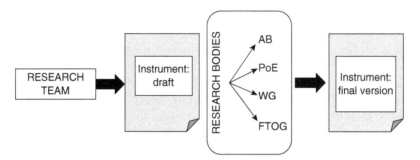

Figure 11.2   Creation of the research instrument drawing on a communicative approach

The questionnaire developed for INCLUD-ED ended with two parts and 62 questions, organised by sets addressed to concrete groups (women, youth, ethnic minorities, migrants and people with disabilities). It was presented to the participants with an introduction which detailed the project objectives and the questionnaire aims. Participants also signed a *consent form* giving them the freedom to participate in the study or to withdraw their data at any time.

There is also another important fact affecting the questionnaire (and all the instruments developed for the project): the language. Since it was used in six different European countries, with different languages, we had to translate it, making sure that all the original questions in English kept their original meaning in the language of the target population. This is especially interesting since some groups had their own cultural jargons. Including people from their groups within the research bodies allowed us to overcome this potential limitation of the instrument due to language misuse.

After obtaining the data using the questionnaire in an online survey (supported by *SurveyMonkey* software), the team created a *Guide for Statistical Analysis* to unify criteria among the partners when working on the data. That solved many potential difficulties due to the different backgrounds, traditions and expertise in doing quantitative analysis. The document stated clearly the aim of conducting such a survey within the frame of the project. Then, a detailed guide was provided to support researchers and technical assistants to work with the microdata files. This guide is the result of a series of meetings, where researchers agreed on the algorithms to use, what kind of statistical indicators to create, which models to generate with the data, etc.

The same procedure applies for qualitative data collection techniques used during the research fieldwork. Overall, for all the studies that involved qualitative data collection (Studies 2, 3, 4 and 6) we conducted a total of 717 in-depth interviews, daily life-stories, focus groups and observations with communicative orientation. Questions, themes, how to address a particular topic, etc., were discussed until reaching a consensus and agreement within the different research bodies presented in Table 11.3. The review on previous literature was always the starting point to produce the first draft, which evolved according to the dialogues and contributions provided until reaching a final version.

Similarly, as in the case of the questionnaires, the qualitative tools were piloted and discussed with different stakeholders. Each partner in their countries piloted the qualitative tools with teachers, families and children in their own languages to make them most culturally appropriate to each context.

Working in this way allowed the INCLUD-ED consortium to face the challenge of working collaboratively, involving schools and communities from different European countries, with different traditions, languages, cultural constraints, etc. This was particularly timely and relevant for the main purpose of the project to go beyond a comparative analysis, but looking for educational actions with a European dimension that could be transferable to diverse contexts. Hence it was crucial to include all perspectives and viewpoints, since the real phenomena is the result of complex situations in which different individuals and diverse groups participate with their own positions and approaches.

We argue communicative methodology provides researchers with tools such as *dialogue, inclusion of everyone's voice, breaking the interpretative hierarchy, universality of speech acts, communicative actions*, etc., to deal with traditional differences between researchers and social actors. This approach has been particularly useful to tackle the diversity of approaches to design tools for data collection and to gather quantitative and qualitative data involving researchers, stakeholders and participants (end-users) in an international and diverse environment, with research teams from around Europe.

11.3.3 ESTABLISHING A GENERAL PROCEDURE FOR CONDUCTING DATA ANALYSIS

When designing a research project researchers usually establish a general procedure for conducting data analysis and convey in the proposal the steps of data analysis (Creswell and Creswell, 2017). This contributes to ensuring accuracy and credibility of their findings. When doing international collaborative research, again, this might become a challenge and creating a common procedure is a particularly useful tool to successfully tackle this issue. For all studies within the INCLUD-ED project, the coordination team developed a *Data Analysis Guide*. This tool was highly useful with regards to the analysis of the quantitative and qualitative data. It was developed by the Project Coordinator in dialogue and collaboration with the research team in various meetings. A coding scheme was produced for the objectives of the different studies. In this particular case, aiming to identify strategies for social cohesion through education, the research team agreed on conducting the analysis of the data collected using this communicative approach and aiming to identify *transformative* and *exclusionary* dimensions in our study.

The communicative data analysis was a novel approach for many of the partners in the consortium. It is based on a double axis of exclusionary and transformative dimensions, which helps to disclose the complexity of reality and aims to avoid simplistic explanations that may categorise a dimension as entirely exclusionary or transformative. One of the most important objectives of communicative research is to focus on going beyond describing and analysing inequalities to ultimately contribute to solutions through dialogue among all agents involved. Codifying the data along the exclusionary and transformative axis might help to achieve this goal, and in the case of this project facilitated the analysis of the educational strategies that contributed to social cohesion and those that deter it (Pulido et al., 2014).

A particular example of a coding scheme is provided (see Table 11.4). This was part of the Study 6, which aimed to study the role of the communities involved in schools that contributed to reduce inequalities and marginalisation, and to foster social inclusion and empowerment. The Data Analysis Guide for this study included the coding scheme and the definitions of the categories.

Table 11.4   Coding scheme: Study 6

	Types of participation and community involvement						Improvements					
	Family education	Decision-making processes	Curriculum and evaluation	Classrooms and learning spaces	Promotion of inclusive practices	Others	Academic results	School coexistence	The participants' opportunities	Transformation of the environment	Overcoming gender stereotypes	Others
	Women (a) Youth (b) Migrants (c), Cultural Minorities (d), People with Disabilities (e)											
Exclusionary dimension	1	3	5	7	9	11	13	15	17	19	21	23
Transformative dimension	2	4	6	8	10	12	14	16	18	20	22	24

The exclusionary dimension refers to the barriers that certain people or groups experience when trying to take advantage of a particular practice or social benefit. If these barriers did not exist, the person or group that wanted to enjoy this benefit might be able to do so. In this particular study this dimension appears through data showing that family and community participation do not contribute to fostering social cohesion and do not promote learning and academic improvements. Instead, the transformative dimension shows how to transform the barriers for the populations studied to access social benefits. In this case, this dimension includes the evidence gathered from the data in which family and community involvement contribute towards fostering social cohesion and improving the learning processes (García-Carrión, Girbés and Gómez, 2015).

The research team also must reach consensus on the categories of analysis, using valid arguments to justify each of the categories proposed. INCLUD-ED organised several virtual meetings, and some face-to-face, with all the participants in the project (AB, PoE, WG and FTOG) to verify and agree on the categories included in the coding scheme, provided as an example.

11.4 ETHICALLY RESPONSIBLE RESEARCH: DEALING WITH ETHICAL RESPONSIBILITY WHEN DOING INTERNATIONAL COLLABORATIVE RESEARCH

Ethics was another key dimension in doing research together internationally, since fieldwork involved human data collection in different countries. In this regard, the entire consortium agreed on responding – at the level of content as well as at the level of scientific and ethical procedure – to the Universal Declaration of Human Rights adopted by UNESCO, to the UN Convention on the Rights of the Child and to the Charter of Fundamental Rights of the EU. Particularly, given the thematic area of the project, some specific articles of the cited international conventions were particularly taken into consideration. Overall, the proposal followed the EU ethical guidelines for research to make sure that it met fundamental ethical principles, including the primacy of the interest and welfare of the human being, informed consent and privacy. Those principals are aligned with the main international codes of ethics, namely *The Nuremberg Code* and the *Declaration of Helsinki*; as well as with good examples in different domains, like the Code of Ethics developed by the International Sociological Association or the Code of Ethics and Conduct from the British Psychological Society and ethics from the British Educational Research Association. Despite these agreements, every institution has their own research ethics board or IRB (Institutional Review Board), whose approval was also required, accounting for each national context and regulations on ethical issues.

Beyond the questions of data protection, privacy, anonymity and consent, this particular international research agreed on our ethical responsibility as public scholars to critically analyse existing strategies in order to disregard the ones that have led to more social exclusion and to shed light on the ones that have led to greater social cohesion. The research team in our project understood ethics not only as part of the scientific standards of rigour and respect for the participants within the study, but also it implies having the responsibility to improve the situations analysed drawing on the research findings. This responsibility also includes the ethical duty to denounce strategies that are leading to educational failure, condemning many vulnerable populations to social exclusion (Cannella and Lincoln, 2018). Doing research in the frame of Social

Sciences and Humanities usually places the researcher in front of that challenge: facing ethics not just as a proper way to act when doing research, but also having in mind the impact of our work as researchers for the target populations (or groups) involved or touched by our research. The consortium took on this duty, along with the shared goal of producing knowledge for and with society.

RESEARCHER CHECKLIST

- Organise a face-to-face meeting as soon as possible with all partners to discuss and agree the design, scientific activities to be conducted and the implementation of the research process.

- With the collaboration of all partners, define key concepts. In the case of the INCLUD-ED project concepts such as community and social inclusion/exclusion were very relevant to share the conceptual basis for the development of the project.

- Discuss and agree a common methodology among all partners. Reflecting upon the methodology with all partners is an essential process when doing international collaborative research.

- Create spaces for dialogue based on serious, reliable and validated procedures, which have the potential to overcome challenges. Communicative methodology is a successful example for managing research in this type of situation. A particularly important lesson learned, drawing on the example used to illustrate this chapter, is the fact that scientific knowledge is co-created between actors (researchers and participants), involved in an egalitarian dialogue oriented for validity claims, rather than for power positions. Creating spaces for egalitarian dialogue (using a communicative organisation of the research process) has the potential to overcome the difficulties emerging from the complexity embedded within international collaborative studies.

- Work *with* rather than *on* the participants especially those from a minority background, as illustrated by the communicative methodology. Involving all participants within the research project has an important ethical impact, since researchers do not look at the participants as objects of study (to be measured, described and analysed) but as subjects that ask researchers to provide scientific, reliable and validated answers to their needs. Researchers serve the participants, not the other way around. A methodological approach may guarantee that researchers do not cross this line and become the 'creators of the reality' as they occupy a dominant position in the process of research (the so-called *interpretative hierarchy* or *methodological gap*).

- Research transforms reality. Research is not a neutral activity. The communicative analysis of the information is always based in the transformative and exclusionary dimensions. This interpretation of reality allows researchers to present the research data guaranteeing the final transformation character. First it presents the main exclusionary information and finally it suggests how barriers can be overcome. The analysis is seconded by participants and also validated by the advisory board, following the premises of the communicative organisation of the research.

11.5 CONCLUSION

In this chapter, we have addressed the challenge of doing international collaborative research across national and cultural boundaries, dealing with the tensions between local particularities and needs emerging from the different local contexts, national frameworks, and even researchers' expertise and experience. We have introduced many examples illustrating how to deal with concrete situations, constraints, difficulties, turning them into possibilities to enrich the research, making it more reliable, inclusive and trustworthy. The communicative methodology draws on postulates including universality of language and action, people as transformative social agents, communicative rationality, disappearance of the interpretative hierarchy and dialogic knowledge (Gómez, Puigvert and Flecha, 2011). Starting from these postulates, researchers discuss, define and reach consensus around the research design, as well as around data collection and data analysis instruments, using egalitarian dialogue, including everyone's voices in doing so, thus breaking the interpretative hierarchy while co-creating knowledge among all participants in the research process. The communicative methodology works because it includes all participants within the research process, from stakeholders to end-users, from researchers to policy makers, everyone who is part of the study. Using this communicative approach enhances reliability, because as we have illustrated throughout this chapter, all participants contribute with their own unique knowledge on the object of study, universalising the analysis performed, making it richer and more accurate with the reality.

To achieve this result while addressing the challenge of doing international collaborative research in diverse contexts, researchers draw on egalitarian dialogue and put this in action across the entire research process, during the research design, data collection and analysis. However, this cannot be taken for granted. The communicative organisation describe in the chapter enables researchers to create spaces for dialogue to arise and to include the voices from different target groups, making the postulates of the communicative methodology more than just sentences or 'statements of intent', but rather real guidelines for researchers to advance in their work.

Research bodies such as the Advisory Board, the Panel of Experts, the Working Groups or the Free-Task Oriented Groups, as presented in this chapter, illustrate a promising way to deal with cultural diversity and complexity when doing research in collaboration with different actors. Then, diversity is not seen as a barrier, but a possibility to enrich researchers' work.

This chapter presents some hints to address diversity and complexity in collaborative research situations, such as doing educational research in different international countries, with different educational systems, populations and cultural traditions. Dealing with such complexity demands serious, rigorous, but also inclusive and participatory methodological frameworks. Using the INCLUD-ED project, we have illustrated how to deal with such challenges in concrete ways. Now it is time for the readers to take a breath, reflect on what was read, and think how to apply it in their own research work.

ADDITIONAL USEFUL READING

Gómez, A. (2017) 'Communicative methodology and social impact', in N. Denzin and M. Giardina (eds), *Qualitative Inquiry in Neoliberal Times*. New York: Routledge. pp. 166–178.

Through this chapter the readers can access a more in-depth explanation about the communicative methodology of research related with social impact. It examines the main postulates of this methodology and the main differences between them and other approaches in terms of organisation of the research, data collection techniques and communicative data analysis. Using two research examples, the chapter illustrates how communicative methodology is directly related with the notion of social impact.

Gómez, A., Puigvert, L. and Flecha, R. (2011) 'Critical communicative methodology: informing real social transformation through research', *Qualitative Inquiry*, *17*(3): 235–245.

This article provides a theoretical framework for communicative methodology and its potential use to inform social transformation through international collaborative research.

Puigvert, L., Christou, M. and Holford, J. (2012) 'Critical communicative methodology: including vulnerable voices in research through dialogue', *Cambridge Journal of Education*, *42*(4): . 513–526.

This paper involves three international scholars who participated in the INCLUD-ED project and deals with the challenges described in this chapter.

Pulido, C., Elboj, C., Campdepadrós, R. and Cabré, J. (2014) 'Exclusionary and transformative dimensions communicative analysis enhancing solidarity among women to overcome gender violence', *Qualitative Inquiry*, *20*(7): 889–894.

Through this article the readers can increase their knowledge of how communicative data analysis is performed in a research project. It is so important to clarify this concrete way to analyse the information, because communicative methodology is oriented toward the social transformation of reality and the way to analyse this reality is basic in order to reach this transformation.

Sorde Marti, T. and Mertens, D. M. (2014) 'Mixed methods research with groups at risk: new developments and key debates', *Journal of Mixed Methods Research, 8*: 207–2011.

This article introduces a Special Issue focused on mixed methods oriented towards social transformation. It includes two papers that reflect on the communicative orientation used in mixed methods research, as used in the project discussed in this chapter.

REFERENCES

Cannella, G. and Lincoln, Y. (2018) 'Ethics, research regulations, and critical social sciences', in N. Denzin, and Y. Lincoln (eds), *The SAGE Handbook of Qualitative Research*. Thousand Oaks, CA: Sage. pp. 83–96.

Creswell, J. W. (1998) *Qualitative Research and Research Design: Choosing Among Five Traditions*. Thousand Oaks, CA: London and New Delhi: Sage.

Creswell, J. W. and Clark, V. L. P. (2007) *Designing and Conducting Mixed Methods Research*. Thousand Oaks, CA: Sage.

Creswell, J. W. and Creswell, J. D. (2017) *Research Design: Qualitative, Quantitative, and Mixed Methods Approaches*. Thousand Oaks, CA: Sage.

Flecha, R. (2006–2011) *INCLUD-ED Strategies for Inclusion and Social Cohesion in Europe from Education*. Sixth Framework Programme, European Commission.

Flecha, R. (2014) 'Using mixed methods from a communicative orientation: researching with grassroots Roma', *Journal of Mixed Methods Research, 8*(3): 245–254.

Flecha, R. (2017) 'Social impact of community-based educational programs in Europe', *Oxford Research Encyclopedia of Education*. Available at: http://education.oxfordre.com/view/10.1093/acrefore/9780190264093.001.0001/acrefore-9780190264093-e-184?print=pdf (accessed 4 February 2019).

García-Carrión, R., Girbés, S. and Gómez, G. (2015) 'Promoting children's academic performance and social inclusion in marginalized settings: family and community participation in interactive groups and dialogic literary gatherings', in L. D. Hill and F. J. Levine (eds), *World Education Research Yearbook*. New York: Routledge. pp. 1–7.

Garfinkel, H. (1967) *Studies in Ethnomethodology*. Englewood Cliffs, NJ: Prentice-Hall.

Gómez, A. (2017) 'Communicative methodology and social impact', in N. Denzin and M. Giardina (eds), *Qualitative Inquiry in Neoliberal Times*. New York: Routledge. pp. 166–178.

Gómez, A., Puigvert, L. and Flecha, R. (2011) 'Critical communicative methodology: informing real social transformation through research', *Qualitative Inquiry, 17*(3): 235–245.

Habermas, J. (1984) *The Theory of Communicative Action: Reason and the Rationalization of Society*. Boston: Beacon.

Mertens, D. M. (2007) 'Transformative paradigm: mixed methods and social justice', *Journal of Mixed Methods Research, 1*(3): 212–225.

Mertens, D. M. (2018) 'Transformative mixed methods and policy evaluation', *Diritto & Questioni Pubbliche, XVIII/1* (Giugno): 247–264.

Ministerio de Ciencia e Innovación (2010) *Conclusions: 'Science against Poverty' Conference*, La Granja, 8–9 April. Available at: www.idi.mineco.gob.es/stfls/MICINN/Presidencia%20Europea/Ficheros/Conferencia_Ciencia_contra_la_pobreza.pdf (accessed 4 February 2019).

Padrós, M., Garcia, R., de Mello, R. and Molina, S. (2011) 'Contrasting scientific knowledge with knowledge from the lifeworld: the Dialogic Inclusion Contract', *Qualitative Inquiry*, *17*(3): 304–312.

Pulido, C., Elboj, C., Campdepadrós, R. and Cabré, J. (2014) 'Exclusionary and transformative dimensions communicative analysis enhancing solidarity among women to overcome gender violence', *Qualitative Inquiry*, *20*(7): 889–894.

Vygotsky, L. S. (1978) *Mind in Society: Development of Higher Psychological Processes*. Cambridge, MA: Harvard University Press.

Wertsch, J. (1990) 'The voice of rationality in a sociocultural approach to mind', in L. C. Moll (ed.), *Vygotsky and Education*. New York: Cambridge University Press. pp. 111–126.

PART V

BRIDGING RESEARCH AND POLICY

12

SHAPING THE RESEARCH PUZZLE IN AN INTERVENTION PROJECT

Lucian Ciolan, Anca Nedelcu,
Cătălina Ulrich–Hygum and Romiță Iucu

12.1 INTRODUCTION: MAKING SENSE OF A RESEARCH COMPONENT IN A DEVELOPMENT/ INTERVENTION PROJECT

This chapter is a reflection and a critical analysis of the challenges specific to the first phases of a research project, in terms of: clarifying the research field and questions in the frame of a development project; anchoring the reflection in a sound theoretical framework; formulating a coherent approach on a topic not yet systematically researched; and building a common understanding of the research field from a socio-cultural perspective. It uses a case study relating to an educational intervention project, still ongoing at the time of writing, to explore how these challenges have been met in practice and how the decision-making process and the basic elements of this specific research have been iteratively shaped.

This multi-method study, still under implementation in Romania, takes place in an international project framework (Romanian-Danish) focused on children's wellbeing. The project is called *Romanian-Danish Centre for Children Wellbeing* (RODAWELL) and is implemented in a partnership between University of Bucharest (Faculty of Psychology and Educational Sciences) and VIA University College, Denmark. The duration of the project is three years (February 2016–February 2019) and it is financed by Velux Foundation.

The project investigates the level of children's wellbeing in kindergartens (age 3–6) and primary schools (age 6–10) in Romania, situated in areas that for economic, social and cultural reasons could be deemed 'at risk'. It aims to propose interventions to improve some of the key parameters of wellbeing, mainly related to social and emotional development.

Here we will analyse the challenges of entering a completely new research field while trying to clarify and formulate accurate and focused research questions and provide a relevant methodological mix for this research, which is situated in a very challenging socio-cultural environment. Overall, the challenge is to find a balance between the research element and intervention/improvement elements in a complex educational project, while trying to find a theoretical grounding for the research, bridging the gaps of an under-researched topic and coming to an understanding of research field from the socio-cultural perspective.

The research component was progressively articulated as part of the interventions, as required by the objectives of the project. From this perspective, it is an applied research project, where knowledge gain is not a goal *per se*, but rather a means to ground a good quality intervention aiming to improve practice.

Many educational projects are initially designed as improvement interventions, to solve problems or to 'fix' current practices, and research comes as an additional component. This is frequently the case with some donor projects where funders are seeking primarily not scientific data, but concrete improvements in educational practice.

12.2 OVERALL PRESENTATION OF THE PROJECT: HOW TO ARTICULATE THE METHODOLOGICAL MIX

RODAWELL was launched as a development/intervention project with the aim to identify and pilot changes in the educational practices focused on children's wellbeing, in kindergartens and schools situated in under-privileged areas. The main objectives of the project are to address young children's wellbeing in at-risk environments, the purpose of the research is twofold:

- to identify vulnerabilities in a contested and neglected terrain in Romanian education – children's social and emotional wellbeing – by collecting, analysing and interpreting data from the field
- to test a designed intervention (called RODAWELL), aiming to improve specific wellbeing indicators, inspired by the local needs, but also by the long-standing and successful experience from the Danish educational system.

The timeline of the project has a classic, staged approach incorporating: needs assessment in schools and kindergartens; design of the intervention and building support mechanisms for implementation; validation by research, revision of the intervention and support mechanisms based on the results from the field; reflection and generalisation in terms of examples of relevant practices and indicated policy measures. There are obviously many challenges in front of a research team at the very beginning of a project, but chief among them is how to focus the investigation and to articulate the selection and combination of methods, taking into account the place of the research in the overall picture of the project.

While researching children's wellbeing at early ages as a factor that impacts their academic achievement, but also their attitude towards school and schooling, we were aware of the multiple facets of the concept of wellbeing and the actual reality it describes. There are different sources influencing the understanding of wellbeing as lived experience. As shown in a recent OECD study (2017: 62), we have proximal sources (psychological, cognitive, social and physical) and contextual sources (education policies, cultural determinants, inequality, etc.). On the other hand, as shown by Cohen (2006: 204), research has demonstrated that, rather than immediate gratification, 'engagement and meaning are the most important and lasting forms of well-being'. It can easily be observed that many of these factors are strongly related to the everyday life of the child, both at home and in educational settings. Therefore, we considered that we have to adapt our methodology to include 'real world research' (see Robson and McCartan, 2015), which can provide a fruitful basis for applied and multi-method research.

This normally leads to the use of multiple methods, either to look at the same variable from a multiplicity of perspectives or to investigate different dimensions of the research problem with different, or adapted, methods. For us this meant that we carefully analysed the mixed methods research design approach, inspired by an already established research tradition, which includes the work of Burke and Onwuegbuzie (2004), Caruth (2013), Creswell (2014), Greene (2007), Guest (2012), Johnson and Christensen (2014), Klette (2012), Ponce and Pagán-Maldonado (2015), Teddlie and Tashakkori (2012) and others.

The research design we have generated includes three elements, based on the following methodological approaches:

- an analysis of the existing *context and needs* of the pilot/intervention schools and kindergartens (case study, interviews, questionnaires for training needs assessment and observation on the field)
- a *quasi-experimental design* with an intervention and a control group on which wellbeing is analysed; based on results, action plans are proposed and implemented, and then multiple measurements are taken
- an *action research design*, supporting the implementation of envisaged interventions coordinated with teachers and strengthened through a consistent training and professional development programme delivered for teachers in pilot institutions (experimental group).

The context and needs analysis revealed two important aspects, both for intervention and for further research. Firstly, we managed to identify four key areas for calibrating the action plans for intervention (learning environment, autonomy, interactions and inclusion). Secondly, we realised that we would face difficulties in 'making space' and building a common understanding for the key concept we came up with, in an institutional culture and educational environment in which social and emotional wellbeing are marginal issues, both in terms of reflection and action.

The four identified areas for interventions framed both the action plans developed by the institutions (with research team assistance), but also the type of support offered by the project team: training, workshops, learning materials, facilitated meetings in schools/kindergartens to monitor and boost implementation.

The first dimension, learning environment, refers here mainly to the physical and ecological dimensions (we have treated social interactions separately), to the way they are managed and used to facilitate a broad perspective, which includes contact with nature, outdoor activities, community awareness, transformation of learning spaces to facilitate learning.

The second dimension, autonomy, refers to children taking ownership of their own learning, individually or by cooperating with others. When children are involved in co-planning, in leading activities and in taking responsibility for parts of the learning process, they gain confidence and self-esteem.

When we talk about the third dimension, interactions, we envisage the quality of relationships built and maintained in the learning environment, both among children, but also among children and adults contributing to their learning.

The growing and wide-spreading risk encountered by young children expose them to marginalisation and exclusion. This is why a key fourth dimension for intervention is related to inclusion. Sustained efforts are needed to see diversity as a resource for the learning process and to identify supporting mechanisms for those having all kind of special needs.

Having the four above-mentioned areas in mind for generating an intervention, a classical quasi-experimental design was articulated, with both experimental and control groups and also with repeated measures (a longitudinal approach), including a total number of $N = 448$ subjects, distributed as shown in Figure 12.1.

The quasi-experimental model includes one baseline measurement and three post-implementation measurements. All measurements were realised with the same standardised scales, envisaging mainly the overall developmental progress, social skills and emotional and behavioural development. A particular additional difficulty of the research process here was the *indirect method of data collection*, from each subject's educators and their parents. The tools used were selected scales from two version of Ages & Stages Questionnaire – ASQ-3 (Squires et al., 2009) and Ages & Stages Questionnaire: Social and Emotional – ASQ:SE-2 (Squires et al., 2015), as well as Social Skills Rating System – SSRS (Gresham and Elliott, 1990) and Strengths and Difficulties Questionnaire – SDQ (Goodman, 1997).

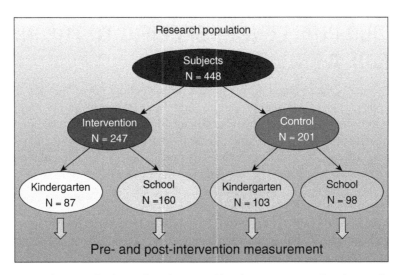

Figure 12.1 Distribution of subjects by educational level in experimental and control groups

In this quasi-experimental design, the effect of the intervention is tested using *gain score analysis*, based on a statistical model which uses multiple linear regression. Gain score analysis refers to the difference between results of different testing occasions, when the measuring instrument is focused on the same trait, attribute or skill. Linear regression is a predictive analysis used to explain the relationship between one continuous dependent variable and two or more independent variables.

We have also organised, as a third methodological pillar, an action research process, which is supporting implementation of the intervention plans designed by each of the pilot institutions to address in a specific way the four dimensions provided by the needs analysis (learning environment, autonomy, interactions and inclusion). The action research process consists in holding facilitation meetings in pilot institutions (the experimental group), according to a specific protocol, and reporting regularly on improvements and challenges. In the first year of the project in each pilot institution we have organised at least two action research meetings each month, facilitated by a professional researcher, and starting with the second year, one meeting per month. After each action research meeting, the facilitator produces a report according to a common structure, documenting the progress in implementing the action plan (an independent variable) and giving just-in-time support for effective transfer of training results on the four dimensions into daily practices in the schools and kindergartens.

By adding a qualitative dimension to the research, we convey a fresh perspective and this helped enormously in creating a shared understanding of the concept of wellbeing and a coherent approach to interventions in the pilot schools.

12.3 FOUR CHALLENGES SPECIFIC TO THE INITIAL STAGE OF A PROJECT

The challenges we have faced in this project are somehow specific to the initial stage, when the planning is still under scrutiny and final decisions are made on how to proceed. One of the most challenging tasks ahead of the team (and the first challenge that we analyse below) was to find the right place for a substantive research in a project designed to focus on intervention at practice level (implementation). Directly related to that was the process of mapping out and understanding the topic of wellbeing in the context, and in correlation with participants' perspectives. The second challenge was the need for continuing reflection by the researchers concerning the choice of a sound theoretical framework for research on such a complex concept as wellbeing. The third challenge brought to attention the difficulties of dealing with an under-researched topic, somehow marginalised both at discourse and analysis levels, with a low level of awareness and understanding among key actors. Finally, the fourth challenge concerned building an understanding of the research field from a socio-cultural perspective, involving two different thinking and research traditions, Danish and Romanian.

12.3.1 FINDING THE BALANCE BETWEEN RESEARCH AND INTERVENTION WHILE MAPPING OUT THE TERRAIN OF THE PROJECT

Given the type of project, and by having as a main focus to validate the interventions to improve wellbeing indicators (clustered in the four dimensions described above), and taking into account the specificity of each educational institution, the decision was made not to standardise the independent variable (the intervention) as is normally the case in experimental designs.

The needs analysis suggested the four key dimensions to be addressed in all institutions, but each experimental group was asked to develop its own intervention plan, according to local and institutional circumstances. Nevertheless, a common framework was set out, informed by the four dimensions and the common principle of challenging daily routines related to those dimensions. The action plans developed at each school or kindergarten level were designed following a series of common training programmes to which teachers and school managers were exposed, addressing exactly the four critical dimensions: child autonomy, learning environment, interactions and inclusion.

In order to address validity challenges, we decided to focus more on intra-group comparison (gain score analysis), although we also made comparisons between experimental and control groups. For the same purpose of increasing validity, we chose to compare and correlate scores for each subject/child obtained from educators, with those obtained from parents' scales, as well as comparing the scores obtained in Romania with similar international research using the same instruments. Not least, adding a qualitative dimension to the process through action research was also a complementary measure to keep our results at a reasonable validity.

Once the three methodologies had been agreed and correlated, we defined the purpose for each of them, as follows:

- the needs assessment leads to identification of the common framework for intervention for schools and kindergartens (the four dimensions)
- the quasi-experimental design involving standardised measurement scales has as a main aim to follow indicators of wellbeing in their evolution, in experimental and control groups
- action research has a twofold perspective: professional development tool for teachers in pilot institutions (enhancing mechanism for the delivered training programmes) and research method, complementing the quantitative measures of standardised scales with the personal experiences of the participating team.

After the preliminary clarification of the research mix and the description of finding the balance between research and intervention, we focus on context mapping.

An intervention requires more than a research design, it requires a careful mapping of the context. Researchers have to approach different layers within the project: practitioners, parents, children, management teams in educational units, stakeholders or decision makers. The underlying premise of understanding and researching wellbeing in educational settings highlights its complex and interrelated nature.

Wellbeing is a networked, summative reality, with no clear-cut borders between its structural dimensions. 'Students' well-being refers to the psychological, cognitive, social and physical functioning and capabilities that students need to live a happy and fulfilling life' (OECD, 2017: 61). Its interrelated nature is in line with the holistic view of the child, promoted for instance by the UN Convention on the Rights of the Child, which sets out that 'concepts of child wellbeing need to be multidimensional and ecological, recognizing both children's outcomes and the conditions they need for their development' (Bradshaw, Hoelscher and Richardson, 2006: 12). This approach is also confirmed by a recent OECD study (2017).

The same comprehensive perspective is also shared by Romanian policy documents, such as that issued by the Romanian Agency for Quality Assurance in Pre-university Education. The document proposes composite indicators of wellbeing, both objective and subjective, as it specifically refers to three main domains of the concept related to: individual, relations and context (Iosifescu, 2015: 93–96). In this way, the document is following the emerging international consensus in arguing that educational wellbeing is multi-dimensional, and includes physical, emotional and social dimensions.

We decided from the very initial phase to address socio-educationally challenged environments and subjects in the RODAWELL Project, in order to promote the principle of socially responsible research. It specifically targets schools with high percentages of educationally and socially at-risk children. 'Many of these children remain invisible, not least because they tend to be not included in child surveys' (Bradshaw, Hoelscher and Richardson, 2006: 6). The intervention is therefore highly inclusive, taking a close look to such diverse categories, frequently overlooked or improperly evaluated by research attempts.

After the clarification of the environment and subjects, mapping the context of the research/intervention revealed the tension between different paradigms at the institutional level: the accountability model (spread at the national level) and the innovative and participative model supported by RODAWELL. The majority of projects in Romania (capacity building, institutional development or professional development) promote the accountability model. Programmes and projects are mainly evaluated using objectives-oriented and management-oriented approaches. RODAWELL promoted a different philosophy of project implementation, grounded on school-based and individual ownership and accountability. Researchers stimulated collaborative efforts and experience sharing, aiming at enhancing communicative styles and productive interactions. Such a participant-oriented approach was surprising (and somehow confusing) for the teachers involved, as it was not part of their previous experience. Most of the earlier projects (experienced by RODAWELL teachers) focused on desirable changes as a 'must'. Teachers were informed from the beginning of the project that they were not supposed to implement some changes formulated by the trainers or researchers but to find out the most suitable changes to improve educational practices within their own schools and kindergartens and specific local community context. For example, instead of simply measuring the level of trainees' satisfaction after the training sessions, the research team asked for authenticity in the action research efforts. Such a focus is in contrast to the regular bureaucratic practices of educational institutions and this approach enabled researchers to support teachers in challenging the frustration, stress and powerless feelings generated by impersonal procedures or authoritarian modes of organisation and control. Researchers tried to follow the quality criteria identified by Guba and Lincoln (1989: 250):

(a) fairness in representing beliefs, values, perspectives of participants
(b) ontological authenticity, by allowing participants to become more aware and to better interpret own experiences
(c) educative authenticity, through which research empowers participants to appreciate and understand how others see the world
(d) catalytic authenticity, in the way research stimulates action and decision making among participants and
(e) tactical authenticity, reflected in empowering stakeholders and participants to act.

By promoting a participatory and empowering approach at every level of the context, the RODAWELL research and intervention model counterbalances the institutional patterns, where many changes are expected to be implemented in a top-down manner.

Designing research 'on the go' is not an easy task. The way methodological choices articulate the research questions is difficult to navigate and needs to take into account time pressures and limitations set by the improvement scope of the project. Understanding the context of the topic and making flexible, multi-method research designs, balancing relevance of research with validity and reliability are key.

12.3.2 CHOOSING A SOUND THEORETICAL FRAMEWORK

A complex and composite construct like wellbeing cannot be properly measured by a sole indicator in a single domain (Borgonovi and Pál, 2016, in OECD, 2017: 60). In order to accurately monitor wellbeing, it is critical, therefore, that measurement tools take into consideration its multi-dimensional nature (OECD, 2017: 60).

In order to properly manage such a composite reality, the RODAWELL approach was grounded on complexity theory (Mason, 2008; Morrison, 2002). This overarching perspective suggests that realities are nonlinear and interconnected. Educational researchers study nested, evolving and intertwining phenomena (Davis and Sumara, 2008) which should be viewed holistically; to atomise phenomena into a restricted number of variables and then to focus only on certain factors is to miss the necessary dynamic interaction of several parts (Cohen, Manion and Morrison, 2007: 34). Davis and Sumara (2008, in Pipere, 2016: 7) argues that complexity-oriented educational research represents an efficient platform to integrate previously disintegrated phenomena like knower and knowledge, representation and presentation, different phenomenal levels of explanation (transphenomenality), multiple discursive perspectives (interdiscursivity) and various disciplinary viewpoints (transdisciplinarity). This specific approach to inquiry and practice allows for different discourses to be used simultaneously in educational studies (Pipere, 2016: 78).

The research design used balances the need for reliability and validity with authenticity. Complexity theory was considered relevant for researching wellbeing within the RODAWELL project given the multi-perspective conceptual insights, but also its methodological preferences. Self-organisation, a key feature of complexity theory, argues for participatory, collaborative and multi-perspective approaches to educational research (Cohen, Manion and Morrison, 2007: 34). Researchers used a nexus between macro- and micro-research in understanding and promoting change. Collecting qualitative accounts based on case study methodology, action research and participatory forms of research made it possible to look at various situations through the eyes of as many participants or stakeholders as possible. This enables researchers to identify different coexisting causes, multiple perspectives and multiple effects to be mapped.

Our focus on children and teachers, working collaboratively with the researchers, fits the action research approach taken. Every action research project should take into account the impact on the lives of people engaged and on the subject of investigation. Wellbeing is a key feature of this project, therefore the wellbeing of the teachers was also a goal of the intervention.

12.3.3 DEALING WITH AN UNDER-RESEARCHED TOPIC

Nowadays, researchers might be overwhelmed by an unmanageable glut of data on a specific topic; they also can be intimidated by the quantity of findings gathered before their own work begins. This has not been the case with the RODAWELL project. Studying educational wellbeing is certainly not a saturated field of investigation within the Romanian context. On the contrary, the topic is under-researched and not analysed thoroughly enough. It is mainly associated with health and psychological dimensions (see Negovan, Glăveanu and Stănculescu, 2016) but ignored by pedagogical literature.

At the same time, although wellbeing is highly situated both in educational discourses and practices in Denmark, the level of scientific conceptualisation is not necessarily that advanced. Apparently, the main reason for this situation is that for a long time wellbeing has been culturally embedded in the daily routines of Danish education, and – as welfare state policy – it has been considered as part of an inner development of education in recent decades.

Children and childhood as research topics are also under-represented. At the end of the twentieth century the developments in the sociology of childhood strongly challenged the understanding of childhood as a stage of passive development (James and Prout, 1997; Mayall, 2000, 2002). Sociology of childhood is not a consistent field in Romania. Elisabeta Stănciulescu's analysis (2010) shows that the child and childhood are not popular topics. Children are explored through the psychological development lens and less as social actors. Understanding childhood as agency had a strong impact on ethos and practices of professionals working with children. Romania did not follow this trend.

In order to identify the realistic level of accumulated knowledge in the field, a literature review was initiated in the early stages of the project. The findings about the current state of knowledge pertaining to the topic indicate clearly a research gap in terms of:

- low level of conceptualisation of wellbeing and childhood within the Romanian educational literature
- visible 'holes' in the body of knowledge on this specific topic within the Romanian pedagogical context
- lack of operationalisation of the concept of wellbeing for study and for effective use in professional practices
- limited and unilateral approaches of the topic; for instance, an association of the concept with health-related issues or a focus on different categories of disadvantages affecting children's wellbeing and not on the overarching concept (see World Vision Romania's study on children's wellbeing in rural areas, Bădescu, Petre and Angi, 2014).

The lack of prior research and the lack of Romanian literature were compensated by a more consistent investigation of the international body of knowledge on the topic, undertaken collaboratively by the Romanian and Danish team. For this purpose, the intercultural composition of the research team was a significant strength of the project. Even though the team encountered different levels of conceptualisation, the cross-cultural approach was highly supportive for reaching a common understanding of the concept, calibrated to the international literature, Danish practices and experiences, and the intervention (Romanian) context.

As researchers, how did we deal with an under-researched topic? Firstly, we made a concept map: we highlighted and made clear the key concepts (wellbeing, autonomy, socio-emotional development, learning environment, inclusive education, outdoor learning) as grounds for intervention and pillars of the research process. Secondly, we introduced the overall issue of wellbeing into the daily discursive practices of the project participants. Thirdly, after making 'space' and 'voice' for wellbeing within the school environment, we encouraged the alignment of discursive approaches, as a platform for compatible or complementary educational practices. The research instruments (questionnaires/inventories) helped practitioners (teachers) to have a clearer focus on the objective indicators (like specific behaviours of children) related to complex lived experience of wellbeing. In this way, a blurry concept became a consistent conceptual ground for researchers, but also for the intervention team (Romanian and Danish experts) and practitioners in schools and kindergartens.

12.3.4 UNDERSTANDING THE RESEARCH FIELD FROM A SOCIO-CULTURAL PERSPECTIVE

Different viewpoints and historically-culturally rooted mindsets about educating, nurturing, rearing children cannot be ignored while defining a research process. On the one hand, researchers see the child mainly as an abstraction. On the other hand, 'growing interest amongst researchers, and others concerned with measuring, still largely overlook inner diversity, possibly because of perceived and real difficulties in structuring such research' (O'Toole and Gordon, 2015: 4).

Within the Romanian–Danish team, the research and intervention topic generated tensions with existing traditions about early education, child perspectives, institutional frames or professional and personal experiences.

Firstly, Romanian and Danish paradigms for early education are obviously very different. The Romanian approach incorporates a strong tradition grounded on the medical-nurturing model from birth to three years, then the dominant teaching-learning model for preschool and primary school levels. The emphasis on academic skills gets stronger as children get older, from preschool to upper levels. The OECD report *Starting Strong II* clarifies the distinction between two dominant approaches. The Romanian professional practices are embedded in the early education approach that means 'centralizing and academic strategy toward curriculum content, methodology and focused cognitive goals' (OECD, 2006: 4). The Nordic countries embrace a social pedagogy approach, which promotes a holistic view on a child's broad developmental goals and context-bound democratic practices.

Secondly, in Denmark and other Nordic countries, the child's perspective is grounded on a shared understanding among professionals and regular people. Inspired by Sommer, Pramling Samuelsson and Hundeide (2010: 30), we operated the distinction between: (1) child perspectives, which direct adult's attention towards an understanding of children's perception, experiences and actions in the world (adult approximation) and (2) children's perspectives, which represent children's experiences, perceptions and understandings in their life-world (children's own expressions).

In order to tailor this concept to the Romanian context, researchers made a distinction between the child-centred versus an adult-centred perspective, which dominates both research and educational interventions. The dominant socio-cultural pattern in Romania consists of a chain-reaction understanding of children as being influenced by family and macro-social changes. Within the educational institutions, at a first glance, children are perceived from the adult's perspective. Only at a second glance, are children perceived on their own. The RODAWELL research broke this pattern. Looking in an authentic way at children's lived reality and exploring the child's world within the educational setting raised tensions and uncertainty for teachers for whom this perspective highlighted some uncomfortable truths. For this reason, researchers needed to adapt, to slow down, to allocate time to reflect, to analyse several times, to reformulate questions. This involved a decanting process within the researcher team. Many adults working with children interpret school life in a functional-structuralist way: educational institutions are part of a wider society and serve to maintain order and consensus, educators are preparing young people for society, discipline is necessary, education is an intergenerational experience, it changes according to societal development, consensus between members of society is reinforced through socialisation. The prevalence of such implicit ideology in teachers is grounded in the communist era, where education was meant to minimise divergent interests or conflicting group values and to give priority to the group, not to the individual. Within such an ideological climate, the content of the educational process was understudied. It was not desirable to explore in-depth topics related to individual motivation, sense of achievement, conflicts or heterogeneity. According to Hendrick (2005), this understanding of childhood is not only specific to totalitarian regimes. The start of compulsory schooling can be connected to such a belief, which is embedded in most large-scale professional interventions. From the state's angle, children are seen as investments for the future of the nation.

Thirdly, given the dominant structural-functionalist interpretation of schooling, researchers had to unfold dichotomies like society versus individual, conflict versus harmony, consensus versus conflict, duty versus wellbeing. Neither Romanian researchers nor practitioners are used to questioning the institutional framework of their daily activity from a qualitative perspective, like time, space and curriculum, interactional and relational point of view. The project pushed participants to see the taken-for-granted world of a school or kindergarten as a critically debatable reality. Many people working in kindergartens and schools perceive the educational settings as well-organised institutional frameworks, run for the benefit of children. Children need to fit into the institutional framework. RODAWELL broke this unquestionable assumption. What if the actual institutional framework is not as functional, beneficial and profitable for children as we (adults in general and teachers, in particular) think it is? Zooming in and out from this complex question revealed the unspoken frustrations or unfulfilled ambitions of teachers. Researchers and teachers jointly formulated questions about how to organise schools and kindergartens in order to support functioning and capabilities that students need to live a happy and fulfilling life. In this respect, the research was a catalyst. Questionnaires on child development completed by teachers and parents and observations on daily activities aggregated a real (and uncomfortable) clash between: (1) what they think the institutional framework is and how it could be perceived and lived by the children and (2) desirable characteristics of school and kindergarten and trends of the social world outside educational units.

Fourthly, another significant part of the socio-cultural contextualisation of the research was to understand the ethos of early education professionals, as they were not only subjects of research, but key creators and influencers of the researched reality. In Denmark, professional ethos and child-centredness gravitate around the idea of habitus, understood as collective shared strategies for action and key theories. In Romania, the mainstream theoretical approach to children and childhood mainly reflects a psychological perspective, built around developmental key stages, with a focus on physical and cognitive abilities. Changes in curriculum (2006, 2011, 2017) reflect a growing awareness about the need for a more comprehensive understanding of children, with a focus on emotional, social skills and multiple intelligences. For most practitioners in schools and kindergarten, socio-emotional development of children is not at the forefront of educational efforts, although it has been part of the core curriculum since 2014.

Fifthly, researchers' own experiences bring additional pieces to the research puzzle. The academic environment, research agenda and practices in educational institutions contributed to shaping the research problem and process. Alongside this, Danish everyday practice is reflected in multi-layered contexts, such as educational settings, family and community context. The child's perspective, wellbeing, feelings of comfort and contentment, indulging in all the good things and people in your life (expressed by the generic Danish word *hygge*) represent ingredients of daily life, not simply normative concepts. All these aspects are taken for granted and embedded into everyday life routines, and it was difficult inside our team to make them explicit and to address them. The Danish researchers claimed difficulties in operationalising these topics, because in their case all these were experienced as socialisation processes. Social and interactional practices, taking benefit from outdoor opportunities and nature as a welcoming environment, are rooted for centuries in Danish lifestyle.

The adventure of articulating a sound research process in an educational intervention project led to four interrelated key challenges to be addressed by the team: articulating the research component in an intervention project while investigating the multi-layered context; having a solid theoretical grounding; dealing with an under-researched topic; and building a deep understanding of the socio-cultural variables (especially perspectives on children and childhood) of the milieu in which research takes place. Evolution and transformation of the international research team thinking and action also form an important part of the whole endeavour, and proved to be a positive side-effect of self-reflection and cooperation in an iterative, 'snowball' type of research process.

RESEARCHER CHECKLIST

In order to ensure consistency and completeness in designing a research project, a checklist for the key points of good practice can be taken into consideration; the following set of questions are extracted from dealing with challenges in the above-mentioned RODAWELL project and can be applied to similar types of educational research situations.

BALANCING BETWEEN RESEARCH AND INTERVENTION WHILE MAPPING OUT THE CONTEXT

As many educational projects begin as interventions to improve something, when trying to add a research dimension we have to be aware that the process is iterative. We need not only flexible designs, but also very flexible and self-reflecting research teams. The following questions have to be clarified:

- What is the target of any knowledge gain process in research embedded in an intervention and improvement project?

- Is the team concerned with identifying research usage at the local/organisational and system level?

- How does the research contribute to the advancement of knowledge in the field? How does it improve the 'state-of-the-art'?

- Is the methodological design appropriate to the research questions? Are they properly investigating what they claim to?

Before formulating any research project, a deep screening of the context is necessary in order to calibrate future decisions in the research team:

- Does the research realistically and rigorously describe the main features of the context?

- Do the research questions, or problems, cover different layers of the educational environments (for example: classroom, school, community, family)?

- Is it clear how the research focus was formulated in order to reflect different perspectives from various national contexts?

CHOOSING A SOUND THEORETICAL FRAMEWORK

The need for a solid theoretical anchoring becomes even more critical when you research not just a new topic for the respective socio-cultural context, but also a complex one which eventually confronts established routines on delicate topics, such as child education and development at early stages. Researchers need to have a good alignment and fine-tuning of the 'lenses' they use, so that the theoretical framework helps both researchers and actors of the project to meet and share the same perspective.

- Is the approach anchored in a relevant overarching research paradigm, understood as a blueprint for the entire inquiry and a clear statement position towards the researched phenomenon?

- Is the theoretical framework adequate to the specificity of the problem (as in the case of a networked concept such as wellbeing, which is difficult to define and even more challenging to measure)?

DEALING WITH AN UNDER-RESEARCHED TOPIC

The enthusiasm of researchers, raised by a challenging topic, can 'take a hit' when it meets the epistemological and social reality in the field, especially when exploring an under-researched area. In this case, screening of the international literature, experience of co-researchers from contexts in which the topic is more generously approached, but also 'accommodating conceptualising conversations' in the research team, are necessary.

- Is the 'information gap spotting' process intensive enough to assure an optimal conceptualisation and operationalisation level of the research field, or research problem? Is there an appropriate reference to the literature?

- Is the research team well-conversant with relevant publications in the field, relevant to the investigation?

(Continued)

(Continued)

UNDERSTANDING OF THE RESEARCH FIELD FROM A SOCIO-CULTURAL PERSPECTIVE

The contextualisation of research in its socio-cultural reality is not a new dimension, but it becomes critically important for knowledge development when you deal with sensitive topics, not sufficiently researched and solidified by patterns in practice developed over time and taken for granted. In these cases, researchers have to be aware they are not just researching a given reality, but they might challenge the reality and reshape it together with the participants. This is also a consequence of combining education intervention/improvement projects with research projects.

- Are underpinning values and operating assumptions taken into consideration (e.g. understanding the child's perspective)?

- Does the research accommodate socio-cultural patterns, especially when undertaken by intercultural investigation teams? How are the epistemological and ontological tensions approached within culturally diverse teams (especially when dealing with challenging concepts)?

- Does the research assure mapping the gap between different social and cultural traditions about nurturing and educating children?

- Is the research problem formulated in clear and explicit terms in order to guide the entire process?

12.4 CONCLUSION

One of the key conclusions after reflecting on the process of articulating a coherent research process (in the initial stage of a comprehensive and diverse project, involving extensive educational intervention) is that iterative construction of design should be accepted as normal. In the large majority of cases the research design is a strict operation happening in advance. Here we had to calibrate and balance the research component with the intervention on practices, and to create a common understanding of the research domain among key actors of the process (especially the multi-national research team and teachers in Romanian schools and kindergartens). All these actions were very much needed, demanding patience, copious reflection and many iterations to arrive at the final framework.

Many educational projects have, as a key component, an intervention focused on improving something; research is attached either as a validation mechanism for an intervention, or as a separate component to accompany the implementation and collect new data. In these cases, before starting the research, we need to ensure that we create a solid and common understanding of the topic and we need to sequentially fine-tune the methodology to fit the reality of the field, the research questions and socio-cultural patterns with potential influence. In this way research becomes embedded, and not an artificial appendix interfering with the other components.

Entering a new and complex research field, collecting data from difficult environments and subjects, managing the threat of misalignment both between researchers and participants and also inside the international research team, calls for a negotiated, but solid theoretical framework. This was essential to allow for meaningful self-reflection, construction of the research problem and questions and to give a common ground for conceptualisation of research, but also interpretation of results.

Existing socio-cultural patterns initially burdened the process of shaping the research problem and design. In counterbalance, this made some topics more visible (control, freedom, democratic practices) and the interventions more sustainable (connecting academic traditions with educational institutions' culture and daily life practices). Triangulation, constant comparison, focus on interpretation and transfer claims make it possible to avoid the misuse of data from different cultural contexts. Fine-tuning research methodology led to the development of non-intrusive data collection activities and customised training sessions (using photos and videos, teachers' and children's narratives). It embraced a triangulation of observers, sources of data, theoretical perspectives of participants and researchers, and mixed quantitative and qualitative methods to interpret data.

Such patterns had a blinding effect in the beginning of the project, as researchers could not see what was taken for granted or what was part of socialisation. Later on these aspects were converted into operational and interpretive tools. Through the project, Romanian teachers and researchers have reinterpreted their own experiences using Danish-inspired tools for understanding children including: focus on freedom, democratic practices, the child as a competent human being, autonomy and cooperation.

The research brought practitioners outside their frame of narrow understanding of school life and enhanced quality criteria for authenticity: fairness, ontological, educative, catalytic and tactical authenticity (Guba and Lincoln, 1989: 250). Consequently, research and intervention activities overcame the psychological perspective on children prevailing in Romania and brought a sociological focus, organically incorporating intergenerational understanding and empowering inter-professional work. It capitalises core values of research traditions from both countries; Danish social education and the Gusti monographic method merged into a coherent research design, without losing the aim of the intervention.

This initial phase of any research project is critical for its quality, but when you face the challenge of articulating the research as part of an intervention, the challenge is even greater. You need a good balance between improvement aims and knowledge growth aims, you need to be flexible in articulating iteratively the research design while being sensitive to both research topic specificity and characteristics of social and cultural milieu. An overarching theoretical framework is needed, first to align the understanding of the research topic inside the team and between researchers and participants, and then to create the ground for researching a reality while trying to transform it.

Alignment was somehow the meta-challenge of this project: aligning the research process with intervention objectives, aligning understanding of the research topic inside the research team and finding a common theoretical framework, and then aligning meanings between researchers and practitioners about an under-researched topic, but very sensitive from socio-cultural perspective. A researcher and a research team should be ready and prepared for all these meta-reflective processes and iterations in the initial stages of a project.

ADDITIONAL USEFUL READING

Coe, R. J. (2017) 'Inference and interpretation in research', in J. Arthur, M. Waring, R. Coe and L. Hedges (eds), *Research Methods and Methodologies in Education* (2nd edn). London: Sage. pp. 44–56.

This chapter approaches types of validity in quantitative and qualitative traditions and confusion around this concept and provides detailed discussions concerning the importance of inference and interpretation in research. Guiding questions about interpretation claims and transfer claims help researchers to make sure that interpretations and inferences from a particular context can be transferred to a range of other contexts, using quality criteria including occasions, instruments, participants, etc.

OECD (2017) *PISA 2015 Results (Volume III): Students' Well-Being*. Paris: OECD Publishing.

The volume represents a recent international study that goes beyond testing and looks at well-being indicators from an international comparative perspective; the study explores a significant set of wellbeing indicators for adolescents, covering issues from anxiety, low performance to engagement or motivation to achieve. The study focuses on illustrating how education can promote both the cognitive skills but also the psychological, social and physical capabilities students need for being happy, which are considered highly relevant for describing a wellbeing perspective in school.

Robson, C. and McCartan, K. (2015) *Real World Research* (4th edn). Hoboken, NJ: Wiley.

The key relevance of this book comes from the fact that it provides the needed elements to carry out an applied research project, with an interdisciplinary approach. Readers find valuable hints on positioning the researcher and strategic decisions needed in the process while facing real-life challenges. This is one of the most comprehensive, but also reality grounded book on educational research.

Swain, J. (2016) *Designing Research in Education: Concepts and Methodologies*. London: Sage.

A large part of this book is particularly recommended for those struggling in the initial phase of a project, both with articulating a coherent design, but also with anchoring research in the context of theoretical and epistemological debates.

REFERENCES

Bădescu, G., Petre, N. and Angi, D. (2014) *Bunăstarea copilului din mediul rural*. Cluj-Napoca: Risoprint. Available at: www.worldvision.ro/bunastare2014.pdf (accessed 11 October 2016).

Borgonovi, F. and Pál, J. (2016) *A Framework for the Analysis of Student Well-Being in the PISA 2015 Study: Being 15 in 2015*. OECD Education Working Papers, 140. Paris: OECD Publishing. Available at: www.oecd-ilibrary.org/docserver/5jlpszwghvvb-en.pdf?expires=1540808641&id=id&accname=guest&checksum=77AFCFBE31D8898AC63207A271D2E9FA (accessed 11 October 2017).

Bradshaw, J., Hoelscher, P. and Richardson, D. (2006) 'Comparing child well-being in OECD countries: concepts and methods', UNICEF. Available at: www.unicef-irc.org/publications/pdf/iwp2006_03_eng.pdf. (accessed 12 September 2016).

Burke, J. R. and Onwuegbuzie, A.J. (2004) 'Mixed methods research: a research paradigm whose time has come', *Educational Researcher*, *33*(7): 14–26.

Caruth, G. D. (2013) 'Demystifying mixed methods research design: a review of the literature', *Mevlana International Journal of Education* (MIJE), *3*(2): 112–122.

Cohen, J. (2006) 'Social, emotional, social, ethical and academic education: creating a climate for learning, participation in democracy, and well-being', *Harvard Educational Review*, *76*(2): 201–237.

Cohen, L., Manion, L. and Morrison, K. (2007) *Research Methods in Education* (6th edn). New York: Routledge.

Creswell, J. W. (2014) *Research Design: Quantitative, Qualitative and Mixed Methods Approaches* (4th edn). Thousand Oaks, CA: Sage.

Davis, B. and Sumara, D. (2008) 'Complexity as a theory of education', *Transnational Curriculum Inquiry*, *5*(2). Available at: http://nitinat.library.ubc.ca/ojs/index.php/tci (accessed 13 March 2017).

Goodman, R. (1997) 'The Strengths and Difficulties Questionnaire: a research note', *Journal of Child Psychology and Psychiatry*, *38*: 581–586.

Greene, J. (2007) *Mixed Methods in Social Inquiry*. San Francisco: Jossey-Bass & Wiley.

Gresham, F.M. and Elliott, S.N. (1990) *Social Skills Rating System (SSRS)*. Circle Pines, MN: American Guidance Service.

Guba, E.G. and Lincoln, Y. S. (1989) *Fourth Generation Evaluation*. Newbury Park, CA: Sage.

Guest, G. (2012). 'Describing mixed methods research: an alternative to typologies', *Journal of Mixed Methods Research*, *7*: 141–151.

Hendrick, H. (ed.) (2005) *Child Welfare and Social Policy*. Bristol: Policy Press.

Iosifescu, Ș. C. (ed.) (2015) *Raportul national privind starea calitătii în unitătile de învătâmânt preuniversitar public din mediul rural*. Bucureşti: Tracus Arte.

James, A. and Prout, A. (eds) (1997) *Constructing and Reconstructing Childhood: Contemporary Issues in the Sociological Study of Childhood*. London and New York: Routledge Falmer.

Johnson, B.R. and Christensen, L.B. (2014) *Educational Research Methods: Quantitative, Qualitative, and Mixed Approaches* (5th edn). Thousand Oaks, CA: Sage.

Klette, K. (2012) 'Mixed methods in educational research', in *Mixed Methods in Educational Research*. Report from the March Seminar 2012. Norwegian Educational Research towards 2020 – UTDANNING2020. Available at: www.uv.uio.no/ils/personer/vit/kirstik/publikasjoner-pdf-filer/klette.-mixed-methods.pdf (accessed 14 February 2019).

Mason, M. (ed.) (2008) *Complexity Theory and the Philosophy of Education*. Oxford: Wiley-Blackwell.

Mayall, B. (2000) 'The sociology of childhood in relation to children's rights', *The International Journal of Children's Rights*, *8*(3): 243–259.

Mayall, B. (2002) *Towards a Sociology for Childhood: Thinking from Children's Lives:*. Maidenhead: Open University Press.

Morrison, K. (2002) *School Leadership and Complexity Theory*. London and New York: Routledge Falmer.

Negovan V., Glăveanu, V. and Stănculescu, E. (2016) 'Mapping psychological well-being: the case of children and adolescents in Romania', in B. Nastasi and A. Borja (eds), *International Handbook of Psychological Well-Being in Children and Adolescents*. New York: Springer. pp. 151–170.

OECD (2006) *Starting Strong II: Early Childhood Education and Care*. Paris: OECD Publishing. Available at: www.oecd.org/edu/school/37519079.pdf (accessed 22 March 2017).

OECD (2017) *PISA 2015 Results (Volume III): Students' Well-Being*. Paris: OECD Publishing. Available at: www.oecd.org/education/pisa-2015-results-volume-iii-9789264273856-en.htm (accessed 21 May 2017).

O'Toole, L. and Gordon, J. (2015) 'Can we measure happy, healthy and meaningful lives?', *Learning for Well-being Magazine*, *1*, published by Universal Education Foundation. Available at: www.l4wb-magazine.org/mag01-art10-otoole-jgordon (accessed 12 April 2017).

Pipere, A. (2016) 'Envisioning complexity: towards a new conceptualization of educational research for sustainability', *Discourse and Communication for Sustainable Education*, *7*(2): 68–91.

Ponce, O. A. and Pagán-Maldonado, N. (2015) 'Mixed method research in education: capturing the complexity of the profession', *International Journal of Educational Excellence*, *1*(1): 111–135.

Robson, C. and McCartan, K. (2015) *Real World Research* (4th edn). Hoboken, NJ: John Wiley.

Sommer, D., Pramling Samuelsson, I. and Hundeide, K. (2010) *Child Perspectives and Children's Perspectives in Theory and Practice*. Dordrecht: Springer.

Squires J., Bricker D.D. and Twombly E. (2009) *Ages & Stages Questionnaires: A Parent-Completed Child Monitoring System (ASQ-3)* (3rd edn). Baltimore, MD: Paul H. Brooks.

Squires J., Bricker D. D. and Twombly E. (2015) *Ages & Stages Questionnaires: Social-Emotional. A Parent-Completed Child Monitoring System for Social-Emotional Behaviors (ASQ:SE-2)* (2nd edn). Baltimore, MD: Paul H. Brooks.

Stănciulescu, E. (2010) 'Children and childhood in Romanian society and social research: ideological and market biases and some notable contributions', *Current Sociology*, *58*(2): 309–334.

Teddlie, C. and Tashakkori, A. (2012) 'Common "core" characteristics of mixed methods research: a review of critical issues and call for greater convergence', *American Behavioral Scientist*, *56*(6): 774–788.

Uprichard, E. (2008) 'Children as "beings and becomings": children, childhood and temporality', *Children and Society*, *22*: 303–313

Williams, T. and Rogers, J. (2016) 'Rejecting "the child", embracing "childhood": conceptual and methodological considerations for social work research with young people', *International Social Work*, *59*(6): 734–744.

13

NAVIGATING MULTI-PERSPECTIVE, MULTI-LEVEL AND LONGITUDINAL RESEARCH

Tamara Katschnig, Corinna Geppert, Mariella Knapp, Michaela Kilian, Sonja Bauer–Hofmann and Tanja Werkl

13.1 INTRODUCTION

This chapter addresses the challenges of setting up and managing a multi-perspective, multi-level and longitudinal method study. It considers the persons involved in the research project, data gathering processes, data analysis and knowledge exchange.

It draws on experiences from a school evaluation project called NOESIS (Niederoesterreichische Schule in der Schulentwicklung – Lower Austrian New Middle School in the School Development Processes). NOESIS was an evaluation project whose overall aim was to investigate if a new school model, the New Middle School (NMS) – which was introduced in 2009 as a new school type in secondary I (10- to 14-year-olds) in Austria – reached the goals that were set, namely, to provide better educational opportunities for all students and to lead as many students as possible to higher secondary education. NOESIS served as an example of how to design a project that can emphasise a multi-level perspective in the complex social circumstances in which schools are situated. Schools can be regarded as complex and ever-changing social environments, relying on the persons directly and indirectly involved in school matters like students, teachers, principals, administrators and family members. Besides these groups of persons, the regional surroundings play a considerable role in creating a space for schools, and schools themselves have implicit rules that create their own school culture. In the evaluation project, it was necessary to try to capture at different levels as many perspectives as possible in order to see how schools and the school model worked.

Besides the groups of persons involved at the micro- and meso-level, legislation also influences each school on the macro-level. In this specific case, Austria's government decided first to implement the NMS as a school trial in which schools could participate voluntarily and receive additional funding for the transformation process. However, in 2012, the NMS was implemented as part of the regular education system and schools were forced to transform. Such circumstances bring challenges: such a transformation process (implementation of a school trial into the regular system) could make a project concerned only with the school trial obsolete. The NOESIS project, however, defined itself as a project dealing with the implementation process and school development processes at the same time. The focus of the NOESIS project was not only on achievement data in terms of standardised assessments or grades. It mainly focused on the conditions for successful educational transitions (moving from one institution to another) and trajectories (development processes within a school career).

To evaluate the complex social situations related to school reforms and to capture the perspectives of the most important persons involved in and affected by the reform, we designed the NOESIS project as a multi-perspective, multi-level and longitudinal project, and hence this chapter deals with the question: what kind of aspects need to be addressed when dealing with the challenge of a multi-perspective, multi-level and large-scale research project within the context of a school evaluation framework?

The challenges are addressed in the present chapter under four major aspects: (1) organisational matters, (2) data collection, (3) data inquiry and (4) dissemination of results.

13.2 THE RESEARCH PROCESS OF THE NOESIS PROJECT

The NOESIS project was a long-term project that was carried out during an eight-year period (2010–2017). The self-declared aim of the school model was to broaden the educational base of all students so that they may have access to more educational opportunities, while at the same time to reduce the number of students with insufficient skills. The key evaluation criteria were organisational measures (time-table, timetable design) and measures of changed didactic strategies. The questions referring to these measures and strategies were: do students notice pedagogical innovations, e.g. team-teaching, changes in the time structure, project learning, individualised instruction, feedback tools, and if so, under which conditions are these strategies perceived as successful? Furthermore, there were questions concerning the performance, transition rates, social integration and the manner in which student flows occurred in the new system. Is there a change in student distribution at the first secondary level? Educational transitions, namely the transition from primary school to secondary school and that from secondary I to secondary II, were meant to be eased through the school reform and educational opportunities for students enriched. Educational aspirations of students were presumed to increase over time and remain stable, so as to retain as many students as possible in the education system, and especially to increase the number of students moving to higher (vocational) education.

The government-funded project was conceived as an impact study to investigate whether and how the educational goals of the implementation had been reached and focused on the opportunities that the implementation opened for the students concerned. Conceptually, it was not designed as a classical summative, value-added and best-practice oriented programme evaluation, but focused rather on the possibilities that were offered to the actors through the implementation process. This has its roots in the capability approach (Sen, 1980, 1992, 2000, 2003, 2009), which suggests that expansion of opportunities is a key element for leading a successful life. In this sense, it was not constructed as an exclusive measurement of achievement data of schools, students and teachers, but was intended to capture as many perspectives as possible. In investigating a school reform, those most concerned needed to be heard, and so this evaluation project emphasised the perspective of students especially. Being in regular contact with schools and by informing them regularly about the results of the project this evaluation can in classical categories be defined as a formative evaluation. With reference to Shadish, Cook and Leviton (1992) and their stages of evaluation theories, the NOESIS-project was oriented on an integration of descriptive knowledge about the use and impact of the school reform as a social programme, but also taking the context and requirements of knowledge thus produced into account (Stage Three Theories).

In this framework of our evaluation research, we speak of institutional players, as those persons who are mostly affected by the reform project. In the same way as the world of students has a different structure from the world of teachers, the world of the family home is composed differently from that of school, and so on. Different methods drawing on different paradigms had to be used to try and capture these multiple perspectives. Hence, the evaluation project was designed as a multi-perspective, multi-level and longitudinal study, separated into four different sections: Transitions, School Settings, Instructional Patterns and Capacity Building, which all used different methodological approaches (see Figure 13.1).

Each section had specific foci, methods and therefore different theoretical assumptions, which allowed an evaluation of the school reform from different points of reference and therefore furnished insights into a complex situation. This also led to challenges when it came to data analysis since direct triangulation or a comparison of data strands was not possible.

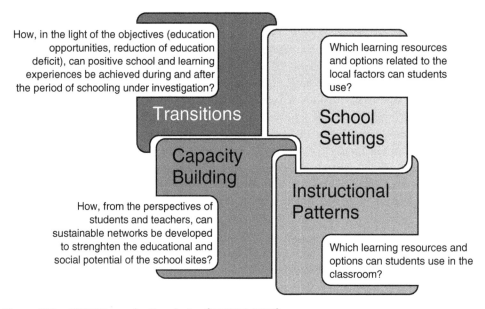

How, in the light of the objectives (education opportunities, reduction of education deficit), can positive school and learning experiences be achieved during and after the period of schooling under investigation?

Transitions

Which learning resources and options related to the local factors can students use?

School Settings

Capacity Building

Instructional Patterns

How, from the perspectives of students and teachers, can sustainable networks be developed to strenghten the educational and social potential of the school sites?

Which learning resources and options can students use in the classroom?

Figure 13.1   NOESIS – evaluation design (NOESIS, 2010)

13.2.1 TRANSITIONS

The first section investigated key factors and conditions for successful educational trajectories from a longitudinal perspective. This was possible by following students, teachers and their parents from the last year of primary school (4th grade) through secondary I to the end of compulsory school (9th grade) and each year asking them to complete questionnaires about their school lives, learning activities, motivation and other out-of-school aspects. Survey data of three cohorts, each consisting of 1500 students and starting in year 1, 2 and 3 of the study were accompanied by questionnaires, completed by their parents and their teachers. Setting up and conducting a longitudinal panel study is very demanding for organisational matters, team-building processes and for acquiring permissions, and these are just a few aspects that will be discussed in this chapter. Another very important issue is the task of avoiding panel mortality, especially the loss of specific groups of persons, which might cause biases in the sample.

In addition to organisational matters, the focus to be set in the data collection had to be decided. Besides collecting achievement data, the main focus of the section was on specific conditions for successful educational transitions and trajectories.

Students' development with respect to soft data (educational aspirations, learning motivation, academic self-concept, wellbeing in school, learning support, cooperation, in- and out-of-school support), as well as achievement data, were taken into account. We used academic achievement (grades) as control variables, but not as the main outcome and not as the main indicator for success, which was a matter of negotiation with the contracting authority right at the start of the project since the project was research on demand (Geppert et al., 2015a, 2015b; Katschnig, Geppert and Kilian, 2011).

In the survey concept students were considered as nested in classes which are nested in schools that are nested in regions, and were taken into account as such while analysing the data, which again is a challenge since advanced mathematics needed to be applied (Raudenbush and Bryk, 2002; Snijders and Bosker, 1999).

13.2.2 SCHOOL SETTINGS

For the second section we gathered information on schools and school sites by using data from national statistics. In this section, we focused on the requirements, resources and options of different schools. Data was collected using telephone interviews and surveys as well as elements of deliberative problem-solving methods (Fung, 2004) and combining their principles with the Delphi method (Linstone and Turoff, 1975) for initiating democratic school improvement processes (Dewey, 1916). Students, teachers, parents, principals and representatives of the local environment of four schools were asked to report about expectations and problems they faced at their school, and about options on how they might change the situation. Data collection, which was carried out in a multiple-step process with feedback loops, took place several times from year 1 to year 4 of the study. Challenges faced in this section related especially to the use of different methods, ensuring that they appealed to participants so as to engage them in the data collection process, to analyse the different data sources within the study and with respect to the data gained in the other sub-studies, and to include the representatives of the local environment in the process. Here, it was especially important to find good ways of providing feedback to all persons involved so as to keep them in the multi-step process.

13.2.3 INSTRUCTIONAL PATTERNS

This strand of the study was interested in the conditions under which the specific measures introduced by the school reform (e.g. suspending achievement-based tracking, new forms of assessment, student-centred individualised learning) were experienced as helpful in meeting learners' needs in heterogeneous classrooms. Drawing on 'herme-neutic phenomenology' as a method for 'researching lived experience for an action-sensitive pedagogy' (van Manen, 1990) the inquiry focused on students' and teachers' narratives in a number of case studies. In year 2 and 3 students in eight schools participated in focus groups and teachers were interviewed. Schools for this section were chosen based on the demographic characteristics of the region, the school and the students involved in the schools, which is why it was particularly important here to have a good statistical database – provided by the Transitions section as well as by data retrieved from the Federal Office of National Statistics (Statistik Austria).

13.2.4 CAPACITY BUILDING

'Students have a lot to tell us that could make school better' (Rudduck, 2007: 591). This was the slogan for perceiving students as experts of their lived world and using their voices to capture their perspectives for school improvement in the fourth section, the peer review study. The intent of the participatory approach of the peer evaluation, in the sense of Kurt Lewin (1948), was to answer the question as to how, from the perspectives of students and teachers, it was possible to develop sustainable networks for strengthening the educational and social potential of the specific school. In year 1 four school sites participated in the NOESIS peer evaluation. In the context of the in-depth evaluation, a group of teachers and students had to visit a partner school in year 2. The student and teacher teams were trained in research methods before the school visit and conducted their own research at the partner school according to their own interests. Teachers authored peer reviews and submitted them independently to the partner school after the school visit, while the outcomes of students' research were written down by the researchers to keep the student workload small (Feichter, 2011, 2012). As a follow-up, group discussions with teachers and principals of the participat-ing schools were held to discuss the impact of the peer evaluation for school developmental purposes. This part of the project was very time-consuming and demanding in terms of organisational, methodological and data collection matters in order to capture the voice of the participating students and teachers.

All four parts of the project led to a broad picture of the research objective. Having four different sections dealing with different perspectives and different methods of data inquiry also meant that there had to be strong boundaries between the four sec-tions to avoid having at the end only specific answers to specific problems, but not a complete picture of the implementation process. Therefore, it was important to have many overlaps, and to connect the sections tightly by steps and levels of analysis, as well as through organisational matters, and the necessary team-building processes. While these four sections must be seen as four parts of a whole, each section also had its own challenges. To avoid over-complexity, this chapter draws attention especially to the Transitions part of the project, the longitudinal study and the special challenges and problems of setting up such a study within the given context, but will also refer to the other parts of the project so as to help researchers who find themselves in more or less similar situations.

13.3 THE MAIN CHALLENGES IN THE EVALUATION PROJECT NOESIS

Challenges in such a multi-perspective, multi-level and longitudinal project were separated into four different aspects, namely, organisation, data collection, data analysis, and dissemination of results.

13.3.1 THE ORGANISATION OF A RESEARCH PROJECT

Concerning organisational matters, various aspects become visible during the research process. First of all, research on demand always means that one has to deal with the tension between accountability to the contracting authority and the principle of freedom of research. Hence, one has to differentiate between basic research and research on demand, which is a significant challenge, especially from the perspective of an evaluation project. Basic or fundamental research mostly refers to original investigations intended to increase the body of knowledge without necessarily focusing on a specific practical goal. Application possibilities of the research results are of subordinate importance, with the pure knowledge gain in the foreground (see OECD, 2002). In contrast, research on demand is applied research and means 'the contractually agreed, paid, time-limited taking on of research and development tasks for a contracting authority by a legally and economically independent contractor, whereby the results obtained are transferred to the contracting authority in connection with specific exploitation rights' (Rüdiger, 2000: 26). The project leader is therefore obliged to provide certain research services to the contracting authority. In university research, the term research on demand often has negative connotations, as it is associated with the latent accusation of doing everything possible to satisfy the contracting authority. It is therefore important to be aware of the accountability to the contracting authority and of freedom of research, and clearly distinguish between the two. Work with publications plays an essential role here. Thus, there should be a clear distinction between feedback reports and publications for the contracting authority or the public, as well as publications within the scientific community.

13.3.1.1 The research team

Such an extensive project with so many different data sources requires more than one researcher. So, another important aspect when dealing with organisational matters is team-building and the distribution of tasks. Especially in the case of an evaluation project running for several years and encompassing different sub-areas, it is vital to cooperate with different specialist divisions, develop a specific organisational structure and define project roles: therefore teamwork is seen as the basic requirement to ensure the success of a project (PMA, 2009). The more people involved, the greater the need from the outset for 'clear objectives, clear allocation of roles, active participation of all members, good communication, rules and standards, motivated team members and clear decision-making authority' (PMA, 2009: 23). A project-start workshop, for example, is ideal for developing and establishing a project-specific identity within the project team, but workshops in general help coordination and communication with all involved, from permanent project members to volunteer students who help perform the data inquiry and who might be able to complete their Bachelor or Master theses within the project. Furthermore, national and international exchanges with colleagues are important, but this is sometimes difficult at large conferences. So the facilitation of international exchanges in the form of workshops can also be seen as crucial. Workshops can open up a setting where one's own project is at the forefront and its results can be presented and discussed from an international perspective and in relation to international research findings. This also affords the possibility of developing important networks and receiving a critical view from an outside perspective. So national and international workshops with researchers who can contribute by addressing challenges in the project are important events, as are regular meetings with the members of the project, and the production of meeting protocols to keep everyone informed about the steps undertaken. In this context, a continuous exchange with the contracting authority is also necessary in order not to lose sight of the common goals.

13.3.1.2 The participants

Another organisational aspect falls under information to participating schools and acquiring permissions. First of all, the schools involved in the project, i.e. principals, teachers, parents and students, have to be informed about the different steps of the evaluation, the aims and how they can benefit from taking part in the evaluation. In our case, we let them know about the next steps at the end and beginning of each school year and right before the planned surveys. Choosing the right language is very important since not everyone is familiar with the scientific language used in such a project. Ongoing information is also essential to keep schools motivated to continue participating in such a panel study (see also Section 13.3.2 on data collection).

Conducting research with children aged nine to fifteen years not only means receiving general permission from the government and the school board, but parents must also allow their children to participate in the study, which goes hand in hand with the need to distribute information. This directly leads to another sensitive issue, namely, compliance with data protection rules, which has to be taken very seriously. One has to be very clear on how to obtain the data, how to anonymise the data and where to store them properly.

Ethical principles must be observed and followed (Fanelli, 2009; UK Research Integrity Office, 2009). From this perspective, three issues are in the forefront: (1) there must be voluntary and informed consent of the participants; (2) anonymity must be guaranteed; (3) any risks for the participants must be identified and eliminated if the benefit of the study is to be greater than the risk (see Mayer, 2007: 156). Therefore, it can be deduced that all participants were previously informed about the survey (by means of information sheets) and participation in the data collection processes was necessarily on a voluntary basis. The data should be anonymised so that no conclusions on the respondent can be drawn. In our case, we anonymised the individual data and the data on the schools and did not make any of the identifiable data public, nor did we provide them to our contracting authority so as to avoid any sort of league-table discussions, which anyway were not possible based on the sort of data we collected. In addition to the information sheet, the participants, or if the research addressed the students, their parents, were asked to sign a letter of consent.

It is important not to burden schools with surveys beyond everyday school activities, so running an exact timeline when to organise what, where, with whom and knowing who would be involved is very helpful, especially since new issues might arise and it may take longer than expected to find solutions.

13.3.2 THE DATA COLLECTION

A main challenge in doing a multi-perspective, multi-level and longitudinal study with three cohorts is to produce data of high quality while at the same time being cost neutral and not too time consuming for the researchers.

To avoid problems in the data collection process, pre-tests were planned and conducted. Pre-tests facilitate obtaining feedback from colleagues and participants about the research instrument used, the research setting and the process of data collection. For longitudinal studies pre-tests are of special interest, because to depict educational trajectories it is necessary to ask the same questions at each point in time. Later changes to the questionnaires limit the possibility of longitudinal statements and raise validity issues. Pre-tests also allow for paying attention to culturally sensitive questions and avoiding them. In Austria, for example, it would be very insensitive to ask questions about income. Hence, it is necessary to consider the importance of raising sensitive issues in the survey, how these can be dealt with and where or when they can be placed in survey waves.

13.3.2.1 Keeping participants in the study

In order to be able to link the data of individual questionnaires, students, teachers, parents and principals at the schools were surveyed and asked similar questions. Here, the task of keeping randomly selected schools over the years and avoiding panel mortality, which is 'the decrease in the size of panel from one wave to the next' (Bailey, 1994: 211), is very important. As long as the content of the survey is interesting or helpful for the respective participants, they are interested in participating. Therefore, it is important to identify the expectations of the survey parties involved and how those expectations can be embedded in the various phases of the implementation. There are often differences in the expectations of participants, schools and the school authority regarding the possible impact of the evaluation. Therefore, it is important from the very beginning to communicate and clarify expectations and interests of the research project (and the contracting authority) and possible benefits for the participating schools. Clarity about the research, but also about the benefits for participants, ensures that motivation is maintained for participation over time. Sometimes it might be difficult to bring all the expectations together, but it seems useful to be sure about the intentions and assignments of the research project. Performing research in schools can often give those to be involved a feeling of being monitored and controlled, which might result in a lack of willingness to participate. Researchers should be aware of these worries and consider strategies for dispelling such concerns. In the NOESIS evaluation we made clear that the results of the study would only be reported on an aggregate level to the school authority, and so it would not have access to results of individual schools, teachers or students. The anonymity of student data was also an important issue because complete anonymity is hardly possible with this type of longitudinal and multi-perspective project. To match the data of the participants and ensure careful and confidential handling of their data we used a sensitive number code that was noted on the questionnaires by the respondents. This strategy also helped us deal with the participants' concerns. Each year, permission to participate was sought again. Even persons who had not given their consent to participate earlier were asked again in the following school year whether they wanted to participate.

Another important strategy to avoid panel mortality is to contact the schools on time. The participating schools, teachers and parents should be informed of the surveys at least three months before each survey. Schools that failed to respond to the information were contacted again by email or by phone.

A telephone and email contact point appeared on all information letters and announcements to ensure that schools and parents were able to directly contact the project coordination team in the event of uncertainty. This established a relationship of trust with the affected groups (teachers, students, parents, principals), which proved to be important for avoiding panel mortality.

Attractive prizes such as tablets, cinema tickets and wireless on-ear headphones could serve as incentives and increase the motivation of the students to participate in the data collection processes.

In addition to collecting information, providing feedback proved to be an important instrument for keeping schools engaged in the project. The kind of feedback that can be given is not only determined by the research design, but also by the groups of persons to be addressed. The possibilities for feedback range from written reports to presentations for parents or teachers, as well as discussions with principals (for more information on this, see the dissemination of results).

13.3.2.2 The need for resources

Data collection processes, especially in a longitudinal project, require many resources and such a multi-perspective, multi-level and longitudinal project can only be planned by acquiring a great deal of external resources in advance. Acquiring additional staff in the form of student apprentices is another possibility for dealing with this challenge. They can collect data at schools, but also enter the data using statistical analysis software. It is necessary to prepare student apprentices well for the survey distribution, and guidance for each work step can be provided by writing down instructions and tasks. This also enables the student apprentices to act in a similar way to researchers and to alleviate possible doubts in the minds of participants. Initial training courses for student apprentices and having contact persons who can be reached by telephone at any time to answer questions is helpful for guaranteeing the quality of the research concerning data collection. A list of the guidelines we used in our project for student apprentices is as follows: (1) guidelines for contacting participating schools, (2) instructions on how to act during the data collection process, (3) guidelines for the confidential handling of data, (4) guidelines for giving feedback to the project team on incidents during the data collection process in schools, (5) guidelines for coding data, (6) guidelines for the data entry, (7) guidelines on how to ensure that data entry is done properly. The inclusion of student apprentices should not only be seen as a resource for researchers, but also as a benefit for the students themselves since they learn how to conduct research in this field. Therefore, they should have the possibility of being integrated into the research project as soon as possible and should be informed about the whole research process (the idea, object and aim of the study, the validation of the instruments and the data analysis procedures). Having an overview of the research enables them to act in line with the project requirements during the data collection process and also guarantees the quality of the data (entry). High quality of data entry is necessary to proceed to the next step, the data analysis procedure, where other challenges may occur.

13.3.3 THE DATA ANALYSIS

Data analysis and the integration of results from different sections may be fraught with pitfalls, especially when dealing with different kinds of datasets, different levels of analysis and multiple perspectives of the persons involved.

In our case, the Transitions section, characterised by the longitudinal panel study, served as a basis. The other sections for which case studies were conducted were used for obtaining a deeper insight into some of the schools included in the longitudinal approach. This meant we had schools where we were able to triangulate data from the longitudinal study and the case studies so as to dig deeper and obtain answers to specific questions.

One important aspect was that the data collection phases happened in parallel and not sequentially and that data integration occurred at the analysis level. Creswell and Plano Clark (2007: 5) point out 'that the use of quantitative and qualitative approaches in combination provides a better understanding of the research process than either approach alone'. Mixing methods therefore provides some more insights into the research process itself. The use of mixed methods, or multiple methods, can even lead to a better understanding of the processes especially when it comes to formative evaluation research of policy reform efforts, as in our case (see also Kelle, 2007).

The integration of the different databases was helpful for identifying the development of the students in the New Middle School by means of the longitudinal data of the transition section and for explaining these developments in accordance with school life and the processes within the school. Here also, the importance of different perspectives (participants – schools – school environment) becomes obvious. The point of integration is therefore at the analysis level and is important for gaining a holistic view of changes during the school reform.

Table 13.1 indicates the different layers and how the sections and methods refer to each other. There are four main groups of interest: principals, teachers, parents and, most importantly, students.

Looking at the school level, three sections collected the data (as can be seen in Table 13.1) from four main groups of interest. (1) In the School Settings section, two schools (principals, teacher, parents and students) were examined using the Delphi method, with the aim to improve the school as a whole by looking at the same problems from different points of view. Linstone and Turoff (1975) describe the Delphi method as a method that should enable group communication processes. The aim is to be able to solve complex issues within the group in an effective way by providing various opportunities to contribute and by using feedback loops. (2) In the Transitions section, teachers, parents and students were asked to fill in questionnaires with the aim of obtaining a better insight into the aspirations and school careers of the students (in nested samples). (3) In the Capacity Building section, data inquiry was aimed at improving instruction at two different schools and obtaining insights into the school culture and the implicit rules in specific schools, whereby teachers and students were examined in a subsample of schools through a peer evaluation process. Teachers observed lessons, while students observed differences at the other school compared to their own school environment by attending classroom sessions and taking pictures of everything they found special or interesting. These pictures were discussed afterwards in focus groups.

Table 13.1 Levels and units of analysis

Principals	Teachers	Parents	Students
Regional Level			
School Settings (Delphi method) in a sub-sample of schools	School Settings (Delphi method) in a sub-sample of schools	School Settings (Delphi method) in a sub-sample of schools	School Settings (Delphi method) in a sub-sample of schools
School Level			
School Settings (Delphi method) in a sub-sample of schools	School Settings (Delphi method) in a sub-sample of schools	School Settings (Delphi method) in a sub-sample of schools	School Settings (Delphi method) in a sub-sample of schools
	Transitions (Survey data) in 16 New Middle Schools	Transitions (Survey data) in 16 New Middle Schools	Transitions (Survey data) in 16 New Middle Schools
	Capacity Building (Peer evaluation) in a sub-sample of schools		Capacity Building (Peer evaluation) in a sub-sample of schools
Classroom Level			
	Transitions (Survey data) in 16 New Middle Schools		Transitions (Survey data) in 16 New Middle Schools
	Instructional Patterns (Focus groups and narrative interviews) in a sub-sample of schools		Instructional Patterns (Focus groups and narrative interviews) in a sub-sample of schools
	Capacity Building (Peer evaluation) in a sub-sample of schools		
Individual Level			
			Transitions (Survey data) in 16 New Middle Schools

Usually all analysis starts with descriptive analyses (in all sections) not only to obtain an overview of the data, but also to correct any errors occurring at the data-entry level, and then proceeds with special analysis steps according to one's research question: in the Transitions section we had to deal with the longitudinal data provided by students, teachers and parents in three cohorts in nested samples, which is why analyses could not be performed by simple inferential statistics, but needed more advanced analyses like Hierarchical Linear Models (HLM) and panel analyses, which challenged the skills of researchers (see Figure 13.2).

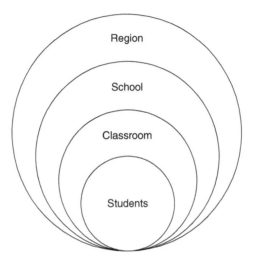

Figure 13.2   Nested samples

Workshops on methodological matters are also helpful for planning the research and the data collection process in advance so as to avoid methodological problems; they also offer a good possibility for establishing contacts with experts in this methodological approach and researchers dealing with similar questions. Such persons can also serve as resources to be consulted in case of problems with data collection and data sampling. Funding for emerging researchers is available at many institutions and should be included in the project budget to provide opportunities for them to participate in such workshops.

Exact planning of data analysis procedures and identifying in advance the software to be used for the analysis can also help avoid wasting time in adapting the data structure to a specific analysis programme.

In order to promote young researchers and to involve them in the research process, we included Bachelor, Master and PhD students of Education from the very beginning of the project, which also can be regarded as a challenge for the analysis process. We had to lead them through a learning process in order for them to know what to do and how to perform the analysis of the considerable amount of material collected. In the majority of cases we had to transform the data files and adjust them first so that inexperienced undergraduates were able to understand how to use the data for their analyses and for the purposes of their own research questions. For PhD students working on larger research projects, it is especially important to focus not only on their own dissertation theses and research questions, but also to bear in mind the overall idea and aim of the whole research project.

13.3.4 THE DISSEMINATION OF RESULTS

A long-term, multi-methodical formative evaluation needs to meet the challenges of providing feedback to different target groups: (1) the contracting authority, policy makers and the general public, (2) the participants of the study, but also (3) the scientific community. In this respect, it is important to consider the objectives to be pursued, the role to be performed as a researcher in this process, and the role and function of data dissemination. Different stakeholders demand various kinds of knowledges. Policy makers or the contracting authority are often interested in governing knowledge. In contrast, schools often require practical knowledge, which should directly address their own school improvement. Researchers should be aware of these diverse expectations but should also have in mind that it is challenging to fulfil all of these requirements, in particular because they often assume education and schooling to be a linear and technological setting, which is not the case. To meet this challenge of informing the public and policy makers in general, the scientific community and also the actual participants of the schools, the following strategies are useful.

13.3.4.1 Contracting authority, policy makers and general public

To inform the contracting authority by periodically issuing working papers and *status quo* reports is a good strategy to address this kind of target group. Reports should be forwarded directly to the contracting authority before publication to give them the possibility to react. Often, it seems difficult to know what stakeholders think about the report as they rarely give feedback on the content and style of it. Therefore, it is important to ask them if the report was helpful for them and if they made changes in the policy strategies based on the reports. To sum up the main results in a clear language and to formulate conclusions and next steps to consider, project leaders should stay in contact with the contracting authority and with policy makers. This can happen in personal meetings, which are also a significant way to directly disseminate the results of the study. Publication of working papers on the project homepage makes the project and the results also accessible to the public. Public relations work in the sense of press releases and articles and maintaining a homepage is also important for keeping participants involved in the research process. It is possible to inform them about the steps undertaken, as well as what happens with the data. This should result in them recognising why it is important and worthwhile to participate.

13.3.4.2 Participants of the study

Participants want and need feedback. When doing research – especially research in schools – feedback to the participants is very relevant. Results are not only intended for presentation within the scientific community, using specialised language, but also need to be provided to those persons involved in the data collection process – in our case principals, teachers, parents and students.

However, to prevent any unintended rankings among schools, it is a good strategy to write feedback not to individual schools (especially if there are small schools), but to write feedback for a cluster of schools. Here it is important to consider the addressee group. It is helpful to summarise the most important results and to formulate them in such a way that the report is understandable for parents, teachers and principals, as well as for students. Scientific terms and vocabulary should be avoided. It is important to ensure that the report is not too complex and that it is constructively critical, offering options for further school improvement. Vivid, self-descriptive graphs and tables are helpful to emphasise results and make the evidence for readers more obvious.

However, the nature of the feedback usually cannot be generalised and is strongly dependent on the objectives and intentions of the research, as well as on the involvement of the participating groups. There are different requirements for feedback. On the one hand there are projects with a summative research character where feedback is only passed on at the end. On the other hand, research projects that have a participatory character, follow action research, or have a strong application-oriented focus – in short, research aimed at involving stakeholders very early and actively, and whose concerns directly address their needs – require early contact with participants, and the feedback is more specific and directed towards the group researched (or co-researchers) and their concrete questions.

Written school feedback should always be accompanied by an oral presentation, or at least there should be the offer of such. Presenting the results at the participating schools themselves is an exciting experience for researchers because it also gives information about the climate in the schools, and receiving feedback from the participants about the evaluation process also indicates the questions with which they actually dealt.

Producing short booklets with the most important results of the project in short form is also a possible strategy to disseminate the results to the participants of the study. It is important to consider a broad target group for booklets and to present not only data-driven results, but also what they mean for the participants.

13.3.4.3 Scientific community

Publishing in peer-reviewed journals is important for discussing and disseminating the research results within a broader scientific community. Therefore sufficient time needs to be allocated for the preparation of such articles (sometimes the reviewing and revision processes take up to two years!). In order to connect to the international scientific audience it is necessary to publish in international journals and submit papers or posters in established international conferences. But such scientific journals may not be read by all stakeholders, so additionally the dissemination to those outside the scientific community would improve through publishing in addressee-specific journals (e.g. magazines of teachers' unions, magazines for school development, and magazines for principals). To address both readers (scientific community and the other stakeholders) we used the strategy in the NOESIS evaluation project to publish an annual book (collected edition) with the main results presented in different chapters and structured by the four sections (Transitions, School Settings, Instructional Patterns and Capacity Building).

RESEARCHER CHECKLIST

KEY LESSONS REFERRING TO ORGANISATIONAL MATTERS

- Research on demand always means that you have to deal with the tension between accountability to the contracting authority and the principle of freedom of research.

- In addition to cooperating with different specialist divisions and developing a specific organisational structure the definition of project roles is important for having clear objectives, active participation of all members, good communication, rules and standards, motivated team members and clear decision-making authority.

- Not only is the publication of new findings necessary in science, but exchanges with colleagues (nationally as well as internationally) are important for seeing one's own results from different perspectives.

- Organisations and persons you work with, e.g. schools (principals, teachers and parents), need to be kept informed about the different steps of the evaluation and about the aim of the project and the data collection processes, the benefits of the evaluation, as well as the data protection processes.

KEY LESSONS REFERRING TO MATTERS OF DATA COLLECTION

- Preparing instruments and conducting a longitudinal panel study is challenging because one cannot change several parts of the research instruments at a later point in time. Pre-tests are necessary to generate high-quality data.

- Plan strategies to avoid panel mortality because participants can get lost at different points in time. The systematic loss of participant groups decreases the reliability and validity of the study.

(Continued)

(Continued)

- Clarify the usefulness and benefits of the study for the participants and try to respond to their demands.

- Think about possible resources which might be useful for your research and which can make it easier to collect data. Bringing in additional staff in the form of student apprentices could be an idea. In this case, make sure that they go through a consistent learning process through assisting you in your study.

KEY LESSONS REFERRING TO CHALLENGES CONCERNING DATA ANALYSIS

- Think about possible networks with other researchers that might be helpful for your research with respect to methodological matters, exchanges about content matters or providing feedback and advice. Plan at which points in your research process exchanges with experts may be helpful for developing your work.

- Be sure to have the necessary skills to deal with different levels of data in your analysis procedures.

- Be aware that your data might be nested data, which will require other methods of data analysis than the ones that rely on independent measures.

- Try to have an overview of the analyses done in sub-projects and identify as many overlaps between different parts of your project as possible.

KEY LESSONS REFERRING TO DATA DISTRIBUTION AND THE COMMUNICATION OF RESULTS

- Publications are important for increasing the project's and the researchers' own visibility and to inform about the project itself, as long as the right language is chosen for the right audience.

- Different forms of publications are suitable for different audiences. Short leaflets might be suitable to inform the public on main findings, while schools/the organisation you work with might require longer reports that help them in their school development process.

- Make sure that you inform your contracting authority about publications, press releases, etc. before making them public so as to give them the possibility to prepare for reactions to requests by journalists.

13.4 CONCLUSION

Setting up a multi-perspective, multi-level and longitudinal research project is challenging since school evaluation research, like most research subjects in the humanities and the social sciences, is very complex. This chapter does not provide the ultimate solution nor does it represent the only way of performing school evaluation research.

Some pitfalls can be avoided by researching only one perspective, or dealing with only one or two levels of analysis. Only one method can be used, but include many perspectives. The project dealt with four different research questions that were answered through four different sections. There could be only one research question to be answered by different methods. This makes it easier to find similarities in data, but also creates tensions if a triangulation fails because of one method producing different results from another. It is necessary to be aware of the benefit of any method used. Using multiple methods does not mean that there are no limitations; quite the contrary is true, but one method might compensate for limitations of another. Research does not have to be performed with multiple-step methods like the Delphi method or peer evaluation as in the case presented, since their analysis is time consuming and complex. For many research questions, a single-step method is enough; however, complex measurements also lead to differentiated pictures of a context and answers to a given question.

Developments can be researched through a quasi-longitudinal study instead of a panel study, i.e. surveying students of different ages at a given point in time. Another option is a longitudinal study without a panel, meaning that the students surveyed might be in the same school or region, but are not necessarily the same students each time. This would limit problems of panel mortality that might cause biases in the dataset, but at the same time would not allow tracking individual developments, but only those at an aggregate level of the class, school or region. To avoid dealing with complex analytical methods like HLM models, students could be selected randomly; however, information about the class context would be missing.

Some organisational challenges might be avoided by researching adults, since parents need to give permission for their children to participate, which could increase the number of participants. This is, of course, problematic in school evaluation research as it limits the perspectives on schooling to a very specific clientele. Some organisational pitfalls might be avoided by doing basic research and not research on demand; however, financial issues need to be clear.

Important when setting up a project using different methods dealing with different perspectives and including longitudinal research is that there is a common ground on which all involved agree. This could be a specific overall aim, like the question whether the implementation of a school model was successful, or a common theoretical background or research paradigm. If there is no common ground, it might be difficult to contain such a complex project and deal with those challenges that occur in any research.

ADDITIONAL USEFUL READING

PROJECT INFORMATION

The following books contain more information about the project and the results of the different sections, as discussed within the scientific community:

Projektteam NOESIS (eds) (2012) *Eine Schule für alle? Zur Evaluation der Niederösterreichischen Mittelschule.* Graz: Leykam.

Projektteam NOESIS (eds) (2013) *Die vielen Wirklichkeiten der Neuen Mittelschule: Zur Evaluation der Niederösterreichischen Mittelschule.* Graz: Leykam.

Projektteam NOESIS (eds) (2014) *Zwischen Alltag und Aufbruch: Zur Evaluation der Niederösterreichischen Mittelschule.* Graz: Leykam.

Projektteam NOESIS (eds) (2015) *Gute Schule bleibt verändert: Zur Evaluation der Niederösterreichischen Mittelschule.* Graz: Leykam.

Projektteam NOESIS (eds) (2016) *Was Schulen stark macht: Zur Evaluation der Niederösterreichischen Mittelschule.* Graz: Leykam.

EVALUATION ISSUES

Hopmann, S.T. (2003) 'On the evaluation of curriculum reforms', *Journal of Curriculum Studies,* *35*(4): 459–478.

This article draws on the history and changes of different patterns and trends in conducting evaluation in the educational field and the consequences connected with thereto. Especially at the beginning of a research project it can be useful when thinking about the research subject.

METHODICAL ISSUES (MULTI-METHOD, MIXED METHOD, MULTI-LEVEL, LONGITUDINAL)

Blossfeld, H. P., Maurice, J. and Bayer, M. (2016) *Methodological Issues of Longitudinal Surveys: The Example of the National Educational Panel Study.* New York: Springer.

Here many challenges when developing questionnaires, collecting longitudinal data and dealing with panel mortality are discussed, taking the German NEPS Panel as an example.

Katschnig, T. and Geppert, C. (2017) *Investigating Multiple Perspectives in a School Reform Process Using a Multiple-Methods Evaluation Approach: A Discussion on the Basis of an Evaluation Project in Lower Austria (NOESIS).* Sage Research Methods Cases. DOI: 10.4135/9781473995871.

This case study exemplifies the design of a formative evaluation project concerned with the implementation of a new school form in Austria and shows how multiple methods were implemented in the NOESIS research project.

Schoonenboom, J. (2014) 'The multilevel mixed intact group analysis: a mixed method to seek, detect, describe, and explain differences among intact groups', *Journal of Mixed Methods Research, 10*(2): 129–146. DOI: 1558689814536283.

This article presents a mixed method from a qualitative perspective. Differences among intact subgroups regarding one construct or effect are first quantitatively identified and subsequently qualitatively described.

Snijders, T. and Bosker, R. (1999) *Multilevel Analysis: An Introduction to Basic and Advanced Multilevel Modeling.* London and Thousand Oaks, CA: Sage.

This introduction about the basic ideas of handling nested data and doing multi-level analyses also helps to deal with data analysis.

Woolley, C. M. (2009) 'Meeting the mixed methods challenge of integration in a sociological study of structure and agency', *Journal of Mixed Methods Research, 3:* 7–25.

By using a combination of methods – questionnaire survey, group interviews and individual interviews – this article offers an example of how maximum integration of datasets can be achieved.

REFERENCES

Bailey, K. (1994) *Methods of Social Research.* New York: The Free Press.

Creswell, J. W. and Plano Clark, V. L. (2007) *Designing and Conducting Mixed Methods Research.* Thousand Oaks, CA: Sage.

Dewey, J. (1916) *Democracy and Education: An Introduction to the Philosophy of Education.* New York: Macmillan.

Fanelli, D. (2009) 'How many scientists fabricate and falsify research? A systematic review and meta-analysis of survey data', *PLoS ONE, 4*(5): e5738. DOI: 10.1371/journal.pone.0005738.

Feichter, H. J. (2011) *Netzwerke und Peers. Peer Evaluation. NOESIS Arbeitsbericht Nr.5.* Available at: www.noesis-projekt.at/uploads/Arbeitsbericht-5.pdf (accessed 29 September 2017).

Feichter, H. J. (2012) 'Capacity building: Netzwerke und Peers. Mehr als eine (An)Sammlung von Daten', in Projektteam NOESIS (eds), *Eine Schule für alle? Zur Evaluation der Niederösterreichischen Mittelschule.* Graz: Leykam. pp. 181–195.

Fung, A. (2004) *Empowered Participation: Reinventing Urban Democracy.* Woodstock, NJ: Princeton University Press.

Geppert, C., Katschnig, T., Knapp, M., Kilian, M. and Hopmann, S. (2015a) 'Mal was Positives von der NMS: Zentrale Ergebnisse der NOESIS-Längsschnittevaluation aus vier Jahren', *Erziehung und Unterricht, 3/4:* 374–383.

Geppert, C., Knapp, M., Kilian, M. and Katschnig, T. (2015b) 'School choice under the pressure of reform efforts', *Studia Paedagogica, 20*(1): 9–28.

Katschnig, T., Geppert, C. and Kilian, M. (2011) 'School transitions – life decisions? Der Übergang von der Volksschule in die Sekundarstufe 1 anhand aktueller Längsschnittdaten (noesis-Studie 2010–2014)', *Erziehung und Unterricht, 9/10:* 920–928.

Kelle, U. (2007) *Die Integration qualitativer und quantitativer Methoden in der empirischen Sozialforschung.* Wiesbaden: VS Verlag für Sozialwissenschaften.

Lewin, K. (1948) 'Action research and minority problems', in K. Lewin (ed.), *Resolving Social Conflicts: Selected Papers on Group Dynamics.* New York, Evanston, London: Harper & Row Publishers. pp. 201–216.

Linstone, H.A. and Turoff, M. (eds) (1975) *The Delphi Method: Techniques and Applications.* London, Amsterdam, Don Mills, Ontario, Sydney, Tokyo: Addison-Wesley Publishing Company.

Mayer, H. (2007) *Pflegeforschung kennenlernen: Elemente und Basiswissen für die Grundausbildung*. Facultas: Vienna.

NOESIS (2010) 'Evaluation'. Available at: www.noesis-projekt.at/evaluation-2/ (accessed 29 September 2017).

OECD (2002) *Frascati Manual 2002: Proposed Standard Practice for Surveys on Research and Experimental Development*. Paris: OECD Publishing. DOI: 10.1787/9789264199040-en.

PMA (Project Management Austria) (2009) *PM Baseline Version 3.0*. Available at: www.p-m-a.at/component/docman/doc_download/3-pm-baseline-3-0-englisch.html (accessed 26 September 2017).

Raudenbush, S.W. and Bryk, A.S. (2002) *Hierarchical Linear Models: Applications and Data Analysis Methods*. Thousand Oaks, CA: Sage.

Rudduck, J. (2007) 'Student voice, student engagement, and school reform', in D. Thiessen (ed.), *The International Handbook of Student Experience of Elementary and Secondary School*. Dodrecht: Springer. pp. 587–610.

Rüdiger, M. (2000) *Forschung und Entwicklung als Dienstleistung: Grundlagen Erfolgsbedingungen der Vertragsforschung*. Wiesbaden: Deutscher Universitäts-Verlag GmbH.

Sen, A. (1980) 'Equality of what?', *The Tanner Lectures on Human Values, Volume 1*, ed. S. M. McMurrin. Cambridge: Cambridge University Press. pp. 197–220.

Sen, A. (1992) *Inequality Reexamined*. Cambridge, MA: Harvard University Press.

Sen, A. (2000) *Development as Freedom*. New York: Anchor Books.

Sen, A. (2003) 'Development as capability expansion', in S. Fukuda-Parr, and A. K. Kumar (eds), *Readings in Human Development*. New Delhi and New York: Oxford University Press. pp. 3–16.

Sen, A. (2009) *The Idea of Justice*. London: Penguin Books.

Shadish, W.R., Cook, T.D. and Leviton, L. C. (1991) *Foundations of Program Evaluation: Theories of Practice*. Newbury Park, CA: Sage.

Snijders, T. A. and Bosker, R.J. (1999) *Multilevel Analysis: An Introduction to Basic and Advanced Multilevel Modeling*. London: Sage.

UK Research Integrity Office (2009) *Code of Practice for Research: Promoting Good Practice and Preventing Misconduct*. Available at: www.ukrio.org/publications/ (27 September 2017).

van Manen, M. (1990) *Researching Lived Experience: Human Science for an Action Sensitive Pedagogy*. London and Ontario: The Althouse Press.

14

MEETING THE EXPECTATIONS OF DIFFERENT ACTORS AT THE SCIENCE–POLICY INTERFACE – MONITORING OF EDUCATION FOR SUSTAINABLE DEVELOPMENT IN GERMANY

Mandy Singer–Brodowski, Antje Brock and Nadine Etzkorn

14.1 INTRODUCTION

The global society in the twenty-first century is facing enormous challenges, such as loss of biodiversity, accelerating climate change and an ongoing divide between rich and poor. Environmental problems have been aggravated to such an extent that scientists refer to the 'Anthropocene' as a new epoch (Crutzen, 2002), where humankind has become one of the major geological driving forces of the earth system. Against the background that ecological challenges can't be addressed independently of the economic and social issues intertwined with them, the United Nations adopted the Agenda 2030 and therewith 17 Sustainable Development Goals (SDGs) in 2015, opening the floor to international strategies for more sustainable development.

Education is seen as decisive in supporting current and future generations in tackling the challenges of sustainability. Therefore, the United Nations announced the Decade of Education for Sustainable Development in the years 2005 to 2014. Its aim was the implementation of Education for Sustainable Development (ESD) at all educational levels and in all nations. The UN Decade of ESD fostered many projects and discussions about how to transform educational institutions and areas in order to address sustainability challenges more comprehensively (UNESCO, 2014a). UNESCO's Global Action Programme on ESD (GAP) (2015–2019) is the follow-up of the UN Decade of ESD. The GAP roadmap states that 'ESD empowers learners to take informed decisions and responsible actions for environmental integrity, economic viability and a just society, for present and future generations, while respecting cultural diversity. It is about lifelong learning and is an integral part of quality education. ESD is holistic and transformational education which addresses learning content and outcomes, pedagogy and the learning environment' (UNESCO, 2014b: 12).

The international and national importance of ESD has increased significantly in recent years, which is mirrored in the fact that ESD is addressed in the framework of the 17 SDGs by the United Nations. Education is seen as a driver for reaching many other SDGs as well (Nilsson, Grigg and Visbeck, 2016). At the international level, progress on ESD was monitored during the UN Decade (UNESCO, 2014a) and is now being implemented via the GAP by UNESCO. On the national level, there has been no (systematic) information on the quality and extent of ESD in Germany until now.

This chapter is based on an educational monitoring project which is grasping the implementation of ESD within the German educational system. Within this chapter, the challenges encountered in the research process will be reflected on, which are mainly caused by the research context and the research design as an indicator-based monitoring project located at the science–policy interface, where different expectations of the involved actors meet.

After describing the research project in more detail, the characteristics of this science–policy interface are introduced. The main challenges will be outlined using a conceptualisation of tensions spanning between simplicity and complexity of the topics and communication of research, and between cooperation and independence within this interface. One challenge was to deal with a broad and complex database consisting of heterogeneous sets of documents, which had to be obtained for

16 different federal states and encompass five different areas of education. The results, however, had to be communicated in an easily accessible and understandable way to different stakeholder groups. Another challenge was related to the balancing act between close cooperation, the co-design of research elements with the different stakeholders in the GAP on the one side, and the requirement of independent scientific research on the other side.

14.2 MONITORING OF EDUCATION FOR SUSTAINABLE DEVELOPMENT IN GERMANY

Policy research in the context of education in general (Lingard, 2013), and Education for Sustainable Development in particular, is increasingly getting more attention (Læssøe, Feinstein and Blum, 2013; van Poeck and Lysgaard, 2015). It can offer valuable insights into the processes and dynamics that can strengthen ESD in a particular area and thereby fruitfully contribute to a mainstreaming of ESD. Precisely, because ESD and its integration into educational systems is a highly political matter, ESD research needs to critically reflect the interplay between policy makers and other stakeholders.

ESD policy-making and research also have to deal with local policies' increasing orientation towards international trends and best practices (McKenzie, Bieler and McNeil, 2015) as a result of emerging international indicators and benchmarking systems. For example, the above-mentioned SDGs, including their education-related goals and their indicatorisation, represent the tendency to orientate educational and sustainability policy towards standardised ways of measurement and governance. From the perspective of science, this tendency contributes to the comparability between different educational systems and sustainability policies. It is also discussed under the term of policy borrowing, in which successful policy strategies are borrowed from respective countries (see e.g. Phillips and Ochs 2003). However, these tendencies also bear the risk of promising a simple transfer of policy strategies from one context to another, and therefore may lead to a decontextualisation of policy strategies and an ignorance of local structures and conditions (see e.g. the discussion about policy mobility in Temenos and McCann, 2012).

Therefore, researchers in the context of ESD (and beyond) should be aware of the impact of their practices, taking into account the risks and limits of scientific evidence, indicator-based research projects, and the tendencies of standardisation and measurability in the sustainability and ESD policy context (Huckle and Wals, 2015; Hursh, Henderson and Greenwood, 2015; McKenzie, Bieler and McNeil, 2015). This chapter is a plea for a critical reflection on doing research at the science–policy interface and will discuss the results and, more broadly, the challenges of ESD-monitoring at the science–policy interface in Germany.

Firstly, we will outline some details about the implementation of the GAP in Germany to enable a deeper understanding of the context of our research project. The Federal Ministry of Education and Research (BMBF) is the coordinating body of the UNESCO GAP in Germany and has set up a differentiated and multi-level implementation structure consisting of a National Platform, six expert forums, partner networks and a youth forum. In addition, there is a system of awarding high-quality activities of ESD in Germany for different groups of actors in the field of ESD (non-formal places of learning, local communities and networks featuring a substantial level of ESD). The winners are being awarded from the BMBF and the German Commission for UNESCO. An international advisor at the German UNESCO Commission and a scientific advisor at the Freie Universität Berlin, Institut Futur, have been appointed to accompany the national implementation process of ESD. In order to monitor the implementation of ESD and the progress that has been made, the research project 'Monitoring of the Global Action Programme of ESD' was set up at the department of the scientific advisor. Its purpose is to advise the ministry, expert forums related to different educational fields, practitioners' networks and other relevant stakeholders for finding effective ways of strengthening ESD.

After setting up the structures of this multi-stakeholder process, the expert forums for each educational field (early childhood education, school, vocational education and training, higher education, informal and non-formal learning/youth and local authorities) began formulating action fields, aims and lists of measures to promote the implementation of ESD specific for the educational sectors for a National Action Plan on ESD. Some authorities from the federal states of Germany are officially represented in the expert forums, as the autonomy of the federal states is very high in educational policy in Germany. On 20 June 2017, the highest decision-making body, the 'National Platform', adopted the National Action Plan on ESD in Germany.

For the design of the national monitoring of ESD, general educational monitoring approaches were reviewed and adapted (Döbert and Weishaupt, 2012; Rürup, Fuchs and Weishaupt, 2016). In the overall debate, educational monitoring can be defined as a systematic and indicator-based observation of the input, output and process aspects of an educational system for the purpose of comparison and quality improvement (Ioannidou, 2010: 163). The monitoring project is based on international (UNECE, 2007, 2014) as well as national indicator sets for ESD (Di Giulio et al., 2011; Michelsen et al., 2011). These indicators have been further adapted to represent the specifics of the different educational fields.

As (educational) monitoring endeavours to create systemic transparency around the state of the art of different aspects of an (educational) system, it cannot provide evidence pertaining to causal interrelations, i.e. that certain policies were the reason for the status quo (Niedlich and Brüsemeister, 2012). Following this assumption, the main purpose of the ESD monitoring project is to provide an observation of the extent of ESD implementation in the German educational system, rather than an evaluation of the GAP strategy in a narrow sense. It is not an outcome assessment regarding, for example, the ESD competencies of learners in order to bring sustainability transitions forward (e.g. Barth et al., 2007; Segalàs et al., 2009; UNECE, 2012; Wiek, Withycombe and Redman, 2011).

The monitoring covers the six educational fields mentioned above while it also takes differences into account at the level of federal states, local authorities and individual institutions into account. The complete monitoring process (three years) encompasses four phases (see Figure 14.1), starting with desk research on the extent of ESD implementation in documents that are central to the German educational system – this desk research will be selectively repeated after one and a half years in phase four. The second phase includes expert interviews to identify central drivers for, and barriers to, implementing ESD in the German education system. The experts were selected for high levels of ESD-related and strategic knowledge in the different educational areas in order to identify leverage points for accelerating the integration of ESD. These leverage points can be described as 'places within a complex system (a corporation, an economy, a living body, a city, an ecosystem), where a small shift in one thing can produce big changes in everything' (Meadows, 1997: 1). A third quantitative research phase focuses on ESD-related knowledge, attitudes, behaviour and general levels of implementation of the educational concept from young people (age 14–24) as well as teachers (total n>3000). This chapter focuses mainly on the potential, the limitations and upcoming challenges of the first phase, the indicator-based desk research.

In preparing the desk research, a synthesis of international indicators for ESD and their adaptation to the specific situation of the education system in Germany was carried out (see Singer-Brodowski et al., 2018: 4f). Based on this set of indicators, a document analysis was conducted in order to analyse the state of implementation of ESD in key documents of the educational sectors mentioned above. The documents (e.g. curricula for the school sector, training regulations for the vocational education sector, and module descriptions in higher education) were analysed via a software-based lexical analysis with MAXQDA. The aim was to identify the extent and, for several types of documents, the context of references to ESD or related educational concepts such as, for example, 'environmental education' or 'global learning' (see Figure 14.2). Our key word list therefore included only educational concepts (with the exception of sustainability and sustainable development). A key word list with thematic contents of ESD, such as climate change or poverty, was only used in the educational area of vocational education and training, as educational concepts in general are rarely used in vocational education and training documents. Apart from this exception, the focus was on educational concepts, as these also imply didactical aspects, e.g. in relation to participative or innovative learning environments that are crucial for ESD (UNESCO, 2014a). Due to the specifics of different educational fields and types of documents, the methodological approach differed slightly in each of them.

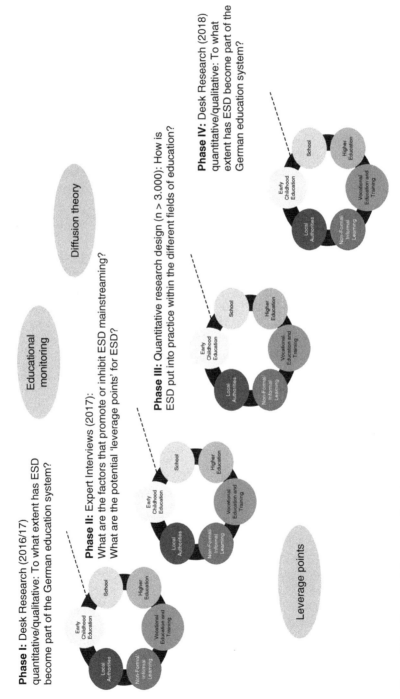

Phase I: Desk Research (2016/17) quantitative/qualitative: To what extent has ESD become part of the German education system?

Phase II: Expert Interviews (2017): What are the factors that promote or inhibit ESD mainstreaming? What are the potential 'leverage points' for ESD?

Phase III: Quantitative research design (n > 3.000): How is ESD put into practice within the different fields of education?

Phase IV: Desk Research (2018) quantitative/qualitative: To what extent has ESD become part of the German education system?

Diffusion theory

Educational monitoring

Leverage points

School
Higher Education
Vocational Education and Training
Non-Formal Informal Learning
Local Authorities
Early Childhood Education

Figure 14.1   Design of the research project

Keywords

- Education for Sustainable Development
- Sustain* + Education
- Sustain*
- Sustainable Development (referring to education)
- Sustainability (referring to education)
- Gestaltungskompetenz (or shaping competence) (see de Haan, 2006)
- Global Development (referring to education)
- Global Learning
- Learning in Global Contexts
- Intercultural Learning
- Development Policy Education
- Environmental Education
- Nature Education
- Intercultural Education
- Ecological Education
- Intercultural Pedagogics
- Nature Pedagogics
- Environmental Pedagogics

Figure 14.2 Key word list for the analysis

Overall, the results of the desk research showed clearly that EDS has been taken up to some extent in certain groups of documents, whereas in many key documents, such as quality standards for educational processes or examination-relevant documents, ESD and related terms have not been explicated at all. The extent varies greatly with regard to the areas of education, subjects, federal states, and how recent the documents are. Educational concepts such as 'environmental education', 'global learning' or 'education for sustainable development' are much more common in early childhood care and education or school education compared to higher education or vocational education and training. In the school system, the range of ESD implementation shows clearly in terms of the variety between the different federal states that were selected. As expected, the results indicate that some school subjects (geography/biology/general studies) have a high affinity for ESD. With the exception of single federal states with just recently updated curricula and a strong interdisciplinary anchoring of ESD, there were only very few references to ESD and related concepts beyond these subjects. In higher education institutions, an increasing integration of sustainability as a concept can be observed, while ESD as an educational concept with its didactical implications is very rare. In the system of vocational education and training, there is a strong bias towards environmental protection resulting from certain policy initiatives in the 1990s which, however, did not result in the uptake of sustainability with its focus on the interdependencies between social, economic and ecological questions. Across all fields of education, it can be stated that the references to ESD and related concepts increased in more recent documents. The findings also indicate that ESD is increasingly prevailing over other educational concepts such as environmental education (see e.g. van Poeck, Vandenabeele and Bruyninckx, 2014).

The experiences of carrying out the desk research and communicating the results of that first research phase showed that divergent expectations from science as well as from policy meet at the science–policy interface.

14.3 TENSIONS AT THE SCIENCE–POLICY INTERFACE

'Tensions at the science-policy interface' summarises the multi-faceted challenges that are typical for this research context as this project was explicitly designed to generate evidence-based knowledge for policy-making based on a comprehensive monitoring of ESD with the aim of further mainstreaming this educational concept. Before elaborating on the tensions, it is helpful to first reflect upon what is meant by 'science' and 'policy'.

14.3.1 DESCRIPTION OF THE SCIENCE–POLICY INTERFACE

Science and policy can be described as groups of different stakeholders or as systems with their own aims, tasks, self-conceptions and rules. The aim of science is to generate knowledge that is systematic and proven in the sense that the knowledge creation is followed by specific rules, and that the processes of data generation, analysis and interpretation are both transparent and, in the case of quantitative studies, replicable. From the perspective of the sociology of science and science and technology studies (STS) (see e.g. Hackett et al., 2008), the past few decades have been characterised by an increasing pressure on science to open up to new forms of participation by non-scientific experts and the wider public. Despite this tendency, in the history of science, a continuous boundary was constructed between scientific knowledge and other forms of knowledge, which has led to a demarcation of science from non-science and thereby to a legitimation of resources and reputation (Gieryn, 1983). This reciprocal, but sometimes contradictory, relation between science or, more precisely, academia, and non-academic fields, is a pivotal basis for capturing and describing this research context.

Concerning politics, a defining characteristic of that field is – according to Geden (2016) – demonstrating the capacity to solve problems, a capacity that will be rewarded by the voters and by which parties can create an advantage over competing actors in this field (Geden, 2016: 48). In addition, most policy makers no longer focus on pure steering or on regulating policy fields, but take a broader view of governing. An increasing diversity of international policy trends, national and regional factors and interest groups influence policy makers as well as administrative staff. Moving within these broader policy environments requires considerable orientation – a factor which also increased the relevance of evidence-based recommendations (Nutley, Davies and Walter, 2002). However, the empirically grounded evidence knowledge base offered by science is not applied by policy makers in a direct way. This evidence base is communicated by policy makers, used for their own interests, and thereby often transformed in a way that was not intended by researchers (Brüsemeister, 2012). A strategy to address this potential challenge was to give concrete recommendations for actions based on the scientific results and to communicate the fragmentariness in the database and the limitations of the results clearly.

Generating and communicating scientific evidence and advice to policy makers and beyond 'takes place within an ecosystem' (Gluckman, 2016) in which the adoption of certain recommendations cannot be guaranteed. Instead of a linear flow of communication and recommendation from science to policy, the science–policy interface is characterised by complex communication, interpretation and negotiation processes. Consequently, the context for the creation of evidence-based policies and the specific role of the evidence base in this process is somewhat nebulous and can be influenced by tensions.

14.3.2 IDENTIFYING TENSIONS AT THE SCIENCE–POLICY INTERFACE IN THE MONITORING OF ESD IN GERMANY

The research project presented here is used to reflect upon the tensions arising from the interplay between scientific and political actors. The tensions encountered can be located between two axes of the science-policy interface (see Figure 14.3). In reflecting upon these tensions, we employ – firstly – some theoretical explanations from educational science, in particular for the elaborations concerning the tensions between simplicity and complexity on the y-axis. Secondly, we reflect more deeply on the tensions between cooperation and independence, referring to research from the field of sustainability science.

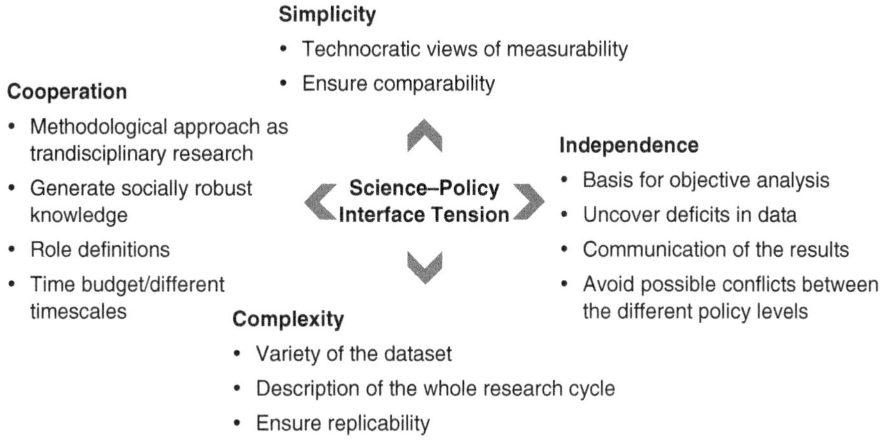

Simplicity
- Technocratic views of measurability
- Ensure comparability

Cooperation
- Methodological approach as trandisciplinary research
- Generate socially robust knowledge
- Role definitions
- Time budget/different timescales

Science–Policy Interface Tension

Independence
- Basis for objective analysis
- Uncover deficits in data
- Communication of the results
- Avoid possible conflicts between the different policy levels

Complexity
- Variety of the dataset
- Description of the whole research cycle
- Ensure replicability

Figure 14.3 Axes of tensions regarding the science–policy interface

The figure is used to systematise the challenges at the science–policy interface in a structured way, bearing in mind that the tensions on both axes are highly interrelated.

14.3.2.1 Tensions between complexity and simplicity

From complex databases to simple stories

The y-axis focuses on tensions between complexity and simplicity that are closely connected to the design of the project as an indicator-based monitoring. To some extent, this type of tension is generic for research as such, ranging from establishing the research design to the point of science communication. In our research project, several points underline the significance of this axis: the comprehensiveness of the monitoring project meant that the results needed to be condensed to a level that could be handled, reproduced and communicated. The database was characterised by a high complexity, e.g. given the five educational areas it encompassed and the federal structure of the educational system in Germany. The quantity and highly diverse set of documents had to be tackled at the level of document selection and acquisition as well as at the level of analysis. We tried to deal with this variety within the dataset from the very beginning of our document analysis by using the indicator set based on international indicator projects for ESD; this guided the selection of relevant documents. At the same time, the wide range of non-scientific stakeholders required a strategy for communicating and disseminating our findings that was sensitive to this diversity. So, the communication of the results demanded simplicity especially when striving for influence on the policy level.

The challenge of comparisons of results

Many of the international ESD indicators focus mainly on the implementation of ESD (topics) at the document level, so the results do not provide information about the level of ESD in actual educational practice (including its quality). For that reason, the narrow view on documents that can be compared, has been complemented with the second and third phase of our monitoring project where the aim was to gain a broader picture of the ESD implementation.

Nevertheless, we tried to deal with the limitations and risks of comparison even in the first phase. The following example illustrates limitations of the comparability of the results of the desk research more clearly: the data sample comprised all the early childhood education plans of the 16 federal states and was analysed in terms of implementation of ESD or related educational concepts. The bar chart (see Figure 14.4) shows a clear ranking between the federal states, with some at the top in terms of numbers of references to the educational concepts, and thereby suggests a clear commensurability. The figure shows not only the absolute number of references to ESD and related concepts, but also the number of pages of the educational plans, as this influences an adequate presentation of the results.

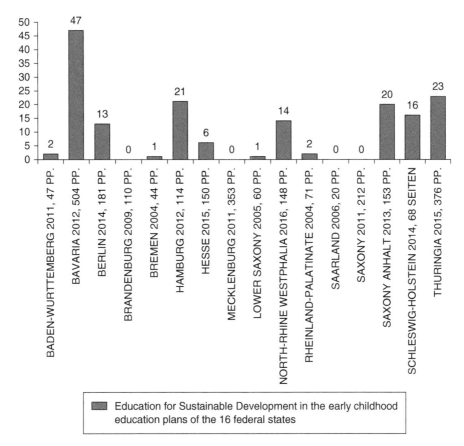

Figure 14.4 ESD and other educational concepts in the early childhood education plans

Some educational plans, however, contain detailed educational approaches on how to empower children in kindergartens to engage with environmental and social issues in the future, but these had not been termed as sustainability or ESD. This problem was addressed by reconstructing and describing the approaches to 'sustainability education' in the wider sense, where possible, via a qualitative analysis. This qualitative contextualisation, however, made it almost impossible to derive a simple story from the results. Here it can be seen that the use of certain indicators might run the risk that value is placed only on what can be measured, thereby losing sight of what counts in the end in education (Biesta, 2009).

The limitations of comparability were even more important in the search for indicators and relevant documents in the field of non-formal learning. The high importance of this educational field for ESD is undoubted and further stressed by the fact that more than 50 percent of all educational activities that were awarded during the UN Decade of ESD in Germany are part of this educational sector

(Deutsche UNESCO Kommission/German UNESCO Commission, 2015). As this is a sector with a high degree of heterogeneity regarding the topics, but also the actors involved (large NGOs as well as self-employed persons), key documents were rare. Furthermore, they lacked internal comparability because of too heterogeneous scopes and aims of the documents, which led to the decision to exclude this educational field from research phase one.

Ensuring replicability through describing the complex research process

The complexity increased as we tried to describe the whole research process for each type of document to ensure replicability of this monitoring phase in order to capture long-term trends in the implementation of ESD. That is why the description of the group of documents, their function within the German educational system, the exact source of the documents, the specific research questions we had regarding the analysis of these documents as well as the methodological procedure of the lexical analysis have been laid out in detail.

The comprehensive documentation as a scientific necessity made the research report very extensive. This publication format diverged to a certain extent from the information relevant for policy-making, decision-making and the educational practitioners or the interested public. We therefore decided to extract the most relevant information from the results in the form of 'executive summaries', which were published much in advance of the more comprehensive research report.

Bridging the gap between science and policy through strategic communication

To reflect on our experiences on a more general and theoretically informed level, we can say that bridging the gap between complexity and simplicity is closely connected with, and widely discussed in the context of, the increasing importance of evidence-based policy in educational research in general. While not being new, the discussion about evidence-based policy is gaining more and more relevance in the education sector, too (Lingard, 2013; Møller, 2017). The international comparison studies were a starting point for a stronger focus on indicator-based educational research projects as a base for quality development in educational systems. They strengthened the need for a productive dialogue between researchers, policy makers, and international organisations and other stakeholders that are striving for quality improvement in educational systems by generating comparable evidence (e.g. European Commission, EACEA, Eurydice, 2017). While an evidence-based quality development is important, it is necessary to discuss the problems and possible challenges of research closely linked to policy processes in terms of the fundamental assumptions underlying large-scale studies such as PISA or TIMMs. They seem to narrow down the view on education (at least in the public perception) to the productivity and quality of educational systems fostering functional competencies in literacy, math and sciences.

Overall, questions of measurability and of reducing complexity to clear and well communicable statements are not only relevant for the general debate around education, but also for the monitoring of ESD, as we have tried to show.

When it comes to evidence-based policy advice in general, politicians refer to research findings, but communicate to the public in an easily understandable way, pointing to some key messages. Researchers therefore have to consider the differences between scientific evidence and governance principles, which results in a strong plea for simplicity (Carney and Oliver, 2017). As policy actors are under strict time limitations and incorporate not only scientific evidence but also values, habits and emotions into their decision-making processes, the literature dealing with the science-policy interface points to reducing ambiguity and complexity in communicating and disseminating scientific results, e.g. through prioritising the most relevant results or using story telling (Carney and Oliver, 2017: 17). Especially when generating research findings by means of qualitative approaches, it becomes even more challenging to communicate results, as they often elude easy uptake in terms of numbers and graphs.

Indicator-based monitoring reduces complexity from the very beginning and thus this approach runs the risk of being reduced to technocratic views of measurability (Biesta, 2007). In particular, doing research about education in the German tradition of 'Bildung', to which the German term ESD ('Bildung für nachhaltige Entwicklung') refers to, might potentially reduce the meaning of this educational concept: 'Bildung' represents a broad and complex process of educative self-formation in many different dimensions and refers, in the Humboldtian sense, to an integrated whole (Bleicher, 2006). Finding indicators for this complex internal process further underlines the proxy nature of the findings. In the document analysis, for example, it remains unclear whether the descriptions in the documents related to ESD and related concepts refer sufficiently to ESD, especially in this ambitious sense of 'Bildung'.

Based on our experiences, therefore, we cannot favour one side or the other of the axis between simplicity and complexity. However, it is essential to discuss the advantages, disadvantages and implications of maintaining or reducing complexity at each stage of the research project.

14.3.2.2 Tensions between cooperation and independence

The other axis of tensions we identified – the x-axis – spans between cooperation and independence and is discussed more often in sustainability research. The challenges connected with the x-axis are also related to the question of the nature and extent of the cooperation with different non-scientific stakeholders in research projects. Clearly, high-quality research requires viewpoints and processes that are as objective as possible. Independence is also crucial for an impartial investigation of the extent and quality of ESD. In addition to this, a certain degree of close cooperation with the different stakeholders involved in the national strategies for ESD implementation was, and still is, indispensable. In order to avoid potential role conflicts, there is a clear need for a demarcation of functions and expectations while creating and maintaining a climate of supportive and constructive interactions.

Transdisciplinarity as a mode of research in sustainability science

Integrating ESD into Germany's educational system requires the cooperation of different stakeholders from policy, science, civil society and educational institutions. On the practical side, this has led to the broad multi-stakeholder process for the implementation of the GAP described above. This cooperation of scientific and non-scientific actors is conceptualised as transdisciplinary research and broadly discussed in sustainability science (for an introduction see Heinrichs et al., 2016). As a problem-oriented approach, transdisciplinary research starts with complex and often wicked societal problems and aims to integrate different forms of knowledge (Jahn, Bergmann and Keil, 2012; Lang et al., 2012). The integration of expert knowledge from different fields aims for making the results more socially robust (Nowotny, Scott and Gibbons, 2001) by co-designing the research project, co-producing knowledge, as well as co-disseminating results (Mauser et al., 2013).

Therefore, we applied a transdisciplinary approach from the beginning: the indicators for ESD have been discussed with members of the expert forums beforehand, drawing on their knowledge and experience in the respective educational areas. During this process, some documents were added to the indicator set, e.g. in the educational area of vocational education and training, we additionally analysed the regulations for advanced further training (in German: 'Verordnungen zu Aufstiegsfortbildungen'). This creation of more socially robust knowledge, was, however, more time-consuming and led to an expansion of the dataset.

Searching for clear-cut role definitions in transdisciplinary cooperation

Another challenge of the project, influenced by close cooperation with politics, administration, stakeholders and science, was the need for clear-cut definitions of roles, including the demarcation of tasks and responsibilities. 'Scientific experts who provide policy advice [...] [should] hold different roles depending on the type of problem and specific background factors' (Spruijt et al., 2014: 22). The role of the scientific advisor of the UNESCO GAP on ESD includes giving recommendations on ESD and its development to ensure that stakeholders are equipped with the best available knowledge to meet the challenges related to a mainstreaming of ESD in Germany. Nevertheless, it was not always trivial to maintain clearly defined roles since there is no clear demarcation line, but rather a continuum between tasks that necessitated a scientific perspective or analysis and those tasks that could be solved 'merely' by, for example, an intensive web search through other non-scientific actors involved. This challenge became even more relevant given that inquiries to certain ESD-related issues followed the time scales of politics that are often not congruent with the time scales of academic analyses.

Coping with different timescales

Fulfilling the expectations of sometimes short-term scientific advice had to be balanced with the time budget for the tasks of the educational monitoring project itself, while the boundaries between both tasks were often blurred. In connection with this, researchers at the science-policy interface have to deal with different timescales in research and in policy (see Nilsson, Griggs and Visbeck, 2016). While political processes often operate within a short-term logic, scientific analyses operate within longer time periods.

These often not easily harmonised timescales of political practices and research processes became apparent in the concurrence of the first research phase of the national monitoring and of compiling the National Action Plan (NAP) on ESD. Because of that, it was not possible to integrate the findings of the desk research into the suggestions of the NAP for all educational fields. While our analysis revealed a considerable lack of implementation of ESD within the descriptions of university modules for future teachers in vocational education and training, the importance of integrating ESD into these key documents has not been explicated in the NAP chapter of vocational education and training. Instead, it was rather implicitly addressed in the section on school education, as teacher education was addressed there in a wider sense. In sum, our analysis could not lead to an adequate tackling of ESD in university modules for future teachers in vocational education and training in the NAP due to the different timescales of the non-scientific and scientific actors.

Necessity and value of an independent monitoring

The above-mentioned example also highlights the importance of the independence of our research project, as we were only able to identify this deficit in data and strategies by using the established and, where necessary, specifically adapted indicator set, thereby identifying areas of high relevance in mainstreaming ESD that have not been tackled by policy strategies. Conducting a research project with a high level of independence was necessary for many reasons. Most of the systematic reports by governments and even UNESCO reports about ESD (e.g. UNESCO, 2014a) are based on self-assessments by the different countries. 'These self-reports tend to be uncritical catalogues that focus on successes, and are silent about problems and failures' (Nazir et al., 2009: 27). As argued at the beginning of this section, this resonates with the logic underlying political action: demonstrating the capacity to solve problems. However, a systematic and even critical investigation of ESD-implementation should also point out areas that are not (yet) successful or that are not visible in the public debate despite its societal relevance.

We have experienced concrete advantages of this independence in the context of communicating the research results to different stakeholders. Given the multi-stakeholder process of fostering ESD and the federal autonomy of the states in implementing this concept, there was a risk of demotivating some actors from the different federal states where comparatively low levels of ESD implementation had become apparent. Precisely because the BMBF coordinates the whole GAP process in Germany, it was decisive that the independent researchers, not the ministry coordinating the implementation, communicated the results.

The same is true for possible tensions between policy actors and actors within civil society organisations, which have been analysed in other research projects (Bormann and Nickel, 2017). Maintaining trust in the impartiality of the research process is of high importance in general, but will be stressed even more in the second phase of the monitoring where expert interviews will also include feedback on the ministry-led GAP-ESD process including potential needs for improvement.

Balancing the different expectations through a transdisciplinary research approach

To reflect on our experiences of the tensions between cooperation and independence on a more theoretical level, we refer to the above-mentioned notion of policy-making that takes place within a whole ecosystem (Gluckman, 2016). The different ESD actors with their specific expertise, time-lines and expectations from this ecosystem were our partners in following a transdisciplinary research approach. We have benefitted from this cooperation in generating more socially robust knowledge (Nowotny, Scott and Gibbons, 2001) that was useful for the different stakeholders and could be connected to their respective professional fields. However, we have also experienced the huge value of scientific independence, especially when it came to communicating our research results. Thus, the expectations of the different stakeholders had to be carefully balanced regarding the aim, context and level of cooperation versus independence. In the end, this is a challenge that concerns many transdisciplinary projects in sustainability research.

Furthermore, the process of establishing sustainability science as a distinct research field and research community was – from the very beginning – interwoven with the normative goal of reaching more sustainable development through scientific evidence and, thereby, a solution-oriented research agenda (Miller et al., 2014). In that sense, independence and impartiality always have to be carefully balanced with a solution-oriented science and the normativity inherent in sustainability science (Scholz, 2017) that always needs to be reflected. With regard to the accelerating problems of unsustainability, the discussions of, and controversies over, how closely scientists should collaborate with policy makers is most visible in the case of the reports by the International Panel on Climate Change (IPCC). Here, the question of the credibility of scientific facts, the communication of uncertainty and the contrast between illustrating scenarios and assessing the consequences are exemplary for the broader sustainability debate.

14.3.2.3 Ethical issues in the monitoring of ESD in Germany

The tensions on the x- and y-axes are also interwoven with ethical issues. One of them lies in the afore-mentioned importance of high research standards in order to ensure the anonymity of the interview partners in the second phase. In order to provide the opportunity for people to give open and potentially critical feedback on the local, regional and national processes, it has to be guaranteed that the interviewees cannot be identified and can fulfil their functions on different levels without having to consider the power structures and the potential consequences for themselves. Another ethical consideration concerns the mentioned consequences of comparative perspectives for those at the bottom end of the distribution, especially against the background that the individual actors or organisations in the federal states, communities, etc. addressed by the study might be successful and effective within the limits of their influence to upscale ESD while the overall performance of ESD in their state or region might, however, be much weaker. This overall performance might, however, be far beyond their realm of individual influence while the less convincing overall performances might even have negative consequences for the individually successful actors or institutions. In conclusion, on the one hand, the ethical considerations refer to the characteristically high importance of communication in the interplay between science and policy in a small scientific and practitioner community. On the other hand, the ethical considerations revolve around general ethical issues in research (ensuring anonymity) and can be found in every research project.

Coming back to the plea for more policy research in the context of ESD (van Poeck and Lysgaard, 2015), the challenges we faced can be understood as different stakeholder's expectations in an environment that is characterised by an increasing interplay between science and policy. The associated tendencies can be theoretically reflected upon in terms of the tensions in evidence-based policy, especially in the sustainability context, where there is a high demand for discussion of normative aspects. As Education for Sustainable Development is also an interdisciplinary research field, it has the potential to use theoretical and empirical work from educational science and sustainability science to deal with the tensions described. In this chapter, we have tried to systematise and reflect on these tensions based on the experiences of our own research project at the science-policy interface. Some concrete recommendations can be instructive for further research projects.

RESEARCHER CHECKLIST

Research projects at the intersection of science, policy and stakeholders offer genuine insights and constitute an inspiring and relevant research context. Researchers have the opportunity to increase the relevance of, and have an impact on, the improvement of educational processes, institutions and policies – even at the nexus of the necessary transformation of our societies towards sustainable development. Their research results can become highly visible and utilisable for quality improvement in different contexts. Based on our experiences in the first phase of our research project, we can give the following recommendations on the two axes: independence and complexity as well as simplicity and cooperation:

- Discuss necessary strategies to reduce the multi-faceted complexity of reality (using indicators and measuring aspects, which are just a small part of the whole picture).

- Bear in mind the implications of this reduction of complexity and make uncertainties and potential shortcomings of the results transparent.

- Reflect the potential effects of the results and – if possible – discuss the possible risks with different stakeholders before publication (regarding e.g. comparisons between different stakeholders).

- Be aware of different expectations of the actors and the usage of your results in a way that you have not intended before.

- Make the role expectations, including the modes of involvement of non-scientific actors, clear from the beginning.

- Clearly demarcate individual work packages and establish robust project management – maintaining permanent expectation management with regard to the role of science in the multi-stakeholder process.

- Be aware of possible delays in research processes from the beginning (such as having to collect data with highly varying accessibility, and consultation processes with different institutions).

- Start with the analysis of small sections of the intended work in order to better extrapolate the necessary time and other resources to complete tasks.

- Consider the difference in timescales between the different sectors, especially at the level of educational policy, where it takes a relatively long time for innovations to diffuse into the structures of education.

- Try to tell simple stories based on your results to communicate your research evidence to policy makers or other decision makers.

Taking these points together, we would highlight the necessity for continuous reflection on the whole research context and the specific challenges presented by working on a project at the science-policy interface.

14.4 CONCLUSION

In this chapter, a national monitoring of Education for Sustainable Development has been used as an example to reflect upon pivotal tensions at the science–policy interface. The location of the project at the science–policy interface, with all the tensions mentioned, offers the potential for a bird's eye perspective on complex phenomena and also provides insights into the mechanisms of implementation. This perspective is helpful in diagnosing the state of the art of ESD and making recommendations. Additionally, the knowledge related to policy and implementation is important for complementing the picture and making it more congruent with the real world in comparison with sector-specific views.

While looking for other possible ways of handling the methodological challenges of this monitoring, large-scale projects in transdisciplinary research processes could provide instructive contexts of learning. Here, the role of the independent project-executing agency is of central importance since they are located neither in the realm of science nor that of policy or practice and can therefore moderate and mediate between the different stakeholders (Defila, Di Giulio and Scheuermann, 2006).

The research context of empirical educational research within the science–policy interface 'doubled' or, more exactly, blended the research-related challenges that come along with each of the two fields, namely the evidence-based and measurability focus from the educational sector as well as the evidence-based focus of policy advice and keeping in mind the diverse audiences involved in this wider research–policy process. This doubling or merging of challenges can lead to an even narrower understanding of ESD – one that is reliably measurable on a large scale in order to satisfy a certain visibility in educational research and an understanding of ESD that is 'catchy' and can be easily communicated in order to be further supported and catalysed by political actors.

While being aware of this possible narrowing down, it was crucial for our approach to monitoring ESD to preserve the high complexity of ESD and at the same time, consider the different needs and logics of upscaling ESD for the different stakeholders. In the communication of our results, we have developed different report formats and communication styles. Given the challenges we described, we could prevent a too 'streamlined' understanding and operationalisation of ESD especially through contextualisation of the analyses, a critical and self-reflexive viewpoint and, most importantly, an understanding of the political goal that is underlying the GAP-ESD process. This viewpoint is not unrealistic, but maintains its huge ambitions of high-quality ESD implementation as encompassing and enriching educational processes at all levels.

ADDITIONAL USEFUL READING

Carney, P. and Oliver K. (2017) 'Evidence-based policymaking is not like evidence-based medicine, so how far should you go to bridge the divide between evidence and policy?', *Health Research Policy and Systems*, *15* (5). DOI: 10.1186/s12961-017-0192-x.

This article summarises results from systematic reviews, critical analysis and theory about evidence-based policy-making in the field of medicine. It recommends some pragmatic strategies to make research results more policy relevant, like story telling in the communication of research results.

Heinrichs, H., Martens, P., Michelsen, G. and Wiek, A. (2016) *Sustainability Science*. Dordrecht, Netherlands: Springer.

This book offers one of the first systematic overviews about theoretical foundations, conceptual assumptions and methodological approaches of sustainability science. The chapters are written by leading scientists in the field and the whole book is edited as a textbook for students in the field, while it serves also as an introduction to the main discourses for interested scientists.

Ioannidou, A. (2010) 'Educational monitoring and reporting as governance instruments for evidence-based education policy', in K. Amos (ed.), *International Educational Governance*. Bingley: Emerald Group Publishing Limited. pp. 155–172.

The author draws on educational monitoring and reporting in the broader context of transnational education policies. She elaborates on using monitoring approaches as a governance instrument and, at the same time, reflects the potential shortcomings of indicator-based research projects.

Lingard, B. (2013) 'The impact of research on education policy in an era of evidence-based policy', *Critical Studies in Education*, *54* (2): 113–131. DOI: 10.1080/17508487.2013.781515.

This article is a valuable starting point for discussing the increasing trend of evidence-informed policy-making in education. The author elaborates extensively on the science–policy interface, while an oversimplified understanding is avoided, where the actors involved in this interface belong to dichotomous communities that have to be bridged or translated to each other. Instead of this, Lingard pleas for an engaged cooperation between science and policy, aiming for different strategies to inform policy through scientific evidence and insights.

REFERENCES

Barth, M., Godemann, J., Rieckmann, M. and Stoltenberg, U. (2007) 'Developing key competencies for sustainable development in higher education', *International Journal of Sustainability in Higher Education*, *8*(4): 416–430. DOI: 10.1108/14676370710823582.

Biesta, G. (2007) 'Why "what works won't work": evidence-based practice and the democratic deficit in educational research', *Educational Theory*, *57* (1): 1–22. DOI: 10.1111/j.1741-5446.2006.00241.x.

Biesta, G. (2009) 'Good education in an age of measurement: on the need to reconnect with the question of purpose in education', *Educational Assessment, Evaluation and Accountability*, *21*(1): 33–46. DOI: 10.1007/s11092-008-9064-9.

Bleicher, J. (2006) 'Bildung', *Theory, Culture & Society*, *23*(2–3): 364–365.

Bormann, I. and Nikel, J. (2017) 'Interconnected case studies on the governance of ESD within the German multi-level education system', *International Review of Education*, *63*(6): 793–809, Special Issue on Education for Sustainable Development.

Brüsemeister, T. (2012) 'Educational governance: Entwicklungstrends im Bildungs-system', in M. Ratermann and S. Stöbe-Blossey (eds), *Governance von Schul- und Elementarbildung. Vergleichende Betrachtungen und Ansätze der Vernetzung* (pp. 27–44). Wiesbaden: VS Verlag.

Carney, P. and Oliver, K. (2017) 'Evidence-based policymaking is not like evidence-based medicine, so how far should you go to bridge the divide between evidence and policy?', *Health Research Policy and Systems*, *15*(5). DOI: 10.1186/s12961-017-0192-x.

Crutzen, P. J. (2002) 'Geology of mankind', *Nature*, *415*(6867): 23. DOI: 10.1038/415023a.

de Haan, G. (2006) 'The BLK "21" programme in Germany: a "Gestaltungskompetenz"-based model for Education for Sustainable Development', *Environmental Education Research*, *12*(1): 19–32. DOI: 10.1080/13504620500526362.

Defila, R., Di Giulio, A. and Scheuermann, M. (2006) *Forschungsverbundmanagement: Handbuch für die Gestaltung inter- und transdisziplinärer Projekte*. Zürich: vdf Hochschulverlag.

Deutsche UNESCO Kommission (2015) *UN-Dekade mit Wirkung 10 Jahre 'Bildung für Nachhaltige Entwicklung' in Deutschland*. Bonn: DUK.

Di Giulio, A. et al. (2011) *Bildung auf dem Weg zur Nachhaltigkeit: Vorschlag eines Indikatoren-Sets zur Beurteilung von Bildung für Nachhaltige Entwicklung. Interfakultäre Koordinationsstelle für Allgemeine Ökologie (Allgemeine Ökologie zur Diskussion gestellt, Nr. 12)*. Bern: Universität Bern.

Döbert, H. and Weishaupt, H. (2012) 'Bildungsmonitoring', in A. Wacker, U. Maier and J Wissinger (eds), *Schul- und Unterrichtsreform durch ergebnisorientierte Steuerung: Empirische Befunde und forschungsmethodische Implikationen*. Wiesbaden: Verlag für Sozialwissenschaften. pp. 155–173.

European Commission, EACEA, Eurydice (2017) *Support Mechanisms for Evidence-Based Policy-Making in Education: Eurydice Report*. Luxembourg: Publications Office of the European Union.

Geden, O. (2016) 'Split zwischen Reden, Entscheiden und Handeln in der Politik', *Energiewirtschaftliche Tagesfragen*, *66*(1/2): 47–49.

Gieryn, T. F. (1983) 'Boundary-work and the demarcation of science from non-science', *American Sociological Review*, *48*(6): 781. DOI: 10.2307/2095325.

Gluckman, P. (2016) 'The science–policy interface', *Science*, *353*(6303): 969. DOI: 10.1126/science.aai8837.

Hackett, E. J., Amsterdamska, O., Lynch, M. and Wajcman, J. (2008) *The Handbook of Science and Technology Studies*. Cambridge: MA: MIT Press.

Heinrichs, H., Martens, P., Michelsen, G. and Wiek, A. (2016) *Sustainability Science*. Dordrecht: Springer.

Huckle, J. and Wals, A. E. J. (2015) 'The UN Decade of Education for Sustainable Development: business as usual in the end', *Environmental Education Research*, *21*(3): 491–505. DOI: 10.1080/13504622.2015.1011084.

Hursh, D., Henderson, J. and Greenwood, D. (2015) 'Environmental education in a neoliberal climate', *Environmental Education Research*, *21*(3): 299–318. DOI: 10.1080/13504622.2015.1018141.

Ioannidou, A. (2010) 'Educational monitoring and reporting as governance instruments for evidence-based education policy', in K. Amos (ed.), *International Educational Governance*. Bingley: Emerald Group Publishing Limited. pp. 155–172.

Jahn, T., Bergmann, M. and Keil, F. (2012) 'Transdisciplinarity: between mainstreaming and marginalization', *Ecological Economics*, *79*: 1–10. DOI: 10.1016/j.ecolecon.2012.04.017.

Lang, D.J., Wiek, A., Bergmann, M., Stauffacher, M., Martens, P., Moll, P., Swilling, M. and Thomas, C. J. (2012) 'Transdisciplinary research in sustainability science: practice, principles, and challenges', *Sustainability Science*, 7(S1): 25–43. DOI: 10.1007/s11625-011-0149-x.

Læssøe, J., Feinstein, N.W. and Blum, N. (2013) 'Environmental education policy research – challenges and ways research might cope with them', *Environmental Education Research*, 19(2): 231–242. DOI: 10.1080/13504622.2013.778230.

Lingard, B. (2013) 'The impact of research on education policy in an era of evidence-based policy', *Critical Studies in Education*, 54(2): 113–131. DOI: 10.1080/17508487.2013.781515.

Mauser, W., Klepper, G., Rice, M., Schmalzbauer, B.S., Hackmann, H., Leemans, R. and Moore, H. (2013) 'Transdisciplinary global change research: "the co-creation of knowledge for sustainability"', *Current Opinion in Environmental Sustainability*, 5(3–4): 420–431.

McKenzie, M., Bieler, A. and McNeil, R. (2015) 'Education policy mobility: reimagining sustainability in neoliberal times', *Environmental Education Research*, 21(3): 319–337. DOI: 10.1080/13504622.2014.993934.

Meadows, D. (1997) *Leverage Points: Places to Intervene in a System*. Available at: http://donellameadows.org/archives/leverage-points-places-to-intervene-in-a-system/ (accessed 6 February 2019).

Michelsen, G., Adomßent, M., Bormann, I., Burandt, S. and Fischbach, R. (2011) *Indikatoren für Bildung für nachhaltige Entwicklung: Ein Werkstattbericht*. Bonn: Deutsche UNESCO-Kommission e.V. (DUK).

Miller, T. R., Wiek, A., Sarewitz, D., Robinson, J., Olsson, L., Kriebel, D. and Loorbach, D. (2014) 'The future of sustainability science', *Sustainability Science*, 9(2): 239–246. DOI: 10.1007/s11625-013-0224-6.

Møller, J. (2017) 'Leading education beyond what works', *European Educational Research Journal*, 16(4): 375–385. DOI: 10.1177/1474904117705487.

Nazir, J., Erminia P., Wallace, J., Montemurro, D. and Inwood, H. (2009) *Climate Change and Sustainable Development: The Response from Education*. Toronto: University of Toronto.

Niedlich, S. and Brüsemeister, T. (2012) 'Bildungsmonitoring zwischen Berichterstattung und Steuerungsanspruch: Entwicklungslinien und akteurtheoretische Implikationen', in A. Wacker, U. Maier and J. Wissinger (eds), *Schul- und Unterrichtsreform durch ergebnisorientierte Steuerung: Empirische Befunde und forschungsmethodische Implikationen*. Wiesbaden: Verlag für Sozialwissenschaften. pp. 75–96.

Nilsson, M., Grigg, D. and Visbeck, M. (2016) 'Map the interactions between sustainable development goals', *Nature*, 534(7607): 320–322. DOI: 10.1038/534320a.

Nowotny, H., Scott, P. and Gibbons, M. (2001) *Re-Thinking Science: Knowledge in the Public in an Age of Uncertainty*. Cambridge: Polity Press.

Nutley, S., Davies, H. and Walter, I. (2002) 'Evidence based policy and practice: cross sector lessons from the UK', *ESRC UK Centre for Evidence Based Policy and Practice: Working Paper 9*.

Phillips, D. and Ochs, K. (2003) 'Processes of policy borrowing in education: some explanatory and analytical devices', *Comparative Education*, 39(4): 451–461. DOI: 10.1080/0305006032000162020.

Rürup, M., Fuchs, H. and Weishaupt, H. (2016) 'Bildungsberichterstattung – Bildungsmonitoring', in H. Altrichter and K. Maag Merki (eds), *Handbuch Neue Steuerung im Schulsystem* (2nd edn) (Educational Governance, 7). Wiesbaden: Verlag für Sozialwissenschaften. pp. 411–437.

Scholz, R. (2017) 'The normative dimension in transdisciplinarity, transition management and transformation sciences', *Sustainability*, 9(6): 991. DOI: 10.3390/su9060991.

Segalàs, J., Ferrer-Balas, D., Svanstrom, M., Lundqvist, U. and Mulder, K.F. (2009) 'What has to be learnt for sustainability? A comparison of Bachelor Engineering education competencies at three European universities', *Sustainability Science*, 4(1): 17–27.

Singer-Brodowski, M., Brock, A., Etzkorn, N. and Otte, I. (2018) 'Monitoring of education for sustainable development in Germany: insights from early childhood education, school and higher education', *Environmental Education Research*, 24(2). DOI: 10.1080/13504622.2018. 1440380.

Spruijt, P., Knolb, A.B., Vasileiadou, E., Devileeb, J., Lebretta, E. and Petersen, A.C. (2014) 'Roles of scientists as policy advisers on complex issues: a literature review', *Environmental Science & Policy*, 40: 16–25.

Temenos, C. and McCann, E. (2012) 'The local politics of policy mobility: learning, persuasion, and the production of a municipal sustainability fix', *Environment and Planning*, 44(6): 1389–1406.

UNECE (2012) *Learning for the Future: Competences in Education for Sustainable Development*. Available at: www.unece.org/fileadmin/DAM/env/esd/ESD_Publications/Competences_ Publication.pdf (accessed 6 February 2019).

UNECE Steering Committee on Education for Sustainable Development (2007) *Indicators for Education for Sustainable Development: Progress Report on the Work of the Expert Group*. Paris: Economic and Social Council.

UNECE Steering Committee on Education for Sustainable Development (2014) *Phase III: Format for Reporting on the Implementation of the UNECE Strategy for Education for Sustainable Development*. Paris: Economic and Social Council.

UNESCO (2014a) *Global Monitoring and Evaluation Report: Shaping the Future We Want*. Final Report. Paris: UNESCO.

UNESCO (2014b) *Roadmap for the Implementation of the Global Action Programme on Education for Sustainable Development*. Paris: UNESCO.

van Poeck, K. and Lysgaard, J. A. (2015) 'The roots and routes of environmental and sustainability education policy research', *Environmental Education Research*, 22(3): 305–318. DOI: 10.1080/13504622.2015.1108393.

van Poeck, K., Vandenabeele, J. and Bruyninckx, H. (2014) 'Taking stock of the UN Decade of Education for Sustainable Development: the policy-making process in Flanders', *Environmental Education Research*, 20(5): 695–717. DOI: 10.1080/13504622.2015.1108393.

Wiek, A., Withycombe, L. and Redman, C.L. (2011) 'Key competencies in sustainability: a reference framework for academic program development', *Sustainability Science*, 6(2): 203–218. DOI: 10.1007/s11625-011-0132-6.

PART VI

GETTING READY FOR AN OPEN FUTURE

15

EDUCATIONAL RESEARCH – A SPACE OF RISK AND UNCERTAINTY

Angelika Paseka, Sofia Marques da Silva, Lucian Ciolan and Marit Honerød Hoveid

This last chapter examines the main research challenges presented in earlier chapters by looking at them in the context of an uncertain and risky future for educational research. Following the ideas of Otto Scharmer (2009), we analyse critically the current situation of educational research before looking for new grounds for the realisation of educational research. The first section will therefore consider various levels and dimensions of uncertainty which can be experienced in carrying out research projects whereas the second section focuses on the role of EERA, how being part of it enhances the opportunities to overcome uncertainties and risks by capacity building and transforming existing limitations.

15.1 UNCERTAINTIES – A MULTI-PERSPECTIVE VIEW ON THE EDUCATIONAL RESEARCH FIELD

The 14 chapters included in this volume make clear that carrying out educational research includes risks and uncertainties. Although this may be true to all types of research, the cases in this volume discussed by experienced researchers indicate that doing educational research has specificities related to the nature of the field, the type of interactions needed to understand social and educational practices, the risky methodological choices, translations and knowledge transferences, among others. Uncertainties arise because our knowledge is not sufficient enough. But even if we accumulate more knowledge, in the dynamics of the *process* of carrying out a research project situations occur that cannot be known in advance. Nevertheless, the process has to go on although there does not exist secure knowledge in a comprehensive sense. Coping with uncertainties demands decision-making. The level of risk involved depends on whether we decide to follow routines and well-known paths or whether we try to cover new ground (Paseka, Keller-Schneider and Combe, 2018). When we address challenges by focusing on uncertainties here, we want to emphasise that entering the field of educational research will bring a variety of situations that researchers need to navigate. From the variety of contributions in this book, it is possible to understand that researchers have to mobilise or develop skills to be able to detect, understand and try to solve challenging situations. Additionally, we are aware of an unequal distribution of resources or conditions, personal, contextual, institutional, political or systemic, which will affect how researchers deal with different levels of uncertainty. Planning is an important and, we would say, almost mandatory component of any research, but Figure 15.1 makes it evident there are at least four levels of decision-making which influence research, the identity as researcher and the uncertainties researchers have to cope with. These levels are: the researcher him/herself, the institutional background, the scientific community, and society and relevant groups that are interested in research.

The multi-faceted nature of uncertainty becomes even more evident by having the following *dimensions* in mind: the content of research, the theoretical background, the methodological approach of research, the research process itself and the research results.

Positioned in the centre of Figure 15.1 is the researcher trying to find their own identity and role in the world of research. This is a process influenced not only by their personal motivation, resources and background, but also by the institution the researcher is part of. Institutions have their own cultures which are influenced by the people working there and also by the scientific community and the social and political decisions concerning research at a macro-level. We do not want to see the researchers dominated by these levels in which their situation is embedded, quite the opposite, researchers can reflect their situation and are able – more or less – to influence the levels as well. How this might happen will be addressed as part of the second section of this chapter.

As a first step, let us look at five different areas in which the researcher has to make decisions and where uncertainties will create challenges. These are not exhaustive, but they highlight some significant areas in which researchers have to make decisions. Our aim is not to say that uncertainties have to be reduced, but rather to show how the tensions created within the five dimensions and between them can become a source

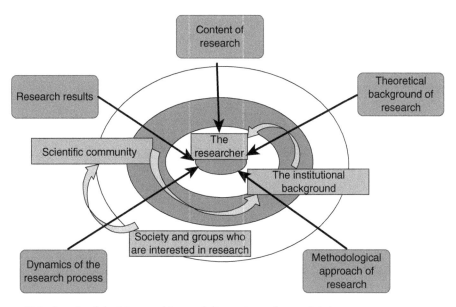

Figure 15.1 Levels of decision-making and dimensions of uncertainty

of productivity and new insight – if you are willing not only to endure the toll but to reflect and explore new ideas.

Uncertainty is played out as part of the *contents* of educational research. The researcher with their interest, imagination, knowledge and energy has to construct an object of research. As part of this search process earlier research results have to be evaluated in order to find a research need, which one is able to address. The general focus of educational research has changed over the years (see Chapter 1). Such changes are influenced by the scientific community as well as by transformations in society. These changes will also have an impact on the institutional background of the researcher, of which they may not be aware. Our point is that educational research institutions are influenced by the society in which they operate and not least by the funding opportunities that are given. Hence, for some content areas, such as those which governments and/or the business sector are interested in, grants for research are more likely to be given. As we pointed out in Chapter 1, the wish to get data concerning the output of the education system is very much emphasised by neglecting other areas of research which remain 'unfunded, incomplete, or generally ignored' (Frickel et al. 2010: 444). Consequently, for a researcher to pursue their personal interest in a defined research area can prove difficult, and even risky, especially if grants are not given for the content area that the researcher is interested in.

Uncertainty also arises when one makes a choice of *theoretical background* for research. Sometimes researchers come into the field with their theoretical 'glasses' predetermined, for others the theories are sought out in the research process. In general, research questions are grounded in a theoretical perspective, which will guide the research process – so choosing a sound theoretical background is an important decision. However, such decisions are influenced by 'theory schools', some of which might have either a good or weak position in one's institution, and likewise in the scientific community. The researcher has to be aware that there are research groups which run journals, organise conferences and are able to spread their research and knowledge in society, whereas others are not so well organised and supported. This underpins the political side of doing research and the inherent power relations, something often omitted from discussion within the research communities. So, how to decide as an emerging researcher? Should one show resistance against mainstream theories, so as not to produce hegemonies or is it better for an academic career to use theories and schools of thought which will help make one's position safer – at least for a while? As an emerging researcher you might not be in a position to make a choice in this. But even for established researchers, following the money and the mainstream trends might be the easier option and it reduces some risks.

Another aspect of uncertainty occurs by choosing a *research methodology*: quantitative or qualitative – that would usually be the first question a researcher has to answer to. Erroneously so, often before the actual research question is decided on – the methodology is chosen first. However, methodology should be in line with the chosen research questions as well as with the theory chosen for the research project. Making the decision about methodology in a research project is also influenced by the institutional background of the researcher and what methods are emphasised in their institution. So, when being new in an institution the researcher tries to find out which research groups already exist, where the experts are and where they might turn to if they need help. Having specific interests, further down the line, a researcher might even explore whether there are colleagues with whom it might be possible to establish an alternative research group and who have specific methodological aspirations. Research methods are influenced by the scientific community and whether there is a clear bias for or against some methods. And of course, the choice of research methodology may also be influenced by research funding. Research funding has the power to foster some methodological approaches over others, for example, the strong emphasis on quantitative evidence-based research carried out by large agencies financed by global players like OECD or EU. As Susan L. Robertson pointed out in her keynote at ECER 2018[1] in Bolzano, there is currently a strong tendency for quantification which enables standardisation and the comparing of national education systems. In a strong research community, and as a generic part of research, this needs critical scrutiny and deliberation. The idea that there is one grand theory, one comprehensive research approach, that would be able to account for education now and in the future cannot be left unchallenged and has to be reconstructed by using historical-hermeneutic methods and methods of social analysis and ideology critique (Klafki,

2002). In other words, using one method will always raise the need for alternative methodological approaches that can help illuminate blind spots and the need for other types of research as well.

Uncertainty will occur in the *dynamics* of a research process, especially when working in research groups. The personal self-interests and ideas of the various researchers and participants have to be negotiated, in this, positions are found and defended – not always knowing how the process will proceed to find a solution that works. As we have already mentioned, these processes are embedded in an institutional frame, the broader scientific community and the even wider societal context. Therefore, there are types of situational and institutional knowledge which are necessary and one has to acquire in order to cope with the uncertainties of a research process. We could also frame this as cultural knowledge, pointing to the need to know the context of the field of research as well as the field where this research itself operates. From an organisational point of view, and in terms of handling such uncertainties, this means handling a lot of 'not-being-able-to-know' or hidden assumptions within the complexity of carrying out a research project.

Uncertainty occurs again when *research results* are presented to specific and diverse audiences. A researcher has to have in mind the various groups, or stakeholders, that the presentation of findings has to address to be able to reach their needs without exactly knowing the reactions. This might be the organisation the researcher is working for, the scientific community, the practitioners or policy makers, the sponsors who enabled the research project as well as the participants. Whereas politicians and bureaucrats are often fond of numbers and figures which enable a quick check concerning, for example, the input and output of an education system, practitioners usually want more detailed inputs. They want, for instance, authenticity by reference to original 'voices' of those who were informants in an interview, or observed in a classroom, and practitioners are often asking for recommendations for their future practice. Additionally, researchers can only partially control what happens with research results, the impact they might have for the future and whether they are a contribution to better understand society and education. Sometimes research results disappear into the desk of those who financed the research project, sometimes research results have a significant impact as they are presented at conferences, published in peer-reviewed journals and even in popularised form in non-scientific journals. If research receives attention and the scientific community decides that the research brings something new to the field, it might attract a lot of further attention. But it can also happen that research results are only discussed in small(er) or local communities of researchers or participants. For the researchers, however, getting more or less attention will probably affect their scientific career since international research cooperation and publication is a common demand today. So, finding the right venue for presenting research results is not always straightforward.

15.2 THINKING IN NEW DIMENSIONS AND THE ROLE OF EERA

Considering the number of uncertainties addressed above it becomes clear that there are lots of challenges for both emerging and established researchers. Most educational researchers must cope with the points raised in the previous section in one form or another, but the stakes are usually higher for those who have not yet achieved a permanent position. This makes the longing for certainties even more acute. However, uncertainties are – to a certain degree – constitutive of doing research. Doing research is something one does in order to address something one does not know, in other words, research is about acquiring new knowledge. Containing all variables is not possible when one ventures into research, and, in addition, the degree of uncertainties is often raised by the context one operates in, whether these are on an individual, organisational, national and international plane. Although many of the risks and uncomfortable sides to uncertainties are addressed above, we also want to underline the productive side of doing research. The tensions and contradictions created by uncertainties and not knowing is one of the main reasons why we do research. Education is a complex field that cannot and should not be addressed as something to be harnessed – but rather as a flourishing field, where new discoveries will always be made.

This book came into being from an idea that started in the EERA council and was developed by four researchers who come from different European countries and who were, at that point, all members of the council. In light of this we would like to look at the role EERA might play in relation to educational research and how EERA might be able to support and strengthen researchers, especially in situations where they experience uncertainties, as accounted for above, and how EERA can offer space for thinking about research in an open future. EERA represents a large community of educational researchers from a variety of research fields across Europe and beyond and it can provide some structures and spaces which might help, especially if you are an emerging researcher. Let us provide some examples.

15.2.1 PROVIDING *SUPPORT* FOR EMERGING RESEARCHERS

Every year since 2011 EERA summer schools have been organised in cooperation between national or regional educational research associations and universities in different European countries. Between 60–70 young researchers, most of them PhD students, come together at universities in various European cities, e.g. Gothenburg (2011), Birmingham (2012), Trondheim (2013 and 2014), Linz (2016 and 2017), Brno (2018 and 2019). In addition to this, various research networks within EERA have organised seasonal schools addressing their field or discipline. All of this takes place with support from the EERA council.[2] These summer or seasonal schools can provide PhD students with an opportunity to meet and have contact with experienced researchers, to network and meet fellow researchers in an international context and, not least, to present their own research and get feedback. Through these initiatives EERA offers several learning opportunities for young researchers by providing a platform to get engaged with and gain entry into an international community of researchers. This happens by inviting experienced researchers as tutors and by bringing together young researchers from all over the world to get advice on current research and PhD projects. This has been proven valuable by a number of emerging researchers (Hoveid, Keiner and Figueiredo, 2014). Such a mentoring process helps students to frame and reflect on uncertainties, encouraging the integration of these uncertainties in the research design. Moreover, mentoring experiences contribute to the development of the quality of educational research by emphasising standards, providing critical discussions and giving opportunities for networking. Preceding the annual ECER (European Conference on Educational research), is the two-day Emerging Researchers Conference. Here emerging researchers are invited to present posters and papers, where they can receive responses from more experienced researchers. For many this is their first international conference, and by acquiring experience in presenting in English, for most not their first language, a first threshold into an international research community is passed. EERA is committed to provide opportunities for emerging researchers, as is often said: they represent the future. Providing a strong and robust research community is part of this commitment as well.

15.2.2 PROVIDING A *SPACE* TO PROMOTE DISCUSSIONS ON ETHICS

Ethical approaches are interconnected with theoretical positioning and methodological options (Beach and Erickson, 2010). These positionalities influence how we deal with uncertainties that may cause ethical controversies alongside which we may also be dealing with specific cross-cultural ethical situations. We may refer to the instability of research settings, to the limits of a specific method or technique to provide data and results with the quality that we need, to the difficulty in portraying research participants with dignity, or to the dissemination strategies. Understanding that we often face sensitive situations, the risk, we believe, especially of causing more harm than good by making realities either visible or invisible, may precisely exist when, due to several constrains, we avoid risky and sensitive topics (Te Riele, 2013).

Rather than starting a discussion on the *dos and don'ts* of ethically sound research, as this is often related to specificities of ethics committees regulations, country or institutional level specificities or to requests concerning applications for projects financing, we would like to highlight how we understand how ethical tensions are intertwined with the specific methodological challenges addressed in educational research. Examples can be found in this book, either when dealing with culturally or politically sensitive research. Therefore, what ethical recommendations may EERA provide?

According to Head (2018), there are several ethical theories: the utilitarian ethical theory that points to the results of research, that the benefits have to be maximised; the deontological ethical theory that aims to establish general rules of behaviour. However, further discussions need to be advanced: who decides what a 'benefit' is and who will benefit? Are ethical conventions protecting those involved in research or causing harm, as symbolically hiding voices and authorship? Following this, Head argues for an ethic of care: 'An ethic of care entails care for the people involved in the immediate process (including participants, funders and sponsors), for colleagues in ethics committees and care for the research itself, for how it is conducted, and for how it is disseminated' (Head, 2018: 7). Therefore, researchers have to protect participants and contexts by assuring anonymity and confidentiality, but also they have to care about 'the impact that ethical decisions and research processes can have on people's lives, or the ways in which participants disclosure can impact on researchers' (Silva, 2013: 96). Some contributions, especially those involving participants in different moments of the research process besides data collection, reflect on particular ethical concerns that are necessary. The proximity that researchers have with contexts and participants while involved in collaborative research inquiries, entail specific skills to deal with power relations, with conflicting positionalities between researchers and participants. This requires 'sensitivity and knowledge' (Hauge, 2013: 146). Researchers will come upon various expressions of ethical dilemmas that hardly can be solved by established frameworks.

The question of the authority of representation is also an ethical concern for us. The issue of how we represent others is addressed in this book and is a concern in educational research as a practice. Representation is present not only when we write, but also when we develop analytical dimensions to produce sound and convincing knowledge. This is especially the case when researchers are engaged in an emancipatory knowledge production process. This is very much aligned with Habermas's (1987) perspective on knowledge-constitutive interests. For the philosopher, science and knowledge should have not only a technical and practical interest, but also an emancipatory interest. The question is: how may one produce transformative knowledge for a better future and for social transformation? There is also some concern related to reciprocity in doing research. How does one think about a model of reciprocity while doing educational research? This has implications for how one incorporates participants' understandings and concepts, recognising them as social actors. Ethical care is about acknowledging participants' competencies, but also acknowledging the existence of asymmetries between researchers and participants, which makes reciprocity nearly impossible to achieve (Young, 1997).

EERA foregrounds, since its foundation, discussions on ethical concerns in educational research, highlighting the impact of recent changes in ethical procedures and how ethics may be attentive to new methods and research contexts. Debates have been taking place in several contexts related to EERA, either in annual conferences, seasonal schools or council meetings. The EERA council has for many years motivated discussion among members, creating a space for sharing good practices developed by national associations with different practices and creating the opportunity for influencing the adoption of ethical recommendations. Exploratory research has been conducted by a group of council members to provide knowledge on the diversity of procedures at European level. However, an EERA perspective on ethics was beyond ethical regulatory guidelines and aimed to respond to ethical discussions coming from structural breaks that are often impossible to prognosticate. Aware of the complexity of doing educational research, EERA, in its diversity, provided members with reflection on ethics as a space of contestation.[3]

15.2.3 PROVIDING A *FORUM* FOR CRITICAL DISCUSSION OF EDUCATIONAL RESEARCH AND RESULTS

There are lots of conferences throughout the year, some of them are very competitive, not only concerning the selection of papers but also concerning the culture. ECER is different, as attested to by the experience of many researchers (Hoveid, Keiner and Figueiredo, 2014). This is for a number of reasons. One is that at ECER so many people from countries all over the world come together because they are inspired by their research and looking for an audience which is interested in a broad spectrum of research – in methodological as well as in theoretical and content-based dimensions. ECER opens space for discussing educational research in a critical context, asking questions like: what kind of knowledge is produced by which kind of research? What are the social, political, practical consequences of our research? How do we define the quality of research – and how it is defined by others, such as the political system with its special interests? How can we protect research from powerful interventions – or are the researchers themselves part of the game?

Such questions force researchers to look at their own research from different perspectives (see Niklas Luhmann, 1993, 1998, who proclaims 'observations of a second order') to find and become aware of blind spots. Alongside this, more general challenges deriving from carrying out educational research have to be discussed and ECER might be a forum offering space and opportunities to do so. Here are some critical issues and questions for further discussions.

Ozga (2008) calls attention to the changing nature of knowledge and governance. The relationship between research and policy is becoming stronger, along with an increase in the commodification of knowledge. What is the impact of such tensions on educational research? Additionally, we have to ask the question of how knowledge creates value and how social and educational sciences drive economic growth. There are several discussions on the value of social sciences and humanities in the landscape of contemporary universities (Collini, 2012). As educational researchers we have to trace the social value of research in *education*. We have a very fragile knowledge about the impact of our research. How do we evaluate the impact of our research? When do we define the type of impact that we want our research to have (beyond neoliberal perspectives on impact and economic growth)?

15.2.4 PROVIDING A *FORUM* FOR THINKING ABOUT A FUTURE FOR EDUCATIONAL RESEARCH

No one knows what the future will bring and what the next main challenges for research in general, and specifically educational research, will look like. However, there seem to be some topics that prevail and, like waves, they push researchers in certain directions. They also influence global players and international organisations that have the power and the money to define areas of research and to finance research projects. Having in mind the topic of ECER 2019 'Education in an era of risk', we have to ask: what are the risks? According to Wolfgang Klafki (1996) six core problems will challenge international education and educational research and may be identified as: peace, environment issues, socially created inequalities, effects of new technologies, effects of intercultural education, and I–you relationships. These key problems are not mentioned explicitly in a current OECD paper (2018); however, in a more generalising way three kinds of challenges are announced which are fundamental in all of the key problems: environmental, social and economic challenges (OECD, 2018).

What does this mean for educational research? These key problems might be a motivation to look for answers. How does one prepare the next generation for coping with such challenges? Concepts for learning have to be developed which help to produce competences that are more than knowledge and skills, but also include the ability to reflect, to be able to handle tensions and dilemmas, and to go critically beyond and under the surface of quick answers. As a further step educational research must critically ask whether the programmes, initiatives and concepts work or whether unintended effects occur which reinforce existing systems and power relations and economic imbalances. To go beyond what can be found on the surface alternative methodologies have to be created and tried out. In this volume some ideas can be found. However, researchers sometimes live a dangerous life if their results and ideas are not in line with the political system of their country. The independence of research is a valuable asset which has to be announced and guaranteed.

EERA and ECER provide a place for open-minded and creative discussions, beyond political pressure, making time to acquire comprehension of an uncertain world. Picking up again the ideas of Otto Scharmer (2009), transferring them to the educational research field and putting educational research in a future perspective, four demands on research are raised which might work as mission statements for EERA: to look critically at the current situation of educational research; to creatively discuss solutions by leaving comfort zones; to experiment with new methods; and to find new common grounds for the realisation of social science research. Having in mind that the landscape we operate in as educational researchers is full of uncertainties, an open question emerges: is there a future for educational research considering the uncertainties analysed above? We would like to say: EERA and ECER can provide a place for deliberations on such a question about research so that we are sure that, yes, there is a future for educational research!

NOTES

1   See www.youtube.com/watch?v=tzrLIAsgDUc (accessed 6 February 2019).

2   See www.eerahistory.eu/season-schools/ (accessed 6 February 2019).

3   See https://eera-ecer.de/about-eera/ethical-guidelines/ (accessed 6 February 2019).

REFERENCES

Beach, D. and Eriksson, A. (2010) 'The relationship between ethical positions and methodological approaches: a Scandinavian perspective', *Ethnography and Education*, *5*(2): 129–142.

Collini, S. (2012) *What Are Universities For?* London: Penguin.

Frickel, S., Gibbon, S., Howard, J., Kempner, J., Ottinger, G. and Hess, D. J. (2010) 'Undone science: charting social movement and civil society challenges to research agenda setting', *Science, Technology & Human Values*, *35*(4): 444–473. DOI: 10.1177/0162243909345836.

Habermas, J. (1987) *Knowledge & Human Interests*. Cambridge: Polity Press.

Hauge, M.-I. (2013) 'Research with young people on female circumcision', in K. te Riele and R. Brooks (eds), *Negotiating Ethical Challenges in Youth Research*. New York: Routledge. pp. 137–148.

Head, G. (2018) 'Ethics in educational research: review boards, ethical issues and researcher development', *European Educational Research Journal*. DOI: 10.1177/1474904118796315.

Hoveid, M., Keiner, E. and Figueiredo, M.P. (2014) 'The European Educational Research Association: people, practices and policy over the last 20 years', *European Educational Research Journal*, *13*(4): 399–403.

Klafki, W. (1996) 'Core problems of the modern world and the tasks of education: a vision for international education', *Education: A Biennial Collection of Recent German Contributions in the Field of Educational Research*, *53*. Tübingen: Institut für Wissenschaftliche Zusammenarbeit. pp. 7–18.

Klafki, W. (2002) 'Characteristics of critical-constructive Didaktik', in B.B. Gundem and S. Hopman (eds), *Didaktik and/or Curriculum: An International Dialogue*. New York: Peter Lang. pp. 307–330.

Luhmann, N. (1993) 'Deconstruction as second-order observing', *New Literary History 24*(4), Papers from the Commonwealth Center for Literary and Cultural Change, pp. 763–782.

Luhmann, N. (1995) *Social Systems*. Stanford, CA: Stanford University Press.

Luhmann, N. (1998) *Observations on Modernity*. Stanford, CA: Stanford University Press.

OECD (2018) *The Future of Education and Skills*. Education 2030. Paris: OECD Publishing. Available at: www.oecd.org/education/2030/E2030%20Position%20Paper%20(05.04.2018).pdf (accessed 14 February 2019).

Ozga, J. (2008) 'Governing knowledge: research steering and research quality', *European Educational Research Journal*, 7(3): 261–272.

Paseka, A., Keller-Schneider, M. and Combe, A. (eds) (2018) *Ungewissheit als Herausforderung für pädagogisches Handeln* [Uncertainty as challenge for pedagogical acting]. Wiesbaden: Springer-Verlag.

Robertson, S. L. (2018) 'Setting aside settings: on the contradictory dynamics of "flat earth", "ordinalization" and "cold spot" governing projects shaping education'. Keynote at ECER 2018, Bolzano.

Scharmer, O. (2009) 'Leadership development is not about filling a gap but about igniting a field of inspired connection and action: ten propositions on transforming the current leadership development paradigm'. Paper for the Round Table Meeting on Leadership for Development Impact. The World Bank, September.

Silva, S. M. (2013) 'Young people and sensitive information: managing protection and dignity', in K. te Riele and R. Brooks (eds), *Negotiating Ethical Challenges in Youth Research*. New York: Routledge. pp. 96–108.

Te Riele, K. (2013) 'Formal frameworks as resources for ethical youth research', in K. te Riele and R. Brooks (eds), *Negotiating Ethical Challenges in Youth Research*. New York: Routledge. pp. 4–15.

Young, I. M. (1997) 'Communication and the other: beyond deliberative democracy', in I. M. Young (ed.), *Intersecting Voices: Dilemmas of Gender, Political Philosophy, and Policy*. Princeton: Princeton University Press. pp. 60–74.

INDEX

Pages in **bold** denote tables, *italics* denote figures